NBA LIST

JAM!

NBA

LIST JAM!

THE MOST AUTHORITATIVE AND OPINIONATED RANKINGS

BY PAT WILLIAMS AND MICHAEL CONNELLY

RUNNING PRESS
PHILADELPHIA · LONDON

Books published by Running Press are available at special discounts for bulk purchases in the United States by corporations, institutions, and other organizations. For more information, please contact the Special Markets Department at the Perseus Books Group, 2300 Chestnut Street, Suite 200, Philadelphia, PA 19103, or call (800) 810-4145, ext. 5000, or e-mail special.markets@perseusbooks.com.

ISBN 978-0-7624-4561-5
Library of Congress Control Number: 2012938751

E-book ISBN 978-0-7624-4686-5

9 8 7 6 5 4 3 2 1
Digit on the right indicates the number of this printing

Designer: Joshua McDonnell
Editor: Greg Jones
Typography: Avenir and Boton

Running Press Book Publishers
2300 Chestnut Street
Philadelphia, PA 19103-4371

Visit us on the web!
www.runningpress.com

You can contact Pat Williams at:

Pat Williams
c/o Orlando Magic
8701 Maitland Summit Boulevard
Orlando, FL 32810
(407) 916-2404
pwilliams@orlandomagic.com

Visit Pat Williams online:
www.PatWilliamsMotivate.com
www.twitter.com/OrlandoMagicPat
www.Facebook.com/PatWilliams.OrlandoMagic

If you would like to set up a speaking engagement for Pat Williams,
please call Andrew Herdliska at 407-916-2401 or e-mail him at aherdliska@orlandomagic.com.

Pat's Dedication

I dedicate this book to Matt Guokas, the longtime player, coach and now commentator. His input on this project was invaluable.

Michael's Dedication

To my beautiful girlfriend, and now wife, Noreen, who tolerated dates being planned around Larry Bird's Celtic schedule. To my life's joy, my son Ryan, for whom sports has been a wonderful bond between father and son. To my father, John Connelly, Jr., who spent his hard-earned money on a basketball court in the backyard in yet another example of putting his kids before himself. To my mother, Marilyn Connelly, who sat and watched as I scored 28 points in a half one night but would have hugged me had I scored none. To my brothers and sisters who are not just my siblings but my friends.

PART 2: GREAT PERFORMERS AND PERFORMANCES

PART 3: COACHES, FRONT-OFFICE, AGENTS, FANS, TRAINERS, AND REFEREES

PART 4: EXPERIENCING THE GAME LIVE AND THROUGH THE MEDIA

Foreword

As Commissioner of the National Basketball Association, it is my privilege to preside over the world's most entertaining sport—a game that is truly international in its scope and appeal. NBA rosters currently boast 75 players who grew up (and up and up!) in 30 countries outside of the United States. We not only have the planet's best athletes, we most assuredly have the tallest!

Were I to be a teacher (and as a league ambassador I suppose I could qualify for the title), I would award our sport four A-pluses for its athleticism, appeal, action, and for the adrenalin rush fans experience night after night watching games. Since you are reading this book, any more proselytizing would be unnecessary.

While I am awarding A-pluses to the game we love, Pat Williams and Michael Connelly have certainly earned theirs for this addictive collection, *NBA List Jam!* Like salted peanuts, you can't stop consuming them after you have "eaten" one. These eclectic lists have been generated by executives, coaches, players, columnists, television and radio commentators, scouts and trainers, and they are sure to stir memories, enjoyment, interest, and debate. They run full-court, covering the league's rich history to its present-day fast-break action.

I do sense that I am "preaching to the choir," for I am convinced, that just like NBA action, you are going to find this book to be "Fan-tastic!"

—David Stern,
National Basketball Association Commissioner

Introduction

From the peach basket to Jumbotrons, from the two-handed set shot to a two-handed tomahawk dunk, the game of basketball has evolved from its early days at a YMCA gym in Springfield, Massachusetts, into an international entertainment entity.

When James Naismith conjured up his notion of an indoor activity in 1891, never in his wildest dreams could he have imagined that his game would be played by athletes who stretch over seven feet in height, jump from free throw line to basket, and come from all corners of the world. From origin to current day, the manifestation of the sport has seen the game played by amazing athletes with vivid imaginations.

Within this spirit of both art and creativity, these players continue to astonish with their ability to manipulate the ball in a fashion that causes us fans to rise from our seats in awe and admiration. From a George Mikan hook shot, to a behind-the-back pass from Bob Cousy, to a Kareem Abdul-Jabbar skyhook, to a George Gervin finger roll, to a Dr. J cuffed dunk, to a Magic Johnson no-look pass, to a Tim Hardaway killer crossover dribble, to a Blake Griffin dunk performed as he looks down at the basket, Dr. Naismith's game continues to evolve.

Since 1946, a wide range of individuals helped build the National Basketball Association into a worldwide sensation. From Spud Webb to Manute Bol, from Red Auerbach to Zelmo Beaty, the sport of basketball has been played at its highest level on a stage we know as the NBA. It is on this stage that the performers have shined beneath the big lights of the LA Forum and Gardens (Boston and Madison Square), bringing their talents to arenas from Toronto to Texas, from Portland to South Beach. Each autumn when the first ball is tossed up from center court, to the championship round later the next spring, the game is played with plot and climax, marvel and mystery, with acts that defy the boundaries of ordinary man.

NBA List Jam! is an effort to capture the game from origin to present, from backcourt to frontcourt, from front office to league office, and from the media to the fans. The book is comprised of lists that rank centers and point guards, dance teams and mascots, players from Texas and players from New York City, and everything in between. The goal of this book is to ink the NBA from era to era, team to team, amazing feat to amazing feat, giving fans of the game the opportunity to agree or disagree while providing interesting points of discussion. The list of those who contributed to this book is so impressive, so diverse, and so special that the authors are humbled and honored to collaborate on this project with them. We hope that you enjoy the book as much as we enjoyed piecing this together.

Top 10 (Plus One) NBA Players from the State of Indiana :: by David Benner

David Benner is the director of media relations for the Indiana Pacers. In 2011, he and his staff were awarded the Brian McIntyre Award for public relations excellence by the Professional Basketball Writers Association. David has been with the Pacers since 1994. The Hoosier State holds a special place in basketball history, including its contribution of fine players to the NBA, like the guys on this list.

10 (tie). Tom and Dick Van Arsdale. Name a more successful twin combination in NBA history. They each played a dozen years in the NBA and split six All-Star appearances (three each) between them. Dick averaged 16.4 points per game and 4.1 rebounds while Tom averaged 15.3 points and 4.2 rebounds. Yeah, we know they make it 11 in a top-10 list, but you can't split these two.

9. Scott Skiles. Considered one of the classic overachievers, Skiles makes this list for a number of reasons: his tenacity on the court, his 11-year NBA career, and his NBA-record 30 assists in a game on December 30, 1990, an Orlando 155–116 victory over Denver. Skiles was also named the Most Improved Player in the NBA that season, averaging 17.2 points and 8.4 assists—doubling his numbers from the previous year. He averaged 11.1 points and 6.5 assists per game over his career.

8. Terry Dischinger. Born in Terre Haute, the 6-7 forward was the NBA Rookie of the Year with the Chicago Zephyrs in 1963. He was also a three-time NBA All-Star who averaged 13.8 points and 5.6 rebounds per game during his nine seasons in the league.

7. Shawn Kemp. He played 14 seasons in the NBA and was a six-time NBA All-Star. Like George McGinnis (below), the 6-10 power forward was both powerful and smooth at the same time. His ability to go out on the floor created matchup problems for all opponents. He averaged 14.6 points and 8.4 rebounds per game and was a second-team All-NBA selection three times.

6. George McGinnis. After starting his pro career in the ABA, McGinnis in 1975 joined the Philadelphia 76ers, a team he represented in two NBA All-Star Games and with a first-team All-NBA selection in 1976. He later earned another All-Star selection with Denver. McGinnis put the power in the power forward position. Over his career, he averaged 20.2 points and 11 rebounds.

5. Dick Barnett. Born in Gary, the 6-4 guard played 14 seasons in the NBA and was part of two NBA championships with the New York Knicks. An NBA All-Star in 1968, he averaged 15.8 points in his career.

4. Clyde Lovellette. The 6-10, 234-pound center/power forward may not be familiar to many, but his record speaks for itself. He was part of three NBA championship teams (one with the Minneapolis Lakers and two with the Boston Celtics) and a four-time NBA All-Star. He averaged 17 points and 9.3 rebounds in his career.

3. Bob "Slick" Leonard. Played in the NBA, coached in the NBA, been a broadcaster in the NBA. But his impact in regards to the NBA rests with there would be no Pacers in the NBA if not for Slick and his wife, Nancy, conducting a telethon to save the franchise when things were dour.

1. Oscar Robertson and 1a. Larry Bird. Talk about the 1 and 1a of Indiana basketball, these two legends define that. The Big "O" was one of the most versatile players in basketball history, averaging a triple-double in a season (stop and think about that for a minute). Bird, well, like Oscar, he was one of the most versatile players in NBA history. With three NBA championships and three MVP Awards, Larry is a bona fide legend.

Top 10 Oklahomans Who Have Impacted the NBA :: by Berry Tramel

Berry Tramel has been a sportswriter and editor for the *Oklahoman* since 1991. He was born and raised in Norman. Long known as a hotbed of football talent, Oklahoma has actually produced a number of top basketball players, some of whom have gone on to fine careers in the NBA, especially these 10.

10. Richard Dumas (Tulsa). Drug-shortened career—just 102 games and 47 starts. But a terror for Phoenix in the 1993 playoffs, when he averaged 10.9 points off the bench in 23 postseason games.

9. Bryant Reeves (Gans). First draft pick in Grizzlies history, No. 5 overall in 1995, played six seasons and averaged 12.5 points and 6.9 rebounds per game for Vancouver.

8. Kevin Pritchard (Tulsa). Nondescript six-year playing career, but then a scout and player personnel director. In three years as Portland's general manager (2007–10), remade the Blazer roster.

7. Jim Barnes (Stillwater). No. 1 overall pick in the 1964 NBA Draft, made All-Rookie in 1965 after averaging 15.5 points per game. Played seven years in the league and averaged 8.8 points a game.

6. Blake Griffin (Edmond). The 2011 NBA Rookie of the Year, a dunking machine who has averaged 22.5 points and 12.1 rebounds per game for the Clippers.

5. Wayman Tisdale (Tulsa). Low-post scorer with a patented turnaround jumper, Tisdale averaged 15.3 points per game over a 12-year career with the Pacers, Kings, and Suns.

4. John Starks (Tulsa). Fairy-tale story, Starks went from sacking groceries out of high school to the 1994 NBA Finals. Starks played 13 NBA seasons but was best known as the second-leading scorer (19.0 ppg) on the Knicks 1994 Eastern Conference champions.

3. Alvan Adams (Putnam City). The 1975–76 NBA Rookie of the Year spent 13 years as a Phoenix Suns center and averaged 14.1 points per game for his career. Averaged 17.9 points and 10.1 rebounds during the '76 playoffs, when the Suns went all the way to the NBA Finals.

2. Mark Price (Enid). The 1993 first-team All-NBA guard and four-time All-Star was one of the best three-point shooters (.402 percent) in league history, and his .904 percent free throw shooting has him going back and forth with the still-active Steve Nash for top spot in that department.

1. Bob Bass (Tulsa). Jumped from coaching Oklahoma Baptist University to the ABA and eventually became a successful general manager who was twice named NBA Executive of the Year and built two solid franchises: the San Antonio Spurs and Charlotte Hornets.

Peter Kerasotis is a University of Florida alum and native of Merritt Island, Florida, who has covered college football and Major League Baseball for a number of publications, including the *New York Times* and *Florida Today*, where his work earned him the 2010 Best Columnist Award from the Football Writers Association of America. The author of the 2005 book, *Stadium Stories: Florida Gators*, has seen basketball grow in popularity in his home state over the past few decades, with Florida serving as home base for an NBA champion and an NCAA men's basketball champion in the 21st century. Here he lists the top 10 NBA players of all time born and/or raised in the Sunshine State.

10. Neal Walk. A former Miami Beach High and University of Florida standout, Walk was the second overall pick in the 1969 NBA Draft and played eight seasons in the league. In 1988, the Florida Gators all-time rebounding leader was told he had a benign tumor encasing his spine. Following surgery, Walk was left without the use of his legs. He then played in the National Wheelchair Basketball Association. In 1990, a White House ceremony officiated by then-President George H. W. Bush honored Walk as the Wheelchair Athlete of the Year. The first basketball player to have his jersey (No. 41) retired by the Florida Gators has gone on to work in the community affairs department of the Phoenix Suns and to gain induction into the Jewish Sports Hall of Fame.

9. Darryl Dawkins. Was one of the first players to renounce his college eligibility and enter the NBA Draft straight out of high school. Dawkins attended Orlando's Maynard Evans High School, where he led his team to the 1975 state championship. The Philadelphia 76ers made him the fifth overall pick in the 1975 NBA Draft. Dawkins went on to play 14 seasons in the league and one with the Harlem Globetrotters. Dawkins was noted for his colorful personality and nicknames, most notably Chocolate Thunder, and his propensity for shattering backboards via explosive dunks, leading to a new NBA rule and the modification of backboards.

8. Derek Harper. After a stellar prep career at West Palm Beach's North Shore High School, where he led his team to the 1980 state championship and was a McDonald's All-American, Harper was a standout for the University of Illinois. During his 17-year NBA career, he scored 16,006 points.

7. Mychal Thompson. Born in the Bahamas, Thompson spent his formative years in Miami, graduating from Miami Jackson High School. After a standout career at the University of Minnesota, Thompson was the first overall pick in the 1978 NBA Draft, becoming the first foreign-born player to achieve that honor. He made the All-NBA Rookie Team and later was part of back-to-back championship teams with the Los Angeles Lakers.

6. Otis Birdsong. Born in Winter Haven, Otis attended school at Winter Haven High School. He was a consensus All-American in 1977, when he led the Houston Cougars to the title game of the National Invitational Tournament. During his 12 NBA seasons, Birdsong made four All-Star teams and scored 12,544 points. He averaged a career-high 24.6 points per game for the Kansas City Kings during the 1980–81 season.

5. Amare Stoudemire. Went straight from Orlando's Cypress Creek High School to the NBA, and then promptly won the 2002 NBA Rookie of the Year Award. Since then Stoudemire has been a six-time NBA All-Star and a first-team All-NBA selection in 2007. He won a bronze medal with the United States men's national basketball team at the 2004 Olympic Games.

4. Mitch Richmond. The Fort Lauderdale native, who attended Boyd Anderson High School in Lauderdale Lakes, was a six-time NBA All-Star and a five-time All-NBA selection. Richmond was the 1989 NBA Rookie of the Year. For his NBA career, he averaged 21 points. As a player for Kansas State, Richmond was selected to the US men's national basketball team, helping them win a bronze at the 1988 Summer Olympics. He was later a member of the US gold-medal team in the 1996 Olympics.

3. Tracy McGrady. The Auburndale native, and cousin to Vince Carter, went straight from high school to the NBA after being named *USA Today*'s prep player of the year. He was the ninth overall pick by the Toronto Raptors in the 1997 NBA Draft. McGrady leads all active players (and is fifth all time) with a 28.5 points per game average in the postseason. He has been selected to the All-Star Game seven times, and named first-team All-NBA twice.

2. Vince Carter. Born and raised in Florida, Carter was a 1995 McDonald's All-American at Daytona Beach Mainland High School. He played three college seasons at the University of North Carolina before leaving for the NBA, where he has been an eight-time All-Star. The prolific scorer, who is known for his creative moves and dunks, earned the nickname Vinsanity. He, along with Julius Erving and Michael Jordan, is the only player to lead the NBA All-Star Game in fan voting three or more times. Carter has scored over 20,000 points so far in his NBA career.

1. Artis Gilmore. Born in Chipley, Gilmore is the only player in the Naismith Memorial Basketball Hall of Fame to have been born and raised in Florida. In college, he led tiny Jacksonville University to the 1970 NCAA Championship Game against powerhouse UCLA. At JU, Gilmore twice led the nation in rebounding and posted a college career average of 22.7 rebounds per game, which is an NCAA record. During his 17-year pro career, he made 11 All-Star teams—five during his time with the ABA and six in the NBA. He was both the ABA's MVP and Rookie of the Year in 1972, and helped the Kentucky Colonels win the 1975 ABA championship. Gilmore, who scored 24,941 points in his pro career, holds the NBA career record with a .599 field goal percentage.

Top 10 New York City Basketball Players to Play in the NBA :: by George Vecsey

George Vecsey is a longtime sports columnist (and now a contributor) with the *New York Times*. He was a junior at Jamaica High in Queens when that school won the city title in 1955. His big moment came when he got in a schoolyard game with Alan Seiden and two other members of that championship team. His side lost.

Vecsey believes he faced a unique challenge in compiling this list, asserting: "Technically, New Yorkers did not invent basketball. However, everybody knows we perfected it, in the old cigar-befouled Madison Square Garden. Our coaches are smarter, our fans are more passionate, and our homegrown players are trickier.

"Tough town. We produced so many basketball players that Tommy Davis of Boys High and Sandy Koufax of Abraham Lincoln High turned to baseball. So narrowing down our great players into a top-10 list is virtually impossible. But if we really had to, here are 10 New Yorkers who could take on the world."

10. Bernard King. Not everybody gets to come home, but Bernard King did. From Alexander Hamilton High in Brooklyn and the University of Tennessee, he played six different tours in the NBA, missing nearly two years after a gruesome knee injury. With his hometown Knicks from 1982 to 1985, he was one of the most explosive small forwards in history.

9. Chris Mullin. The ultimate gym rat from Xaverian High in Brooklyn, he stayed home at St. John's. He rarely left the gym, perfecting his shots in endless practice. Mo never did play for the Knicks, scoring most of his points for Golden State, but the Garden always came alive for his annual return.

8. Connie Hawkins. Blessed with legendary wingspan, he played even taller than his 6-8. From Boys High in Brooklyn and the University of Iowa, he saw his pro debut held back because of his suspension for accepting favors from gamblers. He represents other great city players caught in gambling scandals—Roger Brown of Wingate and Dayton, who was confined to the ABA, and Sherman White of Long Island University, who never made it to the pros.

7. Nate Archibald. All New Yorkers are essentially point guards—a mix of artist and control freak. Dick McGuire, Mark Jackson, Kenny Anderson: Tiny Archibald stands for all of them. Out of DeWitt Clinton High in the Bronx, he went to Texas El Paso and into the NBA, moving as fast as the A train on the express run between 59th Street and 125th Street. In the 1972–73 season, Tiny became the first and only player to lead the NBA in scoring and assists.

6. Billy Cunningham. The Kangaroo Kid. That nickname says it all. He came out of the pouch leaping, went to Erasmus Hall in Brooklyn (right after Streisand took the Underground Railroad to North Carolina). Then he dominated the NBA and ABA until he blew out a knee at 32. With modern surgery, he could have played more years.

5. Lenny Wilkens. He chose to play in the Catholic Youth Organization as a sophomore and junior, and then started only half a season for Boys High. After starring at Providence, he became a silky guard who willingly gave up the ball for four pro teams. Opponents knew the lefty would not drive right, but nobody could stop him anyway. Smart and gentle, he became a great coach.

4. Dolph Schayes. Out of DeWitt Clinton High in the Bronx, Schayes stayed home at New York University, and then eluded the Knicks to play in upstate Syracuse. He brought a new element to pro ball—a big man who could shoot. At 6-8 he could pop a set shot, and also drive to the basket, particularly the year he played with a cast on his reset wrist.

3. Bob Cousy. This slender magician from Andrew Jackson High in Queens and Holy Cross brought elegance to the clumsy, earnest NBA with his thoroughly functional blind passes, bounce passes, and behind-the-back flips. In the schoolyard, if you got too flashy, a teammate could wither you with one word: "Cousy!"

2. Julius Erving. All right, he came from Roosevelt High on Long Island, but if the city cannot claim Brooklyn-born Michael Jordan, then it has territorial rights to Doctor J. Also, he played at the Rucker, the ultimate city tournament. After a stay at UMass, he validated the ABA, and then won an NBA championship (and dunk contests) with the 76ers. His baseline levitation from behind the basket in the 1980 NBA Finals—around Kareem—remains an NBA classic.

1. Kareem Abdul-Jabbar (aka Lew Alcindor). He left New York for UCLA after drawing national attention at Power Memorial High in Manhattan, but he always remained a son of the city, identifying with Jackie Robinson and Wilt Chamberlain's joint in Harlem, Small's Paradise. Fate provided great teammates wherever he played, and Kareem became the dominant big man of his era.

Ryan Baker is a native of the south suburbs of Chicago and graduate of the University of Illinois. He serves as the longtime sports anchor for the CBS affiliate in the Windy City.

10. Derrick Rose. The Simeon Career Academy graduate was the 2009 NBA Rookie of the Year for the Bulls, the youngest MVP in NBA history (age 22 in 2011), and possibly the most athletic point guard in NBA history.

9. Dwyane Wade. Grew up on the South Side of Chicago and attended Harold L. Richards High School. Was the fifth pick of the 2003 NBA Draft and proceeded to lead the Miami Heat to the 2006 NBA championship while winning honors as the Finals MVP. He is a seven-time All-Star, 2010 All-Star Game MVP, two-time All-NBA first team selection, and 2009 NBA scoring champion.

8. Terry Cummings. The Carver High School great went on to star at DePaul University before entering the NBA. He was the 1983 NBA Rookie of the Year with the Los Angles Clippers, a two-time All-Star, and finished his career averaging 16 points and 7 rebounds per game.

7. Cazzie Russell. Student of Carver High School, Russell went on to be the first overall pick of the 1966 NBA Draft by the New York Knicks, won a championship with the Knicks in 1970, and was an NBA All-Star.

6. Glenn "Doc" Rivers. The Proviso East High School superstar went on to become an NBA All-Star, winner of the J. Walter Kennedy Citizen Award, NBA Coach of the Year, and NBA champion coach for the Boston Celtics.

5. Maurice Cheeks. The Chicago native, who attended DuSable High School, is 10th on the all-time NBA assists list, was an NBA champion with the Philadelphia 76ers, a four-time All-Star, four-time All-Defensive first teamer, and served as head coach of the Portland Trail Blazers and Philadelphia 76ers.

4. Mark Aguirre. Born and raised in Chicago, Aguirre attended George Westinghouse College Prep before leading DePaul University to the Final Four. The top overall pick of the 1981 NBA Draft (by the Mavericks), he became a two-time NBA champion with the Pistons, three-time All-Star, and ended his career averaging 20 points per game.

3. Tim Hardaway. The Chicago native who attended Carver Area High School was a five-time NBA All-Star, an All-NBA first-team pick, and a player posted career averages of 17 points and eight assists per game.

2. George Mikan. Born in Joliet, Illinois, Mikan attended Chicago Archbishop Quigley Preparatory Seminary before matriculating to DePaul University. He went on to the NBA and was voted into the Hall of Fame. He won seven NBA titles, Rookie of the Year, MVP, four NBA All-Star selections, a spot on the 50 Greatest Players in NBA History list, and inspired the "Mikan Rule."

1. Isiah Thomas. The great point guard grew up on the West Side in North Lawndale and attended St. Joseph's School. He went on to become a Hall of Famer, two-time NBA Champion with the Pistons, NBA Finals MVP, 11-time All-Star, two-time All-Star Game MVP, three-time All-NBA first team pick, 50 Greatest Players in NBA History honoree, NBA head coach with the Indiana Pacers and New York Knicks, and front-office executive for the Toronto Raptors and New York Knicks.

Top 10 NBA Players from Philadelphia's Big 5 :: by Dick Jerardi

Dick Jerardi is the longtime and highly decorated college basketball writer for the *Daily News* in Philadelphia. This list represents his take on the top 10 NBA players to come out of Philadelphia's top five collegiate men's basketball programs—La Salle, St. Joseph's, Villanova, Temple, and the University of Pennsylvania—famously known as the Big 5. Despite having conference affiliations in the Big East, Atlantic 10, and Ivy League, these Big 5 teams take the time each season to compete against one another in a round-robin city series that showcases the City of Brotherly Love's fierce rivalries and tradition of developing great basketball players.

10. Lionel Simmons (La Salle University). Only the great Paul Arizin had a better start to his pro career than the L-Train, the seventh overall pick in the 1990 NBA Draft. Playing for Sacramento, Simmons averaged 18.0 points and 8.8 rebounds in his first season, 17.1 points and 8.1 rebounds in his second, and 17.9 points and 7.2 rebounds in his third. A great passer for a forward, he filled up box scores, getting 135 steals and 132 blocks in his second season. Very bad knees limited him to seven seasons and 5,833 points.

9. Kerry Kittles (Villanova University). Scored 7,165 points in seven seasons for New Jersey and one injury-plagued, shortened season for the Los Angeles Clippers. He averaged between 12.9 points and 17.2 points a game in his Nets career. One of the fastest guards of his era, he played in the 2002 and 2003 NBA Finals and had a career average of 14.1 points a game.

8. Jameer Nelson (St. Joseph's University). The Philly point guard in the Guy Rodgers tradition has scored over 6,500 points and dealt over 2,500 assists in his first eight NBA seasons, all with Orlando. He made the 2009 All-Star team after leading the Magic to an NBA-best 33-8 record at midseason. The 2004 National College Player of the Year is a great leader who shoots 46 percent overall, nearly 40 percent from the arc and 81 percent from the foul line.

7. Jim Washington (Villanova University). A double-double machine in his 11 seasons with St. Louis, Chicago, Philadelphia, Atlanta, and Buffalo. Scored 8,168 points and had 6,637 rebounds. He averaged a double-double in four different seasons. In the 1967–68 playoffs for the Bulls, he averaged 17.2 points and 15.0 rebounds.

6. Mike Bantom (St. Joseph's University). Scored 8,568 points in nine seasons for Phoenix, Seattle, Indiana, Philadelphia, and the Nets. He averaged 12.1 points and 6.4 rebounds. In 1976–77 for the Nets he averaged 18.6 points and 8.6 rebounds. A key member of the United States 1972 Olympic team, he was strong, tough, and relentless around the glass.

5. Tom Gola (La Salle University). A big man with little-man skills, Gola played 10 seasons for his hometown Warriors and then for the Knicks. He played in four All-Star Games, scored 7,871 points, and had 5,617 rebounds. He averaged 11.3 points, 8.0 rebounds, and 4.1 assists, and appeared in five NBA All-Star Games between 1960 and 1964. Was elected to the Hall of Fame, as much for his wonderful college career (NCAA and NIT championships), as for his solid NBA career.

4. Larry Foust (La Salle University). Scored 11,198 points in 12 NBA seasons. He played in seven NBA All-Star Games in the 1950s. Over his NBA career, he played for Fort Wayne, Minneapolis, and St. Louis. He averaged nearly a double-double for his career, with 13.7 points and 9.8 rebounds per game. Was an incredibly reliable player who could be counted on to put his numbers up just about every night.

3. Guy Rodgers (Temple University). Brilliant point guard played for Philadelphia, San Francisco, Chicago, and Milwaukee over 12 seasons. Scored 10,415 points and had 6,917 assists. Rodgers was a great passer who was unstoppable with the ball on the fast break. The Philadelphia native played in four All-Star Games during the 1960s. He averaged 18.6 points and 10.7 assists in his eighth season, and then 18.0 points and 11.2 assists in his ninth.

2. Eddie Jones (Temple University). Played 14 seasons, scoring 14,155 points while averaging double figures for 12 consecutive seasons, mostly for the Lakers and Heat. For his career he averaged 14.8 points. Over five seasons from 1999 to 2004, he averaged 20.1, 17.4, 18.3, 18.5 and 17.3. Great defender (1.620 steals) and amazing athlete who made 1,546 threes. He was a three-time All-Star.

1. Paul Arizin (Villanova University). Member of the All-Star team in each of his 10 NBA seasons for the Philadelphia Warriors and was named MVP of the 1952 All-Star Game. He scored 16,266 points while averaging 22.8 points and 8.6 rebounds in his Hall of Fame career. He was a three-time first-team All-NBA selection. Arizin was at his best in the postseason, averaging 24.2 points in 49 playoff games. He was a great shooter, scorer, and one of the league's earliest stars. He was selected as one of the 50 Greatest Players in NBA History.

The 10 Most Impactful NBA Players from the Big Ten :: by Clark Kellogg

Clark Kellogg played basketball for Ohio State University, where he was named Big Ten MVP for the 1981–82 season. The eighth overall pick of the 1982 NBA Draft, Special K made the league's All-Rookie team and established himself as a fine NBA player, averaging 13.9 points and 9.5 rebounds per game for the Indiana Pacers before his playing career ended after only five seasons due to knee problems. The Cleveland native then moved into broadcasting, working for Prime Sports, the Big East Network, ESPN, and CBS, where he's served for almost two decades and risen to the position of lead college basketball analyst. Kellogg has also been a TV analyst for the Indiana Pacers since 1990. Here, he lists the best 10 players that the Big Ten has contributed to the NBA over the years.

10. Mychal Thompson (University of Minnesota). The Gopher was a two-time All-American before becoming the first overall pick in the 1978 NBA Draft by the Portland Trail Blazers. He was selected to the NBA All-Rookie Team and was a two-time NBA champion (1987 and 1988) with the Los Angles Lakers.

9. Glen Rice (University of Michigan). The all-time leading Wolverine scorer, Rice led his Michigan team to the 1989 NCAA championship. He was selected fourth overall in the 1989 NBA draft by the Miami Heat. He went on to become a three-time NBA All-Star and one-time champion (in 2000 with the Los Angeles Lakers) while scoring over 18,000 points for his career.

8. Chris Webber (University of Michigan). The leader of the famous Fab Five at Michigan, Webber led the Wolverines to the NCAA Finals in 1992 and 1993. He was the first overall pick in the 1993 NBA Draft. He became a five-time NBA All-Star, the Rookie of the Year in 1994, and averaged over 20 points a game during his 831-game career.

7. George McGinnis (University of Indiana). The Hoosier was a six-time ABA/NBA All-Star who scored over 17,000 points during his career in the two leagues. He led the Indiana Pacers to two ABA championships (1972 and 1973).

6. Walt Bellamy (University of Indiana). Bellamy was the first overall pick of the 1961 NBA draft by the Chicago Packers. The four-time All-Star scored 20.1 points for his career and claimed 13.7 rebounds a game. He was voted into the Hall of Fame in 1993.

5. Kevin McHale (University of Minnesota). Considered by some as the greatest low-post player in NBA history, the Gopher joined the Celtics in 1980 as the third overall pick in the draft and formed one third of Boston's famous Big Three with Larry Bird and Robert Parish. Over his Hall of Fame career he won three NBA championships while scoring over 17,000 points.

4. Jerry Lucas (Ohio State University). Jerry Lucas was a three-time All-American in Columbus, Ohio. In the NBA he was a six-time All-Star and won a championship with the New York Knicks in 1973. He was inducted into the Hall of Fame in 1980 and later voted one of the 50 Greatest Players in NBA History.

3. Isiah Thomas (University of Indiana). The point guard from Chicago led the Hoosiers to the 1981 NCAA championship. Drafted by the Detroit Pistons with the second overall pick in the 1981 draft, Thomas became a 12-time All-Star, led the Pistons to two championships (1989 and 1990), and was voted into the Hall of Fame.

2. John Havlicek (Ohio State University). Part of the famous Ohio State 1960 NCAA championship team, along with Jerry Lucas and Bobby Knight, "Hondo" was drafted by the Boston Celtics and became a 13-time NBA All-Star. A key part of eight Celtic championship teams, he eventually earned Hall of Fame induction and inclusion on the 50 Greatest Players in NBA History roster.

1. Magic Johnson (Michigan State University). The Spartan led his team to the 1979 NCAA championship over Larry Bird and Indiana State, and then came to the NBA, where he revolutionized the game with his Showtime skills in Los Angeles. Johnson's Laker teams won five championships while he gained three MVP Awards, a dozen trips to the All-Star Game, Hall of Fame induction, and a nod as one of the 50 Greatest Players in NBA History.

Top NBA Players from Original Big East Teams :: by Bill Raftery

Bill Raftery, the former La Salle University basketball captain and head coach of Seton Hall, has become one of the great ambassadors for college basketball during his over three decades as a television broadcaster. He started his TV career on ESPN's *NCAA Tonight* during the 1980 men's basketball tournament and currently calls Big East games on the network's *Big Monday*. He's also worked for CBS as an NCAA basketball and NBA analyst, called New Jersey Nets games for over two decades for Fox Sports, and worked for the Big East Network. He was given the Curt Gowdy Media Award by the Basketball Hall of Fame in 2006.

Below, Bill offers his expert take on the best NBA players to come out of the Big East. Founded in 1979, the conference quickly established itself as an elite men's basketball power and training ground for pro players. The league has had numerous ups and downs and realignments over the years. For this list, Bill focuses on players who came into the NBA from one of the original seven Big East members—Syracuse, Connecticut, Boston College, Seton Hall, Providence, St. John's, and Georgetown—since the conference was established.

14 (tie). Roy Hibbert (Georgetown University) and Rudy Gay (University of Connecticut).

Hibbert is a Hoya who was drafted by the Toronto Raptors in 2008, and then traded to Indiana, where he is on the verge of a double–double career in the pivot. Rudy Gay was drafted in 2006 by the Houston Rockets, and then traded to Memphis, where he has developed into a go-to guy who averages over 17 points a game.

12 (tie). Caron Butler (University of Connecticut) and Ben Gordon (University of Connecticut).

Caron Butler starred at UConn before making his way to the NBA as the 10th overall pick (by the Miami Heat) in 2002. He has averaged over 16 points a game over his first decade in the league. Ben Gordon was born in London, grew up in New York, and starred at UConn. In the NBA he is instant offense. He was voted the NBA Sixth Man of the Year in 2005.

10. Derrick Coleman (Syracuse University).

The power forward with limitless talent was a force to be reckoned with when he wanted to be reckoned with. He was NBA Rookie of the Year in 1991 and played on some of the best New Jersey Nets teams. Five times in his career he averaged a double-double for a season.

9. Richard Hamilton (University of Connecticut). The most out-standing player in the 1999 Final Four, Hamilton was drafted by the Washington Wizards, won a championship with Detroit, and has played in three NBA All-Star Games.

8. Mark Jackson (St. John's University). The point guard from Brooklyn stayed at home to play college ball before bringing his game to the NBA, where he dished out over 10,000 assists and scored over 12,000 points with a variety of shots, including a teardrop from the paint.

6 (tie). Alonzo Mourning (Georgetown University) and Dikembe Mutombo (Georgetown University). The two Hoya centers brought their game to the NBA after stellar college careers. Mourning played in seven All-Star Games, was twice named Defensive Player of the Year (1999 and 2000), and won a championship with Miami (2006). Mutombo was four-time Defensive Player of the Year (1995, 1997, 1998, and 2001), warding off would-be shooters with his wagging finger.

4 (tie). Ray Allen (University of Connecticut) and Allen Iverson (Georgetown University). Ray Allen might be the greatest shooter in NBA history. He owns the three-point shooting record and earned himself a ring in Boston. Allen Iverson thrilled fans at Georgetown and for years in Philadelphia with his fearless and relentless attacks of the basket. Over his NBA career he scored almost 25,000 points, and was Rookie of the Year (1997) and league MVP (2001).

3. Carmelo Anthony (Syracuse University). His stay in upstate New York was brief but impactful. After leading the Orangemen to the national cham-pionship in 2003, he was drafted third overall by Denver, where he starred for eight years before being traded to the Big Apple, where he hopes to bring the Knicks their first title since the 1970s.

2. Chris Mullin (St. John's University). Born to shoot, the left-hander from New York stayed home at St. John's before matriculating to Golden State, the Dream Team, and Springfield, Massachusetts—where he was inducted into the Hall of Fame in 2011.

1. Patrick Ewing (Georgetown University). The first overall pick in the 1985 NBA Draft didn't disappoint. He never won a ring but did everything else for the Knicks. He played in 11 NBA All-Star Games, scored almost 25,000 points, and grabbed over 11,000 rebounds while thrilling all at Madison Square Garden.

The 10 Players from the SEC Who Had the Greatest NBA Careers :: by Jeff Turner

Jeff Turner was a star at Vanderbilt in the early 1980s. In 1984, he won a gold medal on the Bobby Knight-led US Olympic team. The New Jersey Nets made him the 17th overall pick of that year's NBA Draft. He stayed in the NBA for 10 years and played in three postseasons, including in 1995, when he contributed to Orlando's run to the NBA Finals. On the task of putting together this list, he said, "This turned out to be much more difficult than I had first thought. This list leaves out many former SEC standouts who went on to have great NBA careers."

10. Dale Ellis (University of Tennessee). I spent three years in college chasing Ellis off of screens! Thank goodness we didn't have a three-point line in college at that time. Dale went on to play 17 years in the NBA and finished his career with 19,004 points. He is top 10 all time in three-point FGs made and attempted. In 1987 he was selected as the league's Most Improved Player after improving his scoring average from 7 to 24 points per game.

9. Pat Riley (University of Kentucky). Pat's nine-year playing career was highlighted only by being a part of the 1972 NBA champion Lakers. His significant impact on the league comes from his 24 years as the head coach of the Lakers, Knicks, and Heat. Riley is the only coach to take three different teams to the NBA Finals and has won five championships—four with the Lakers and one with the Heat. He was selected NBA Coach of the Year three times.

8. Cliff Hagan (University of Kentucky). Hagan played 10 seasons with the St Louis Hawks and was selected to the NBA All-Star team five times. In 1958 he combined with Bob Pettit to lead the Hawks to the NBA championship over the Boston Celtics. He scored 14,780 points in his Hall of Fame career.

7. Dan Issel (University of Kentucky). The Horse comes in at No. 7 on my list based on his 15-year NBA/ABA career. Dan was a seven-time All-Star who put up big scoring numbers throughout his Hall of Fame career. He ranks ninth all time on the combined NBA/ABA scoring list, with 27,842 points.

6. Bernard King (University of Tennessee). Admittedly, it is hard for me as a Vanderbilt Commodore to vote for another Volunteer, but I will put aside my bias for King. A four-time All-Star in his 14-year NBA career, King was a scoring machine, leading the league in 1984–85 at 32.9 points per game. He finished his career with 19,655 points.

5. Pete Maravich (LSU). Hall of Famer, Pistol Pete played 10 years in the NBA after a legendary three years at LSU. Arguably, the greatest ball handler of all time, Pete brought fans to the games to see what amazing things he would do with a basketball. He inspired players of my generation to try new skills that were previously branded as "showboating." Pete finished his career with 15,948 points and was an All-Star five times.

4. Bob Pettit (LSU). Played 11 years in the NBA and in 11 All-Star Games! Petit was one of those special players whose work ethic and talent combined to make him the NBA's Rookie of the Year in 1955, a two-time NBA Most Valuable Player, and eventual Hall of Fame selection. He led the St. Louis Hawks to the NBA title in 1958. He scored 20,880 points in his career, which works out to 26.4 points per game, and pulled down 12,849 rebounds, which works out to 16.2 rebounds per game.

3. Dominique Wilkins (University of Georgia). The most spectacular slam dunk artist ever, I swear I saw the bottom of his shoes as he jumped over me one time! The Human Highlight Film was a two-time NBA Slam Dunk Contest champion whose high-flying dunks overshadowed the fact that he was one of the most prolific scorers in the 1980s. He led the NBA in scoring in the 1985–86 season, averaging 30.3 points per game. Dominique was selected to the All-Star team nine times in his 15 NBA seasons and finished his career with 26,668 points and a Hall of Fame induction.

2. Charles Barkley (Auburn University). Listed at a generous 6-6, Sir Charles was one of the most unique power forwards to play the game. His strength and power around the basket combined with his ability to run the floor made him a matchup nightmare. Voted the league's Most Valuable Player in 1993, Charles was an 11-time All-Star. In his 16-year career, Barkley amassed 23,756 total points and pulled down 12,541 rebounds.

1. Shaquille O'Neal (LSU). This is the easiest choice of all. In 19 seasons, Shaq won four NBA championships, two scoring titles, one league MVP, three Finals MVPs, and was selected to the All-Star team 15 times! His combination of power and speed made him almost impossible to stop one-on-one, which opened up shots for teammates like me. He ranks sixth on the all-time NBA scoring list with 28,596 points.

Top NBA Players from Texas Colleges ::
by Bob Hill

Bob Hill served as an NBA head coach for the Indiana Pacers, New York Knicks, San Antonio Spurs, and Seattle SuperSonics. In the 1994–95 season, Hill led the Spurs to the best record in the league, 62–20.

14. Ricky Pierce (Rice University). The Texas native attended Rice University before starring in the NBA, where he was the two-time Sixth Man of the Year (1987 and 1990) and scored almost 15,000 points during his 16-year pro career.

13. Terry Teagle (Baylor University). Teagle scored 2,189 points for the Baylor Bears before his 11-year pro career, during which he scored almost 8,000 points for the Lakers, Houston, Detroit, and Golden State.

12. LaMarcus Aldridge (University of Texas). Aldridge was a McDonald's All-American, matriculated to Texas, and then was drafted second overall by Portland, where he has averaged over 17 points and over seven rebounds a game in his first six seasons.

11. LaSalle Thompson (University of Texas). Thompson played at Texas in the early 1980s before heading to the NBA, where he played in 985 games and scored 7,806 points.

10. Zelmo Beaty (Prairie View University). Beaty was selected by the St. Louis Hawks with the third overall pick in the 1962 NBA Draft. He played in both the NBA and ABA. During his career he played in five All-Star Games and won an ABA championship with the Utah Stars while scoring over 15,000 points.

9. Luke Jackson (University of Texas-Pan American). Jackson was a forward/center on the 1967 NBA champion 76ers. Luke averaged 11.0 points and 11.7 rebounds in the 15-game postseason during Philadelphia's run to the title.

8. Maurice Cheeks (West Texas State). Cheeks came to the 76ers in the second round of the 1978 NBA Draft and became one of the greatest point guards of all time in the NBA. He led Philadelphia to a 1983 NBA championship.

7. Slater Martin (University of Texas). Martin scored 49 points in a 1949 game against TCU for the Longhorns, who later retired his No. 15. In the

NBA he won five championships—four with the Minneapolis Lakers and one with the St. Louis Hawks. He played in seven NBA All-Star Games and is a member of the Hall of Fame.

6. Tim Hardaway (University of Texas-El Paso). The five-time NBA All-Star came out of UTEP in 1989 and electrified NBA fans with his killer crossover dribble, drives to the basket, and dishes to teammates Chris Mullin and Mitch Richmond as part of the Golden State triumvirate known as Run TMC.

5. Kevin Durant (University of Texas). The Longhorn burst onto the NBA scene as an immediate superstar, revitalizing the Seattle SuperSonics/Oklahoma City Thunder while making those teams viable contenders. He won the NBA scoring three times in his first four years in the league and also won the 2008 NBA Rookie of the Year Award.

4. Nate "Tiny" Archibald (University of Texas-El Paso). Tiny Archibald had one of the great seasons in NBA history in 1972–1973, when he led the league in both scoring and assists. Tiny was a six-time All-Star and won an NBA championship with Larry Bird in Boston in 1981.

3. Clyde Drexler (University of Houston). Clyde the Glide swooped into the NBA from Houston and wowed fans in Portland with his cutting attacks to the hoop and graceful play. After a stellar career in the Northwest, he went home to Houston where he gained selection to his ninth and tenth All-Star Games, and won an NBA championship in 1995 with the Rockets.

2. Elvin Hayes (University of Houston). The Cougar center averaged over 31 points a game in college and slayed Lew Alcindor in the Astrodome before bringing his game to the NBA, where he eventually migrated to Washington and led the Bullets to a championship in 1978 with his deadly turn-around jump shot from the elbow. The Hall of Famer scored over 27,000 points and played in 12 All-Star Games.

1. Hakeem Olajuwon (University of Houston). A charter member of Phi Slamma Jamma, the Houston Cougar center was drafted by the Houston Rockets first overall in 1984 and proceeded to lead his team to consecutive NBA championships in 1994 and 1995. During his pro career Hakeem was a two-time Defensive Player of the Year, a one-time NBA MVP, a two-time Finals MVP, and a 12-time All-Star.

Tom Nissalke has been a coach and announcer in the NBA for five decades. He was named Coach of the Year in the NBA (for the 1976–77 season with the Houston Rockets) and in the ABA (for the 1971–72 season with the Dallas Chaparrals). He also coached both the ABA's Utah Stars and the NBA's Utah Jazz. He later became an announcer for the Utah Jazz broadcasts. Here, he details the long, proud, and vastly underrated contributions of Utah colleges to NBA rosters.

10. Jimmer Fredette (Brigham Young University). It would take about 10 pages to list all of Jimmer's awards during his brilliant career at BYU. He was the country's leading scorer, National Payer of the Year, Wooden Award Winner, Naismith Award winner, the Oscar Robertson trophy winner, and on and on! Can he be like the others on this list and make a name for himself in the NBA? The jury is out on him right now, but I think he will do well. A star? Maybe not.

9. Nate Williams (Utah State University). Nate was built like Superman and could have gone the same route as Cornell Green, another former Aggie great who turned to football. He played during some of Utah State's greatest years. Williams was picked in the 1971 NBA hardship draft and played almost nine years in the league. His best season was 1973–74, when he averaged 16 points per game with the Kansas City Kings.

8. Fred Roberts (Brigham Young University). A terrific college player at BYU, along with Danny Ainge and Greg Kite, Fred played his entire four years in college, averaging 15 point per game during some very good years at BYU. He was a very successful journeyman, playing 13 years in the NBA. His most productive were the five seasons (1988–93) he spent with the Milwaukee Bucks.

7. Andrew Bogut (University of Utah). Bogut was another former Utah collegian to be named Player of the Year, All-American, Wooden Award winner, All-Conference, and whatever other honors were out there. After his brilliant career at Utah he was picked first overall in the 2005 NBA Draft by the Milwaukee Bucks. As a pro he is considered one of the best passing big men in the game. Because of some injury problems, he has lost significant playing time. If he stays injury-free, he could be among the top centers in the NBA for years to come.

6. Mike Newlin (University of Utah). Tough, feisty, hard-nosed—these adjectives were applied to Mike during his career at the University of Utah, and later during his 11-year pro career. Newlin was All-Conference at Utah, besides being a fine student. Most of his NBA playing days were spent in Houston, where his Rockets backcourt partners were Hall of Famer Calvin Murphy and John Lucas. He finished his playing days in New York with the Nets, and later the Knicks. His top scoring output in a game was 52 points during his time with the Nets.

5. Mel Hutchins (Brigham Young University). The only "old-timer" on my list played in another era but was a standout. At BYU he was an NCAA All-American and was the second overall pick in the 1951 NBA Draft by the former Tri-Cities Blackhawks (later the Milwaukee franchise). He was the NBA Co-Rookie of the Year in 1952, played in four All-Star Games, and was forced to retire in 1958 due to a knee injury after a seven-year career.

4. Andre Miller (University of Utah). Looking for a fine point guard to run your team? Andre has been that for 14 years in the NBA. He became a starter as a freshman at Utah, and then became the team leader and an All-American. He led the Utes to the 1998 NCAA championship game, which the Utes lost to Kentucky, 73–69. George Karl, his head coach in Denver, said Andre is the smartest point guard he ever coached.

3. Keith Van Horn (University of Utah). Keith is considered by many to be the University of Utah's greatest player. He was All-Conference, All-American, and the all-time leading scorer for the "U" and the conference. He was the second overall draft pick and was a major contributor to both the Nets and Mavs' conference championship teams. Could he have been even a better pro? Maybe? Though 16 points per game was pretty good.

2. Tom Chambers (University of Utah). Tom was a very good player at the "U" but became an even better player as a pro. He led the San Diego Clippers in scoring his rookie year and was traded to Seattle, and later to Phoenix, where he achieved NBA stardom. He was the MVP of the 1987 NBA All-Star Game and was selected to four All-Star teams. During his Phoenix years Chambers and future Sacramento Mayor Kevin Johnson were one of the great pick-and-roll duos in the league.

1. Danny Ainge (Brigham Young University). What hasn't Danny Ainge done? He was a great student and athlete at BYU, a two-time NBA champion and standout with several teams, and is now the Majordomo with the Boston Celtics. As an All-American at BYU he is best remembered for his coast-to-coast drive to beat Notre Dame in 1981. In the NBA Danny was a key player on two great Celtic teams, as well as for the Suns and Blazers. He later coached the Suns, was an NBA TV broadcaster, and was selected as the 2008 NBA Executive of the Year.

Top NBA Players from the Ivy League ::
by Fran Dunphy

Fran Dunphy coached the University of Pennsylvania men's basketball team from 1989 to 2006. During his 17-year tenure, he won 310 games, including one in the NCAA tournament over Nebraska, and 10 Ivy League championships. Coach Dunphy is currently the head coach of Temple University, but remains a scholar of Ivy League basketball history.

13. Matt Maloney (University of Pennsylvania). The guard with a coach for a father (John Maloney assistant at Temple) played the game with a high basketball IQ. As a Houston Rocket, Maloney started at point guard as a rookie. He was named to the second team All Rookie squad in 1997. He played six years, scoring over 2,000 points and registering almost 900 assists.

12. Ernie Beck (University of Pennsylvania). The 1953 All-American was chosen by the Philadelphia Warriors with their territorial selection in the 1953 draft. He went on to play in the NBA for seven years, winning a championship with the Warriors in 1956.

11. Jeremy Lin (Harvard University). After the 2010 Harvard graduate was waived by Golden State and Houston he arrived in New York and electrified not only Madison Square Garden, but the entire NBA. His Lin-sane game was a surprise to everyone in the sports world except himself.

10. Dave Wohl (University of Pennsylvania). The Quaker point guard led his college team to a No. 3 national ranking in 1971. He was drafted in the third round of the 1971 NBA Draft and proceeded to play in the league for seven years, scoring over 2,500 points and dishing out almost 1,500 assists. After his playing career he coached the New Jersey Nets for three seasons and was an executive with the Miami Heat.

9. Chris Dudley (Yale University). The Bulldog center was chosen in the fourth round by the Cleveland Cavaliers in 1987. He went on to have a 16-year NBA career in which he recorded over 1,000 blocks, 5,000 rebounds, and almost 3,500 points.

8. David "Corky" Calhoun (University of Pennsylvania). This Quaker led his college team to a three-year record of 78-6 before the Phoenix Suns made him the fourth overall pick in the 1972 NBA Draft. He played in the NBA for eight years, winning a championship with the Trail Blazers in 1977.

7. John Hummer (Princeton University). The Tiger played for Pete Carril at Princeton before being drafted by the Buffalo Braves in the first round of the 1970 NBA draft. He enjoyed a six-year NBA career with Buffalo, Chicago, and Seattle.

5 (tie). Armond Hill (Princeton University) and Brian Taylor (Princeton University). Armond Hill was a New York City point guard before matriculating to Princeton. In 1976 he was named Ivy League Player of the Year and was chosen by the Atlanta Hawks with the ninth pick of the NBA Draft. He went on to have a productive eight-year NBA career.

After a two-year career at Princeton in which he scored 1,239 points, Brian Taylor left after his junior season to play for the New York Nets in the ABA, where he won two championships and was Rookie of the Year. Over his 10-year ABA/NBA career, Taylor scored 7,868 points.

4. Rudy LaRusso (Dartmouth College). The 6-7 center is the greatest player in Dartmouth history. He led the Big Green to an Ivy title in 1959 on a last-second shot. He was drafted by the Minneapolis Lakers in 1959 and migrated with the team to Los Angeles, where he played before being traded to the San Francisco Warriors. The four-time All-Star averaged 15.6 points a game and grabbed 9.4 rebounds over his 10-year, 736-game NBA career and was considered a first-rate defender.

3. Jim McMillian (Columbia University). As the greatest player in Columbia history, the 6-5 forward led the Bears to a No. 6 national ranking in 1968. He was drafted by the Lakers in the first round in 1970, and was an integral part of their 1972 championship and 33-game winning streak. Over his nine-year NBA career, Jim scored over 8,700 points while hitting over 48 percent of his shots from the field.

2. Geoff Petrie (Princeton University). The Tiger star was drafted by the Portland Trail Blazers with the eighth overall pick of the 1970 draft. He shared Rookie of the Year honors with Dave Cowens that season, averaging almost 25 points a game. He once scored 51 points in a game (a then-Portland record) and would later have his No. 45 retired after playing in two All-Star Games. Following his playing career he became a team executive. Twice he was awarded Executive of the Year Awards (1999 and 2001) as president of the Sacramento Kings.

1. Bill Bradley (Princeton University). One of the greatest college players ever, Bill Bradley scored 2,503 points (30.2 a game), led the Tigers to the 1965 Final Four (where he was MVP), and won a gold medal in the 1964 Olympics. After two years as a Rhodes Scholar, he joined the New York Knicks, who chose him with the second overall pick of the 1965 NBA Draft. As a Knick, he won two championships, played in one All-Star Game, and was subsequently voted into the Hall of Fame. Following his career he served as a United States Senator for 18 years.

Top 10 NBA Players from Black Colleges
:: by Nick Anderson

Nick Anderson played in the NBA for 13 seasons, including 10 for the Orlando Magic—the team that made him its first-ever draft pick in 1989. The guard/forward averaged in double figures in each of his 10 seasons in Orlando and remains the team's all-time leading scorer. Dubbed St. Nick for his off-court charitable efforts, Anderson now works in the Magic's community relations department.

Anderson played his college ball at the University of Illinois, a major program that reached the Final Four during his time there. Here, he pays tribute to 10 players who made it in the NBA after playing at colleges established to serve the higher education needs of the nation's black community.

10. Al Attles (North Carolina A&T). The former Bulldog guard was the fifth-round pick of the Philadelphia Warriors in the 1960 NBA Draft. Eleven years later he had played in two NBA finals and been a consistent contributor to the Philadelphia and San Francisco Warriors. But Attles' greatest NBA contribution came as the head coach of the Golden State Warriors, a team he led to 557 wins and the 1975 NBA championship.

9. Dick Barnett (Tennessee A&I). After a storied career at Tennessee A&I, Barnett was drafted in the first round of the 1959 NBA Draft by the Syracuse Nationals. During his 15-year pro career he scored over 15,000 points and won championships with the New York Knicks in 1970 and 1973.

8. Charles Oakley (Virginia Union University). One of the great power forwards in NBA history, Oakley played in almost 1,300 games, scoring over 12,000 points and grabbing over 12,000 rebounds while playing primarily for the Chicago Bulls and New York Knicks.

7. Luscious "Luke" Jackson (University of Texas-Pan American). The powerful forward was the first-round pick of the Philadelphia 76ers in 1964. He was a significant contributor to the Sixers' 1967 championship team while playing alongside Wilt Chamberlain in the frontcourt.

6. Ben Wallace (Virginia Union University). The determined Wallace was one of the great rebounders of his generation. Four times he was named NBA Defensive Player of the Year and won a championship with the Detroit Pistons in 2004. He left his mark on the game despite being undrafted coming out of Virginia Union.

5. Zelmo Beaty (Prairie View A&M University). Beaty was the first-round pick of the St. Louis Hawks in 1962. Over his career he averaged a double-double (16 ppg and 10.4 rpg) while playing in five All-Star Games (two in the NBA and three in the ABA).

4. Bob Love (Southern A&M). The three-time NBA All-Star was originally a fourth-round pick of the Cincinnati Royals in the 1965 NBA Draft. He eventually landed in Chicago, where he became a favorite of the Windy City fans. His No. 10 was retired by the Bulls.

3. Sam Jones (North Carolina Central University). This five-time All-Star was a vital cog in the Celtic dynasty machine. The clutch-shooting guard was part of 10 NBA championship teams in Boston from 1959 to 1969. He scored over 15,000 points and was voted into the Hall of Fame in 1984.

2. Earl Monroe (Winston-Salem State). Earl the Pearl thrilled the NBA and fans in both Baltimore and New York. The four-time All-Star with the patented spin move was not only one of the great showmen in league history, but also one of the league's greatest players.

1. Willis Reed (Grambling State University). Sure, he limped onto the Madison Square Garden floor for Game 7 of the 1970 finals, but he was more than that great moment. The seven-time, All-Star and league MVP (1970) was the leader and heart of the New York Knicks' greatest years, which culminated in two championships (1970 and 1973) and shook Madison Square Garden like it never had been shaken before.

Bill Foster served as head coach of Duke men's basketball team from 1974 to 1980. He led the team to the Final Four and then the final game of the NCAA tournament in 1978—when he was named Coach of the Year by the National Association of Basketball Coaches—as well as to two ACC tournament titles and an ACC regular-season title. The Pennsylvania native was the first coach to lead four different programs (Duke, Rutgers, South Carolina, and Utah) to 20-win seasons.

Faced with the difficult task of choosing the top 10 NBA players to come out of Duke, Foster chose 15 of them. He said, "These lists were never one of my favorite things to do—visiting the dentist or having an operation was right up there in a tie for first. The different eras and the team successes have been legendary. Many players were involved and when I counted the number of Duke players that ever played in the NBA, I found the numbers coming up to approximately 54. I made several phone calls, including ones to Jon Jackson (current associate athletic director, media relations at Duke) and to Johnny Moore (president of Moore Marketing in Durham, NC, who has been a valuable person in Duke athletics since the time I was there). I needed their confirmation for this article. From the media relations office at Duke, here is some interesting information: number of Duke players chosen in the first round of the NBA Draft from 1985 to present under the watch of Duke Head Coach Mike Krzyzewski—23 (16 of them lottery picks), which is the second most of any college basketball program.

"Because of the restrictive numbers allowed in a list like this, there are a lot of very good former Duke players who are not included below, but that's the way it goes."

15. Johnny Dawkins (played in NBA 1986–95). Current head coach at Stanford University played for three NBA teams: San Antonio, Philadelphia, and Detroit.

14. Gene Banks (1981–87). Played for San Antonio and Chicago, and is currently an assistant coach with the Washington Wizards.

13. Danny Ferry (1990–2003). Started in Cleveland, and then moved to San Antonio, where he won a championship ring.

12. Mike Dunleavy, Jr. (2002–present). Long and productive career in the NBA with Golden State, Indiana, and Milwaukee.

11. Shane Battier (2001–present). Played for Memphis, Houston, and Miami, becoming a valuable player with his all-around "team" game and his outstanding defensive play.

10. J. J. Redick (2006–present). Orlando Magic guard has improved his game as a shooter/scorer and valuable player with each passing year.

9. Mike Gminski (1980–94). "The big guy" proved to be an outstanding shooter and very durable player over the course of his lengthy career (14 seasons) in the NBA while playing for New Jersey, Philadelphia, Charlotte, and Milwaukee.

8. Corey Maggette (1999–present). Has averaged over 16 points per game during his career with Orlando, the LA Clippers, Golden State, Milwaukee, and Charlotte.

7. Luol Deng (2004–present). Very steady performer with the Chicago Bulls received the NBA Sportsmanship Award in 2007.

6. Christian Laettner (1991–2006). Played with Minnesota, Atlanta, Detroit, Dallas, Washington, and Miami (and who can forget his shot in the fading seconds for Duke to defeat the University of Kentucky in the NCAA tourney in 1992). He was a very steady NBA performer.

5. Carlos Boozer (2002–present). Former second-round pick has played for Cleveland, Utah, and Chicago, as well as in the 2007 and 2008 NBA All-Star Games.

4. Elton Brand (1999–present). A double-double man who has been a solid NBA performer for Chicago, the Los Angeles Clippers, and Philadelphia. He was named Rookie of the Year in 2000 (along with Steve Francis), to the NBA All-Rookie Team, to the NBA All-Star Game in 2002 and 2006, and won the NBA Sportsmanship Award in 2006.

3. Jack Marin (1966–77). A player with Baltimore, Houston, Buffalo, and Chicago, Marin made the NBA All-Rookie Team in 1967, and the NBA All-Star Game in 1972 and 1973. What a shooter! I've often felt that when Jack would be 75 years old, he could get up at 3 a.m. and make eight out of ten from three-point range.

2. Jeff Mullins (1964–76). A very steady, all-around performer for three different NBA teams— St. Louis, San Francisco, and Golden State. Won a championship ring with the Warriors, the team he was with from 1971 to 1976. Earned NBA All-Star selections from 1969 to 1971.

1. Grant Hill (1994–present). A star for Detroit, Orlando, and Phoenix, Grant Hill has gained too many honors to list, but here are a few of the most important ones he has received during his illustrious career: All-NBA Team (1996–2000); NBA Rookie of the Year (1997); IBM Award (1997); NBA All-Rookie Team (1995); NBA All-Star Game selections (1995–98, 2000, 2005); and the NBA Sportsmanship Award (2005, 2008, and 2010).

University of North Carolina Tar Heels Who Impacted the NBA :: by Stuart Scott

Stuart Scott is a longtime on-air ESPN personality who serves as an anchor on the network's flagship *SportsCenter* program, and has been the lead host on its NBA programming. He also writes a column for *ESPN the Magazine*. He graduated from the University of North Carolina in 1987 and still bleeds baby blue.

13 (tie). George Karl and Larry Brown. Both individuals were fine basketball players at North Carolina and in professional basketball (each played in the ABA and NBA), but the two basketball lifers have left greater footprints as coaches. Both Brown and Karl have won over a 1,000 NBA games, with Brown also earning an NBA title with the Detroit Pistons in 2004.

12. Rasheed Wallace. Always interesting, always unpredictable, Wallace scored over 15,000 points in a career that included four All-Star Games and a championship with the Detroit Pistons in 2004.

11. Mitch Kupchak. Kupchak was a piece of the puzzle in two NBA championships (Washington in 1978 and the Los Angeles Lakers in 1985) as a player, and then as a general manager he built two championship Laker teams (2009 and 2010).

10. Charlie Scott. The first African-American ever awarded an athletic scholarship at North Carolina, Scott joined the ABA after a stellar college career and was a dominant scorer before matriculating to the NBA, where he was a three-time All-Star with the Phoenix Suns before coming to Boston to win a championship.

9. Vince Carter. An eight-time All-Star, Carter has scored over 20,000 points during his high-flying NBA career.

8. Brad Daugherty. Daugherty was a 1986 All-American. He was subsequently selected by Cleveland with the first overall pick of the 1986 draft. And though his brilliant NBA career was prematurely hijacked by a balky back, he left his mark on the league with five NBA All-Star appearances while leading the Cavaliers to some of their glory years.

7. Antawn Jamison. The 1998 NCAA Player of the Year has played in two NBA All-Star Games and scored over 19,000 points in his pro career.

6. Bobby Jones. One of the great defending forwards in NBA history, Jones won a championship in Philadelphia while being coached by fellow Tar Heel Billy Cunningham.

5. Sam Perkins. The sweet-shooting left-hander scored over 15,000 points in the NBA during a steady and effective career that stretched to 1,286 games.

4. James Worthy. The forward, who ran with the Showtime gang of Los Angeles in the 1980s, won a championship in North Carolina with Michael Jordan and Sam Perkins. For his pro career, Worthy won three NBA championships and played in seven All-Star Games.

3. Billy Cunningham. The Hall of Famer played in Chapel Hill in the early 1960s. He was chosen in the first round of the 1965 draft by Philadelphia, where he won a championship and played in four All-Star Games. Later as a coach he led the Sixers to their second championship.

2. Bob McAdoo. After scoring 19 points a game in the 1971–72 season at North Carolina, McAdoo was selected second overall in the NBA Draft by Buffalo, where he would earn Rookie of the Year status (1973) and MVP honors (1975). The five-time All-Star and three-time scoring champion won two NBA titles with the Los Angeles Lakers later in his career.

1. Michael Jordan. It all started with a jump shot against Georgetown in the 1982 NCAA title game and ended in the NBA, but only after six NBA championships, five MVPs, 14 All-Star visits, and 10 scoring championships. Now that is Tar Heel basketball at its best.

Bobby Cremins served as head coach from 1981–2000 of the men's basketball team at Georgia Tech, where he was a three-time ACC Coach of the Year and in 1990 was named Naismith College Coach of the Year. Over his career he has won over 500 games and earned a trip to the Final Four in 1990. The floor of the Yellow Jackets gym is called "Cremins Court." He retired in 2012 after four decades as a college basketball coach.

10. Tom Hammonds. One of the finest young men I have ever coached and definitely one of the strongest. The 14-year NBA veteran scored over 3,500 points while grabbing 2,243 rebounds. He appeared in 21 NBA playoff games. While enrolled at Georgia Tech, Hammonds scored over 2,000 points and won a gold medal with the US national team in the 1986 FIBA World Championship.

9. Travis Best. He was a great scorer who also could defend. The left-handed point guard had a 10-year NBA career. During the 2000 NBA Finals, the Pacer averaged 5.8 points per game against the Los Angeles Lakers. For his career he scored over 5,000 points while distributing almost 2,500 assists.

8. Jon Barry. We found him out of a junior college in Texas. He was fearless and very confident. In college and the NBA he was a great shooter with superior range. During his 14-year career, he was a top-10 three-point shooter year in and year out. Over his 821 games, he scored 4,715 and won a title with the 2003 Detroit Pistons.

7. Chris Bosh. Chris is the perfect team player. His talent, intelligence, and will to win made him a pleasure to watch. The seven-time All-Star has averaged close to 20 points and 10 rebounds per game over his nine-year career. Was a member of the 2008 US Olympic Team that went 8–0 and won the gold medal. He is the Raptors all-time leader in points, total rebounds, offensive rebounds, defensive rebounds, free throws made, blocks, minutes, games started, and double-doubles.

6. Dennis Scott. Absolutely incredible range and a natural point forward. The Orlando Magic made this great shooter the fourth pick of the 1990 draft. Over his 10-year career he scored over 8,000 points. He set an NBA record by making 267 three-pointers in 1995–1996.

5. Matt Harpring. Played football, baseball and basketball in high school. He missed all the summer camps so we almost didn't recruit him. Toughest kid I ever coached. The one-time quarterback of Georgia Tech played in the NBA for 11 years. He averaged 11.5 points a game (7,645 points) over his career. In 2002–2003 he averaged 17.6 points a game.

4. John Salley. Smartest player I have ever coached and great personality. The forward was the first player in NBA history to win a ring with three separate teams. He played for 11 years and scored 5,228 points, claimed 3,356 rebounds and ranks 85th in NBA history with 985 blocks. A valuable postseason player, Salley participated in 134 playoff games.

3. Stephon Marbury. Incredible talent, unstoppable at times. Because of his upper body strength he was a very good defensive player also. The 13-year NBA player scored over 16,000 points (19.3 per game) and dished out 7.6 assists a game. He was a two-time All-Star.

2. Kenny Anderson. Best ball handler I have ever coached or seen. He could pass and score with anybody. The point guard had over 10,000 points and 5,000 assists during his 14-year career. He started in the 1994 All-Star Game and scored 6 points. Anderson is the all-time assists leader of the New Jersey Nets, who chose him with the second pick in the 1991 draft.

1. Mark Price. The complete package. Mark was a very spiritual person and had incredible determination. I loved when he was on the free throw line at the end of a game. The 12-year NBA star had almost 11,000 points and 5,000 assists over his career. He finished with a .904 free throw shooting percentage, placing him second on the league's all-time leader list. In 1988–1989, he became the second player, after Larry Bird, to join the NBA's 50-40-90 Club for those who shot at least .400 from three-point range, at least .500 from the field, and at least .900 from the free throw line in a single season (three players have done it since). He twice won the Three-Point Shootout and was a four-time All-Star. Price was named first-team All-NBA after the 1992–93 season. He played for the US national team, also known as Dream Team II, in the 1994 FIBA World Championship, winning a gold medal.

Top NBA Players from Wake Forest
:: by Ernie Accorsi

Ernie Accorsi was the longtime NFL general manager of the New York Giants, Cleveland Browns, and Baltimore Colts. Accorsi graduated from Wake Forest University in 1963.

10 (tie). Jeff Teague and Al-Farouq Aminu. Teague was an outstanding player in college and has become a solid NBA guard who is a good shooter and playmaker. Aminu is a powerful frontcourt presence with a big upside.

9. Darius Songaila. The Lithuanian was the first international player in Wake Forest's rich basketball history. Songaila has become a solid NBA performer over the years.

8. Dave Budd. A very underrated NBA rebounder and defensive specialist for some mediocre New York Knicks teams in the first half of the 1960s. Tough as nails and scored more than he was expected to with some very big point nights. Was a senior at Wake when Len Chappel and Billy Packer were sophomores. If Dave had one more year there, when Chappel and Packer led the Deacons to the Final Four in 1962, it could have meant a national championship for the school. He was that kind of clutch player.

7. Len Chappel. The power forward was a first-team All-American and one of the leading scorers in the country when he led Wake Forest to the 1962 Final Four. Chappel was the first-round draft choice of the Syracuse Nationals (which became the Philadelphia 76ers) and fourth overall in that year's NBA Draft. Chappel was big for his time (6-8) and had a huge wingspan. He was a good inside rebounder and respected power player, but what set him apart from most big men was his shooting touch. He could drift outside and shoot long-range jumpers, pulling the big man guarding him out of the pivot. He had a solid, 10-year NBA career for several clubs, probably enjoying his best years for the New York Knicks, including his 1963–64 All-Star season.

6. Frank Johnson. He was an outstanding pure shooter, especially with the three-point shot in the new rule's early years. He was quick and could score. He played the same way in the pros as he did in college. Later, he became head coach of the Phoenix Suns.

5. Josh Howard. The 2003 ACC Player of the Year is an outstanding all-around NBA player. He has been a valuable starter and contributor for the Dallas Mavericks, Washington Wizards, and Utah Jazz.

4. Rodney Rogers. A wonderful NBA forward and even better person whose career was cut short by a tragic accident. A force off the boards and as an inside scorer, he was the inspiration and best player on some very good Wake Forest teams.

3. Muggsy Bogues. Truly one of the most remarkable college and professional athletes in history. I was with the Baltimore Colts when I saw a note in the *Baltimore Sun* that the 5-3 Bogues had received a grant in aid to play at Wake Forest. My reaction? How could the *Sun* allow such a glaring typo to run in all of their editions. Well, it wasn't a typo—he was 5-3, and yet no one in the ACC or the NBA could handle him. Just an extraordinary, quick, dynamic player who made his mark in NBA history.

2. Chris Paul. How can Chris Paul become one of the greatest players in the NBA when countless other players coming out of his college have his size and stature and don't make it? Well, besides extraordinary physical talent, quickness, explosion, floor vision, shooting ability, court presence, and tremendous intelligence, there is an intangible that all of us who try to evaluate athletes cannot quantify, but we "feel." That intangible is "heart." He has that in abundance. He's the guy you want on your side. What a great player and person this young man is.

1. Tim Duncan. Simply, in my view, the best forward to ever play in the league. A first-ballot Hall of Famer with incredible character and a pure winner. I had the humbling experience of being inducted into the Wake Forest Hall of Fame with Tim Duncan. I didn't get top billing on that one. When I spoke, I said, in 35 years in the National Football League, searching for people to build my teams around, trying to find great players and people, I had never come across anyone with Hall of Fame credentials in every category—personal, character, and physical. As a general manager you dream about acquiring a person and player like Tim Duncan. The greatest tribute I ever heard to Duncan came from college coaching great Rick Pitino, who was not successful as head coach of the Boston Celtics. He said, "If we had won the coin toss and had the opportunity to pick first and draft Tim Duncan, I would still be coaching the Boston Celtics." There's not much to say after that.

Top 10 NBA Players from Syracuse University :: by Sean McDonough

Sean McDonough is one of the most talented and versatile announcers in the business. Son of the *Boston Globe*'s famed sportswriter Will McDonough, the ESPN broadcaster has called the Masters, US Open tennis, Major League Baseball, the NFL, college football, and NCAA basketball over his career. A 1984 graduate of Syracuse University, McDonough remains a big fan of the college program that has consistently attracted and developed some of the finest basketball talent in the country.

Honorable Mention. Etan Thomas; Rafael Addison; Marty Byrnes; Jason Hart; Wes Johnson.

10. Hakim Warrick. The 2005 All-American was chosen in the first round by the Memphis Grizzlies. And though he is still compiling numbers in the NBA, Hakim has already scored almost 5,000 points during his seven-year career.

9. John Wallace. The forward averaged 7.6 points and 2.8 rebounds per game over a seven-year career. In 1997–98, he had a strong season with Toronto, averaging 14 points and 4.5 rebounds a game.

8. Louis Orr. One of the classiest players ever to come out of Syracuse, the smooth forward scored over 5,500 career points in the NBA. He had a nice season with the Knicks in 1984–85, when he averaged 12.7 points and 4.9 rebounds a game.

7. Danny Schayes. The son of the great Dolph Schayes, Danny had a solid NBA career himself, with 8,780 career points (7.7 a game) and 5,671 rebounds (5 a game). The forward was a rock-solid veteran who had some good seasons in Denver.

6. Billy Owens. The 1991 All-American was chosen third overall by the Sacramento Kings in the 1991 NBA draft. Over 10 seasons, Owens scored more than 7,000 points, grabbed more than 4,000 rebounds, and dished out 1,704 assists. He was selected to the NBA All-Rookie Team in 1992.

5. Rony Seikaly. The first-round pick of the Miami Heat scored just under 10,000 points (14.7 a game) and grabbed 6,424 career boards (9.5 a game) during his NBA career. Seikaly was a top-seven rebounder in the league for five straight years.

4. Sherman Douglas. The General had an excellent pro career, highlighted by his patented floater in the middle of the lane. He scored 8,425 career points (11 a game), dished 4,536 assists (5.9 a game), and hauled down nearly 1,700 rebounds.

3. Derrick Coleman. Most people, including me, consider his NBA career to be a big disappointment due to the enormity of his talent. Hard to imagine what he might have achieved had he been fully engaged. But he still scored nearly 13,000 points (16.5 a game), had more than 7,200 rebounds (9.3 a game), and blocked more than 1,000 shots. He was Rookie of the Year in 1991 and an All-Star in 1994. There are a lot of guys who would like to have had that kind of disappointing career.

2. Carmelo Anthony. Perhaps he will someday be regarded as a better NBA player than Bing, but not yet. The five-time All-Star has plenty of career left, barring injury. So far he is averaging about 25 points a game for his career.

1. Dave Bing. Easy choice. The Hall of Famer was named one of the 50 Greatest Players in NBA History. Bing was a seven-time All-Star, NBA Rookie of the Year, and led the league in scoring in 1968. For his career, the classy Bing averaged 20 points and 6 assists a game.

Top NBA Personalities from St. John's University :: by Dr. Richard Lapchick

Dr. Richard Lapchick is a professor at the University of Central Florida and the chair of the DeVos Sports Business Management Program. His father was Joe Lapchick, a Hall of Famer regarded as the game's first agile big man during his days playing on the original Celtics and as a renowned coach of both the New York Knicks and the St. John's University basketball team. On ranking this list, the younger Lapchick writes: "I put my Dad 10th with modesty. These SJU men played a combined 146 seasons as players and coaches, and averaged almost 15 seasons each."

10. Joe Lapchick. He coached the Knicks for 10 seasons, winning 326 games and leading his team to the NBA Finals in three consecutive years (1951–53). His biggest impact on the NBA had to be his 1950 signing of Nat "Sweetwater" Clifton—the first African-American given an NBA contract. He sandwiched his Knicks tenure as head coach of St. John's where he led his team to four national championships and 335 wins in all.

9. Billy Paultz. From River Edge, New Jersey, Billy Paultz attended St. John's University from 1968 to 1970. While at St. John's, Paultz had a career double-double, averaging 12 points and 10.1 rebounds per game. Paultz went on to spend 15 seasons in both the NBA and ABA. While in the ABA, Paultz won the 1974 championship with the New York Nets and was a three-time All-Star who was later voted a member of the ABA All-Time Team.

8. Kevin Loughery. Kevin Loughery was born in Brooklyn, New York. He attended St. John's University from 1960–62. While there, Loughery's teams posted a combined record of 41-10 under head coach Joe Lapchick. Loughery went on to play 11 seasons in the NBA and followed that with a 21-year coaching career. Kevin Loughery went on to win two ABA Championships as head coach of the New York Nets in 1974 and 1976.

7. LeRoy Ellis. Born in Far Rockaway, New York, LeRoy Ellis played center for St. John's University. While there, Ellis won the Haggerty Award, which was given to the New York area's top men's Division I basketball player. After his time at St. John's, Ellis went on to play 14 seasons in the NBA. He was a member of the 1972 Los Angeles Lakers, a team that not only won an NBA championship, but set an NBA record for the longest win streak in league history at 33 games.

6. Jack McMahon. From Brooklyn, New York, Jack McMahon was the captain of the first St. John's team to reach the final of the NCAA Tournament. While at St. John's, McMahon scored 1,162 points, an average of 12.8 per game. After his time at St. John's, McMahon went on to play eight seasons in the NBA, where he won an NBA championship with the St. Louis Hawks in 1958. After his playing career Jack McMahon was a coach for 11 seasons.

5. Mark Jackson. Born in Brooklyn, New York, Mark Jackson played for St. John's from 1983–87. Jackson is St. John's career leader in assists, with 738. As a junior, Jackson recorded 328 assists, an NCAA single-season record at that time. During his senior season, Mark Jackson won the Big East Defensive Player of the Year and was a second-team All-American. Jackson played in the NBA from 1987–2004 and began his coaching career with the Golden State Warriors in 2011.

4. Malik Sealy. Malik Sealy was born in the Bronx, New York. While attending St. John's University, Sealy scored 2,402 career points, which is second in school history. During his junior season, he led St. John's to the Elite Eight. For his senior season, Sealy averaged 22.6 points per game and was named a second-team All-American. Sealy is St. John's all-time leader in steals. Malik Sealy spent eight seasons in the NBA, before dying in a car accident at age 30.

3. Dick McGuire. From the Bronx, New York, Dick McGuire attended St. John's University from 1943 to 1944 and from 1946 to 1949. While at St. John's, McGuire was a two-time winner of the Haggerty Award. McGuire spent 11 years in the NBA, where he was selected as an All-Star seven times. McGuire went on to coach basketball for nine seasons. Dick McGuire was inducted into the Naismith Memorial Basketball Hall of Fame in 1993.

2. Bill Wennington. Bill Wennington was born in Montreal, Quebec. He attended St. John's University from 1981 to 1985, during which time he made an appearance in the Final Four. Following his time at St. John's, Wennington played in the NBA from 1985 to 2000. During his career, he was able to win three consecutive NBA championships with the Chicago Bulls—in 1996, 1997, and 1998. Bill Wennington was inducted into the Quebec as well as the Canadian Basketball Hall of Fame.

1. Chris Mullin. Born in Brooklyn, New York, Chris Mullin attended St John's University from 1981 to 1985. He was a three-time winner of the Big East Basketball Player of the Year Award, as well as the John Wooden Award, which is given to the most outstanding men's college basketball player each year. Mullin went on to play from 1985 to 2001 and became a five-time NBA All-Star. In 2011 Chris Mullin was named to the Naismith Memorial Basketball Hall of Fame.

Top 10 NBA Players from Georgetown ::
by Matt Guokas

A former NBA player and head coach, broadcaster Matt Guokas has seen plenty of great Hoyas in the NBA over the decades. Here are the 10 he's seen the most from.

10. Roy Hibbert. The Hoya center played four years in Washington D.C. before being chosen by the Indiana Pacers in the first round of the 2008 draft. Every year since joining the league he has improved and is on the verge of dominance. In 2012, he was selected to his first NBA All-Star team.

9. Jeff Green. A special 6-9 player who can put the ball on the floor or shoot the three-pointer, Green spent three years as a Hoya before being drafted with the fifth overall pick of the 2007 NBA Draft. The forward played in Seattle, and then in Oklahoma before being traded to the Boston Celtics. Health issues have sidetracked a career in which he has already scored over 4,000 points.

8. Othella Harrington. The lefty shooting forward/center had a 709-game NBA career in which he scored 5,212 points.

7. David Wingate. After a stellar college career that featured a national championship and another trip to the NCAA Finals, Wingate played in the NBA for 15 years while scoring over 4,000 points.

6. Reggie Williams. The slender cutting guard/small forward known as Silk averaged a career high 18.2 points a game in the 1991–92 season and went on to score 7,508 points over the course of his 10-year NBA career.

5. Eric "Sleepy" Floyd. After scoring over 2,300 points in college, Floyd had an outstanding NBA career in which he scored over 12,000 points. The guard set two playoff records: points in a quarter (29) and points in a half (39—on his way to 51 points for the game). In 1987, he played in his only NBA All-Star Game.

4. Dikembe Mutombo. He came to Georgetown from the Democratic Republic of Congo and when he finished playing basketball in the United States in 2009 the eight-time NBA All-Star had established his legacy as one of the most feared defenders the game has ever seen. He won four NBA Defensive Player of the Year Awards and is second all time in career blocks.

3. Allen Iverson. The 6-0 star from Hampton arrived on the Georgetown campus and electrified the country with his fearless offensive game and lightning-quick hands on defense. He went on to be one of the greatest stars in the long history of the Philadelphia 76ers, winning the MVP Award in 2001 while leading his team to the NBA Finals. The 11-time All-Star led the league in scoring four times.

2. Alonzo Mourning. The center scored 2,001 points in college and was a standout player over his NBA life. He was the two-time NBA Defensive Player of the Year and won a championship with the 2006 Miami Heat. Alonzo scored over 14,000 points and grabbed over 7,000 rebounds while being named to seven NBA All-Star Games, despite having to overcome significant health issues during his career.

1. Patrick Ewing. From the school that has produced more elite NBA centers than even UCLA, Ewing is the best. Coming out of Cambridge Rindge and Latin in Massachusetts, Ewing accepted an offer to play for John Thompson in Georgetown. It was a perfect marriage. Thompson harnessed the raw skill of Ewing while sparking intensity that manifested itself in rim-shaking dunks and ferocious blocked shots. After a college career that included a national championship, Ewing played for the New York Knicks for 15 years in a Hall of Fame career that included frustrating runs at a championship that he would never realize. Ewing was named one of the 50 Greatest Players in NBA History.

Top 10 NBA Players from Ohio State :: by Jack Nicklaus

The greatest golfer in the sport's history attended Ohio State from 1957 to 1961. While a Buckeye he won the US Amateur twice (1959 and 1961), as well as the 1961 Big Ten and NCAA individual titles. During summer break in 1960, Nicklaus competed in the US Open and finished second, just two strokes behind Arnold Palmer while setting a scoring record for an amateur. The Golden Bear is an avid sports fan and was an all-around athlete growing up. He was a standout in football, track, baseball, and was an All-Ohio Honorable Mention basketball player in high school and was even recruited to play basketball in college before pursuing his golf career at Ohio State. He remains a passionate follower and supporter of all things Ohio State athletics.

"To choose the top 10 NBA players that played their college ball at Ohio State is quite a challenge," says Nicklaus. "Like any Buckeye fan, I would like to include a lot more than just 10. So, I decided to break the players into two groups: the top five and then a collection of the Best of the Rest."

The Best of the Rest. Mike Conley; Gary Bradds; Kelvin Ramsey; Tony Campbell; Clark Kellogg; Larry Siegfried; Arnie Risen; Michael Redd; Dick Schnittker; Evan Turner.

5. Herb Williams (played for Ohio State 1978–81). A 2,000-point scorer at Ohio State, played in over 1,000 games in the NBA, where he scored almost 12,000 points and grabbed over 6,500 rebounds.

4. Neil Johnston (1947–48). An NBA Hall of Famer who played in six All-Star Games, won three league scoring titles, and led the league in rebounds. He also won a championship with the Philadelphia Warriors in 1956. At Ohio State, he was not only a center on the Buckeye team but a star pitcher on the baseball team. Along with being an NBA star, he also pitched for the Philadelphia Phillies.

3. Jim Jackson (1989–92). The 1992 College Player of the Year, two-time Big Ten Player of the Year, and two-time All-American had his No. 22 retired in honor of his efforts in Columbus. After his junior season, he was drafted fourth overall by the Dallas Mavericks. Over his career, he scored over 12,000 points, including his best season in 1994–95, when he averaged 25.7 points a game.

2. Jerry Lucas (1960–62). The high school phenom chose Ohio State over 149 other college suitors. He went on to lead the 1960 team to the national championship. Over his three-year college career, Jerry Lucas scored 1,990 points. He was drafted by the Cincinnati Royals, but won a title with the New York Knicks in 1973. One of the great rebounding forwards in league history, Lucas averaged 15.6 boards a game and once collected 40 in one game. Along with being elected to the Hall of Fame, he also is considered one of the 50 Greatest Players in NBA History.

1. John Havlicek (1960–62). The eight-time NBA champion won an NCAA title in 1960 with Buckeye teammates Jerry Lucas, Bobby Knight, and Larry Siegfried. Known as Hondo in Boston, Havlicek played in 13 All-Star Games and is the Celtics' all-time leader in points scored and games played—scoring 26,395 points (20.8 points per game) and playing in 1,270 games (17th all-time in the NBA). Havlicek became the first player to score 1,000 points in 16 consecutive seasons, with his best season coming during the 1970–71 NBA season when he averaged 28.9 points a game.

Top 10 NBA Players from the University of Michigan :: by Matt Guokas

Matt Guokas played for a decade in the NBA, and then served as a head coach in the league for seven more seasons. Along the way, he tangled with plenty of Wolverines. Below, he selects the top NBA players to come out of the University of Michigan.

11. Phil Hubbard. The first-round pick of the Detroit Pistons after a college career that included a third-team All-American selection, Hubbard played in 665 NBA games. His best season was in 1984–85, when he averaged 15.8 points and 6.3 rebounds for the Cleveland Cavaliers.

10. Gary Grant. After scoring 2,222 points in Ann Arbor, the point guard was drafted in the first round of the 1988 NBA Draft and played in the league for 13 years. He had his best season in 1989–90, when he averaged 13.1 points and 10.0 assists per game.

9. Jalen Rose. From the moment the sweet-shooting lefty left high school at Southwestern, he was trying to live up to expectations. From the hysteria of the Fab Five and throughout his NBA career, Rose delivered, but not always to the level that many hoped. He played for 13 years for a half dozen NBA teams, while scoring over 13,000 points and playing in 59 playoff games.

8. Juwan Howard. He's played in over 1,200 games, scored more than 16,000 points, and played for nine different teams. The worst thing that happened to Juwan Howard was being overpaid in Washington. People would never let him forget that his check exceeded his production. He played in one All-Star Game and was paid over $150,000,000 for his career.

7. Campy Russell. The Wolverine forward was chosen in the first round by the Cleveland Cavaliers in the 1974 draft. Michael Campanella Russell played in one All-Star Game and averaged 15.8 points a game over his 566-game career.

6. Rickey Green. The 6-0 guard came out of Michigan in 1977 after scoring 1,184 points in two seasons. He played in one All-Star Game and twice led the NBA in steals and three times finished in the top 10 in assists over his 14-year pro career.

5. Jamal Crawford. When he walks into an arena Jamal thinks he's within range. He has always been instant offense in the mold of World B. Free, Vinnie

Johnson, and Downtown Freddie Brown. He has scored over 12,000 points in his career; won the Sixth Man of the Year Award for the 2009–10 season, and has a game high of 52 points on his résumé.

4. Cazzie Russell. The two-time All-American out of Michigan was selected first overall in the 1966 draft by the New York Knicks. He played in one All-Star Game and played on the 1970 championship Knicks team. Over his 817-game career, Cazzie scored 12,377 points.

3. Glen Rice. After scoring a school record 2,442 points and leading Michigan to the 1989 national championship, Rice was chosen fourth overall in that year's NBA Draft by the Miami Heat. Over his career he played in three All-Star Games and scored over 18,000 points, many from three-point land (he had 1,559 three-point field goals). In 2000, he won his one and only NBA championship ring with the Los Angeles Lakers.

2. Chris Webber. One of the greatest talents to ever play the game, C Webb appeared in five All-Star Games, won the 1994 Rookie of the Year Award, and was always on the verge of superstardom. For his career, he produced excellent numbers: 20.7 ppg, 9.8 rpg, and 4.2 apg. With over 17,000 points in his career, he will someday have his name enshrined.

1. Rudy Tomjanovich. Rudy T, a two-time All-American, was chosen second overall in the 1970 NBA Draft by the San Diego Rockets. His team and he migrated the next year to Houston, where he played the rest of his 768-game career. The five-time All-Star is the third leading scorer in franchise history and had his No. 45 retired by the team. He would ater come back to the Rockets as their head coach and lead them to two championships.

Top 10 NBA Players from Michigan State
:: by Matt Guokas

Matt Guokas's career as an NBA player, head coach, and broadcaster has lasted long enough to see all the guys on this list play in person. Michigan State is no little brother to its in-state rival, the University of Michigan, when it comes to college basketball. The Spartans have been one of the elite NCAA men's hoops programs, especially since the 1995 arrival of Tom Izzo, who has guided his team to six Final Fours since becoming head coach, and won a national title. MSU has also placed many fine players in the NBA, including the guy at the top of this list who would probably make the NBA version of Mount Rushmore.

11. Eric Snow. The tough but understated second-round pick played in the NBA for 846 games and 13 seasons. During that time Snow scored 5,791 points and established himself as a solid defender and passer, gaining a second-team All-NBA Defensive selection and finishing in the top 10 in assists three times. The dependable point guard was a key player in Philadelphia's drive to the 2001 NBA Finals, soldiering on through the postseason on a broken ankle.

10. Sam Vincent. The first-round draft pick of the Celtics in 1985 won a ring in Boston as a backup point guard. After a seven-year playing career in which he averaged double figures in scoring in three seasons, Vincent would be chosen by the Charlotte Bobcats as their head coach.

9. Jay Vincent. Sam's older brother was a member of the Spartans 1979 NCAA championship team. The sharpshooting forward would later lead the Big Ten in scoring twice before being chosen in the second round of the 1981 NBA Draft by the Dallas Mavericks. He was selected to the NBA All-Rookie Team and established himself as a dependable NBA scorer who averaged 15.2 points per game while tallying 8,729 points for his career.

8. Morris Peterson. The lefty shooting forward was Big Ten Player of the Year before being drafted into the NBA in the first round by Toronto, where he played the majority of his 11-year career. Mo Pete scored 7,628 points and became a fan favorite in Canada.

7. Johnny Green. The Spartan center was the first-round pick of the Knicks in 1959. Over his four-time All-Star career he twice led the league in field goal percentage and scored over 12,000 points while hauling down over 9,000 rebounds.

6. Jason Richardson. The fifth overall pick in the 2001 NBA Draft has averaged in double figures for scoring his entire 11-year career, and averaged over 20 ppg in three seasons. The multidimensional Richardson led the league in three-point field goals for the 2007–08 season. Two seasons later he averaged 19.8 ppg during Phoenix's postseason drive to the Western Conference Finals.

5. Scott Skiles. The intense and tough point guard left Michigan State as the school's all-time leading scorer, with 2,145 points. He was named first-team All-American before being drafted by the Milwaukee Bucks in the first round of the 1986 draft. Over his pro playing career he had over 6,000 points and more than 3,000 assists. He holds the record for most assists in a game (30) and is in the league's all-time top 10 for free throw shooting percentage. Following his playing career, he has served as the head coach of the Chicago Bulls, Phoenix Suns, and Milwaukee Bucks.

4. Kevin Willis. Potentially the most underrated power forward in NBA history, Willis had an amazing career. He played 1,424 games while scoring over 17,000 points and grabbing almost 12,000 rebounds. The seven-footer was a key part of the fine Atlanta Hawks teams of the 1980s.

3. Steven Smith. At Michigan State he scored over 2,000 points and went on to be responsible for more than 13,000 points during a 942-game NBA career. He won a championship in 2003 with the San Antonio Spurs and once led the league in three-point shooting. He was chosen to play in the 1998 All-Star Game.

2. Zach Randolph. The amazing talent left East Lansing after just one season, during which the Spartans made the Final Four. In the NBA his game has been as good as his personality has been inconsistent. In 2004, he was named Most Improved Player. He currently is playing in Memphis, where he seems to have found a balance between decorum and game.

1. Magic Johnson. The man with the effervescent smile and game that matches it led the Spartans to a national championship in 1979. He was selected first overall in that year's NBA Draft by the Los Angeles Lakers and he took over the town. He went on to win five NBA championships and be chosen league MVP three times. During his career the point guard with the high dribble and no-look passes played in 12 All-Star Games and nine NBA Finals series while simultaneously reviving a franchise and a league.

Top NBA Players from Indiana University
:: by Matt Guokas

Former NBA player and head coach, and current broadcaster Matt Guokas started playing in the league around the same time as Jon McGlonklin, and Matt's father and uncle played in the league years before Slick Leonard established himself as an NBA regular. If you're not familiar with McGlonklin and Leonard, and/or are interested at all in the great tradition of Indiana Hoosiers in the NBA, let the knowledgeable Matt Guokas tell you all about it in the following list.

12. Eric Gordon. After one year at Indiana, Gordon left for the NBA in 2008. The 20-year-old guard wasn't out of his depth, making second-team All-Rookie. Gordon has averaged around 18 points a game over his first four NBA seasons and appears to be on the verge of perennial All-Star status.

11. Bob "Slick" Leonard. The Indiana star played in the NBA from 1956 to 1963 while scoring over 4,000 points. He would later become coach of the Indiana Pacers and lead the team to three ABA championships. He continued to coach the team after the ABA-NBA merger, guiding the Pacers through their first four seasons in the league.

10. Quinn Buckner. A loyal solider of Head Coach Bobby Knight, Buckner was a key cog in the Hoosiers' undefeated national championship season in 1976. He became a solid NBA guard and defensive standout with the Milwaukee Bucks before coming to the Celtics and winning a championship alongside Larry Bird in 1985.

9. Mike Woodson. The 6-5 guard/forward was chosen in the first round of the 1980 NBA Draft by the New York Knicks. He went on to score almost 11,000 points during an 11-year NBA career.

8. Calbert Cheaney. Born and bred in Indiana, Calbert was predestined to go to school in Bloomington. When he was done at Indiana University, he had scored 2,613 points—an IU and Big Ten record. He was chosen by the Washington Bullets in the 1993 draft, but never realized the success he had in college. Still, he was a solid pro who averaged 9.6 points a game over an 825-game NBA career.

7. George McGinnis. After just one college season—in which he led the Big Ten in both scoring and rebounding—the big center was drafted by the Indiana Pacers of the ABA. McGinnis would have a spectacular career in the alternative league before coming to the NBA, where he played in three All-Star Games as a forward. His No. 30 was retired by the Indiana Pacers.

6. Kent Benson. The two-time All-American who played on the undefeated 1976 NCAA championship team as a junior was chosen first overall in the 1977 NBA Draft by the Milwaukee Bucks. His NBA career didn't live up to the hype generated by his scholastic days; but over 680 games, the forward did score 6,168 points.

5. Jon McGlonklin. The Indiana Hoosier graduated in 1965 and became the lifeblood of the Milwaukee Bucks. The shooting guard played with zest and helped lead the Bucks to their only championship in 1971, along with teammates Oscar Robertson and Kareem Abdul-Jabbar. McGlonklin continued his connection with the Bucks for decades as part of the club's broadcast team.

3 (tie). Dick and Tom Van Arsdale. The twin brothers grew up in Indianapolis. They would go on to play together for the University of Indiana before each enjoyed a stellar NBA career. The brothers appeared in a total of six NBA All-Star Games while playing 921 and 929 games respectively, and scoring almost 30,000 points between them.

2. Walt Bellamy. The Hall of Fame center graduated from Indiana after averaging 15.5 rebounds and over 20 points a game. He played in the NBA during the era of the great centers, and he more than held his own. The Chicago Packer was named 1962 NBA Rookie of the Year after averaging 19 rebounds and scoring 31.6 points a night. The 1960 Olympic gold medalist scored over 20,000 points and hauled down over 14,000 rebounds during a pro career that included four NBA All-Star Games.

1. Isiah Thomas. The point guard out of Chicago led Hoosier Nation to a national championship in 1981. His greatness would be on display throughout his NBA career as the leader of the two-time champion Detroit Pistons Bad Boys. His Hall of Fame career would include 12 All-Star appearances, almost 19,000 points, and a Finals MVP Award in 1990.

After playing a decade in the NBA, Matt Guokas became an NBA head coach for seven seasons, during which time he helped evaluate college talent and saw his club draft Chris Webber, Shaquille O'Neal, Dennis Scott, and Bison Dele.

Home to one of the nation's top men's college basketball programs, the University of Kansas has produced plenty of great hoops talent over the years. Here, Guokas offers his evaluation of the Jayhawks that soared highest.

10. Drew Gooden. The athletic 6-10 forward played three years in Kansas, where he scored 1,526 points, before becoming the fourth overall pick in the 2002 NBA Draft. He has averaged double figures in scoring per game in each of his 10 pro seasons, along with almost eight rebounds a contest.

9. Kirk Hinrich. The sharpshooter guard entered the NBA as a lottery pick in 2003 after a heralded college career at Kansas. He made the NBA All-Rookie Team, has twice finished in the top 10 in total assists, and has scored over 8,000 points during his first nine years in the league.

8. Nick Collison. The All-American led the Jayhawks to two Final Fours and scored 2,097 points during his college days before coming to the NBA in 2003. During his first eight years in the league he has scored over 4,000 points and pulled down over 3,500 rebounds.

7. Danny Manning. The amazingly athletic 6-10 center/forward with the passing skills of a top point guard led the Kansas Jayhawks to an unexpected national championship in 1988. After a college career in which he scored 2,951 points, Manning became the first overall pick in the 1988 NBA Draft and seemed primed for a run to the Hall of Fame. But his pro career was hampered by injuries that required him to have both his knees reconstructed. Despite his physical restrictions Manning still played in two NBA All-Star Games and was awarded the Sixth Man of the Year Award in 1998.

6. Darnell Valentine. The speedy guard played nine seasons and in over 620 games in the NBA, where he scored exactly 5,400 points. He averaged a career best 12.5 points for the Portland Trail Blazers in the 1982–83 season.

5. Bill Bridges. The three-time NBA All-Star out of Lawrence averaged exactly 11.9 points and 11.9 rebounds over his 926-game pro career, during which he won a title with the Golden State Warriors in 1975.

4. Jo Jo White. The sharpshooting point guard of the Boston Celtics arrived in town in 1969 after a tour of duty in the National Guard. He was part of two NBA championship teams, including one in 1976, when he was Finals MVP. Jo Jo played in seven All-Star Games and scored over 14,000 points.

3. Clyde Lovellette. The center/forward came to the NBA after three years of All-American play in Kansas, where in 1952 he became the only player to ever lead the nation in scoring the same season his team won a national championship. He went on to win three NBA championships—one with the Minneapolis Lakers, and two with the Boston Celtics. The four-time NBA All-Star scored almost 12,000 points during his pro career and was voted into the Hall of Fame in 1988.

2. Paul Pierce. The Celtic great cemented his place in Boston folklore when he led the team to its 17th championship in 2008. During that playoff run he out-dueled LeBron James in Game 7 of the Eastern Conference Finals, in Larry Bird-like fashion, forever endearing himself to the Boston fans. During his pro career he has scored over 22,000 points on his way to certain enshrinement in the Basketball Hall of Fame.

1. Wilt Chamberlain. The likes of him were never seen before in college basketball, nor in the NBA. The records he holds for his professional career are so mighty and many that this book has a list dedicated to just the most remarkable of them. Author of the 100-point individual single-game performance and other wonders, the Big Dipper thrilled basketball fans in Lawrence, Kansas, and, after a stint with the Harlem Globetrotters, took his amazing act across the country for NBA fans to marvel at.

Top NBA Players from UCLA :: by Andy Hill

Andy Hill is a motivational speaker and author whose unique success as president of two media companies, CBS Productions and Channel One Network, was based on lessons he learned from Coach John Wooden as a member of three UCLA NCAA champion men's basketball teams (1970, 1971, 1972).

10 (tie). Russell Westbrook and Kevin Love. Both these guys have a chance to crack the top five before they are done. But three years in the league is just not enough time to place them higher.

9. Sidney Wicks. Sidney had the ability to crack the top five, but his career seemed to slide downhill. The guy was a four-time All-Star, but he never was better than his first year in the league when he was named NBA Rookie of the Year and averaged 24.5 points and 11.5 rebounds a game. Those are Hall of Fame numbers, but Sidney did not have a Hall of Fame career.

8. Kiki Vandeweghe. One of the most underrated players in NBA history. If rebounding and defense didn't matter, Kiki might have been in the Hall of Fame. Averaged nearly 20 ppg, shot over 50 percent from the field and made nearly 89 percent of his free throws.

7. Baron Davis. Here's a guy with all the ability in the world. He is 25th on the all-time list of three-point shooters. Just not sure I'd want him on my team. Despite one great playoff with the Warriors, Baron is like Sidney Wicks—a transcendent talent who should have been better.

6. Marques Johnson. The winner of the first Wooden Award as a collegiate, this five-time NBA All-Star averaged nearly 20 ppg and scored nearly 14,000 points. A great team player whose career was cut short by injuries.

5. Jamaal Wilkes. If Baron Davis is the guy you do not want on your team, Jamaal Wilkes is the guy you DO want on your team. What a travesty he is not in the Hall of Fame. A two-time NCAA champion in college, Jamaal was NBA Rookie of the Year for the 1974–75 season, when he helped the Golden State Warriors win their only NBA title. The kind of guy you had to see play every day to understand his greatness. John Wooden's favorite player—that's good enough for me.

4. Reggie Miller. A bit brash for a Bruin, but one of the clutch performers of all time. Second all time in three-point shooting. No one not named Michael Jordan made more dramatic clutch shots than Reggie. More than 25,000 points in his career. One ring and he would be No. 2 on this list.

3. Bill Walton. If he'd never been injured, Bill might have given Kareem a run for the top spot. As it is, I'd probably knock him down behind Reggie if he wasn't my best friend. (That's gotta count for something, especially considering what Pat Williams paid me to do this—nothing!). He was the NBA MVP in the Portland Trail Blazers dream season and NBA Sixth Man of the Year on perhaps the greatest Celtic team ever. Simply more fun to watch than any big man ever.

2. Gail Goodrich. After a legendary college career in which Gail put on the greatest show in the history of the NCAA Finals (apologies to Bill Walton, but he knows this is true) in 1965 when he dropped 42 or Michigan, lots of folks thought Gail was too small to make it in the NBA. Hard to measure heart and determination, as Gail went on to a Hall of Fame career in which he scored over 20,000 points and was a part of the 1971–72 Laker championship team that won 33 straight. The third-highest-scoring lefty in NBA history.

1. The Captain—KAJ. No explanation necessary.

Top Players Who Went Directly from High School to the NBA :: by John Nash

John Nash has been an NBA executive for the last three decades, during which time he has been general manager of the Philadelphia 76ers, Portland Trail Blazers, Washington Wizards, and New Jersey Nets. Like every other NBA GM who served between the Supreme Court's 1971 ruling on the Spencer Haywood hardship case and David Stern's successful effort to protect younger players with the adoption of the "one year out of high school rule" almost 35 years later, John Nash had to extend his player evaluation efforts to high school players—kids who might want to skip college to play in the pros. Many young players tried and failed to make that giant leap, but some succeeded. Here are the ones, in John's view, who succeeded the most spectacularly.

He admits that this list was difficult to finalize, not just due to the subjective task of evaluating which players performed best in the NBA, but also due to trying to figure out exactly which players qualified for the list. In John's words: "Dirk Nowitzki may not qualify because he played in Germany before the NBA and entered the NBA at age 19. Shawn Kemp is also a question mark because he did not play immediately after high school but arrived a year later. Hence I listed 15 just to be safe."

Honorable Mention. Al Harrington; J. R. Smith; Kendrick Perkins; Andray Blatche; Lou Williams; Darryl Dawkins.

15. Andrew Bynum. If not for injuries, he would likely rank higher. His numbers are modest because he plays on a team where he is not the first or second option, but he is a premier talent and among the best of the current crop of NBA centers.

14. Josh Smith. Outstanding on the defensive boards and as a shot blocker, Josh is a superior athlete who can contribute offensively as well. He can make a midrange face-up jumper to keep the defense honest.

13. Rashard Lewis. Rashard didn't get to play immediately. But when he finally did, his ability to score at both forward positions made him a difficult matchup. His perimeter shooting has improved over the course of his career.

12. Al Jefferson. Al flourishes with his back to the basket and is one of the elite post-up players in the game. He is a very good rebounder who is capable of playing both power forward and center.

11. Jermaine O'Neal. When given the chance to play full-time with the Pacers, he demonstrated uncanny ability to score in the post and was a presence on the boards and as a shot blocker.

10. Monta Ellis. Despite his relative lack of size, the 6-3, 175-pound player is a prolific scorer at the shooting guard position and handles well enough to play as a scoring point guard. He is a volume shooter who loves the transition game.

9. Amare Stoudemire. Amare is an offensive force who added perimeter shooting to his inside power game. His great physique enables him to rebound and block shots as well.

8. Tracy McGrady. His size and length combined with his skill made him a nightmare to guard. Injuries compromised his career, but at his best he was as good as it gets. He excelled in transition and in a set offense.

7. Shawn Kemp. A tremendous combination of power and skill, he was an imposing sight when attacking the basket. Kemp had great hands and ball skills for a man with a 6-10, 230-pound physique. He also became a good midrange shooter.

6. Dwight Howard. With tremendous physical quickness for a man his size, he makes any starting five he graces a playoff contender because of his shot-blocking and rebounding abilities. He catches anything around the basket.

5. Dirk Nowitzki. Dirk is the best shooting seven-footer in the history of the game and a deadly face-up shooter. The 11-time All-Star and 2007 NBA MVP is outstanding in the clutch from the floor and at the free throw line.

4. Kevin Garnett. After a two-decade pause in high schoolers trying to make the quantum leap to the NBA, Garnett ignited another surge in the phenomenon by becoming the fifth overall pick in the 1995 NBA Draft. His success at both ends of the floor—and on the backboard and as a shot blocker, places him among the elite players of all time.

3. Moses Malone. Perhaps one of the hardest-working players of all time, Moses was relentless around the basket as a scorer and rebounder. The three-time NBA MVP was also clutch at the line in close games in the fourth quarter.

2. LeBron James. Physical superiority coupled with tremendous skill make LeBron almost unstoppable on the offensive end. His scoring ability is well-documented, but he is an excellent passer, too.

1. Kobe Bryant. Kobe has all of the ingredients: incredible skill matched by incredible determination. The best offensive and defensive player on the floor during most of his career.

Top 10 Foreign Players in the NBA
:: by Leigh Montville

The great *Boston Globe* columnist and *Sports Illustrated* writer Leigh Montville has the profound ability to articulate sport in print as well as anyone ever has. Along with his insightful columns, he has written several sports books including bestsellers *The Big Bam* and *The Biography of an American Hero*. For a man who needs no introduction, he wanted to add an introduction to this list himself. So let's turn it over to him now:

"I picked the players on this list the same way the Little League coach in the old neighborhood always selected the players on his team. There have been tryouts—every game, every season any foreign-born player has played in the NBA has counted—and most of the best players are on the list. Some personal favorites also have been included.

"You know how it is. Your own kid always has to play. Your sister's kid has to play. Then there is the friend of a friend of your boss. Both of his kids have to play. The big kid has to play because he might become something good if he ever gains some coordination. The kid whose mother wears the tank tops and the tight jeans certainly has to play.

"Apologies go out to a bunch of terrific players like Detlief Schrempf (Germany), Vlade Divac (Serbia), Pau Gasol (Spain), and Tony Parker (France). They definitely all should have been on the list. They simply didn't know the right people. What can I say? This is the American way."

10. Kresimir Cosic (Yugoslavia). OK, so he never played in the NBA. He was too good, too early, turned down a bunch of offers because he could make more money in Europe. The important fact is that he was the Jackie Robinson of this list, the trailblazer, the first good European basketball player to make a name in the United States. Six-feet-eleven, owner of a zany shoot-first offensive game, he left his hometown of Zadar, Croatia to play three years at Brigham Young University, 1971-73. He was twice an All-American, played in four Olympics. I once asked him if he was afraid when he left home for Utah. He said Zadar was a seafaring town. Men would leave the house, say they were going for a pack of matches, and come home 25 years later.

9. Manute Bol (The Sudan). I wrote a book about him. That puts him on the list. Seven-feet-seven. Could have been a much better player if his fingers weren't deformed from a birth defect. He couldn't palm the ball, couldn't dunk without using two hands. Still the best story ever. Came from the jungle to the NBA for 11 seasons. Couldn't read or write. Couldn't drive a car. Didn't know how to hold a pencil. Did just fine in civilization. Did better than fine.

8. Sarunas Marciulionis (Lithuania). The Grateful Dead. Tie-died tee shirts. There doesn't have to be any other reason. No, there doesn't.

7. Drazen Petrovic (Croatia). Not the best, no. Not one of the 10 best, no. Another trailblazer. He showed the NBA that a European guard could play in the NBA. Overlooked, shoved to the end of the bench at the start of his career in Portland, he had become a genuine star with the New Jersey Nets by the time of his death at 28 in a car crash in 1993. He showed that the Europeans could come to the league and light up the floor from the three-point arc. They didn't have to be pituitary wonders. This was a moment.

6. Yao Ming (China). Even if he didn't play in eight All-Star games, even if he didn't slam his 7–6 body against Shaquille O'Neal—a sci-fi matchup when seen by normal men—he would be on any list on his cultural impact alone. Safe to say he was the first native Chinese personality most of America ever invited into its homes. He was charming, literate, damned funny. He also was surprisingly nimble for a man that large. His early retirement with foot problems left us wondering how good he might ever have become.

5. Manu Ginobili (Argentina). I covered the Pan-Am Games in Mar del Plata, Argentina in 1995. Tickets to the basketball final were in such demand that organizers padlocked the sellout crowd inside the building to keep the people outside the building from breaking inside. (Fire laws? Didn't seem to be any.) The Argentinians then dismantled a rag-tag US team, 98-85, for the title as the crowd stood and sang Spanish songs for the entire game. There was the feeling that some great Argentinian ballplayer would come along, the product of this kind of fever. Manu Ginobili came along and has been wonderful, a unique NBA talent for the San Antonio Spurs.

4. Dikembe Mutombo (Democratic Republic of the Congo). I interviewed him for Sports Illustrated. He was playing for the Nuggets. He lived an expatriate life, a huge rented condo with very little furniture. His goal was simple—"When the Nuggets play in a city, I want to see the sign out front, 'Mutombo Here Tonight.' " That never really happened, but he was a terrific big man. A shot blocker. A blithe spirit.

3. Hakeem Olujuwon (Nigeria). How good was Hakeem the Dream? He was chosen first in the 1984 NBA draft that included Michael Jordan, Charles Barkley and John Stockton. Eventually paired with Ralph Sampson as "The Twin Towers," he brought two NBA championships to Houston. He scored almost 27,000 points, a bunch of them with his back-to-the-basket "Dream Shake" that freed him for either a mid-range jumper or a drive to the basket.

2. Dirk Nowitzki (Germany). No big man ever has shot as well from the outside. A seven-foot, three-point threat. (Try to guard that at your own peril!) He became the face of the Dallas Mavericks franchise, brought the team all the way to the NBA title. Nowitzki once said his first NBA season was "like jumping out of an airplane and hoping the parachute would open." The parachute opened.

1. Steve Nash (Canada). The idea that a foreign-born player could be the best point guard in the NBA was once laughable. Point guard is the instinctive position, the playground position, the All-American-Apple-Pie position. A foreigner? OK, he did grow up in Canada, which is pretty close, and he did polish his many skills at Santa Clara, which is in California, but Nash is foreign and enjoyed a long stretch as the best guard in the game. The Vancouver, British Columbia native still is an All-Star at age 39, a modern-day Bob Cousy, master of the no-look pass, a distributor of the basketball. He exceeded Cousy as a long-distance shooter and a hard driver to the basket. Twice he was picked as the MVP in the NBA. That is as good as a basketball player can be on this planet, no matter where he was born.

Rick Sund has been a general manager in the NBA since 1979, when he took over the post of the Dallas Mavericks at age 29. He has held similar roles with the Seattle SuperSonics, Detroit Pistons, and Atlanta Hawks. Rick has seen a lot of drafts during his career, and is a student of the game who's knowledgeable about the NBA drafts that occurred even before he was born.

In his words: "The NBA Draft has evolved dramatically since it began in 1947, ranging from as many as 20 rounds to its current two-round format, from territorial rights to coin flips to lottery picks to sleepers. During that span, a unique yet important category of players has emerged: those who went undrafted but had a significant impact on the league.

"Two legendary undrafted players fall into their own unusual category. George Mikan, the NBA's first great big man, was assigned to the Minneapolis Lakers in 1946, one year prior to the advent of the draft, while Connie Hawkins's rights were given to Phoenix in 1969, after he had been prevented from entering the league for several years due to an alleged college rules infraction. Due to their unique circumstances, I omitted them from my top 10.

"Here is my list of the top 10 undrafted players of all time."

10. David Wesley. Wesley was an outstanding "shooting" point guard, who averaged 12.5 ppg and 4.4 apg over his 14-year, 949-game (plus 55 playoff-game) career. He tallied almost 12,000 career points and dropped in 1,123 three-pointers. He was also a stout defender, finishing in the top 10 in steals per game twice.

9. Udonis Haslem. Still playing in the NBA, this hard-nosed power forward has scored more than 5,500 points and pulled down more than 4,500 rebounds in nine seasons, all with the Miami Heat. He surprised the league as an undrafted rookie, earning All-Rookie second-team honors in 2004, and has played in three NBA Finals, winning rings in 2006 and 2012. He's played in almost 600 regular-season games, starting close to 400 of them.

8. Raja Bell. This Florida International collegian crew attention from NBA scouts with his stellar play in the minor leagues. When he got his chance in the NBA, he parlayed it into an NBA career that's gone 11 years, and still counting. This defensive standout has made the league's All-Defensive Team twice, and actually led the league in three-pointers made in 2006–07, also finishing in the top 10 in that category in two other seasons.

7. Bo Outlaw. This undersized power forward spent 15 years in the NBA with four teams, piling up 914 career games played. His longevity was a result of his competitiveness, relentless effort, and intangibles. Despite being just 6-8, he recorded an impressive 1,193 career blocked shots. He also ranks ninth in NBA history in field goal percentage (.567).

6. Avery Johnson. This current NBA head coach wasn't drafted, but played in the league for 16 years, recording an impressive 637 regular-season starts. He was in the NBA's top 10 in total assists four times, including a career-best 9.6 apg in 1995–96. He went on to finish his career ranked 32nd in league history in assists (5,846), and helped lead the Spurs to their first championship in 1999.

5. Darrell Armstrong. This six-foot undrafted point man brought tremendous energy to the court, taking Most Improved Player and Sixth Man Award honors in the same year (1999). Armstrong was one of the most accurate free throw shooters in NBA history (20th of all time, at .871). He was part of eight playoff teams and saw 51 games of postseason action.

4. Bruce Bowen. Bowen's longevity in the NBA, primarily with San Antonio, focused on his lockdown defensive ability, along with his three-point shooting prowess. He was named to the NBA's All-Defensive Team eight times, including five first-team honors. Bowen led the NBA in three-point percentage in 2002–03, and was an integral part of three Spurs championship teams.

3. Brad Miller. Despite a tremendous college career at Purdue, Miller went undrafted. But he proved all the scouts wrong, grinding out a 13-year-and-counting NBA career. He has played in over 850 regular-season games, earned two All-Star berths, and averaged over 11 points and 7 rebounds a game. His passing ability has made him a versatile offensive threat at both power forward and center.

2. John Starks. While Starks gained notoriety as one of the league's best substitutes with the Knicks (making an All-Star appearance in 1994 and winning the league's Sixth Man Award in 1997), he also started 420 of his 866 career regular-season games. Known for his competitiveness and defensive ability, he also led the league in three-pointers made in 1994–95, and ranks 36th all time.

1. Ben Wallace. This 15-year blue-collar veteran is a rare player who has made an impact on the floor simply with his defense and physical presence. Wallace won the NBA Defensive Player of the Year Award a record-tying four times. He has five All-NBA Teams, four All-Star Games, and two rebounding titles to his credit so far, and also helped lead the Pistons to the NBA title in 2004.

Basketball Minor Leaguers Who Went on to Make Great Impacts :: by Eric Musselman

Eric Musselman is a product of a basketball family. His father, Bill Musselman, worked as a head coach for over a quarter century in the Western Basketball Association (WBA), Continental Basketball Association (CBA), American Basketball Association (ABA), and in the NBA. Eric followed in his footsteps, coaching both in the minor leagues and in the NBA for over two decades. Below, Eric lists some players, coaches, officials, and executives who followed similar paths to distinguishing themselves in the basketball and sporting world.

Honorable Mention. Players: John Starks; Bruce Bowen; Darrell Armstrong; Charlie Criss; Chris Childs; Billy Ray Bates; Manute Bol; Spud Webb; Avery Johnson. Executives: Jim Tooley; Terdema Ussery. Officials: Tommy Lasorda; Earl Strom; Mendy Rudolph; Jake O'Donnell; Duke Callahan; Bill Kennedy; Steve Javie.

15. Anthony Mason. Spent 1990–91 in the Continental Basketball Association before starring for the New York Knicks and Charlotte Hornets.

14. Paul Arizin. When the NBA's Philadelphia Warriors moved to San Francisco in 1961, the Hall of Famer chose to stay in Philadelphia, playing three years with the Eastern League's Camden Bullets.

13. John Chaney. The longtime Temple Owls coach played for the Eastern League's Sunbury Mercuries, and later coached the Williamsport Billies. The Hall of Fame coach was renowned for producing teams of great discipline.

12. Jim Boeheim. Long before he became head coach of the Syracuse men's basketball team, Boeheim was a star for the Scranton Miners of the Eastern League in the 1960s. At Syracuse University he was NBA Hall of Famer Dave Bing's backcourt mate. As the Syracuse head coach he developed many top NBA players.

11. Jack McCloskey. In the 1953–54 season he was the Eastern League MVP. He played one game for the Philadelphia Warriors during the 1953 season. From 1972 to 1974 he was the head coach of the Portland Trail Blazers before leading the Detroit Pistons as general manager for 13 years in the NBA, where he became known as Trader Jack. Piston teams he constructed won the NBA championship in 1989 and 1990.

10. Flip Saunders. Ranks second in the CBA with 253 career victories as a head coach. Would later coach in the NBA with the Minnesota Timberwolves, Detroit Pistons, and Washington Wizards. He is known for his ability to create advantageous offensive matchups for his players. He was a great college point guard at the University of Minnesota.

9. Bill Musselman. Won four consecutive CBA titles coaching the Tampa Bay/Rapid City Thrillers and Albany Patroons. He later became the first head coach of the NBA's Minnesota Timberwolves. His Albany Patroons team was the best in the history of minor-league basketball. During his time in the minors, Musselman helped develop four future NBA head coaches (Rick Carlisle, Sidney Lowe, Scott Brooks, and Sam Mitchell) and coached NBA players Micheal Ray Richardson, Tony Campbell, Scott Roth, and Lowes Moore.

8. Rick Carlisle. Played on the greatest minor-league team in history with the Albany Patroons. Won an NBA championship as the head coach of the Dallas Mavericks and is head of the NBA Coaches Association.

7. Tim Legler. The Omaha Racers star later became an NBA player with the Washington Bullets. The highlight of his NBA career was his winning the Three-Point Shootout during NBA All-Star weekend. Tim is currently a sportscaster on ESPN.

6. Mario Elie. Worked his way up through the minor leagues, becoming known as the Alphabet-man due to playing in several minor leagues (the USBL, WBA, CBA). He wore a half dozen NBA uniforms over the course of a decade in the league. Elie was a lunch-pail worker who developed into a three-point threat. Went from a Division II program in college to the minor leagues to becoming a contributor to three NBA championship teams.

5. Paul Silas. Played for the Wilkes-Barre Barons before joining the St. Louis Hawks and going on to play for 16 years in the NBA, where he played in two All-Star Games and won three titles.

4. George Karl. Coached the Montana Golden Nuggets in the CBA, where he was Coach of the Year in 1981 and 1983. He later coached the league's Albany Patroons, a club he led to a 50–6 record in the 1990–91 season, when he earned his third CBA Coach of the Year Award. Coach Karl later became a head coach with the NBA's Milwaukee Bucks, Seattle SuperSonics, and Denver Nuggets. He was the seventh coach in NBA history to record 1,000 wins.

3. Hubie Brown. One of the greatest clinicians in the history of sports, Hubie Brown has his PhD in X's and O's. Brown is a two-time NBA Coach of the Year—the honors separated by 26 years—and led the Kentucky Colonels to the ABA Championship in 1975. Brown was inducted into the Basketball Hall of Fame in 2005. Coach Brown played for the Rochester Colonels of the Eastern Professional Basketball League before they folded after just eight games. He averaged 13.8 points per game, but was best known as a good defender.

2. Dr. Jack Ramsay. Played in the Eastern League in 1950–51 with the Harrisburg Senators, averaging 11.8 points in 20 games. Went on to coach at St. Joseph's (1955–66), taking them to 10 postseason tournaments and a Final Four. He also led the Portland Trail Blazers to the 1977 NBA title. His pressure defense philosophy impacted throughout the Eastern seaboard. Still going strong as an NBA commentator.

1. Phil Jackson. The former New York Knick coached the CBA's Albany Patroons for five years before winning 11 championships as an NBA head coach. He is one of the greatest coaches of all time in any sport. Was able to handle superstar players and blend them into a team that played within a system.

Best All-Time NBA Point Guards
:: by Matt Guokas

During his time as an NBA player and head coach, Matt Guokas either played against, played with, coached against, or coached for all but two of the guys on this list—and he's offered plenty of insight on those two during his subsequent time as an NBA broadcaster. Matt's expert eye and firsthand experiences tell him that these are the best floor generals to ever lead their troops into NBA battle.

13. Maurice "Mo" Cheeks. The essence of class and command, Cheeks directed the great Sixers teams of the late 1970s and early '80s, including Philadelphia's 1983 NBA championship team. He was named to four NBA All-Star Games and four NBA All-Defensive Teams.

12. Mark Jackson. The St. John's product could make a good pass or score with his great touch floater in the paint. While dishing over 10,000 assists the 1988 NBA Rookie of the Year made everyone around him better.

11. Guy Rodgers. Guy Rodgers was one of the league's first great floor leaders. From 1958 to 1967, he was either first or second in the league in assists. Rodgers played in four NBA All-Star Games while representing his hometown Philadelphia Warriors and the Chicago Bulls.

10. Tony Parker. The Frenchman wasn't picked until 28th overall in the 2001 NBA Draft, but paid almost immediate dividends to the San Antonio Spurs. He was an integral part of three Spurs championship teams, excelling as both a passer and scorer. He was voted MVP of the 2007 NBA Finals and probably still has a few more years in the league ahead of him.

9. Bob Cousy. Not many athletes revolutionize their sports. But the Cooz did just that from the point guard position while running the Celtics 1960s dynasty like a maestro. His style of dribbling and passing had never been seen before, nor had the level of dominance of his Boston Celtics, the team he led to six championships from 1957 to 1963.

8. Jason Kidd. The kid from the University of California made any team he played for better—a lot better. In his prime he had the potential to notch a triple–double every game. During his career he has worked hard, added an outside shot to his arsenal, and played in three NBA Finals and 10 All-Star Games.

7. Walt Frazier. When Clyde walked on the court, there was no doubt who was in command. He ran the floor with style while leading his Knicks to NBA championships in 1970 and 1973. He was also a great defender who made seven NBA All-Defensive Teams.

6. Lenny Wilkens. His exceptional leadership skills on the court translated into a Hall of Fame career as a player, and as a coach. The nine-time NBA All-Star ranks 11th in career assists and twice led the league.

5. John Stockton. To see John Stockton run the pick-and-roll with teammate Karl Malone was to see perfection. The guard out of Gonzaga came into the league undervalued and left the league a 10-time All-Star, the NBA's all-time assists leader (with 15,806), and an imminent Hall of Famer.

4. Steve Nash. The guard from Canada is a unique blend of distributor and scorer. He can beat you off the dribble or draw a double team and set up a team-mate in his favorite spot. When you're a two-time MVP, you must be pretty good.

3. Isiah Thomas. Isiah was always a leader. From the blacktop courts of Chicago to Hoosierland to Detroit, Thomas's only goal was to beat you. He was the driving force behind the Pistons' consecutive NBA championships in 1989 and 1990.

2. Nate "Tiny" Archibald. He led the league in both scoring and assists for the 1972–73 season. What more needs to be said? But I'll add that he won an NBA championship with the Celtics in 1981 and appeared in six All-Star Games.

1. Magic Johnson. The versatile 6-9 Michigan State product could have played any of the five positions on the court, and sometimes did. But mostly he played point guard and did it better than anyone ever has. He was the perfect leader for Showtime in Los Angeles, with his engaging smile and great court imagination. Magic led his Lakers teams to five championships. He was a three-time league MVP, two-time All-Star Game MVP, and three-time NBA Finals MVP.

Top Shooting Guards in NBA History
:: by Del Harris

Del Harris has been a head coach and assistant coach in the NBA for almost five decades. He was the head coach of the Milwaukee Bucks, Houston Rockets, and the Los Angles Lakers. He took the Rockets to the 1981 NBA Finals and won NBA Coach of the Year honors in 1995 during his stint in LA.

In determining this list of top shooting guards, Harris considered the candidates in the contexts of the times they played in. "It is a matter of discussing eras (what percentages in shooting was prevalent in a specific era, points scored in the era, shots attempted, etc) and various other factors, including All-Star Game appearances and that there were far fewer teams in early eras than there are today.

"Some current players may well be better than those listed below, but it is hard to put a current player ahead of players who have completed their careers. Also, swing players are difficult to define. I could have considered swing players guard/forward or point guard/shooting guard: George Gervin, LeBron James (he is a great combo man at 1-2-3-4, and like Magic, I imagine he could compete at 5 most nights), as well as Walter Davis, Paul Arizin, and Oscar Robertson, whom I would put on the all-time point guard list, considering he had the ball all the time and averaged right at 10 assists a game."

13. Dennis Johnson. Was one of the best defenders of shooting guards ever to play. He still managed to score 14 points per (17 in the postseason) and made five All-Star teams.

12. Mitch Richmond. Shot .455 while averaging 21 a game and playing in six All-Star Games.

11. Calvin Murphy. Was one of the best pure shooters I ever saw play. He was one of only two players less than six-feet tall to play over 1,000 games in the NBA. He shot at .482 and averaged 21 per game.

10. Sam Jones. Sam shot it .456 and averaged 19 points a game over his 12-year career in the NBA while making the All-Star team five times, despite the fact that he played on a Celtic team that already had two or three All-Stars every year with bigger names. At one time or another he was a teammate of Bob Cousy, Bill Sharman, Frank Ramsey, Bill Russell, John Havlicek, Tom Heinsohn, and Bailey Howell—all Hall of Famers. He was a true shooting guard who was best of friends with the backboard, a bank-shot specialist.

9. Earl Monroe. He shot it .464 and brought a new dimension to ballhandling for a shooting guard. He averaged 18.8 on a team that was so well-balanced in scoring, with Walt Frazier, Jerry Lucas, Willis Reed, etc.

8. Bill Sharman. Was the best shooter of his day. He was an .883 free throw shooter and shot .426 from the field for his career, which ran from 1950 to 1961. He averaged 17.8 for the regular season and 18.5 in his 10 consecutive postseasons with the Celtics. There are two remarkable facts that must be considered here in evaluating Sharman:

The NBA did not have a team shoot as high as 40 percent from the field until 1959, when one team managed to shoot .410. Sharman shot .456 that same year. It wasn't until the year after Bill retired that all teams in the league would shoot better than 40 percent.

He was a pure shooter who averaged 18 points a game on a team that had a shooting point guard, Tommy Heinsohn, who shot whenever he could get one off, and with others who scored as well, like Ed McCauley, Frank Ramsey, and then Bill Russell.

7. Dwyane Wade. This is his ninth year and I could say waiting for a current player this good to have played 10 years before being considered is unfair. Wade will be an all timer, if he isn't already. His stats are significant. He already has 15,000 points and eight All-Star Game appearances at age 30.

6. Ray Allen. Has had a long enough career as well, and his stats and All-Star appearances in an expanded league are also impressive. Allen is a true shooting guard.

5. Kobe Bryant. His is a clear-cut top-10 shooting guard, much like Michael Jordan. His current career is long enough to qualify. His stats and All-Star Game appearances speak for themselves.

4. Dave Bing. He shot .441, averaged over 20 per game, played in seven All-Star Games, and was one of the best during his time.

3. Hal Greer. He was a .452 shooter in his day, averaging 19.2 points a game, and played in 10 All-Star Games.

2. Jerry West. At times has been called a point guard, but there were no such designations in his era and point guards don't lead the league in scoring. He was a shooting guard.

1. Michael Jordan. Pretty clear-cut decision here.

Top 10 Rebounders of All Time

:: by Rick Barry

Rick Barry was named one of the 50 Greatest Players in NBA History. A 12-time All-Star in the ABA and NBA, Barry scored over 25,000 professional points, had three sons play in the NBA, and won a championship in 1975, when he was named NBA Finals MVP.

10. Dwight Howard (7,664 total rebounds/12.95 rebounds per game average). Awesome physical specimen who I expect to continue to board at this rate or better. That is why I picked him over Elvin Hayes and Tim Duncan, despite both being outstanding for their whole careers.

9. Dennis Rodman (11,954/13.12). Same as Jerry Lucas below. Rodman was a relentless rebounder, but lacked Lucas's offensive skills.

8. Elgin Baylor (11,463/13.55). One of the best rebounding small forwards ever, as well as one of the greatest offensive players ever.

7. Walt Bellamy (14,241/13.65). A superb all-around player who happened to have to play against Wilt, Russell, Lucas, and Thurmond.

6. Wes Unseld (13,769/13.99). The best rebounding center who wasn't very tall.

5. Bob Pettit (12,849/16.22). One of the best rebounding power forwards in the history of the league, along with being an outstanding scorer.

4. Nate Thurmond (14,464/15.0). Remember, he played a couple of seasons with Wilt and as a reserve with the Bulls and still amassed an impressive number of boards.

3. Jerry Lucas (12,942/15.61). Relentless is the best way to describe Jerry's approach to rebounding, along with dedication. He once had 40 rebounds in a game, a record for a forward. He also was an outstanding offensive player.

2. Bill Russell (21,620/22.45). The player who had the most impact on a team's success through his defense and rebounding skills.

1. Wilt Chamberlain (23,924/22.89). Wilt was an amazing athlete who did incredible things on both ends of the court.

Top 10 NBA Shot Blockers of All Time
:: by Swen Nater

Swen Nater played in the ABA and NBA for 11 years. The UCLA product was the 1974 Rookie of the Year in the ABA, and the following season led the league in rebounds, with 16.4 per game. He also led the NBA in rebounds in the 1979–1980 season, when he averaged 15.0 boards a game. For his professional career he averaged 14.5 rebounds and 15.6 points a game.

On preparing this list, he said: "I have been asked to rank the top shot blockers of all time. The top two are easy but the other eight are very difficult to rank in order because intimidation is such a huge part of the effectiveness. But I'll try. Mind you, these may not be in order of total shots blocked for a career. Factors that were considered were intimidation, keeping the ball in play, and total blocks.

"It's too bad this list is limited to NBA careers, because the second-best shot blocker I ever saw was my UCLA teammate Bill Walton (whose pro career was too impacted by injuries to make this list). He had the intelligence of a Bill Russell, starting fast breaks with his blocks. He was also very selective. Here was Bill's strategy as he told it to me: 'I try to block my man's first shot. Then I don't have to worry about him anymore. I just fake at him the rest of the game and worry about helping everyone else out.'

"I should have changed my name to Bill. Perhaps I'd be in the top 10."

10. Tim Duncan. I'm supposed to put David Robinson here because he had way more blocks than Tim Duncan, his teammate. But I think Duncan was more of an intimidator. His hand was always there.

9. Patrick Ewing. Ewing blocked shots at their apex. When players go to block shots right after the ball leaves the shooter's hand, the shooter has time to adjust the shot. But when they release a shot they think is going in, and someone like Ewing jumps to the top of the backboard and blocks it, they think about that the next time. With Ewing, no shot was safe, even if it looked good.

8. Alonzo Mourning. Tenth all time in number of blocks, I list him eighth because of his tenacity and love for the block. Alonzo would be No. 3 if he would have kept the ball inbounds. But he just loved the crowd's approval. Too bad.

7. Bobby Jones. How do you put a forward above Kareem, David Robinson, and Patrick Ewing? Bobby Jones holds no shot-blocking records, but he blocked the shots of some of the greatest forwards of his day—on the run. He kept the ball in play and the opponents knew that every time they shot, his hand was there.

6. Mark Eaton. I'm listing Mark higher than some might because I know the man and watched him play against my team, the Lakers. Before the game, Pat Riley would remind us, "When Eaton is in there, you might have to make two more passes to get the shot you want." Mark's effectiveness in blocking shots was that he was always there. That huge hand was always up and he had great timing. He also kept the ball in play.

5. Dikembe Mutombo. Noted for shaking his finger after blocking a shot, Dikembe was truly an intimidator. Nobody wanted to see that window-washer finger waving after shooting the ball.

4. Hakeem Olajuwon. With 3,830 blocks, this Hakeem was perhaps the most athletic center we've ever seen. He was quick to the block, was also selective, and you just never knew where he was coming from. Like Bill Russell, he got to some shots that seemed impossible to block.

3. Nate Thurmond. All of his career, Nate was overlooked because of the dominance of Wilt Chamberlain and Bill Russell in his era. Nate blocked a ton of shots, perhaps almost as many as Wilt and Bill, but no shot-blocking stats were kept in his era. Nate also kept the ball in play and was selective.

1. Bill Russell and 1a. Wilt Chamberlain. What is "shot blocking" in basketball? Today, we marvel at high jumpers like Dwight Howard as they slap a shot into the seventh row, and then stand erect, gazing into the seats to soak in the marvel of the crowd. Consequently, on every basketball playground and American basketball court, young men and women mimic those heroes of swat. Yes, shot blocking today is swatting the ball out of bounds.

Call me old fashioned, but to me "shot blocking" is just that—it's "blocking" a shot from going to the basket, not swatting it out of bounds. Shot blocking is keeping the ball in play. You see, I grew up watching Chamberlain and Russell. Now don't Google them to see how many shots they blocked because when they played, that statistic was not kept. But it is estimated they both blocked about six shots a game, far more than any player has since.

But Wilt and Bill "blocked" shots, they didn't swat them out of bounds. Russell was the best because he directed the block to a teammate (usually Bob Cousy) to start a fast break. For Russell and the Celtics, a blocked shot was like an outlet pass. No, it was more like a turnover because of the element of surprise that left the other team at an immediate positional disadvantage. A ball swatted out of bounds merely goes back to the other team.

In my book, because Bill Russell averaged about six blocked shots per game and kept them in play (more than Wilt), he is the most effective shot blocker of all time. I read once that an opposing player said, "When I went up for a shot, I knew Bill Russell blocked six shots per game. The problem was I wasn't sure if the one I was shooting was going to one of them."

Along the same lines, Russell said, "The idea is not to block every shot. The idea is to make your opponent believe that you might block every shot."

Arguably the most intelligent basketball player ever to lace up a pair of sneakers, Russell approached blocking shots strategcally. He felt opting to not try to block a certain shot (but perhaps faking toward the shooter) was more effective in the long run than trying to block everything. In other words, he messed with the minds of the opponents. And he kept the ball in play rather than swatting it out of bounds.

Top 10 Old-School NBA Players Who Would Have Been Great Three-Point Shooters Today :: by Matt Guokas

NBA broadcaster Matt Guokas was formerly a player and head coach in the NBA. He played for Philadelphia's 1967 NBA championship team, with Wilt Chamberlain. Following his 10-year playing career, he served as a head coach for seven seasons for the Philadelphia 76ers and Orlando Magic.

Guokas never got the chance to test his three-point shooting prowess during his NBA playing days, which ended a few years before the trey became part of the NBA game in 1979. Here he cites 10 players from the pre-three days he believes would have flourished beyond the arc.

10. Larry Costello. The last of the great two-handed set shooters. He could beat you off the dribble and shoot a little floater or get all the way to the rim. That set up his jab step and set shot.

9. Kevin Loughery. Like most of these shooters, Kevin did not jump very much on his outside shot. He benefitted from playing with Earl Monroe, Gus Johnson, and an all-purpose player, Jack Marin, to set up wide-open looks from the perimeter.

8. Wali Jones. He had a jackknife-type shot, during which he kicked out his legs to draw fouls. Most of his corner shots were just inside the sideline. Wali usually took those when he was tired, and on a miss he was coming out of the game.

7. Gail Goodrich. The UCLA product had a scorer's mentality. He used the high pick-and-roll to his advantage. If the defender went under the screen, Gail would stop and pop. Good drives for medium shots set up that outside shot. It didn't hurt that he played with Elgin Baylor, Wilt Chamberlain, and Jerry West for a good part of his career.

6. Jerry West. The Laker legend was one of the great 16–18-foot jump shooters of all time. He usually took two dribbles to get his rhythm and get into his shot. Not known for being a spot-up shooter, but with all of his skill, Jerry would have found a way.

5. Bill Sharman. He was a 2-guard in the 1950s before that term even existed. Used screens very well and played very effectively without the ball off Bob Cousy and Bill Russell. Bill was the founding father of the day-of-game shootaround, so no one would have practiced the three more than him.

4. Rudy Tomjanovich. His favorite shot was the 45-degree left-wing bank shot. You don't see the modern player do that intentionally. Rudy T would've only had to step back about two paces to be a very effective three-point shooter, and he had the rest of the offensive game to set that up.

3. Sam Jones. See Rudy T above. Sam had an all-around offensive game, but he would always gravitate to that favorite spot on the left wing. Celtic teammates Bob Cousy, K. C. Jones, John Havlicek, and Bill Russell all did a good job of finding Sam there.

2. Dolph Schayes. Pardon the comparison from one era to another, but Dolph was similar to Larry Bird—except he didn't pass as much. Dolph had a two-handed over-the-head set shot. He had three-point range back in his day.

1. Pete Maravich. Consummate scorer and shotmaker. He had the ballhandling and the ability to get to the hoop. If Pistol could get an extra point for shooting form a little farther out, he would have found a way.

Top 10 NBA Sixth Men of All Time
:: by Scott Howard-Cooper

Scott Howard-Cooper has been an NBA reporter for *Sports Illustrated*, ESPN.com, the *Sacramento Bee* and NBA.com. Below he lists the top specialists in the art of being a team's top reserve player—the guy brought off the bench to add an offensive spark or shut down an opposing scorer or create matchup problems or give his team a shot of energy or change of pace or . . . the guy known as the sixth man.

10. Jason Terry. He went from the opening lineup most of his first eight seasons, to making himself invaluable as a Mavericks reserve the next four and exemplifying the sixth man mantra: it matters who finishes games, not who starts them. Terry became an unquestioned finisher who tore through defenses. He also won the award as the league's top bench player for the 2008–09 season, and two years later became an NBA champion.

9. Detlef Schrempf. He sported a distinctive flattop and German background (Schrempf moved to the United States before his senior year of high school and starred at the University of Washington). But, really, no gimmicks, Schrempf was one of the unique talents of his generation because of his special game, the way he could shoot from the perimeter at 6-9. In 1992–93, he was the only player to finish in the top 25 in points, rebounds, and assists. He might have become more than a two-time NBA Sixth Man of the Year Award winner had that success not turned into seven consecutive seasons as a starter.

8. Ricky Pierce. Although he played for eight franchises, Pierce is best known for his work in Milwaukee and Seattle in the middle of his career, and for making himself into one of the top reserves of the 1980s and '90s. He won Sixth Man of the Year twice within four seasons, both with the Bucks, during a stretch of averaging at least 18 points a game in five of seven campaigns.

7. Frank Ramsey. He became the original sixth man a few seasons after Red Auerbach arrived in Boston and started to build the Celtics' machine. Ramsey was such an integral part of Boston's seven championships in his eight seasons that he made the Hall of Fame despite averaging just 13.4 points a game and inspired the Celtics to retire his No. 23.

6. Vinnie Johnson. The nickname says it all. The Microwave would come off the bench and immediately inject offensive heat as a needed boost to a Pistons roster that prided itself on defense and toughness. The real impact statement: his scoring average improved from the regular season to the playoffs in Detroit's 1989 and 1990 postseason drives that led to NBA titles.

5. Bobby Jones. One of the underrated players of his generation, if not any era, Jones was a star as a defensive forward so respected on that side that he never averaged more than 15.1 points and still made the All-Star Game four times. He was the first winner of the NBA Sixth Man of the Year, claiming the inaugural award for 1982–83, the same season the 76ers won the championship.

4. Michael Cooper. A rare combination among reserves of suffocating defender and electric offensive showman—thanks in part to the Coop-a-Loop lobs to the rim he would finish with a slam. Even as a Defensive Player of the Year for the 1986–87 season, Cooper didn't just accent Showtime while in a supporting role to eventual Hall of Famers. He helped define it.

3. Manu Ginobili. For all the years of life on a yo-yo—going from reserve to starter to reserve to starter courtesy of Spurs Head Coach Gregg Popovich—Ginobili's impact has not wavered. He has been a critical part of three NBA titles (2003, 2005, and 2007), once as a constant in the opening lineup and twice as a part-time starter and key bench contributor. But opponents came to know without uncertainty that Ginobili could beat them, especially in the playoffs, as well as anyone.

2. Kevin McHale.* The asterisk refers to his being a starting power forward—among the historic Big Three of the Celtics front line with Larry Bird and Robert Parish—in the four greatest statistical seasons of his Hall of Fame career. But McHale easily finished with more reserve appearances than starts over his career and averaged at least 18 points a game in four different seasons while primarily coming off the bench. The up-and-under played very well in any role.

1. John Havlicek. It's difficult to break the 1-2 tie; McHale and Havlicek were easy calls for the Hall of Fame, as both played key roles off the bench for championship teams, and both were Boston favorites. But as one of the originals as sixth man, Havlicek's success—while unselfishly accepting the role others would have taken as a slapping demotion—eventually gave the job prestige. He made the sixth man a popular spot.

Top 10 Hook Shots :: by Tommy Heinsohn

Tommy Heinsohn has enjoyed a distinguished career that's stretched across six decades and included major accomplishments as an NBA player, head coach, and broadcaster. The six-time All-Star won eight championships as a center/forward with the Boston Celtics, and then two more as the team's head coach. He has worked as a broadcaster in Boston-area radio and TV since the 1960s, and went national in the 1980s, serving as a color commentator for the CBS television network.

The 6-7 Hall of Famer often found use for the hook shot during his playing days, and laments that more players don't employ it today. In his words: "The sweeping hook shot was an unstoppable weapon when used in the normal flow of the play because it would naturally bring the offensive player away from the defender. Why is the era of the hook shot history? Because there are too many little guys coaching."

10. Manu Ginobili. In this day and age, the guard from Argentina has the closest thing to an old-school hook shot. Whenever he gets angled off the basket, he uses the hook shot off the backboard to score.

9. Magic Johnson. The Laker guard would use the hook shot when he needed it. Taught to him by Kareem Abdul-Jabbar, Magic used the "baby hook" in the 1987 Finals in the Boston Garden to virtually clinch the championship.

8. Neil Johnston. The NBA center starred for the Philadelphia Warriors. He was the league's most dominant scorer in the early 1950s, using his sweeping right-handed hook to win the scoring title three times. That was until Bill Russell showed up.

7. Wilt Chamberlain. Wilt used the hook shot as part of his arsenal. He relied on the fallaway jumper, but could swing into a hook shot when he needed it.

6. Tony Lavelli. The renowned player from Yale who came to Boston in 1949 not only had a great hook shot, but played the accordion at halftime of Celtics games for the Boston Garden crowd.

5. Tom Heinsohn. Tommy could get the hook shot off against any defender. If the clock was running down, it was the perfect weapon to guarantee a good shot. Tommy could shoot it from the right corner but mostly used it as part of his drive to the hoop. (*Note: Tommy didn't include himself on his own list, but he deserves to be here, so the book's authors added him*).

4. George Mikan. The first superstar of the NBA led the league in scoring three straight years in the 1950s while leading the Minneapolis Lakers to five championships. Taught by legendary DePaul Coach Ray Meyer, Mikan could shoot the hook shot with either hand.

3. Cliff Hagan. The one-time Celtic was traded to the St. Louis Hawks with Easy Ed Macauley for the rights to Bill Russell. His hook shot was used for his intermediate shot as part of his drive, as opposed to a low-post move. Hagan used it all the way to the Hall of Fame.

2. Bob Houbregs. The 6-7 University of Washington grad could shoot the hook shot from almost anywhere, including the corner, which is now three-point land. He was voted into the Hall of Fame in 1987.

1. Kareem Abdul-Jabbar. His skyhook was one of the greatest weapons in NBA history. Kareem hit a devastating game winner in Game 6 of the 1972 Finals against my Boston Celtics team, sending the series back to Milwaukee, where we won in seven games.

Top 10 NBA Passers of All Time
:: by Matt Guokas

Matt Guokas is a veteran NBA broadcaster, and former NBA head coach and player who competed against some of the greatest passers in the league's history during the 1960s and 1970s. His father, Matt Guokas, Sr., and his uncle, Al Guokas, played in the league before him.

"I've been watching the NBA since 1952," says Guokas. "I learned the game from my father, who was a terrific 6-3 passing center in the late 1930s at St. Joseph's College. Passing has always fascinated me more than any other part of the game. There are so many players that could be on this list, but this is a very good group that spans the 1950s to the present day."

10. Bob Cousy. Coming out of nearby College of the Holy Cross in 1950, he was initially considered too small and slow by Boston's Red Auerbach. But the Houdini of the Hardwood eventually won the Celtics boss over and proved to be easily the flashiest and most clever passer of his era. When Bill Russell joined the Celtics in 1956, a dynasty began to form and the best fast break in the game was born. Russell's defense and rebounding and shot blocking started it all, with Cousy taking advantage by getting farther up the floor. It was exciting and unstoppable, and ultimately propelled the Boston Celtics to six championships with Cousy.

9. Guy Rodgers. He electrified college fans as a floor leader for the Temple Owls in the mid-1950s, when he teamed with a fabulous shooter, Hal Lear, and led the Owls to two Final Fours. Though he stood only 6-0, he was stocky and strong, which allowed him to get to any spot on the floor he wanted to and helped make Rodgers maybe the best ball handler ever.

As a first-round pick of the Philadelphia Warriors he demonstrated his ability to draw defenders to set up high-quality shots for teammates, though it didn't hurt that Wilt Chamberlain was one his teammates for most of his pro career. Guy coupled fundamentals with flair better than anybody of that era. He played in four NBA All-Star Games and finished first or second in assists in the league each year from 1959 to 1967.

8. Oscar Robertson. The Big O was racking up triple-doubles in the 1960s before that was even a basketball term. Don't forget that in those times defense was an afterthought and there were many more possessions. Nevertheless, Oscar would be just as great today. He was only 6-5 but used his lower body to back you down, and once another defender took a peak, he made them pay with his passes. I wish that he passed even more often, rather than regularly pour in 30-plus on me when I was trying to guard him.

7. Ernie DiGregorio. Here's another too slow/too short/can't shoot player who had the uncanny ability to always make the right pass. His college coach, Dave Gavitt at Providence, and first NBA coach, Dr. Jack Ramsay with the Buffalo Braves, both knew how to get around his weaknesses and utilize Ernie D's biggest strengths—passing and playmaking. DiGregorio won Rookie of the Year for the 1973–74 season, when he led the NBA in assists. He was the best I ever saw or played with at delivering perfectly to the shooting pocket at just the right time.

6. John Stockton. Looked like a choirboy from Gonzaga, but was as competitive as all get-out. Played until he was 40, because he took care of himself and Jerry Sloan kept a tight rein on his minutes. He distributed nearly 18,000 assists in the regular season and playoffs. The pick-and-roll was around forever, but John and Karl Malone gave it a whole new meaning. It was so successful because of its "randomness" during the course of the game and it's execution at crunch time. Stockton probed the defense until he could find the open man. Some have even suggested that he was the nastiest screener of all time.

5. Nate Archibald. Tiny was a solid middle-distance jump shooter and that set up his fabulous penetration moves to score, get fouled, or make an easy pass. Being a lefty with a great change of pace in the open floor helped make him the only player in the history of the NBA to lead the league in scoring (34.0 ppg) and assists (11.4 apg) in the same season (1972–73), and ultimately get him elected to the Hall of Fame.

4. Steve Nash. How many other defensively challenged, 6-3 players have won back-to-back NBA MVP Awards? After a mediocre start to his career in Phoenix and Dallas, Nash began to thrive under Coach Don Nelson's loosey-goosey, wide-open style. His change of pace, probing, and excellent ball-handling have made him fun to play with and fun to watch. The Canadian's extraordinary passing abilities and accomplishments (he's led the league in assists six times so far) have been set up, in part, by his being one of the best-ever shooters from the field, the foul line, and from beyond the arc.

3. Jason Kidd. I'm not so old school that I couldn't find more than one player for this list who played in the 21st century. Jason was a great passer when he came into the league in 1995, and he is still doing it at age 38. He never seemed concerned about getting shots or scoring. Not only has he been a volume assist man, he knows how to set the tempo. The handful of years that Kidd has played with a running team, he's orchestrated the fast break as well as anybody who has ever played. Just about every great player over the last 17 years would say that Jason Kidd is the guy he would most like to have as a teammate.

2. Tom Boerwinkle. Who? As a seven-footer with some very good Chicago Bulls teams in the 1970s, Tom was a space eater, fair scorer, and an outstanding defensive rebounder. But while players such as Bill Walton, Johnny "Red" Kerr, Arvydas Sabonis, and even Wilt Chamberlain were all considered very good passing centers, Tom was head and shoulders above that group. His knack for hitting cutters—straight and backdoor—and screen slippers, along with his ability to deliver passes to players in stride make him the best passing center of all time in my book.

1. Earvin "Magic" Johnson. No. 1 is easy for me. If you polled fans, journalists, and players— young and old—who saw him play, they would concur. And most importantly of all, Magic loved doing it. He got more of a kick from a good or great pass than any field goal he ever scored. A 6-9 point guard, he had tremendous timing and feel and ability to see the play develop before anyone else could, giving him that extra edge. Magic Johnson defined the Showtime Lakers of the mid-1980s. On the fast break with Worthy, Scott, and Cooper as his wingmen, he made the Lakers worth the price of admission every night.

Top 10 Passing Big Guys :: by Tom Tolbert

Tom Tolbert played eight years in the NBA before retiring and becoming a network TV broadcaster for NBA games. He has worked for ABC, NBC, and ESPN. The forward/center averaged less than one assist per game during his pro career, though he does know how to spot a good passer playing one of the frontcourt positions, and rates these 10 as the top of all time in the NBA.

10. Chris Webber. Good all-around player who could get the ball to the open man. He took pride in his passing. For his career he had over 3,500 assists.

9. Alvan Adams. The center's game included hitting cutters like Paul Westphal and Dick Van Arsdale, finding them in the perfect spot to score.

8. Wes Unseld. The league has never seen anyone like him. He could get a rebound and twist in midair and rocket a two-handed pass the length of the court. Unseld was one of the greatest outlet passers in NBA history.

7. Kevin Garnett. At times he's been accused of being too unselfish. But part of his game includes drawing defenders and passing to open teammates. Garnett was a believer in the team concept and he has proven that by accumulating over 5,000 assists.

6. Vlade Divac. The center brought the European game to the NBA, which meant moving the ball to the open man. He was a very clever player with a complete game. At age 35, he averaged 5.3 assists a game.

5. Arvydas Sabonis. A big hulking kid who came to the NBA after his prime had passed. He did everything well. He could have been one of the greatest NBA centers of all time.

4. Wilt Chamberlain. Later in his career Wilt took a great interest in passing. He took passing as a challenge and went on to lead the league in assists in 1967–68, averaging 8.6 a game. Though his passing was very selective; he would only pass to players who could score and wouldn't take two dribbles before shooting, thus costing him an assist.

3. Bill Walton. He did everything well. There was nothing that he couldn't do, including passing. He was best in the low post with the ball in his hands, allowing cutters to use him as a pick, and then he would cleverly drop the ball over his head to his teammate for a layup.

2. Johnny "Red" Kerr. He was a high-post center with incredible vision. He could thread a pass to a cutter with a "carver's touch" by utilizing his radar vision.

1. Tom Boerwinkle. The center seemingly had eyes in the back of his head. He had the ability to anticipate cutters before they cut and would lay the ball perfectly into their hands.

Hall of Famer Wayne Embry was a five-time NBA All-Star center/power forward and a vital member of the Boston Celtics 1968 championship team. In 1972, he became the first African-American NBA general manager—a position he would hold with three NBA teams over the next four decades—and in 1994 became the first African-American NBA team president. He was twice named NBA Executive of the Year (1992 and 1998).

As Cleveland's team president and general manager he was instrumental in turning the long-dormant Cavaliers into one of the better teams in the NBA. The key move in that revival may have been Embry's shrewd 1986 acquisition of the No. 1 overall pick in the NBA Draft, which he converted into center Brad Daugherty, who would go on to play in five NBA All-Star Games.

Embry not only was a very good NBA center, he knows how to spot other good centers. The attributes he looks for in the ideal center: size (the taller the better); strength; physical and mental toughness; ability to play with back to the basket; good hands to catch the ball; cerebral (good decision maker); vision; good footwork; quickness; and jumping ability.

"Along with the above attributes the center must have a good understanding of the game," according to Embry. "Offensively, the center is first a passer. The team should be able to run its offense through the center. The center should be able to score with his back to the basket using hook shots, both hands, power, spin moves, and turn-around jump shots, and jump shots facing from high post. The center should be able to set a good pick and either pop or roll to the basket. The center must be a good rebounder. Defensively, the center has the responsibility of protecting the basket.

"In rating the centers for this list, I have considered these factors. All of the above are vital to winning and a reason why all teams covet an effective center. No NBA team has won a championship without an effective center."

10. Patrick Ewing. He was effective on the low post and he developed the jump shot facing the basket. He played with great heart, making him a winner at the collegiate level and in the pros. He was one of the best all-around centers.

9. Bob Lanier. Perhaps the best shooting touch of players at any position. He used his big frame to establish low-post position. His body allowed him to create space to shoot hook shots. He was a leftie, but was equally effective with his right hand. He was one the first centers to go out on the floor and shoot the jump shot. He was a space eater in the paint defensively, which allowed him to protect the basket and be a good rebounder.

8. Shaquille O'Neal. From head to toe maybe the strongest center to play the game. He was nearly impossible to stop once he started his move to the basket. He scored mostly on power moves to the basket, however he did develop a decent jump hook later in his career. Defensively, he protected the lane through intimidation. Like most great centers he made teammates better because he demanded double and triple teams.

7. Nate Thurmond. Nate is considered one of the best defensive centers of all time. He was a very good shot blocker and very good rebounder. Although defense was his strength, he was an adequate scorer. He scored mostly facing the basket, and he was one of the first to develop the jump hook.

6. David Robinson. He was a great defender and perhaps the best shot blocker since Bill Russell. Offensively, he used finesse and quickness to score in the low post with a jump hook and spin moves to the basket. He could also turn and face the basket and take his defender with the dribble.

5. Moses Malone. He was a relentless worker who simply outworked his opponents. He was perhaps the best offensive rebounder to play the game. He had a great knack for the ball and just went and got it. Perhaps not as skilled as other top centers, but he made up for it with hustle. He was a "blue-collar" worker. What he did wasn't pretty. He just did it.

4. Hakeem Olajuwon. Being a soccer player in his childhood helped him develop exceptional footwork that made him effective on both ends of the floor. Largely because of his quickness, he developed many ways to score in the post and could take opponents out away from the basket and drive around them. He defended the post and was a good help defender.

3. Kareem Abdul-Jabbar. A combination of height, skill, and great footwork made him an unstoppable offensive force. He perfected the hook shot known as the skyhook that was impossible to stop. This made him a great back-to-the-basket scorer. Not only did he score, he made teammates better because he commanded double- and triple-teams, and he was a very good passer out of the post. Although his height dictated that he be a center, Kareem would have been great at any position. His length bothered opponents at the defensive end.

2. Wilt Chamberlain. Wilt was the greatest offensive center in the history of the NBA because he possessed height, strength, athleticism, and skill. Wilt was the strongest to play the game. Because of his strength, he was able to establish low-post position and was impossible to move. Wilt averaged over 30 points and almost 23 rebounds per game in a 14-year career. No other NBA player has scored 100 points in a game or averaged 50 points per game in a season.

1. Bill Russell. His quickness, instincts, and desire to block, change, and discourage shots revolutionized the game. He was the best shot blocker that has played the game. When he blocked shots he always kept the ball in play. That, with his rebounding ability, meant the Celtics always had more possessions than their opponents. His points per game average wasn't as high as many other centers, however, he triggered the fast break and the Celtic offense ran through him. With his all-around play he led his team to 11 championships in 13 years.

Harvey Pollack is the longtime director of statistical information for the Philadelphia 76ers. The man known as Super Stat has been affiliated with the NBA since the league's inception in 1946 and is considered one of the leading statisticians in all of sports. He was awarded the John W. Bunn Lifetime Achievement Award by the Basketball Hall of Fame in 2002. The author of the annual *Harvey Pollack's NBA Statistical Yearbook* noted that, "Wilt Chamberlain had 128 listings for records after he retired in 1973. I have picked out the best of them, in my opinion."

Best of the rest. Just to name a few other Wilt records: he averaged 50.4 points a game in the 1961–62 season; Wilt scored 65 points or more in a game 15 times, and 50 points or more 118 times; before blocked shot stats were kept, he unofficially had numerous games of 20 or more, including 25 blocks in one game against Boston; Wilt's career league mark of the most 50-point and 60-point games still stands, as does his record for seasons leading the league in rebounding (11), and most consecutive games with triple-doubles (11).

9. Field goal streak. Over the course of a four-game stretch, none of which were played in Philadelphia, Wilt sank 35 consecutive field goal attempts before missing. The streak covered games on February 17 vs. Cincinnati in Cleveland, on February 19 in St. Louis vs. the Hawks, on February 24 vs. Baltimore at a game played in Pittsburgh, and ended on February 28 against Cincinnati in Syracuse.

8. No foul outs. Wilt retired early, at the age of 36, and yet played in 1,045 regular-season games, 160 playoff games, and 13 All-Star Games for a total of 1,218 games. In his career with the Philadelphia Warriors, San Francisco Warriors, Philadelphia 76ers, and the LA Lakers, he never fouled out of a game. Bill Russell actually fouled out of 33 games and Michael Jordan 14.

7. Most points in a single season. Wilt is the only player ever to score 4,000 points in a season, tallying 4,029 in 1961–62. He also had two seasons in which he scored over 3,000 points. Only Michael Jordan also cleared the 3,000 mark, and he did it just one season (1986–87) and played in 82 games that season, whereas Wilt did it in 79 or 80 games.

6. Iron man streak. In the 1961–62 season, when the league schedule was 80 games, Wilt played every minute of every game—regulation and overtime— with the exception of eight minutes in one game, for a total of 3,882 minutes.

Referee Norm Drucker ejected Wilt from the last eight minutes of a game for disputing a call to prevent a perfect 3,890.

5. Assist leader. In the latter stages of his career when he wasn't scoring heavily, Wilt decided to improve his passing. The result was that he became the only center to lead the league in assists, pulling off the feat in his final season (1967–68) with the Sixers. He also is the coholder of the Sixers club mark of 21 assists in a single game.

4. Quadruple double-double. Wilt is the only one ever to accomplish the deed of a quadruple double-double—tallying at least 40 points and 40 rebounds in the same game. He did it when starting just his third game as a rookie, and went on to accomplish it a total of four times that first year of his career. He did it a total of five times over the course of his career. No one else has done it even once.

3. Triple double-double. Since the league started in 1946, there has been only one triple double-double performed by an NBA player. Wilt did that on February 2, 1969, against the Detroit Pistons. His totals were 22 points, 23 rebounds, and 21 assists. No player has ever even approached that feat before or since, and it may be the most difficult one to duplicate.

2. Rebound record. Another Wilt feat that may never be matched happened in Philadelphia on November 24, 1960, when Wilt captured 55 total rebounds (it wasn't until years later that rebounds came to be identified as offensive or defensive). His opponent in the paint that night: defensive ace Bill Russell of the Boston Celtics.

1. The single-triple. No doubt about it: Wilt's greatest feat was scoring 100 points in a single game. He did it against New York in Hershey, Pennsylvania, on March 2, 1962. The Philadelphia Warriors won the game 169–147. Wilt made 36 of 63 shots from the field and an amazing 28 of 32 from the foul line. No one has ever approached his scoring performance that night.

NBA Records that Wilt Chamberlain Doesn't Hold :: by Harvey Pollack

Wilt Chamberlain holds over one hundred NBA records, but he doesn't hold every NBA record. Stat guru Harvey Pollack cites the most significant individual NBA marks that the Big Dipper didn't set.

Best of the rest. Most seasons leading league in assists: nine by John Stockton of Utah; most assists in single game: 30 by Scott Skiles for Orlando vs. Denver on December 30, 1990; most career steals: 3,265 by Stockton; most assists in career: 15,806 by Stockton; most blocked shots in single game: 17 by Elmore Smith for LA Lakers in 1973—the year after Wilt retired.

9. Most Consecutive Games Played: 1,192. A. C. Green accomplished this feat while playing for four different teams (the Los Angeles Lakers, Dallas Mavericks, Miami Heat, and Phoenix Suns). His streak ran for 15 years—from November 19, 1986, to April 18, 2001.

8. Most minutes played in a single game: 69. Dale Ellis set this mark playing for Seattle against Milwaukee on November 9, 1989. This was a five-overtime game. In the same game Xavier McDaniel played 68 minutes for Seattle. Next in line with 64 minutes in four-overtime games are Norm Nixon, playing for the Lakers at Cleveland, and Eric "Sleepy" Floyd, playing for Golden State vs. New Jersey.

7. Most seasons leading the league in scoring: 10. Michael Jordan paced the league from 1986–1993, and from 1995–1998.

6. Most career points: 38,387. Kareem Abdul-Jabbar (aka Lew Alcindor) reached this mark during his six seasons with Milwaukee (1969–70 to 1974–1975) and 14 seasons with the Los Angeles Lakers. Karl Malone, with 36,928 points, and Michael Jordan, with 32,292, are next in line.

5. Most consecutive games scoring in double figures: 866. Michael Jordan scored at least 10 points in games he played in from March 25, 1986, to December 26, 2001. Next in line are Kareem Abdul-Jabbar during his time with the LA Lakers (787 games) and Karl Malone (574 games) while playing for Utah.

4. Most career three-point field goals: 2,612. Ray Allen rang up this trey total from 1996 to 2011, while playing with the Milwaukee Bucks, Seattle

SuperSonics, and the Boston Celtics. Next in line, with 2,560, is Reggie Miller of the Indiana Pacers.

3. Most career triple-doubles: 181. Oscar Robertson set this statistical standard for all-around play while playing a decade with Cincinnati and four years in Milwaukee. In the 1961–62 season with Cincinnati, he had 41 triple-double games while averaging a triple-double in points (30.8), assists (11.4), and rebounds (12.5) for the season. Magic Johnson sits in second with 138 career triple-doubles.

2. Most seasons leading the league in free throws made: 8. Karl Malone of the Utah Jazz hit more one-pointers than anyone in the 1988–89, 1989–90, 1990–91, 1991–92, 1992–93, 1996–97, 1997–98, and 1998–99 seasons. Adrian Dantley was next in line with five seasons (1977–78, 1980–81, 1981–82, 1983–84, and 1985–86).

1. Most consecutive years leading the league in rebounding: 7. Dennis Rodman set this mark while playing with three different teams. He led the NBA in rebounding in 1991–92 and 1992–93 with Detroit; in 1993–94 and 1994–95 with San Antonio; and in 1995–96, 1996–97, and 1997–98 with Chicago. Moses Malone did it five straight seasons while with Houston and Philadelphia. While Wilt led the NBA a total of 11 seasons in rebounding, he never strung together seven of them in a row.

Top 10 Small Guys Who Came Up Big
:: by Mike Fratello

Mike Fratello is not only the Czar of the Telestrator but also one of the winningest coaches in NBA history, with 667 wins which included the glory days of the Atlanta Hawks in the 1980s. In 1986, he was named the NBA Coach of the Year.

10b. Earl Boykins (5-5). The Eastern Michigan University product went undrafted in 1998 despite being second in the nation in scoring at 26.8 points. He was signed as a free agent and went on to have a twelve-year NBA career with multiple teams, with his best season being 2006-2007 when he averaged 15.2 points per game in stints with Denver and Milwaukee. Despite his size, he was fearless and strong. He was able to bench press 315 pounds at the weight of 133 pounds.

10a. Charlie Criss (5-8). The dynamic guard played college at New Mexico State University before embarking on a professional career which included time with the Washington Generals, Atlanta Hawks, San Diego Clippers and Milwaukee Bucks. He averaged 8.5 points per game and 3.2 assists for his career.

9. Tyrone "Muggsy" Bogues (5-3). The shortest player to ever play in the NBA, the Wake Forest product was chosen 12th overall by the Washington Bullets in the 1987 NBA draft. For his career, Bogues averaged 7.7 points and 7.6 assists per game.

8. Anthony "Spud" Webb (5-7). Spud went to North Carolina State and was a fourth-round pick of the Detroit Pistons in 1985. He average 9.9 points per game for his career along with winning the 1986 slam dunk contest. He also mentored 5-9 Nate Robinson in the skilled event which Robinson won three times.

7. Michael Adams (5-10). The Boston College guard was the third-round pick in 1985 of the Sacramento Kings. Over his career, Adams averaged over 15 points with his best season coming in 1990-1991 when he averaged twenty-five points a game. He had a career high of 54 points in a game and once had nine steals in a game.

6. Daron "Mookie" Blaylock (6-0). In 1988, he led Oklahoma to the NCAA title game. In the 1989 NBA draft he was chosen 12th by the New Jersey Nets. The thirteen-year veteran was voted onto the 1994 All-Star team. He was a two-time All Defensive Team selection and twice led the league in steals. Over his career he averaged 13.5 points, 6.7 assists and 2.3 steals per game.

5. Kevin Porter (6-0). Porter went to St. Francis University before playing in the NBA for ten seasons. Four times he ed the league in assists. He once had 29 assists in a game. He was a key player on the 1975 Washington Bullets team that lost in the finals to the Golden State Warriors.

4. Thomas Terrell Brandon (5-11). The 1991 Pac 10 Player of the Year while playing at the University of Oregon was the 11th pick in the 1991 draft of the Cleveland Cavaliers. The two-time All-Star played in the league for 11 years from 1991-2002 for Cleveland, Milwaukee Bucks and Minnesota Timberwolves averaging 13.8 points per game and 6.1 assists with a high scoring season of 19.5 points per games. Five times he dished out 16 assists in a game.

3. Calvin Murphy (5-9). The shortest player ever inducted into the NBA Hall of Fame (1993 Class), the three-time All-American from Niagara University averaged 33 points for his school. He had a 14-year NBA career. He was named to the 1979 All-Star team and was one of the greatest free-throw shooters in NBA history. Murphy was a world-class baton twirler who was "bullied into it" by his mother and six sisters. In the eighth grade he won the National Championship for baton twirling.

1. Nate "Tiny" Archibald (6-0). Tiny went to University of Texas El Paso and played three years for coach Don Haskins. He was a second-round pick of the Cincinnati Royals in the 1970 draft. Archibald had a 15-year career with his best year coming in the 1972-1973 season when he led the NBA in both assists and points—the only player ever to accomplish this duo. The point guard was a six-time All-Star and three-time NBA first team. He averaged 18.8 points and 7.4 assists per game and was a member of the NBA's 50th anniversary team. Nate won a title with the Boston Celtics in 1981.

1. Isiah Thomas (6-0). Often listed at 6-1, his true height was 6-0. The youngest of nine children, he played two years at Indiana University where he led the Hoosiers to the 1981 National Championship. Isiah was the second pick of the 1981 draft by the Detroit Pistons for whom he played between 1981 and 1994. For his career he played in twelve All-Star games, was a three-time NBA first-team selection and led the Pistons to back-to-back championships in 1989 and 1990. Thomas averaged 19.2 points and 9.3 assists per game and was named to the NBA's 50th Anniversary team.

Best NBA Thieves :: by Jack McCallum

Jack McCallum was the primary NBA writer for *Sports Illustrated* for almost three decades. In 2005, he won the Curt Gowdy Award for print media from the Basketball Hall of Fame. Jack possesses one of the most impressive catalogues of articles ever accumulated by a basketball writer, along with the byline for several acclaimed books on basketball, including *Seven Seconds or Less, Dream Team,* and *Unfinished Business.* Below, he lists the NBA players most skilled at stealing possession from their opponents.

12. Karl Malone. You didn't think of the Mailman as a steals guy. But he was an excellent anticipator, caused havoc by swatting at the ball when his man started to dribble, and, needless to say, held on to most of what he got his hands on.

11. Hakeem Olajuwon. He is the only other big man besides Malone in the NBA's top 10 of total career steals. The Dream, fleet-footed as they came for a center, was a Nightmare to his opponents, coming out of nowhere to spoil many an entry pass. He was slick enough to get many of his steals off of lane-intruding small men, too.

9 (tie). Magic Johnson and Larry Bird. Okay, it's cheating just a little to put these guys together, but they were essentially the same defender: While relatively slow of foot when guarding their own guy, they were masters at committing larceny in the passing lanes, and they did it at crunch time, too.

8. Clyde Drexler. The Glide wasn't always the most assiduous lockdown defender. But he had astonishingly quick hands and feet, and, most importantly, when he made a perimeter steal you could reliably bet he would finish with a thunderous dunk at the other end.

7. Maurice Cheeks. Like the fog in the Carl Sandburg poem, Mo did his thievery "on little cat feet"—quietly, efficiently, and in the shadow of the rim-rattling dunks of Julius Erving and the jackhammer interior play of Moses Malone. His defense was a major, albeit overlooked, part of Philadelphia's highly successful teams of the early 1980s.

6. Walt Frazier. The NBA didn't record steals back in Clyde's early days with the Knicks, and I'm not sure how accurately the stat was when the practice finally began in 1973–74, Frazier's seventh season. But no one was as adept as Clyde at the "pure steal," i.e., subtly flicking the ball away from a dribbler without fouling.

5. Jason Kidd. J-Kidd was an all-around thief. He could strip you in the open court, come behind and knock it away, sneak into a passing lane, or use his strong hands to rake it away from a big man. And he's still doing it at age 39.

4. John Stockton. The Hall of Fame Jazz point guard retired as the NBA's all-time steals leader. He had two seasons (1988–89 and 1991–92) when he led the league in both steals and assists, a level of production that is truly astonishing. He was still a first-rate thief even in his last season, when, at age 40, he had 137 steals.

3. Alvin Robertson. No one was a tougher defender than this hard case from Arkansas. Four of the top 11 single-season steals records belong to Robertson, and that includes 1985–86, when he had 301 steals, still a record. Not coincidentally, he had a quadruple-double (20 points, 11 rebounds, 10 assists, 10 steals) in a game that season.

1. Michael Jordan and 1a. Scottie Pippen. MJ could be on here alone since he ranks second behind Stockton. But his deadliest work was done in conjunction with Pippen, with whom he had almost a secret language—when to double, when to trap, when to swoop in for the kill. No duo has ever been better.

The All-Time NBA All-Defensive Teams
:: by Billy Cunningham

Billy Cunningham came out of Brooklyn, New York, and matriculated to the University of North Carolina before starting his Hall of Fame pro career. The five-time All-Star led the ABA in steals for the 1972–73 season. He won an NBA championship in Philadelphia as a player (1967) and as a coach (1983).

(It should be noted that the NBA's Defensive Player of the Year Award started in 1983, whereas the selection of the league's All-Defensive Team began after the 1969 season.)

Honorable Mention. Kobe Bryant. Through will and determination Kobe plays the game on both ends of the floor. He has averaged 1.49 steals a game for his career. He is a nine-time first-team NBA All-Defensive selection and two-time second teamer. By the time his career is over, he will almost certainly have earned a spot alongside the 15 players on the teams below.

THIRD TEAM

5. Nate Thurmond. He was so good that the Warriors traded Wilt Chamberlain to make room for him in their starting lineup. For his career, Thurmond averaged 15 rebounds a game.

4. Tim Duncan. Quiet, steady, complete—the Spurs great was selected to 13 NBA All- Defensive Teams over his career.

3. Bobby Jones. The well-schooled Tar Heel came to the NBA and, with timing and effort, consistently frustrated the other team's best forward. Jones was named to the NBA All-Defensive first team eight times and to the second team once.

2. Michael Cooper. The perfect piece of the puzzle for the Showtime teams of the Los Angeles Lakers. The defensive specialist who could knock down the three was an eight-time All-Defensive honoree and was voted Defensive Player of the Year in 1987.

1. Walt Frazier. The Knick known for style and offense was also a tremendous defender who would cover the other team's best player, no matter what position he played. Clyde was seven times voted to the NBA All-Defensive Team.

SECOND TEAM

5. Wilt Chamberlain. Simply through size and athleticism the Big Dipper could dominate the paint on both ends. They didn't record blocks in his day, but his 22.9 rebounds per game career average is certainly an indication of his dominance.

4. Gus Johnson. The longtime Washington Bullet dominated the paint, pulling down almost 13 rebounds game.

3. Scottie Pippen. The "Bull in the shadow" had plenty of game of his own to be proud of. He was selected first-team NBA All-Defensive eight times and twice placed on the second team. He led the league in steals in 1995 and recorded 1.96 steals a game for his career.

2. Jerry Sloan. The man—who combined talent, intensity and unstoppable resolve— competed every night, on every possession.

1. Norm Van Lier. The guard was a great on-ball defender. He was a three-time first-team All-Defensive and five-time All-Defensive second teamer.

FIRST TEAM

5. Bill Russell. No. 6 is considered by most to be the greatest defender in NBA history. He played before statistics could validate his greatness, so I will submit:
> Exhibit A: 11 NBA championship rings
> Exhibit B: 21,620 career rebounds (22.5 per game)

The recurring image of him blocking a shot and directing the ball to a teammate for a fast break is enough for me.

4. Hakeem Olajuwon. Hakeem the Dream was a five-time first-team All-Defensive and four-time second-team selection. He was awarded the Defensive Player of the Year twice (1994 and 1995). He also ranks 23rd all time in steals per game (1.75) and has more recorded blocks (3,830) than any player in NBA history.

3. Dennis Rodman. The relentless rebounder and defender was voted seven times first-team All-Defensive and once to the second team. In 1990 and 1991, he was awarded the NBA's Defensive Player of the Year Award.

2. Michael Jordan. The greatest two-way player in NBA history, Jordan was selected first-team All-Defensive nine times. In 1988, he was the winner of Defensive Player of the Year. He is third all time in steals per game, with 2.35, and led the league in steals three times.

1. Jerry West. Near the end of the Laker great's career, the NBA started naming players to an annual All-Defensive Team. West was selected to the first team five times. Like every thing he did, he was superior at playing defense.

Top 10 NBA Floppers :: by Richie Adubato

Richie Adubato was a three-time NBA head coach with the Detroit Pistons, Dallas Mavericks, and Orlando Magic. He is now the color man for Orlando Magic radio. He notes that "flopping" has become an intricate part of the NBA and a tactic used on both ends of the floor. It has developed into an art form that can have an impact on winning and losing. Some players deserve a Screen Actors Guild card for their "heroics" in the flopping department.

10. Derek Fisher. Excellent clutch shooter and leader of the Lakers and Thunder, he is a small NBA guard who uses the flop in situations where he is screened by bigger opponents.

9. Paul Pierce. Modern day Celtic great who loves pressure shots in clutch. Uses flop (flares arms to give the impression he was hit) on offensive end when guarded closely while attacking the basket.

8. Reggie Miller. All-Star and a great clutch shooter who is league's second all-time three-point shooter. Perfected flop on three-point shot by kicking out his legs, making him more impossible to guard.

7. Glen "Big Baby" Davis. The power forward is a strong inside player with limited athleticism. He utilizes his strength and body to fool bigger opponents, using the flop to help him defend opponents.

6. Anderson Varejao. The Brazilian forward is an aggressive, intense defender known for his hustle and as a great help-side defender. He will use flopping style to increase chances of getting referees calls.

5. Zaza Pachulia. Center is strong and physical. Guards more athletic centers using positioning to stop opponents and often outguesses man he's guarding to get to the spot first and flop.

4. Dennis Rodman. Great rebounder and defender who used flopping style in many ways.

3. Manu Ginobili. All-Star player who plays with reckless abandon and utilizes the flop on offense, and on defense when taking a charge.

2. Vlade Divac. The Los Angeles and Sacramento center was an excellent European player who was known for flopping in many situations.

1. Bill Laimbeer. The Piston center in championship years utilized the flop when he anticipated charges in the lane. Would try to intimidate opposing center with flop. An example occurred in a playoff game against Portland. He elbowed Kevin Duckworth, causing the Blazer to react by throwing a punch. Laimbeer flopped to the ground and Duckworth was ejected.

Best Pure-Shooting Lefties in NBA History :: by Doug Collins

Doug Collins was the first overall pick in the 1973 NBA Draft by the Philadelphia 76ers. The four-time All-Star played his entire career with the 76ers. He has gone on to coach four NBA teams. One of the few backcourt players to post a career field goal percentage of over .500, Collins rates the best left-handed pure shooters in league history—players whose unshakable confidence and sweet strokes allowed them to consistently hit shots from anywhere on the court.

10. Troy Murphy. The smooth-shooting left-hander out of Notre Dame could use both hands around the basket or pull his defender out of the paint and shoot the three.

9. Chris Bosh. The six-time NBA All-Star has averaged 20 points a game for his career.

8. Nick Van Exel. The University of Cincinnati product seemed to have unlimited range. The NBA All-Star scored 12,658 points in his career.

7. Bob Lanier. The first overall pick in the 1970 NBA Draft, Lanier was one of the first centers to score away from the basket, where he used his soft touch. He scored over 19,000 points while averaging 20.1 per game during his 14-year career.

6. Sam Perkins. His nickname was Big Smooth. In his 1,286 NBA career games, Perkins scored over 15,000 points.

5. Dick Barnett. The lefty out of Tennessee State was the fourth overall pick in the 1959 NBA Draft by the Syracuse Nationals, and went on to win two NBA championships with the New York Knicks (1970 and 1973).

4. Jack Marin. The two-time All-Star from the Baltimore Bullets and Houston Rockets once led the NBA in free throw shooting percentage and was voted to the 1966–67 All-Rookie Team.

3. Michael Redd. The Ohio State scorer made himself into a great shooter with hard work. In November 2006, he set the Milwaukee Bucks franchise record, scoring 57 points in a game.

2. Gail Goodrich. The smooth-shooting left-hander from UCLA was also a scorer who averaged almost 19 points a game over his 1,031-game career.

1. Chris Mullin. The St. John's product was born to shoot. Over his NBA career with the Golden State Warriors and Indiana Pacers, the Hall of Famer shot .509 from the field and .865% from the line.

The 10 Individuals Who Most Impacted My Career :: by Ann Meyers-Drysdale

Ann Meyers Drysdale is a member of the Naismith Memorial Hall of Fame. She was a standout at UCLA and became the first woman to sign an NBA contract when she inked a deal with the Indiana Pacers in 1979. She is an announcer, president of the WNBA's Phoenix Mercury, and vice president of the Phoenix Suns.

10. Jack McCloskey. Jack was the assistant coach for the Indiana Pacers and was very positive with me. He went on to be general manager of the Detroit Pistons during their championship years.

9. Bob Leonard. Coach Slick Leonard was the head coach of the Indiana Pacers from 1968 to 1980. During that time he led the franchise to three ABA championships. He was also my coach during my tryout with the Pacers.

8. Johnny Davis. He supported me in my tryout with the Indiana Pacers. I knew him from USA Basketball.

7. Pete Newell. Pete became a friend and mentor who I could talk basketball with. I partnered with him on a Tall Women's Camp for footwork. He escorted me for the Naismith Hall Of Fame induction.

6. Sam Nassi. He was the owner who signed me to the Indiana Pacers as a free agent in 1979 and in doing so opened the door in so many ways.

5. Wilt Chamberlain. He was a friend and supporter of women in sports. I used to play racquetball with him at UCLA and in pickup games.

4. Julius Erving. Julius became a friend and confidant of the game. We went into the Naismith Hall of Fame together in 1993.

3. Bill Russell. The Celtic great was a winner and played defense. He became a friend. I did some broadcasting with him and we went into the FIBA Hall of Fame together.

2. John Havlicek. I always loved his style and the way he became a friend. Years after watching him, we became friends.

1. Dave Meyers. I learned so much from my brother Dave. He was not only my sibling but also my idol. He taught me how to compete.

NBA Teammates Who Most Impacted My Life :: by Chet Walker

Chet Walker was a seven-time All-Star during his 13-year NBA career. The 6-6 forward known as Chet the Jet won an NBA championship with the great 1966–67 Philadelphia 76ers team, and scored almost 19,000 career points while playing in Syracuse, Philadelphia, and Chicago.

10 (tie). Clifford Ray (Bulls) and Norm Van Lier (Bulls). Clifford is a very intelligent man and one of my best friends in the whole world. He's a very creative guy who is a great cook and has a great voice. He is one of the league's best big man coaches because he is so intelligent. Norm was an intense little guard who could make his teammates better. He was a sensitive soul and quite insecure. He passed away a few years ago and I miss him to this day.

9. Jerry Sloan (Bulls). He was a savage competitor and the hardest worker I've ever been around. He played just as hard in practice as he did in the games.

8. Bob Love (Bulls). I had great respect for him. Bob had a handicap because he stuttered. However, he didn't let it bother him. When you were talking with Bob, you had to have patience with him. He just seemed happy with who he was. The good news is that Bob overcame his stuttering problem and became a good public speaker.

7. Hal Greer (76ers). He was difficult to get to know because he was introverted and insecure in some ways. I guess you would call him a little antisocial. He was perhaps the best midrange jump shooter who ever played the game.

6. Wali Jones (76ers). Here is a guy who lived in the moment. Wali was very spontaneous and believed you only live once, so enjoy every day of your life. He was a very creative person and that's how he played basketball. He was a wild man on the court.

5. Billy Cunningham (76ers). He believed in securing one's financial independence after your NBA career was over. Billy did a great job at that and made a lot of money over the years through his wise investments.

4. Luke Jackson (76ers). He was the best teammate you could ever have. Big Luke believed in the team concept and always said, "Never be bothered if you are unappreciated."

3. Wilt Chamberlain (76ers). The big fella had a great imagination. He always wanted to be bigger than life. Wilt wanted to make you believe that he was much, much more than a basketball player and could do anything he set his mind to. Also, Wilt was very sensitive and insecure in many ways.

2. Johnny Kerr (Syracuse Nationals). He was the ultimate teammate and always played within the concept of the team. John believed you could be a better player if you looked to pass the ball first.

1. Alex Hannum (76ers Coach). He convinced me that I had what it takes to be a great player. Also, Alex was not afraid to be your friend because he was secure in who he was.

Top NBA Duos (and Trios) :: by Mark Price

Mark Price played guard from 1986 to 1998 in the NBA, where he was a four-time All-Star. Born and raised in Oklahoma, Price starred at Georgia Tech before leading the Cleveland Cavaliers through their glory years of the late 1980s and early 1990s. He was named first-team All-NBA for the 1992–93 season and remains the all-time league leader in free throw shooting percentage. Among the top 10 in the NBA in assists per game in five of his NBA seasons, Price knows what it means to work effectively with teammates. Below he lists the top duos and threesomes who played the game as one.

11. LeBron James, Dwyane Wade, and Chris Bosh. They all brought their talents to South Beach with big games and big personalities, with only final results to be determined.

10. Shawn Kemp and Gary Payton. Shawn Kemp was one of the greatest talents the league has ever seen. When paired up with teammate Gary Payton, the twosome led Seattle through a period of excellence by dominating opponents with superior athleticism, an awesome inside-outside game, and swarming defense.

9. Oscar Robertson and Lew Alcindor (later Kareem Abdul-Jabbar). In Milwaukee, Lew Alcindor was an unstoppable young phenom who meshed with clever veteran Oscar Robertson, a legend in desperate search of his first ring—which he earned along with his young superstar center in 1971.

8. Isiah Thomas and Joe Dumars. The guard tandem led Detroit's Bad Boys to back-to-back championships in 1989 and 1990. Thomas brought flash and steely determination; Dumars covered the other team's scorer while adding a steady offensive game that earned him the NBA Finals MVP Award in 1989.

7. Jerry West and Elgin Baylor. The great duo thrilled the NBA, and especially Los Angeles, with their amazing collective talents. They played together for the Lakers from 1966 to 1971, and appeared in three NBA Finals series together.

6. Kobe Bryant and Shaquille O'Neal. The twosome led the Lakers to three championships, but could have won many more if their personalities didn't clash and cause the breakup of the two greatest players of their generation.

5. Larry Bird, Kevin McHale, and Robert Parish. The three joined forces to play the game as perfect complements to one another. On the offensive end Bird had a complete game and could play off McHale. the greatest low-post player in league history, while Parish served as a weak- side outlet who could consistently hit a 15-foot jump shot. Defensively, the length and athleticism of Parish and McHale allowed Bird to freelance in passing lanes and disrupt opposing offenses.

4. Magic Johnson and Kareem Abdul-Jabbar (aka Lew Alcindor). A young, rambunctious Magic Johnson came to Los Angles in 1979 and revived the veteran center, Abdul-Jabbar. Combined, the two utilized each other's skill sets all the way to five championships.

3. John Stockton and Karl Malone. The two Utah Jazz greats were the essence of teamwork. Stockton was the great passer and Malone was the great scorer. The two would have been All- Stars without each other, but not the legends they became together. To see the two work the pick-and-roll was to watch perfection in action.

2. Bill Russell and Bob Cousy. Though Cousy was a six-time All-Star and a fan favorite in Boston, he had yet to realize an NBA championship. That was until Bill Russell arrived in Boston from the NCAA champion University of San Francisco and Olympic champion United States men's basketball team. Together, the Houdini of the Hardcourt and Russell, the greatest defender in league history, combined to form the core of the greatest dynasty known to American team sports.

1. Michael Jordan and Scottie Pippen. While one cast the shadow and the other one played within it, the two needed each other to thrive. Together, they possessed a game with skills the likes of which had never been seen before in the league. When their partnership was over, they both had earned six championship rings.

Individuals of Jewish Faith Who Most Impacted the NBA :: by Marc Berman

Marc Berman is a writer for the *New York Post* who has covered the New York Knicks since 1998. He previously covered the CBA's Albany Patroons—back when they were coached by Phil Jackson, George Karl, and Bill Musselman. The Associated Press Sports Editors Award winner authored the book, *Living Without Ew*, about the New York Knicks after the Patrick Ewing era.

Honorable Mention. Amare Stoudemire.

13. Marty Blake. The longtime NBA draft scout extraordinaire also spent a decade as an executive with the Atlanta Hawks.

12. Ben Kerner. Kerner was the longtime owner of the Hawks who moved the team from the Tri-Cities to Milwaukee to St. Louis, where the team won the NBA championship in 1958.

11. Abe Sapperstein. The owner/coach of the Harlem Globetrotters was an integral part of the NBA's growth. He organized doubleheaders that included NBA teams, allowing the league exposure they were desperate for. The Globetrotters were also responsible for introducing the sport to the world.

10. Ernie Grunfeld. The first-round NBA Draft pick out of the University of Tennessee, where he teamed up with Bernard King for the "Bernie and Ernie Show," Grunfeld would play for nine seasons before serving as an executive for the New York Knicks, Milwaukee Bucks, and Washington Wizards.

9. Bill Davidson. The longtime Detroit Pistons owner brought his franchise three NBA titles (1989, 1990, and 2004), as well as a privately built arena, the Palace.

8. Abe Pollin. The longtime owner of the Baltimore Bullets/Washington Bullets/Washington Wizards was a partner in the team's acquisition in 1964 and would realize the pinnacle of the sport in 1978 when his Bullets won the NBA championship.

7 (tie). Dolph Schayes and Dan Schayes. The father-and-son tandem combined to score over 27,000 points and grab over 17,000 rebounds in the NBA. Dolph, the father, was a 12-time All-Star, won a championship in 1955 with the Syracuse Nationals, and was voted into the Hall of Fame.

5. Eddie Gottlieb. The Mogul was the first coach of the Philadelphia Warriors before buying the team. He eventually sold the team to San Francisco. He was the driving force of the NBA rules committee for a quarter century. Gottlieb is a member of the Hall of Fame.

4. William "Red" Holzman. Hall of Famer Holzman won an NBA title in 1951 as a player with the Rochester Royals and would later lead the New York Knicks to two championships, in 1970 and 1973, as a head coach.

3. Larry Brown. A great ABA player, Brown went on to win championships as a college coach (Kansas) and as an NBA coach (Detroit Pistons). He has won over 1,000 NBA games and is a member of the Hall of Fame.

2. Arnold "Red" Auerbach. The Celtic maestro led the Green to 16 championships—nine as a coach and seven as an executive. With lit cigar and rolled-up program, the NBA Hall of Famer revolutionized the game while creating the greatest sports dynasty ever.

1. David Stern. Over the course of his three decades as NBA commissioner, Stern transformed the American sport into a global mega-entity.

Reverend Ryan is the Pastor of the College Park Presbyterian Church in Orlando. Before his call to the ministry, he worked with the Orlando Magic in promotions and is currently involved with the team as a minister.

10. Avery Johnson. "Didn't get the Memo." Someone must have forgotten to give Avery the memo that said he was too small for the NBA, that only college All-Americans can win championships, and that every locker room you walk into isn't a church. Avery never got that memo because all he does is share the good news of the Gospel in every room he walks into. Every day is Sunday and every locker is a pulpit for Avery Johnson because Avery Johnson is a Christian.

9. Terry Cummings. "Silent Servant." Teddy Roosevelt famously said, "Speak softly and carry a big stick." This could describe Terry Cummings. He spoke softly but the words he said were powerful and would stick with you. He was not demonstrative or demanding of attention but rather a silent servant of Christ Jesus. He let his actions do his talking; he let his service in the name of Christ be his calling card. He spoke softly, but for those who heard him, those words stayed with them for a lifetime.

8. Wayman Tisdale. "All Smiles." There are smiles and then there was Wayman Tisdale's smile. His smile lit up any room he walked into. It seemed like he was always smiling, no matter what the situation was, on or off the court. His life was always in perfect harmony, playing basketball or making music because his relationship with Christ was always first in his life. The reason he was always smiling was because he knew Jesus personally and intimately and now eternally; there can't be a better reason to smile.

7. Monty Williams. "Heart of a Champion." In sports, it's all about heart; it's all about what's on the inside of a player that determines whether they will win or lose. Even though Monty Williams' physical heart may not have been perfect, his spiritual heart is. Monty will "win" because his heart is focused and obedient to Jesus Christ, and that's what makes him a winner in God's eyes. Whether he was playing or coaching, Monty Williams will always be "winner" because he has the heart of a champion, a heart for Christ.

6. Mark Jackson. "Action Jackson." Whether it was on the playgrounds of New York, at St. John's University or in the NBA, Mark Jackson was a man of action, on and off the court. He never sat back and waited for things to happen, he made them happen and this applied to his faith as well. He was more than a "hearer" of the word but rather a "doer" of the word. From sharing the Gospel with teammates, coaches and fans or founding and leading a church in Los Angeles, Mark Jackson has been, and will always be, "Action Jackson."

5. Mark Price. "The Price is Right." There are a few things in life that you can count on: death, taxes and Mark Price at the foul line. Mark Price was one of the NBA's most accurate free throw shooters in history. To be that consistent and accurate took lots and lots of practice. The same was true in Mark's walk with God. He practiced every day, reading the scripture praying and praising God in song. The reason why Mark's faith was so strong was because he was right with God through a personal relationship with Jesus Christ as his savior.

4. AC Green. "Outspoken not Outdated." In a world of high fashion and trend-setting lifestyles, many said AC Green was outdated in his view of life. Though many around him led promiscuous lifestyles, he believed in abstinence. AC was outspoken on why he chose to live as he did: his relationship with Jesus Christ. His goal of pleasing God was greater than his goal of pleasing himself or impressing others with false bravado. Being obedient to the word of God is never outdated and AC Green was outspoken when it came to living his faith.

3. Pete Maravich. "Breakdown to Breakthrough." He could do anything on the basketball court and he could buy anything off it and yet, "Pistol" Pete Maravich was an empty man for most of his life. He tried to fill his life with so many worldly things that just didn't work: basketball, possessions, drugs, alcohol and even false religion. It wasn't until he had a breakdown of his body and life that he experienced a breakthrough, knowing the person of Jesus Christ as his Lord and savior. A life once empty was now full, if only for a short time, of the hope and grace of Christ.

2. Bobby Jones. "Common Name, Uncommon Faith." In a profession that values and markets catchy nicknames for players, Bobby Jones' name seems just too common. Though his name may be common, his faith was not. It was Bobby Jones who first requested a chapel service before games when he played for the Philadelphia 76ers and since that day athletes, in many sports around the world, have been impacted by the Gospel. His name is not in the headlines but his heart is in Christ and his impact on professional sports is ongoing. Common name, but uncommon faith.

1. David Robinson. "Measuring Stature." We often measure a person's stature by how tall they are and David Robinson is tall, 7–1. He has an impressive resume: served our country in the Navy, won two NBA championships, MVP awards and numerous others. What gives him such stature is his walk with Christ and how he lives that every day. From leading his family, to building Christian schools, to mentoring young people, David Robinson stands tall because he has knelt before the throne of his Lord and King, Jesus Christ.

Top 10 Current NBA Players Under 28
:: by Peter May

Peter May was the longtime Celtics beat writer for the *Boston Globe*. He also contributes to *Hoop Hype*, ESPNBoston.com, and now writes for *The New York Times*. Peter has authored several basketball books, including his last venture, *Top of the World*, on the Celtics' 2008 run to the NBA championship.

10. LaMarcus Aldridge, Portland Trail Blazers. He may be the most underrated big man in the NBA. It's mostly because of where he plays. Portland is not exactly a major media market and the Blazers have not had a good recent playoff run that would introduce the casual fan to this guy's remarkable talents. If he played in New York, his face would be on city buses.

9. Kevin Love, Minnesota Timberwolves. As versatile a big man as there is in the NBA these days—and he's got the Beach Boys in his family tree! Love has been a double-double machine for the Timberwolves since he stepped onto the court and he can hurt you from both inside and outside. It will be interesting to see where he goes in a few years if there's no improvement in Minnesota.

8. Marc Gasol, Memphis Grizzlies. He isn't quite the best player in his own family, but he is one of the top three young centers in the league. His game has improved exponentially since he came to the Grizzlies in the trade for his brother, Pau. The Lakers wouldn't redo that deal—Pau got them a couple titles. But the Grizzlies were going nowhere with Pau. They may be going somewhere with his younger brother.

7. Blake Griffin, LA Clippers. If you had to pick a power forward to build your team around, he would be your guy. He has a dynamic personality to go with his dynamic game and promises to be a force in the NBA for years to come. His dunks get all the attention, but he has a very serviceable offensive game around the basket and, of course, is a rebounding machine. He is power personified in the low post.

6. Chris Paul, LA Clippers. Maybe you could flip-flop him with Griffin, but most observers will tell you that a first-rate point guard is more critical than a first-rate power forward. And the Clippers seemed to break through with the arrival of Paul, who is so creative and effective with the ball. He isn't just a great passer. He can score and he is usually among the league leaders in steals.

5. Andrew Bynum, LA Lakers. If it were not for his fragility and suspect wheels, he would be up there near the top. He has a very good offensive game. He rebounds. He blocks shots. He's still learning the game because he just turned 25 in October 2012. Remember when Kobe Bryant wanted Jason Kidd instead of Bynum. He'd have two fewer rings if that deal had gone down.

4. Derrick Rose, Chicago Bulls. The youngest MVP in NBA history and, one could argue, the best point guard in the NBA. He is so fast with the ball and is unafraid to take it to the basket, contorting himself into every possible position. He's getting better as an outside shooter, has always been an excellent distributor, and has accepted his role as the leader of the Bulls. He's your point guard of the future.

3. Dwight Howard, Orlando Magic. What is it about this guy that turns so many people off to his obvious greatness? He should be the hands down No. 1 pick for the future NBA Team of the Universe, but there is a certain *je ne sais quoi* about him. There are simply too many games where he doesn't assert himself as he should. And then there are the free throws. Having said all that, 29 other NBA teams would gladly take on those shortcomings and go with him.

2. Kevin Durant, Oklahoma City Thunder. Maybe we should put him at 1a. instead of at No. 2. He is going to ensure that the Thunder remains a major player in the NBA for years to come. He is as smooth and effortless a scorer as we've seen in some time, and he seems to have the perfect personality for his team and the city. He basically won the 2010 Worlds for the United States. A certifiable keeper.

1. LeBron James, Miami Heat. A tough choice over Durant, but the King is simply the most explosive and versatile player in the league. He covers so much ground that it's impossible to overstate his value. He puts up numbers that rival Oscar Robertson's production in his prime. The only thing missing from the résumé is a championship, and until he gets one his detractors will hold it as a sign that he's overrated. Not in my book.

Ken Berger is the NBA columnist for *CSBSports*.com. He came to CBS Sports following successful stints with the Associated Press and *Newsday*. How good is Ken Berger? The AP named him one of the top five columnists in the country in 2011.

10. Kareem Abdul-Jabbar, Los Angeles Lakers, 1987–88. In the best season ever by a 40-year-old player, Abdul-Jabbar averaged 14.6 points and 6.0 rebounds while shooting .532 from the field and helping the Lakers win the last championship of the Showtime era. James Worthy was MVP of the Finals, where the Lakers beat the Pistons in seven games.

9. Wilt Chamberlain, Los Angeles Lakers, 1971–72. At age 35 and a decade after his 100-point game, Chamberlain averaged 14.8 points and 19.2 rebounds while playing in all 82 regular-season games, two years after appearing in only 12 games due to a devastating knee injury. Wilt shot .649 from the field and was MVP of the Finals, where the Lakers beat the Knicks in five games.

8. Karl Malone, Utah Jazz, 2002–03. In the highest-scoring season ever by a 39-year-old, Malone averaged 20.6 points and 7.8 rebounds, and played 81 games. The Jazz, however, lost in the first round of the playoffs for the third straight season, this time to the Sacramento Kings.

7. Kareem Abdul-Jabbar, Los Angeles Lakers, 1985–86. Abdul-Jabbar's best season at 35 or older was marred by losing to the Houston Rockets in five games in the Western Conference Finals, which marked the only time in an eight-year stretch that the Lakers failed to make the NBA Finals. But the 38-year-old Abdul-Jabbar played 79 games and averaged 23.4 points, 6.1 rebounds, and 3.5 assists while leading the Lakers to a 62-20 record.

6. Alex English, Denver Nuggets, 1988–89. English's 26.5 points per game in the 1988–89 season make him the owner of the highest scoring average in NBA history among players who started a season at 35 or older. The 35-year-old English shot .491 from the field and .858 from the foul line. The Nuggets lost to the Suns in the first round of the postseason.

5. Karl Malone, Utah Jazz, 1999–2000. The 36-year-old Malone continued to get better with age, averaging 25.5 points and 9.5 rebounds while playing all 82 games and shooting .509 from the field. He also led the Jazz to the Western Conference Semifinals, where they lost to Portland.

4. Elgin Baylor, Los Angeles Lakers, 1969–70. Baylor, 35, averaged 24.0 points and 10.4 rebounds. The only other 20-10 season ever recorded by a player 35 or over was Patrick Ewing's 1997–98 campaign—but Ewing only played 26 games that season. Baylor played 54 games, averaging 41 minutes and led the Lakers to the Finals, where they lost in seven games to the Knicks.

3. Karl Malone, Utah Jazz, 1998–99. One of the best 35-and-over players in NBA history, Malone averaged 23.8 points and 9.4 rebounds while winning league MVP honors at age 35. Malone played 49 of 50 games in the lockout-shortened season, which ended for the Jazz with a loss to the Portland Trail Blazers in the Western Conference Semifinals.

2. Michael Jordan, Chicago Bulls, 1997–98. Jordan wasn't 35 when the season began, reaching the milestone on February 17. That made him 35 for about half of an historic season that saw him average a league-leading 28.7 points, capture the regular-season and Finals MVP Awards, and capture his sixth championship with the Bulls with that iconic elbow jumper over Utah's Bryon Russell. As Marv Albert would say, "It counts."

1. Kareem Abdul-Jabbar, Los Angeles Lakers, 1984–85. At age 37, Abdul-Jabbar played 79 games, averaged 22.0 points and 7.9 rebounds, and was MVP of the Finals, where the Lakers beat the Celtics in six games. He also shot .599 from the field. Among those who recorded the 50 highest-scoring seasons for players 35 and older, only Artis Gilmore (.623 in 1984–85 at age 35) and Shaquille O'Neal (.609 In 2008–09 at age 36) shot better.

Top 10 Most Colorful Players in NBA History :: by Stan Van Gundy

Stan Van Gundy has served as the head coach of the Miami Heat and Orlando Magic, and led both to multiple playoff appearances. He has never endured a losing season in his seven-plus years in the NBA, during which time he has compiled a career winning percentage of close to .650. The brother of former NBA head coach and current TV commentator Jeff Van Gundy, Stan has interacted with a lot of great characters and exciting players during his time as an NBA coach and fan. Below, he offers his 10 most colorful NBA players, along with some words of wisdom on the game and its fans:

"The attraction of the game of basketball to fans around the world consists not only of the display of such a beautiful game, but also the unparalleled entertainment value offered by athletes of great imagination and physical gifts. Those listed below have proven themselves the best of the best when the lights come on."

Honorable Mention. Ernie DiGregorio; Isiah Thomas; Jason Kidd; Mahmoud Abdul-Rauf; Paul Westphal; Vince Carter; World B. Free; Rajon Rondo.

10. Jason Williams. Known as White Chocolate, the point guard could wow you with his look-away passes, behind-the-back (and sometimes around-the-back) dribbles, and alley-oop passes from anywhere on the court.

9. Walt Frazier. The king of cool in the coolest city could make people pay attention by walking into a restaurant or driving to the hoop.

8. Dominique Wilkins. His ability to take off from anywhere inside the free throw line and punish the hoop with a tomahawk dunk kept people from going to the concession stand.

7. Earl "the Pearl" Monroe. With a spin dribble like no other, the Pearl was a magician at getting his shot or getting one for a teammate in the perfect position.

6. Bob Cousy. His nickname—the Houdini of the Hardcourt—said it all. He specialized in behind-the-back passes, leading the fast break, and one-handed running layups. His moves not only were never before displayed in the league, they hadn't even been imagined. The Cooz was the league's first showman.

5. David Thompson. Skywalker was said to be able to take a quarter off the top of a backboard. The North Carolina State great wowed crowds with a vertical leap unseen in the NBA before that time.

4. Michael Jordan. His greatness for winning didn't mean he couldn't also put on a show. With his arsenal of horizontal dunks, layups in traffic while suspended in the air with his back to the basket, and double-pump reverse layups, His Airness was a must-watch every time he stepped on the floor (somewhere Craig Ehlo is waking up in cold sweats).

3. Magic Johnson. He was the captain of Showtime in Hollywood. He could lead the break with a high dribble, spin on an unsuspecting defender, throw a court-length bounce pass, or embarrass an opponent with a look-away dime.

2. Julius Erving. From his free-throw-line dunk in the ABA All-Star Game, to his cuff dunk over Michael Cooper, to his up-and-under reverse layup victimizing poor Laker Mark Landsberger, the good Doctor would bring people from their seats every time he touched the ball.

1. Pete Maravich. With droopy socks and a mop of black hair, Pistol Pete could wow the crowd and opponents with his between-the-legs dribbles, behind-the-back passes, or double-pump scoop layups.

My Favorite Darryl Dawkins Dunk Names
:: by Ken Hussar

Ken Hussar is a comedian and a motivational speaker who has coauthored a number of books on life's levity and ways to improve one's plight, including *Nothing But Winners*, with Pat Williams—the man responsible for drafting the irrepressible Darryl Dawkins. A player of vast talent and imagination, Dawkins could not only do things like shatter a backboard with a thunderous dunk, he could poeticize about his efforts. The list consists of Ken's favorite names used by Sir Slam to title his different dunks, along with some interesting facts about Darryl and his career.

10. Spine Chiller Supreme. Darryl Dawkins was an amazing talent that came straight from high school into the NBA.

9. Greyhound Bus (went coast to coast). The massive center measured 6-11 and 251 pounds.

8. Rim Wrecker. Twice in his career the massive Sixer broke a backboard with a dunk.

7. Look Out Below. As a result of his dunks, the NBA converted to break-away rims.

6. Dunk You Very Much. The center also went by the aliases Sir Slam, Dr. Dunkenstein, and Chocolate Thunder during his career.

5. Candyslam. Darryl played in three NBA Finals.

4. Earthquaker Shaker. When Walt Frazier saw him at the draft, he said of Dawkins' high school instructor, "I bet his teacher called him, Mr. Darryl."

3. The Go-rilla. Dawkins reported that he was a resident of the planet Lovetron.

2. In Your Face Disgrace. For his career Dawkins scored 8,733 points and averaged 6.1 rebounds a game.

1. The Chocolate-Thunder-Flying, Robinzine-Crying, Teeth-Shaking, Glass-Breaking, Rump-Roasting, Bun-Toasting, Wham-Bam-I-Am-Jam. This famous dunk occurred against the Kansas City Kings in Bill Robinzine's face. It sent backboard glass flying and Robinzine running.

Top 10 ABA Players You've Probably Never Heard of :: by David Twardzik

Dave Twardzik played for the Virginia Squires of the ABA and the Portland Trail Blazers of the NBA. In 1977, he was the point guard of the champion Portland team. Following his playing career he has served in both coaching and the front office of several teams.

Honorable Mention. Louie Dampier; Bob Netolicky; Larry Jones; Cincy Powell; Mack Calvin; George Carter; Ralph Simpson; George Thompson; many others I'm sure I'm leaving out.

10. Donnie Freeman. Unbelievably quick, Freeman was able to get his own shot no matter who defended him. He was a creative scorer off the dribble who was able to stop on a dime and get off deadly midrange jump shots. Donnie had an uncanny ability to draw fouls and get off a quality shot, and hit tough acrobatic shots. He seemed to never miss free throws, especially at crunch time. He was also a very good passing lane defender. He was a five-time All-Star and won an ABA championship with Indiana.

9. Freddie Lewis. Was the facilitator on the powerful Indiana Pacer teams. He sacrificed his own personal stats to keep everyone else on the Pacers involved and happy. He was a very good defensive player, especially in passing lanes with his ability to anticipate. Freddie made big plays at both ends of the floor. He could beat you off the dribble, drive to the hoop, or stop and hit pull-up jumpers with his midrange game. The bigger the game, the better he played. He was a deadly free throw shooter, four-time All-Star, All-Star Game MVP, and three-time ABA champion with Indiana, including in 1972, when he was playoff MVP.

8. Doug Moe. Known more for his coaching career, Doug was also a winning basketball player. He had great basketball IQ and great work ethic, and was fearless. He was the type of player guys loved to play with but hated to play against. There was nothing sexy about his game. He wasn't that fast and couldn't jump very high, but he competed every minute. He took pride in his defense, never letting his man get an easy shot. He was an excellent passer and was constantly on the move. The three-time All-Star won a championship in Oakland.

7. Ron Boone. The Utah star had one of the sweetest jump shots ever seen in either league. With a high arc, he elevated his shot and was instant offense with range anywhere on the court. He could overpower smaller defenders or could shoot the three effectively, though he preferred to abuse his defender by scoring with a midrange game. You could count it whenever he stepped to the free throw line, where he shot .837 for his career. He was a true iron man, playing in over a thousand consecutive games. He was a four-time All-Star and won a championship with Utah.

6. Jimmy Jones. He had a game that was very similar to those of Walt Frazier and Oscar Robertson. A true point guard at 6-4 who was an unbelievable one-on-one player, Jones was a tough matchup for smaller guards because he liked to back them down. He had an extremely high basketball IQ. His midrange game was lethal. He had good quicks and was a very efficient player who could fill up a stat sheet. In 1969, the six-time All-Star averaged 26.6 points per game.

5. Warren Jabali. The powerfully built shooting guard was a unique combination of strength and athletic ability. He loved the physical part of the game. He would overpower guards and was too athletic for most small forwards. He could score in a variety of ways and added the three-point shot to his game in his third year. He had the ability to play multiple positions. He was an explosive leaper with no weakness and could defend, score, rebound, and pass. He was Rookie of the Year, a four-time All-Star, an All-Star Game MVP, and a playoff MVP and ABA champion with Oakland in 1969.

4. James Silas. Tough-as-nails and physical, Silas competed every night. He was another difficult defensive assignment for the guards, overpowering the points and out-quicking the off-guards. Physical at both ends of the floor, Silas was a tough defender who could score in a variety of ways. He was capable of getting his own shot, constantly hitting tough shots with defenders in his face. He scored mostly from drives and midrange jumpers, and was known for his late-game heroics. He would literally take over the game in the fourth quarter. Once he got on a roll, no defender was going to be able to stop him, irregardless of his size or quickness. And don't think about fouling him—Silas shot .855 from the line in his career. He made two All-Star squads and a pair of All-ABA Teams.

3. Willie Wise. He was the definition of consistent. Wise didn't possess great athletic skills but what set him apart from other players was his extremely high BB IQ, his feel for the game, and an unquenchable work ethic. He was always one or two passes ahead of the play. An unbelievable one-on-one player. Wise was able to get his own shot and capable of scoring in a variety of ways. He could post up, turn and face, put it on the floor, and had an excellent midrange. A very good rebounder at both boards, he was also a tenacious defender who took a lot of pride in his defense. He actually liked to defend, and could have been the best wing defender in the ABA—and maybe the best two-way player, too. He made All-Rookie, two All-Defensive Teams, and two All-ABA Teams, in addition to being a three-time All-Star and champion with Utah.

2. Mel Daniels. A true center who was the ultimate competitor. The paint was his office and he owned the paint. Opposing players paid a price for driving to the basket or trying to score inside. He was a physical presence and loved to defend, as well as a very good rebounder. Daniels would rebound in traffic and outside his area with very good hands—if he touched the ball, he caught the ball. He had a high basketball IQ and was an enforcer who always had a teammate's back. In a word: WINNER. A seven-time All-Star, two-time ABA MVP, and three-time ABA champion.

1. Roger Brown. In a word: SMOOTH. Roger was the most efficient player in the league. There was never any wasted movement. He had a great demeanor on the floor and would never get rattled. He played at his own pace. His basketball IQ was off the charts. He was a great one-on-one player who could get anywhere he wanted off the dribble and create any shot when he wanted. Like all great ones, he made the game look easy. He was an excellent shooter who once hit 21 field goals in a row. He was a four-time All-Star, three-time ABA champion, and a playoff MVP.

Top 10 Non-NBA Athletes :: by Eric Gordon, Jr.

Note: Eric Gordon, Jr. is a 6-3 guard from the University of Indiana who has taken the NBA by storm, averaging over 18 points a game in his first four years in the league with the Clippers and Hornets, and with his star still rising. While the NBA may represent the greatest collection of athletes in the world, Eric offers his list of great athletes from around the world who compete in other sports or leagues.

10. Usain Bolt. He keeps winning the 100-meter dash.

9. Michael Conley. He was my AAU coach. He did the triple jump in the Olympics. His son, Mike Conley, Jr., plays for the Memphis Grizzies.

8. Albert Pujols. A great baseball player from our time.

7. Babe Ruth. You always hear about him when anyone talks about baseball, so he has to be in there.

6. Peyton Manning. I'm from Indianapolis, and I would still say that he's one of the best of all time.

5. Lisa Leslie. As far as women, I believe she is one of the greatest athletes.

4. Roger Federer. He's always been my favorite tennis player. I still would say that he is the greatest of all time.

3. Michael Phelps. He is for sure up there as one of the best of all time.

2. Lance Armstrong. He has proven to be the best cyclist out there.

1. Muhammad Ali. He is definitely the best boxer of all time and I think that is probably the toughest sport.

Top 10 NBA Cities :: by Tyreke Evans

Tyreke Evans is one of the hottest young stars of the NBA. In 2009, the Memphis State product was the 4th overall pick of the Sacramento Kings in the NBA draft. Evans validated their selection by earning the 2010 Rookie of the Year award.

10. Phoenix. If I get into golf, I'll go to Phoenix. It's nice and green.

9. Toronto. It is a very beautiful, clean city.

8. Chicago. I like to shop downtown in Chicago.

7. Dallas. I like the nightlife and the city.

6. Philadelphia. It's close to home, so I get to see my family.

5. Houston. I like the atmosphere of the city.

4. Memphis. I went to school there, so I have a lot of great memories.

3. Miami. Just like my number one pick below, I love the weather and the beach.

2. New York. I'm an east coast guy, and New York is beautiful.

1. Los Angeles. I love the weather, and being near the beach.

Top Major League Baseball Players Who Also Played Pro Basketball :: by Ed Randall

Ed Randall is one of the principal baseball reporters in the country. For decades he has brought the sport to fans on ESPN, MLB Network, Sirius Radio, and many other outlets. Below, he lists the best of an exclusive group— Major League Baseball players who also played in the top pro basketball leagues of their eras.

14. Cotton Nash. Cotton Nash was a right-handed first baseman/outfielder who signed with the Los Angeles Angels in 1964. He made his major-league debut in September 1967 with the Chicago White Sox and was hitless in three at-bats. In 1969, he was back up with the Billy Martin-led Minnesota Twins and had two hits in nine at-bats. The following season, he made it back to the Twins for four at-bats with one hit and two RBIs. Lifetime, he batted .188 with three hits in 16 at-bats. The 6-5 University of Kentucky product played four seasons as a forward in the NBA and ABA, where he averaged 8.5 points and 4.9 rebounds in the 1967–68 season.

13. Hank Biasetti. Biasetti was born in Beano in northeastern Italy. That small town is located near Slovenia and north of Venice. A 27-year-old left-handed first baseman, Biasetti had a major-league career that lasted 21 games with the 1949 Philadelphia A's. He had 24 at-bats and gathered two hits, both doubles, for a lifetime average of .083. But, somehow, he scored six runs and drove in two. His pro basketball career consisted of being drafted by the Boston Celtics in 1947, and then scoring six points in six games for the Toronto Huskies.

12. Dick Ricketts. A right-handed pitcher who signed with the St. Louis Cardinals in 1955, Ricketts reached the majors for his one and only season in June 1959. In 12 games, he pitched $55^{2/3}$ innings, giving up 68 hits and 42 runs (36 earned), with 30 walks and 25 strikeouts. He won once, lost six times and had a 5.82 earned run average. He fared better in the NBA, where the 6-7 forward/center was the first overall pick in the 1955 Draft, and averaged 9.3 points and 6.3 rebounds during three seasons with the St. Louis Hawks and Rochester/Cincinnati Royals.

11. Dave DeBusschere. The Detroit native made his major-league debut with the Chicago White Sox in 1962. The right-handed hurler appeared in 12 games with no record, pitching 18 innings while giving up only five hits. But had a bit of a control problem, walking 23 batters. In 1963, he appeared in 24 games with 10 starts, pitching $84^{1/3}$ innings, with 53 strikeouts and a more palatable 34 walks while winning three, losing four, and posting a respectable 3.09 earned run average. He finished his two MLB seasons with a career 3-4 record and 2.90 ERA. His Hall of Fame NBA career with the Pistons and Knicks included two NBA titles and being named to eight All-Star Games, six NBA All-Defensive Teams, and as one of the 50 Greatest Players in NBA History.

10. Chuck Connors. Long before he gained fame as the title character in *The Rifleman* on television, Chuck Connors had one hitless at-bat with the 1949 Brooklyn Dodgers. He resurfaced two years later with the 1951 Chicago Cubs at age 30. In 66 games, the left-handed first baseman gathered 48 hits—two of them home runs—along with 18 runs batted in while posting a .239 average. He didn't fare any better in pro basketball, where the 6-5 Connors averaged 4.5 points a game in little over a season with the Boston Celtics. But then again, nobody on the planet remembers Chuck Connors, who acted in dozens of films and TV shows after he retired from professional sports, for his baseball or basketball careers.

9. Danny Ainge. Danny Ainge was drafted by Toronto Blue Jays in the 15th round of the 1977 MLB Draft, the expansion team's first. He made his major-league debut in May 1979 at age 20. The right-handed hitter played in 87 games at second base, batting .237 with two homers and 19 runs batted in. In 1980, he was in 38 games, mostly in center field, batting a career-high .243, with four RBIs. In 1981, a season interrupted by a 50-day player strike, he appeared in 86 games, primarily at third base, batting .187 with 14 RBIs. In his three MLB seasons, he batted a composite .220 with two homers and 37 runs batted in. Ainge did much better in the NBA, scoring almost 12,000 points in nine seasons while making the 1988 All-Star Game and winning NBA titles in 1984 and 1986 with the Boston Celtics.

8. Howie Schultz. Howie Schultz was a 20-year-old right-handed first baseman when he made his major-league debut with the Brooklyn Dodgers in 1943. He had 49 hits in 45 games, batting .269 with a homer and 34 runs batted in through the end of his first season. The next year was his best—playing in 138 games, batting .255, with 32 doubles, 11 homers, and 83 RBIs. In May 1947, he was purchased by the Philadelphia Phillies, and batted .223 with six homers and 35 RBIs for them. In May 1948, he was placed on waivers and claimed by Cincinnati, where he batted .167 in 36 games and 72 at-bats. He was gone from the majors for good at age 25. In six seasons and 470 games, he had 383 hits with 24 homers, 208 RBIs, and a .241 average. The following year, the 6-6 Schultz launched his NBA career, which lasted three seasons, during which time he played for three teams (the Anderson Packers, Fort Wayne Pistons, and Minneapolis Lakers) and averaged 5.3 points a game.

7. Mark Hendrickson. The left-handed starter was drafted five times before Toronto chose him in the 20th round of the 1997 draft. He was 28 years old when he advanced to the major leagues in August 2002. He pitched for the Blue Jays in 2002 and '03, for the Tampa Bay Devil Rays from 2004 to 2006, when he was dealt to the Los Angeles Dodgers. He was in LA through 2007, pitched a year for Florida in 2008, and then joined Baltimore in 2009. He remained with the Orioles until September 2011, when he was released at age 37. In 10 seasons, he was 58-74 with a 5.03 earned run average. The 6-9 forward/center out of Washington State was drafted by the Philadelphia 76ers in 1996, and played sparingly for four NBA teams over the next four seasons, averaging 3.3 points per game.

6. Frank Baumholtz. The left-handed hitting outfielder signed with the Cincinnati Reds in 1941. He did not make his major-league debut, though, until after World War II, at age 28 in 1947, when he had 182 hits in 154 games and a .283 average. After three seasons in Cincinnati, he played six years with the Cubs, batting .325 in 1952 and .306 in 1953. He concluded his career with a pair of seasons with the Philadelphia Phillies. In 10 big-league seasons, he had 1,010 hits in 1,019 games, with 25 homers, 272 runs batted in, and a .290 average. Just before his MLB debut, the 5-10 Ohio University product managed to fit in a season of pro basketball for the Cleveland Rebels of the Basketball Association of America (BAA), a forerunner of the NBA. He averaged 14.0 points a game, which was good enough to gain him second-team all-league honors for the 1946–47 season.

5. Steve Hamilton. The left-handed pitcher out of Morehead State in Kentucky signed with the Cleveland Indians in April 1958 and debuted in the big leagues in 1961. He was dealt the following season to the Washington Senators, who traded him to the Yankees the year after that. He appeared in the 1963 and '64 World Series and spent eight of his dozen seasons in the Yankee bullpen before moving on to the Chicago White Sox, San Francisco Giants, and Chicago Cubs, winning 40 games and closing 31 for his career. He is most remembered for occasionally throwing a blooper pitch known as the Folly Floater. The 6-6 Hamilton played in the NBA before moving to baseball. The eighth overall pick in the 1958 NBA Draft by the Lakers, he averaged 4.5 points a game in 82 games over the course of two seasons.

4. Gene Conley. Right-handed pitcher Gene Conley holds the singular distinction of being the only player to have played on a World Series winner (the 1957 Milwaukee Braves) and for an NBA champion (he won three titles with the Boston Celtics in 1959, '60, and '61). He was THE two-sport player before Bo Jackson was even born. He signed with the Milwaukee Braves in 1951 and pitched 11 years in the majors, from 1952 to 1963 with Milwaukee, Philadelphia, and Boston. He had five seasons of double-digit wins and won 91 games overall. After being drafted in the 10th round of the 1952 NBA Draft, Conley played a season with the Celtics, but then took a five-year sabbatical to concentrate on baseball.

But he came back to play five seasons with the Celtics and Knicks between 1958 and 1964 while continuing to play Major League Baseball. The 6-8 center/forward averaged 5.9 points and 6.3 rebounds a game during his NBA career.

3. Ron Reed. Ron Reed came out of Notre Dame to sign with the Milwaukee Braves in 1965. The right-handed pitcher enjoyed 19 seasons in the big leagues, winning 146 games, making him the winningest MLB pitcher to have played in the NBA. He had seven seasons of double-digit wins, with a high of 18 for the National League Western Division champion Atlanta Braves in 1969, when he also made the All-Star Game in the first season of divisional play. He pitched in 13 National League Championship Series games for the Braves and Phillies, along with four divisional series games. He appeared in two World Series games for the Phillies in 1980, when they won it all, and three games in the 1983 World Series, which Philadelphia lost in five games to the Orioles. Reed compiled a 1.69 ERA for the World Series games he pitched in. The 6-5 forward didn't reach the NBA playoffs in his two seasons (1965–66 and 1966–67) with the Detroit Pistons, though he did average 8.0 points and 6.4 rebounds a game before retiring from basketball to concentrate on baseball.

2. Dick Groat. Dick Groat was a two-time All-American baseball and basketball player at Duke University before signing to play shortstop for the Pittsburgh Pirates shortly after graduating in 1952. Over 14 seasons, he batted .286 and was selected to eight All-Star teams. He was the National League batting champion in 1960 and was named the league's Most Valuable Player as the Pirates upset the Yankees in the World Series. Four years later, he was a member of the world champion St. Louis Cardinals who, like the Pirates, also beat the Yankees in seven games. Groat was the first basketball player to have his jersey (No. 10) retired by Duke and won the UPI Player of the Year Award in college basketball in 1952, when he was selected third overall in the NBA Draft by the Fort Wayne Pistons. He averaged 11.9 points a game for the Pistons in his one NBA season, which was cut short by his enlistment in the military. He returned to Major League Baseball after his two years of military service, but not to the NBA.

1. Lou Boudreau. Lou Boudreau played only briefly in the National Basketball League, the league that merged with the Basketball Association of America to form the NBA in 1949. But the Hall of Famer is easily the best pro basketball player ever to play in Major League Baseball. He was an All-American at Illinois in the two sports before switching to baseball exclusively in 1939. At age 24, he was named manager of the Cleveland Indians, becoming the youngest MLB skipper in history. He made seven All-Star teams at shortstop and won the 1948 American League MVP Award. In 1970, he had his No. 5 retired by the Indians and was elected to the Baseball Hall of Fame.

For over three decades, Sam Smith has covered the NBA and the Chicago Bulls for the *Chicago Tribune,* and now does the same for the Chicago Bulls website. In 2011, he was presented the Phil Jasner Lifetime Achievement Award for his career's contributions. In addition to his media responsibilities, he is the author of two books, including the best-selling *The Jordan Rules.*

10. June 16, 1993. Jordan scores 55 points to give the Bulls a 3–1 Finals lead in what becomes a six-game series with John Paxson's winner. Jordan sets the all-time NBA Finals scoring record in the series, averaging 41 points, a feat all the more delicious because it came not only against big-talking buddy Charles Barkley, but also because Jordan was guarded by Dan Majerle, a favorite of Jordan's Bulls foil, Jerry Krause, who always would tell Jordan about Majerle's great defense.

9. February 12, 1985. In the first game after the famous 1985 All-Star Game, when Jordan allegedly was the victim of a freeze-out by Isiah Thomas and his pals, the Bulls hosted the Pistons and won in overtime. Jordan had 49 points, 15 rebounds, 5 assists, and 4 steals—all team highs—while Thomas had a quiet 19 points and shot 5-15. It would be the first of many Jordan duels with Thomas and the Pistons, and an early peek at Jordan's driving motivation against various slights, perceived and otherwise.

8. March 28, 1995. Jordan completes his dramatic comeback from almost two years in retirement to play baseball with 55 points in Madison Square Garden in his fifth game back, while also assisting Bill Wennington on the winning basket. For the biggest stage and the most media, Jordan once again saves his best—and ends the questions about whether he could be as good as he once was.

7. June 3, 1992. In the game made famous by Jordan's shrug after making his sixth three-pointer in the first half, MJ scored 35 first-half points in a domination of the Trail Blazers that led to a six-game Finals win and the Bulls' second NBA title. Although Jordan was voted MVP that season, some were saying Portland's Clyde Drexler had done more for his team. And having Drexler on their roster had convinced the Trail Blazers that they could pass on Jordan in the 1984 NBA Draft and instead go for a center. Jordan always was one never to forget and always anxious to make his case. And points.

6. February 7, 1988. Jordan gained unofficial acceptance of the mythical torch of league excellence and showmanship from Dr. J as Jordan dominated All-Star weekend. He won the Slam Dunk Contest with a Dr. J-style dunk, taking off from the free throw line, and then led the Eastern stars to victory by scoring 40 points—the second most ever by one player in an NBA All-Star Game to Wilt's 42 in 1962.

5. June 11, 1997. Jordan's 38 points and game-winning three-pointer (while playing 44 minutes despite a devastating case of food poisoning from room service pizza) won Chicago the pivotal NBA Finals Game 5 for a 3–2 Bulls lead over the Jazz in the series. (Though one has to ask: who orders pizza in Utah?) The Bulls then returned to Chicago to wrap up their fifth championship as Jordan passed to Steve Kerr for the winner.

4. April 20, 1986. In the most prolific playoff scoring game ever, Jordan poured in 63 points against the team many regard as the best ever, the 1986 Celtics. It was afterward that Larry Bird famously said it was "God disguised as Michael Jordan," as Jordan established himself as the game's greatest scorer since Wilt Chamberlain.

3. June 12, 1991. Jordan finally gets that first, elusive NBA title—the one his critics in the 1980s said he was too selfish and too much a scorer to ever get. He celebrates in tears with his father, James. Dominating on-court rival Magic Johnson throughout the series, Jordan has the famous switch-hands layup in Game 2, the final shot to send the game into overtime in Game 3, and the seminal trust moment in Game 5 when Jordan passed repeatedly to John Paxson to thwart the Lakers' pressure tactics. Jordan would score 30 points in Game 5 to average 31.2 in the series. But he also had 5 steals, 2 blocks, and 10 assists. He would average 11.4 assists in the series and become the versatile threat that would prove unbeatable in every Finals he played in the rest of his career.

2. May 7, 1989. The shot to win the first-round series over the Cleveland Cavaliers. There may never have been a more frequently shown first-round playoff series winner. But that win effectively cemented the Bulls' championship-era core and assured their future league domination. Magic Johnson had labeled those versatile Cavs "the team of the '90s" and they were 6-0 over the Bulls in games that season. The Bulls then would go onto the Eastern Conference Finals. But the talk had been if they'd lost in the first round that the team could be broken up. Little remembered was Jordan missing two late free throws to lose Game 4, thus making Game 5 another famous atonement.

1. June 14, 1998. The shot to win the 1998 championship against the Utah Jazz. Has there ever been any better conclusion to a career (he didn't really come back to play for the Wizards, did he?). Maybe Ted Williams's home run in his final at-bat. But it wasn't just Jordan's final shot—Jordan stole the ball from Karl Malone as Malone was attempting to effectively put the game away for the Jazz on the previous possession. Jordan then drove full court and hit the famous pull-up over Bryon Russell.

My Top 10 Favorite Athletes
:: by Stephen Curry

Stephen Curry is the son of retired NBA sharpshooter Dell Curry. After wowing the sports world with his amazing run at Davidson College, Curry was the seventh pick in the 2009 NBA Draft by the Golden State Warriors and hasn't disappointed, averaging over 17 ppg during his first two seasons. He has also registered numbers that are top 10 in three-point shooting, assists, and steals—and he's only getting better.

10. Michael Jordan. MJ—best player in my sport. I learned a lot from him.

9. Seth Curry (my brother). No. 30 for Duke, he's an up-and-coming star. I have a Fathead poster of him in my room.

8. Sam Mills. He is my all-time favorite Carolina Panthers player. He did a lot to start the organization.

7. Cam Newton. He's the future of the Carolina Panthers, my hometown team. And I'm a die-hard Carolina fan.

6. Fred McGriff. My grandmother was a huge Braves fan and always had TBS and Turner Sports on the television when I was growing up. I loved those Braves teams with David Justice and Ryan Klesko and McGriff and that whole squad.

5. David Ortiz. I'm a huge Red Sox fan and he's done a lot for that team and made me happy.

4. Arnold Palmer. I'm a big Palmer fan, not only for what he did on the course but what he did in the cafeteria as well (see ESPN commercial).

2 (tie). Tiger Woods and Phil Mickelson. Golf's my second favorite sport to basketball and these two stand out.

1. Dell Curry (my father). He is the all-time leading scorer in the Charlotte Hornets organization. And he's family, as well.

The Greatest NBA Postseason Single-Game Performances :: by Marv Albert

Marv Albert has been announcing basketball games for almost a half century, earning himself the nickname the Voice of Basketball, along with several Emmys and induction into the Basketball Hall of Fame, which awarded him its Curt Gowdy Media honor in 2004. The Brooklyn native was the New York Knicks play-by-play man for 37 years, and has served the same function for the New Jersey Nets on the YES Network since 2005. He has been TNT's lead NBA announcer since 1999. Albert has worked Super Bowls, Stanley Cup Finals, Wimbledon, the Breeders Cup, March Madness, and the World Series. He has also done play-by-play for the NBA Finals, as well as numerous other NBA playoff games. Here is his list of the greatest individual NBA playoff performances of all time.

11. Bill Walton. In Portland's title-clinching Game 6 win over Philadelphia in the 1977 NBA Finals, Walton had 20 points, 23 rebounds, 7 assists, and 8 blocks, leading the Blazers to their only championship after trailing the Sixers 2–0 in the series.

10. Tom Heinsohn. In Game 7 of the 1957 NBA Finals, the Celtics' rookie forward scored 37 points and grabbed 23 rebounds in the 125–123 double-overtime victory over the St. Louis Hawks that secured Boston its first NBA championship.

9. Jerry West. In Game 7 against the Boston Celtics in 1969, West had 42 points, 13 rebounds, and 12 assists. The Lakers lost the game and series, but West was named MVP of the Finals—the only time in league history that a player from a losing team was so honored. For West, this was his sixth appearance in the Finals and sixth loss, having also gone down to the Celtics the previous five times. The Lakers actually had a 3–2 lead in the series but lost Game 6 in Boston, and then again back in Los Angeles, despite the spectacular triple-double by West.

8. Larry Bird. In Game 6 of the 1986 Finals against Houston, the great Celtic forward submitted a clutch performance to lead Boston to their 16th NBA championship. For the game, Bird registered a triple-double, with 29 points, 11 rebounds, and 12 assists.

7. Michael Jordan. Thirty-five points and six three-pointers against Portland in the FIRST HALF of Game 1 in the 1992 Finals set the record for both the number of points and number of three-pointers registered in a single half of a Finals game.

Michael was not one to take many three-pointers, but I recall that he came out earlier that day to shoot three-pointers hours before the arena had opened its doors. I was courtside to broadcast the game for NBC, along with The Czar—Mike Fratello—and Magic Johnson, and it was amusing to see Michael look over at us and shrug his shoulders, as if to say, 'I can't believe I'm doing this.'

6. James Worthy. In 1998, the Lakers became the first team since the 1969 Boston Celtics to repeat as champions. Led by Big Game James, who was accountable for 36 points, 16 rebounds, and 10 assists in Game 7 of the Finals, LA defeated Detroit. Worthy was named Finals MVP after the Lakers came from down 3–2 in the series to win Game 6 by one point, and then take Game 7 behind Worthy's legendary performance.

5. Bob Pettit. The St. Louis forward scored 50 points in the Hawks NBA Finals-clinching Game 6 victory over Boston in 1958. The Hawks were the one team that could challenge Bill Russell's Celtics, and after losing a tough Finals Game 7 to Boston the previous year, the Hawks realized redemption by winning their only NBA title behind Hall of Famer Bob Pettit's dazzling performance, in which he scored 19 of the Hawks' last 21 points to shock the Celtics.

4. Willis Reed-Walt Frazier. The combined exploits of these two New York greats in Game 7 of the 1970 NBA Finals led the Knicks to their first NBA title by beating the Lakers at Madison Square Garden. Willis, who sat out Game 6 in Los Angeles with a painful thigh injury, provided the inspiration with his emotional hobbling entrance just moments before the start of the game, and then hit two early jump shots to set the tone. But it was Walt "Clyde" Frazier who dominated the game with 36 points and 19 assists, capping off one of the most memorable games in NBA history.

3. Bill Russell. In Game 7 of the 1962 Finals, the Celtic center scored 30 points and was responsible for a remarkable 40 rebounds in an overtime win over the Lakers to win the title. For Red Auerbach and Boston, it was their fourth of what would be eight straight championships.

2. Michael Jordan. Playing with a severe case of the flu, the great Bull came up with 38 points, 7 rebounds, and 5 assists to spark Chicago to a decisive Game 5 win in Utah in the 1997 Finals. Prior to the game, due to MJ's dehydration and exhaustion, the Bulls had their doubts as to whether Jordan would even dress for the game. But he played through it and was helped by teammates to get back to the bench each time-out. The win sent the series back to Chicago with the Bulls up 3–2. Two days later they won their fifth title in seven years.

1. Magic Johnson. The 20-year-old rookie was forced to play center in Game 6 of the 1980 Finals to fill the void left by an absent Kareem Abdul-Jabbar, the six-time NBA MVP sidelined with an ankle sprain. In Abdul-Jabbar's place, Magic scored 42 points, grabbed 15 rebounds, and dished 7 assists to beat the 76ers. Magic's remarkable performance led the Lakers to the road victory over the Sixers and earned Los Angeles the first of its five NBA championships in the 1980s.

Top 10 Greatest Moments in NBA All-Star History :: by Chris Broussard

Chris Broussard is an NBA analyst for ESPN. He serves as a regular on the network's *NBA Fastbreak* studio show and *First Take*. He also began appearing on ABC's *NBA Countdown* pregame show in the 2011–12 season. The Louisiana native started covering the NBA in the mid-1990s for the *Akron Beacon Journal* before doing the same for the *New York Times*. He now writes for *ESPN Magazine*. The Oberlin College grad has experienced dozens of great NBA All-Star Game moments over the past few decades as a reporter and as a fan. Here are the 10 he recalls best.

10. Spud Steals the Show (1986). In the biggest (no pun intended) upset in Slam Dunk Contest history, 5-7 Spud Webb beats his air-walking teammate, 6-7 Dominique Wilkins. Webb stunned everyone with his wide assortment of dunks, including a 360. On his last slam—with the crowd chanting, "Spud! Spud!"—he tossed the ball in the air, caught it off the bounce, and dunked it backwards.

9. Hodges Catches Fire (1991). In a shooting display so incredible that in 27 years not one of the greatest shooters in league history has come anywhere near matching it, Craig Hodges sinks 19 straight shots in the Three-Point Shootout en route to winning his second of three straight contests. Larry Bird, the event's only other three-time winner, owns the second-most prolific consecutive-shot streak of 11.

8. MJ's Last Hurrah (2003). Mariah Carey serenaded him in a skintight "Wizards 23" dress, Vince Carter gave him his starting position, and Michael Jordan did his part in giving the basketball universe what it wanted. With the score tied in overtime and everyone—even perhaps his opponents—wanting Jordan to nail the last shot in his 13th and final All-Star appearance, MJ got the ball on the right block and sank a fadeaway jumper over the outstretched arms of Shawn Marion with just seconds remaining. Unfortunately, due to an inexplicable and ill-timed foul by Jordan's East teammate Jermaine O'Neal moments later, the West was allowed to tie it and go on to win in a second overtime. Still, with the 39-year-old Jordan scoring 20 points and hitting the "should've-been" game-winning shot, it was a night to remember.

7. Larry Legend Talks Trash, Then Backs It Up (1986).

Larry Bird burst into the locker room two minutes before the contestants in the league's first-ever Three-Point Shootout (then called the Long-Distance Shootout) were to be briefed on the rules. Nearly a half hour late for the meeting, Bird strolled through the room in silence, staring at his competitors. Then, as he was wont to do, he began playing mind games. "Man, who's coming in second?" he said. It was a good question, because with Bird on his "A" game, no one else stood a chance. In the final, Bird hit nine straight shots, beating runner-up Craig Hodges by 10 points.

6. The Doctor Ushers in the Dunk Contest (1984).

Give him credit for showing up. Julius "Dr. J" Erving, arguably the greatest dunker of all time, was in his 13th pro season, a few weeks shy of his 34th birthday. But when the NBA wanted to liven up its All-Star Game by adding a dunk contest, Doc didn't let his age or weary legs stand in the way. Eight years after he'd won the legendary event in the ABA with his famous foul line slam, he took on a crew of relative youngsters, including 24-year-old Larry Nance. The 6-10 Nance, dunking two balls at once, edged Dr. J in the finals. But make no mistake, the Doctor, far from his high-flying best, still provided the spark needed to turn the event into an annual spectacle.

5. Vinsanity Reigns (2000).

For all intents and purposes, it was over after one dunk. Vince Carter, who once famously hurdled a seven-footer while dunking, opened the Slam Dunk contest with a reverse 360 windmill. No one—not Jordan, not Doc, not Dominique—had ever done it before, and no one has done it since. The contest went on to have other great moments (for instance, Vince catching a bounce pass, shifting it between his legs, and jamming; and Carter putting his entire forearm in the rim after another slam) but the crowd's eruption made it clear that the outcome was decided after his first dunk.

4. "It's a Bird, It's a Plane . . ." (2008).

Centers are not supposed to win dunk contests. They're too big, too clunky. Well, in 2008, Dwight Howard killed that noise by putting on one of the most creative and spectacular performances the contest has ever seen. After nearly a quarter century of NBA Slam Dunk Contests, we thought we'd seen it all. But Howard came up with several innovative, never-before-seen dunks, including The Superman, in which he donned a red "S" cape, leaped off two feet from a foot behind the dotted line, caught an alley-oop pass from teammate Jameer Nelson, and hurled the ball into the rim like a pitcher throwing a fastball. Although there were also tremendous dunks from Gerald Green and Jamario Moon in that contest, Superman won going away.

3. Michael vs. 'Nique (1988). In perhaps the most hotly contested Slam Dunk Contest in league history, the two most electrifying dunkers of their era went head-to-head in Chicago. Jordan, with the home fans cheering his every gyration, wowed with his incomparable grace and hang time, while Dominique Wilkins's scintillating power jams left even the Jordan faithful in awe. Jordan, down heading into his last dunk, emerged victorious when he danced in midair while flying from the foul line for the final flush. Dominique graciously accepted his second-place finish, though to this day, many believe he was robbed.

2. The 50 Greatest Players in NBA History (1997). Grant Hill, Hakeem Olajuwon, Karl Malone, and their All-Star counterparts were working their wonders on the court, but the real stars of this show were sitting in the stands. Wilt, Magic, The Doctor, Clyde, Kareem, Bird—men known by one name, or by their nicknames—were the headliners, as the past came together with the present in this grandest of basketball events. On the 50th anniversary of the NBA, the league named its 50 Greatest Players in NBA History, and all but three of them converged on Cleveland to be celebrated at halftime.

1. Magic's Triumphant Return (1992). Three months after announcing his retirement because of HIV and playing in his first NBA game in nearly eight months, Magic Johnson showed he still had it—and then some—by putting on one of the most inspiring and emotional performances in American sports history. Scoring 25 points and dishing out nine assists, Johnson led the West to a 153–113 rout. He closed the game with three consecutive three-pointers as he went one-on-one in fun-loving matchups with one-time rivals and friends Michael Jordan and Isiah Thomas.

Top 10 Current NBA Players :: by Ian Thomsen

Ian Thomsen is a senior writer at *Sports Illustrated*, where he's covered the NBA full-time since 2000. In the 1990s, he spent six years writing about international basketball (and other sports) for the *International Herald Tribune* in Paris. In the 1980s, Thomsen helped cover the Magic vs. Bird NBA Finals for the *Boston Globe*. He has seen a lot of great players over the years, but this is his list of the best NBA players as of the start of the 2011–12 season.

10. Pau Gasol. He had a poor 2011 postseason, but the Lakers could not have won the previous two titles—or held onto Kobe Bryant, perhaps—without trading for Gasol in 2008. He is the world's most versatile big man, as he proved while leading Spain to the 2011 FIBA World Championship title. He may not knock you down, but he'll beat you every other way.

8 (tie). Deron Williams and Chris Paul. Their rivalry has been back-and-forth since the 2005 NBA Draft, when Williams went No. 3 to the Jazz ahead of Paul at No. 4 to the Hornets. The mistake is to rate them as anything other than dead even; whenever one has appeared to grab a momentary advantage, the other has surged ahead. Williams, who was traded in 2011 to the Nets, is rated by many coaches as the league's most complete point guard, with the size, skills, and athleticism to win by all imaginable means, while Paul is the NBA's most inspirational leader, with the explosive athleticism to make winning plays at both ends of the floor. And the best is still to come, as neither one has peaked.

7. Dwyane Wade. Few players have a better understanding of how and when to make the big play, which is why the Miami experiment will ultimately succeed with Wade, the ruthless finisher complementing LeBron James as the league's most creative playmaker. Wade overcomes his size (he's much shorter than his 6-4 listing) by attacking incessantly, raising concerns that he may shorten his career. But few (only six, actually) are better right now.

6. Dwight Howard. He's the last of the frightening low-post centers, which leads to needless criticism of Howard's offensive skills. The NBA rulebook has changed to favor perimeter slashers at the expense of big men, which hinders the credit Howard deserves for his improving footwork and shooting. In the meantime he influences the game as few can by protecting the rim, covering the glass, and outrunning opponents to both ends of the floor.

5. Kevin Durant. Here is a young scorer who inspires his teammates and celebrates their success. Durant has improved every year, at first in his individual game and more lately as a leader. He's an explosively athletic version of Dirk Nowitzki, with a shooting stroke that is audaciously smooth—and sooner rather than later it will be Durant's turn to tear through the postseason, as Nowitzki did in 2011.

4. Derrick Rose. The rules changes that have opened up the driving lanes to the basket could have been invented with Rose in mind. He has quickly become the prototypical scoring point guard who attacks because he can and scores as an afterthought (his selfless priority is to enable and elevate his teammates). Like James Bond in a tuxedo, this is a quiet gentleman who isn't afraid to deploy all of his weapons, humbly, of course.

3. Kobe Bryant. No player of this era is more accomplished and—despite 15 seasons of NBA mileage—it is entirely within his means to reclaim No. 1 on this list. So Bryant isn't the explosive scorer he used to be; instead he has become the wisest title contender in the league, with the skills, understanding, and ruthless ambition to execute plays of any and all kinds. He may yet equalize and surpass the six titles won by Michael Jordan, and what a historical debate that would create.

2. LeBron James. Going into the 2011 NBA Finals, James appeared to be the best postseason player in basketball—defensively and offensively, as a playmaker and as a finisher, a slasher with three-point range in the clutch. Look for him to solidify his post-up game and fulfill himself in an NBA Finals. Never mind his off-court decisions, at 6-8 James has the skills to be a bigger version of Michael and Kobe, with the passing skills of Magic Johnson built in.

1. Dirk Nowitzki. *"Don't worry! In Year Four, you'll become an annual All-Star; by 28 you'll be MVP. You'll change the game for NBA big men, and just as they're shifting to the perimeter you'll be learning to destroy them in the paint. No one will be better in crunch time, you'll be more resilient than you ever dreamed, and your worst losses will inspire you to become the most important international player in history—the first true import to lead an NBA champion."*
When Nowitzki was a nervous 19-year-old German, sitting by Don Nelson's swimming pool the night before he decided to gamble on emigrating to the NBA, wouldn't it have been nice to tell him how it was going to turn out? Humble as he is, he would not have believed a word of it—which explains how he earned his place atop the game.

Jerry Sloan is one of the most competitive players and coaches in the history of the game. He coached one team (the Utah Jazz) for longer (20 years) and to more regular-season wins (1,127) than any other head coach in NBA history. He was inducted into the Hall of Fame as a coach in 2009, two years before he retired.

As a player, Sloan had his No. 4 retired by the Chicago Bulls, the team he played on for eight seasons, during which time he was named to two NBA All-Star teams. A dogged defender known as Spider, he earned two second-team and four first-team All-NBA Defensive selections. Below is his dream NBA Final Four, with the numbers indicating the players' positions.

In Jerry's words: "Dr. Naismith would come back from the dead to watch this tournament. The problem would be finding an arena big enough to accommodate the millions of other fans who would be desperate to attend this event. The good news is I would get to coach all four of these teams. Why not? It's my tournament."

TEAM FOUR

5: Shaquille O'Neal.

4: Charles Barkley.

3. Dominique Wilkins.

2. Steve Nash.

1. Dennis Johnson.

Shaquille O'Neal is the most immense NBA specimen since Wilt Chamberlain. With Shaq occupying space, Steve Nash has the choice to deliver to Barkley or Dominique—two of the greatest athletes ever to play the forward position. What a treat it would be to watch. Oh, by the way, DJ might be the most critical player on this team, the guy with the vital job of shutting down the other team's 2-guard (Jordan, West, or Kobe).

TEAM THREE

5. Kareem Abdul-Jabbar.

4. Tim Duncan.

3. Rick Barry.

2. Kobe Bryant.

1. John Stockton.

For the tournament John Stockton would certainly average over 20 assists a game. The point guard's only problem would be deciding whether to give the ball to Duncan on the wing, Kareem on the low post for the skyhook, Rick Barry for a three-pointer, or to Kobe on the clear out.

TEAM TWO

5. Wilt Chamberlain.

4. Karl Malone.

3. Julius Erving.

2. Oscar Robertson.

1. Jerry West.

It's not often that an All-Star team has both a guard (Robertson) and a center (Chamberlain) who led the NBA in assists for a season. Oscar (a six-time NBA assists leader) and Wilt (who did it once) both were great distributors of the ball. Jerry West might be the purest player, Karl Malone the greatest scorer from the power forward position, and Dr. J the most creative forward in league history.

TEAM ONE

5. Bill Russell.

4. Larry Bird.

3. Elgin Baylor.

2. Magic Johnson.

1. Michael Jordan.

Talk about a Dream Team. Can you imagine Bill Russell blocking a shot, controlling possession, and then outletting the ball to Magic, who would throw a court-long bounce pass to Larry Bird, who would immediately throw a no-look pass to Elgin Baylor, who would take the ball to the basket and hang in the air, drawing defenders, before dropping the ball to Michael Jordan, who would score on a double-pump reverse layup? It's possible that four of the players could record triple-doubles in the same game, and Russell would certainly account for 20-plus rebounds.

Players Who Kept Me Up the Night Before We Played Them :: by Bill Fitch

Bill Fitch is one of the greatest coaches in NBA history. Not only did he win the title with the Celtics in 1981, he did a great job with the Cleveland Cavaliers, bringing the team to the 1976 Eastern Conference Finals. He also guided a young Houston team to the 1986 NBA Finals.

12 (tie). Alex English and Dan Issel. They said that the Denver altitude made it tough on you, but it was really these two guys who killed you. Doug Moe, their coach, would get his team running and they could kill teams. Alex and Dan were both good all-around players—you just didn't hear enough about them.

10 (tie). Andrew Toney and Karl Malone. With Philly we'd just let Dr. J get his points, and then this kid Toney would come along and just tear you apart. He'd be a Hall of Famer if his feet had stayed healthy. Malone was just a very good power forward in a league that had a bunch of them. He was so consistent. He'd get his points and rebounds every night and didn't take nights off.

8 (tie). Walt Frazier and Pete Maravich. We feared Frazier more as a defender than anything. If a player was hot, whatever the position he was playing, Red Holzman would just switch Frazier over on him and that was it. Maravich was an offensive machine. You would do the best you could to keep him under control, but at any time he could erupt.

7. Oscar Robertson. I coached against Oscar at the end of his career. What made him so tough was that he could play any position. I would be up all night studying film, trying to figure out how to stop him at all five positions.

6. Bob McAdoo. He could put up huge production on the board and did it every night. The only one who could stop him was The Barber—the leather-lunged fan in Detroit who would ride everyone to distraction.

5. John Havlicek. On John's 40th birthday he was in town in Boston. He came to our practice and I threw him into the scrimmage. Our regular players were drenched in perspiration and worn out. John wasn't even sweating.

4. Nate Archibald. What a great little player he was. He had his best days in Cincinnati and Kansas City. I coached him in Boston late in his career. He didn't have to carry the whole load, so we used him primarily as a passer.

3. Larry Bird. I lived and died with him. I lived when I coached him early in his career. When I coached against him, I was dying. The only way to stop him was with a gun, and they wouldn't let me bring it to the gym.

2. Kareem Abdul-Jabbar. He perfected that skyhook and it was unstoppable. I think I was the first coach to bring in three guys to try to stop him.

1. Wilt Chamberlain. When I was coaching the Cavaliers, the Lakers were in town at our old arena. Wilt stole the ball and was out front for a breakaway. As he got up in the air he hit the front of the rim with the ball and fell flat on his back. I rushed up and down the bench and told our players, "Don't anybody laugh." All I needed was for Wilt to get mad and he would punish us even worse.

Top NBA Coaches of All Time
:: by Bob Ryan

Bob Ryan is considered by many to be the greatest basketball writer of all time. The former *Boston Globe* scribe won the 2000 AP Sportswriter of the Year Award, along with many other awards. In addition to his newspaper writing, Ryan penned several books, including collaborations with NBA greats Bob Cousy, John Havlicek, and Larry Bird.

Honorable Mention (i.e. Toughest Omissions). John Kundla; Bill Fitch; Lenny Wilkens; Jerry Sloan; Bill Sharman; Hubie Brown; Doug Moe.

10. Larry Brown. A head coach at age 32. Brown has coached 10 ABA and NBA teams, won three ABA and one NBA Coach of Year awards, and finally won an NBA championship with Detroit in 2004. Considered to be one of the game's great teachers, to the point where many suggested he would have been happy with endless practices and no games. They were kidding. Perhaps.

9. Jack Ramsay. Entitled his book, *A Coach's Art*, which befits a man with a PhD. Intense, cerebral man who really did have artistic vision of the game. Fulfillment was his 1977 champion Trail Blazers, built around Bill Walton, but his Buffalo Braves teams were works of hoop art, as well.

8. Red Holzman. Fame rests with Knicks teams of 1969–74, but that's enough. Won titles in 1970 and 1973 with teams built on great team defense and great ball movement. Laid-back to the max. Red once said, "We win, I'll have a steak and a scotch. We lose, I'll have a steak and a scotch." He wasn't kidding. Won 696 games. Lost 604. Lotta steaks. Lotta scotches.

7. Don Nelson. Greatest Coach Not To Have Won A Championship. Fearless offensive innovator. Would try anything. Coached some of the most exciting NBA teams ever, winning a record 1,335 games along the way.

6. Chuck Daly. Transformed Pistons from glitzy finesse team to two-time champions who would hurt you. Chosen as coach of 1992 Dream Team because of people skills. Said best asset a coach can have is "bad hearing" and likened regular-season coaching to flying a plane coast to coast in violent weather.

5. Gregg Popovich. Originally groomed to be an executive, he took over Spurs from Bob Hill in the 1996–97 season and coached them to four championships. A bluntly honest, no-frills guy who has coached a no-frills team. Having Tim Duncan hasn't hurt, but, like Auerbach and Jackson, possesses the requisite people skills to coach great players.

4. Dick Motta. Coached six teams and won a title with Washington in 1978, but did best work with early '70s Bulls. Absent a 24-second clock, would have won there at least twice. Master of defense and forward-centric offense. Once told me, "I've been in this league 16 years, and not once have I ever had the ball thrown into the pivot with the expectation the guy would score."

3. Pat Riley. From broadcast booth alongside Chick Hearn to assistant to Resident Genius in about a year. Supervised Showtime Lakers, presided over team leadership transition from Kareem to Magic and then reinvented himself as defense–oriented coach in New York and Miami.

2. Phil Jackson. The Tex Winter Triangle Offensive aside, no one played mind games better than the Zen Master. Had great players, such as Jordan, Pippen, O'Neal, and Bryant, true, but pushed buttons masterfully. Had Jordan not retired for those two years, he'd probably have 13 titles, rather than 11.

1. Red Auerbach. Do people realize he quit at age 48? Won nine titles and lost to St. Louis in the 1958 Finals during a 10-year stretch. Might easily have won more. He's No. 1 over Phil Jackson because he did it all with no assistant, no traveling secretary, no help at all. Recognized the unique genius of Bill Russell, who has said more than once he would never have been the player he was in any other uniform.

10 Things You Never Knew About Phil Jackson :: by Charley Rosen

Charley Rosen is an NBA analyst for Fox-sports.com and the author of 17 sports books. Two of those books were collaborations with this list's subject. During the early to mid-1980s, Rosen served as an assistant to Phil Jackson when the future Hall of Famer was the head coach of the Continental Basketball Association's Albany Patroons.

10. He's an excellent cook. Phil is devout in his belief that breakfast is indeed the most important meal of the day. Whenever he's not on the road, he'll take special pains to prepare and cook his specialty—pancakes made from scratch that includes at least a dozen ingredients (buttermilk, eggs, whole-wheat flour, wheat germ, flax seed, fresh berries in season, etc.). So diligent is he about cooking them perfectly that he fries only one pancake at a time. No wonder they're always scrumptious!

9. When serenaded by the house band in Mexican restaurants, he'll tip the musicians $50 to play "My Way." This should not be seen as proof of a bloated egotism. Instead, it's a sign of his fierce individualism. Indeed, in his own quiet way, Phil is proud that he's never taken the easy, well-worn path, and has always remained true to himself.

8. Since he really doesn't see himself as being a celebrity, only two personalized items adorn the walls of his home in LA. One is a large, framed poster filled with caricatures of all the members of the Knicks 1973 championship team. Phil's portrait overemphasizes his broad, bony shoulders, his thick moustache, and his whimsical grin. The other is a large drum cymbal dedicated to him and autographed by the Grateful Dead, circa the early 1990s.

7. His favorite radio program is _Prairie Home Companion_. The corny-_cum_-clever humor and down-home songs resonate with the wholesome, semi-rural, 4-H environment of his childhood in Montana and North Dakota.

6. Phil and his older brother Joe handcrafted the main residence in PJ's current homestead in Montana. Although they did have some help with the foundation, the plumbing, and the electrical system, over the course of three summers the Brothers Jackson erected, roofed, floored, and finished a cozy, attractive weatherproof house that's as livable as it is unique. The property also contains several other attractive contractor-built houses for the annual off-season visitations of Phil's five children and six—and counting—grandchildren.

5. During a Knicks practice in the early 1970s, Phil completed the most unusual pass in the history of the game. He was on the wing of a three-man full-court fast-break drill, with Walt Frazier in the middle. As Phil reached the far foul line and made the required diagonal cut, Frazier flipped a pass in his direction, fully expecting PJ to catch the ball and cruise to the hoop for the layup. However, while still on the run, Phil abruptly crouched and turned his back to the ball. He then let the ball bounce off his butt and redirected it straight into Frazier's hands. Clyde was laughing so hard that he missed the chip shot.

4. Despite his calm, Zen-like exterior, Phil is a ferocious competitor. Whether he's playing penny-ante card games, thumb wrestling, foosball, tiddly-winks, and certainly on the hardwood, Phil wants to win—period! On at least two occasions, he's deliberately inflicted a bony knee to the respective thighs of opponents who were getting the best of him in pickup games. In fact, the primary reason why he got along so well with Michael Jordan was that the two of them were the most competitive individuals in the entire Bulls organization.

3. Phil was nearly killed by George McGinnis. At 6-8 and a lean 225 pounds, Phil was often required to defend bigger, stronger players. To hold his own against the 6-8 McGinnis, who had muscles on his muscles and weighed at least 260 in his prime, Phil had to make maximum use of his long arms (38-inch sleeve length) and pointy elbows. During one game, McGinnis warned Phil to keep his "bows sheathed," but to do so would have prevented PJ from playing even cursory defense. Suddenly, McGinnis had enough and, without warning, quickly directed a massive fist at Phil's face. There wasn't even time to duck, but instinctively Phil's entire body simply went limp and he collapsed to the floor. The punch grazed the top of Phil's head, but had it connected, Kermit Washington's assault on Rudy Tomjanovich would have seemed like a love tap.

2. As a player, and certainly as a coach, Phil had a contentious relationship with referees. In fact, at best he considered them to be a necessary evil. At worst, they were biased, mean-spirited jerks. During his tenure as coach of the Albany Patroons in the Continental Basketball Association, Phil was suspended for two games for spitting on the head of a bald ref during an argument. And his last official action in the CBA was to hurl a chair (à la Bobby Knight) on to the court after he was thumbed out of his final game for protesting an egregiously bad call.

1. In his younger days, Phil was an extremely talented baseball player. He once pitched a one-hit, 12-strikeout shutout for the University of North Dakota. Phil was also a superb hitter. He was a teenager playing for an American Legion team in an exhibition game when he clouted a line-drive double off the left-centerfield wall against one of the greatest pitchers of all time—the legendary Satchel Paige!

Top 10 NBA Coaches with Big 5 Roots
:: by Andy Jasner

Andy Jasner was a columnist for the *Philly Sports Daily* and the son of the late, great Phil Jasner, a Basketball Hall of Fame sportswriter who covered the Philadelphia 76ers and Philadelphia's Big 5 for the *Philadelphia Daily News*. In addition to staging the nation's most celebrated ongoing college basketball city series, the Big 5—which consists of La Salle University, Villanova University, the University of Pennsylvania, Temple University, and St. Joseph's University—has served as a staging ground for numerous fine coaches who have gone on to the NBA. Here, Andy offers a look at the best of them.

Honorable Mention. Bob Weinhauer; Don Casey; Dick Harter.

10. Mike Fratello. The Czar honed his coaching skills as an assistant under Rollie Massimino at Villanova from 1975 to 1978. Fratello was an NBA head coach for three teams (the Atlanta Hawks, Cleveland Cavaliers, and Memphis Grizzlies) from 1980 to 2007. Fratello qualified for the playoffs 11 times and finished with an impressive career record of 667-548. In the 1986–87 season, Fratello guided the Hawks to a 57-25 record and was named NBA Coach of the Year by five different organizations.

9. Chris Ford. Ford starred at guard for Villanova from 1969–72 and was inducted into the Big 5 Hall of Fame in 1977. Ford would later become a head coach in the NBA with the Boston Celtics, Milwaukee Bucks, Los Angeles Clippers, and Philadelphia 76ers. Ford compiled a career record of 323-376 in parts of 10 seasons, five with the Celtics. His best season came as a rookie head coach in 1990, when he led the Celtics to 56 victories.

8. Jim O'Brien. O'Brien led Saint Joseph's to two NCAA Tournament appearances and one NIT berth as a player in the early 1970s. He went on to become an NBA head coach for nine seasons with the Boston Celtics, Philadelphia 76ers, and Indiana Pacers. O'Brien finished with a career mark of 303-327 and 14-17 in the playoffs. In 2002, his Celtics dropped a hard-fought six-game series to the New Jersey Nets in the Eastern Conference Finals.

7. Jack McKinney. The highly successful Saint Joseph's assistant and head coach went on to become the NBA Coach of the Year in 1980–81 with the Indiana Pacers. The Pacers finished 44-38. The year before, McKinney suffered a horrific crash on his son's bicycle 14 games into the 1979–80 season as head coach of the Lakers. McKinney's Pacers were swept in the playoffs by the Philadelphia 76ers in 1981, but that didn't diminish the fabulous job he'd done. McKinney won 136 career games as a head coach in the NBA.

6. Jack McCloskey. The former University of Pennsylvania coach was inducted into the Big 5 Hall of Fame in 1994. McCloskey's teams at Penn went 87-53 in the Ivy League and captured the school's first Philadelphia Big 5 title in 1963. McCloskey left Penn with an overall record of 146-105. McCloskey was the head coach for the Portland Trail Blazers for two seasons (1972–74) before becoming a highly successful NBA executive, most notably with the Detroit Pistons in the 1980s and early '90s.

5. Paul Westhead. The former head coach at La Salle won 142 games between the years 1970–79. He hit legendary status when he guided the Los Angeles Lakers to an NBA championship in 1979–80. Westhead took over when Jack McKinney was injured in a bicycle accident. Oh, have we mentioned that Magic Johnson was a rookie that season with the Lakers? Still, Westhead was in the right place at the right time. And he took full advantage. Westhead also coached the Chicago Bulls and Denver Nuggets, but nothing ever came close to that experience with the Lakers.

4. Matt Guokas. Born and raised in Philadelphia, Guokas played for Saint Joseph's and was the 76ers' first-round draft choice in 1966. He helped the Sixers win the 1966–67 NBA championship. Guokas eventually became head coach of the expansion Orlando Magic from 1989 to 1993. The 1992–93 season was special, as Guokas led the Magic to their first-ever .500 season at 41-41. Guokas also coached the 76ers for nearly three seasons, posting a 54-28 mark in the 1985–86 season. The Sixers were 6-6 in the postseason that year and fell to the Milwaukee Bucks in seven games in the Eastern Conference semifinals.

3. Jimmy Lynam. A three-year starter at Saint Joseph's, Lynam went on to record a 65-28 record as head coach on Hawk Hill, including a remarkable run to the Elite Eight of the NCAA Tournament in 1981. Lynam would become a terrific head coach in the NBA for 10 seasons with the Los Angeles Clippers, 76ers, and Washington Bullets. Lynam won 329 career games, with his best season coming in 1989–90 with his 76ers going 53-29 and falling to Michael Jordan and the Chicago Bulls in five games in the Eastern Conference Semifinals.

2. Jack Ramsay. From 1955 to 1966, Ramsay led Saint Joseph's University to an unbelievable record of 234-72, seven Big 5 titles, and 10 postseason berths. Ramsay was just as amazing as an NBA head coach, highlighted by a championship he won with the Portland Trail Blazers in 1977. He would take his teams to the playoffs in nine of the next 10 seasons and was inducted into the Basketball Hall of Fame in 1992. Ramsay won 864 career games as an NBA head coach with the 76ers, Buffalo Braves, Trail Blazers, and Pacers, and registered 16 appearances in the playoffs. Impressive indeed.

1. Chuck Daly. Daly took over as Penn's head coach in 1971 and went 125-38 in six seasons, with a staggering 20-5 record in Big 5 games. Daly won two NBA championships with Detroit's Bad Boys, leading the Pistons to back-to-back championships in 1989 and 1990. Daly won 638 regular-season games in his NBA career, and 75 more in the playoffs. Daly also guided the Dream Team to a gold medal at the 1992 Olympics in Barcelona. One of Daly's greatest strengths was meshing strong personalities. That was quite evident in his time with the Pistons and with the Dream Team, arguably the best collection of talent ever assembled on one team.

Top 10 Chuck Daly "Dalyisms"

:: by Brendan Suhr

Brendan Suhr partnered with Chuck Daly as assistant coach of the Bad Boys era Detroit Pistons when they won back-to-back NBA championships in 1989 and 1990. Brendan has coached in over 2,500 NBA games.

10. "12 O'clock Rule." When you lose a game, feel sorry for yourself, be mad at your players, etc., but at midnight, you have to move on and get your team ready to play the next day.

9. "Nobody looks bad in a blue suit." Chuck loved to dress, and he loved blue suits. He believed he was better at fashion than he was at coaching.

8. "All decisions are 50/50!" We all want to be right 95 percent of the time, but in reality the BEST you should ever expect to be is right 50 percent of the time. We would take Isiah out of the game and VJ would go in and make five shots in a row, and you would think that putting one of the NBA's greatest players back in would be a no-brainer, but only 50 percent of the time it is. Trust your instincts and knowledge, when you make your decisions.

7. "Get past MAD." Don't hold grudges against your players. Also, your job is to get the team ready for the next game, especially after a loss. The coaches that "master" this concept in the NBA have the most success, because they focus on the next play. We got upset by Miami, then an expansion team, by two points. We were embarrassed and mad. Three nights later, we played the same team again and we won by over 40 points.

6. "Whatever." When Chuck didn't want to give an honest response to a question, he would respond with "Whatever." But, it had so many meanings, you could insert it everywhere and you can't get in trouble. When we were the Bad Boys in Detroit, we were playing the Bulls in the playoffs and a writer from Chicago asked Chuck if he felt Rick Mahorn, Bill Laimbeer, Dennis Rodman, Mark Aguirre, Isiah, etc. were "dirty" players who were trying to hurt Jordan and Pippen? His terse response was, "Whatever." End of interview and he never answered the question.

5. "Make it a one-day story. Never get into a fight with a person who buys ink by the barrel." Don't argue with the media, you can't win. Don't make them one of your enemies. It will turn into several days instead of one.

4. "Coaching is like flying an airplane—there is going to be a lot of turbulence, but your job is to land the plane safely." During the season, there are going to be a lot of ups and downs, but as the coach you have to understand you have to remain calm and poised and remember the goals that you have established for the team. On the road to each championship season, we had major turmoil occur, but Chuck landed the plane safely.

3. "I'm not a pessimist, but rather an optimist with experience." Bob Ryan, the great sports columnist from the *Boston Globe*, dubbed Chuck, "The Prince of Pessimism," because of his negativity. The above Dalyism was Chuck's response at the press conference that day. It was an awesome line. When we were up, 3-0, in the 1989 NBA Finals against the Lakers, Magic and Byron Scott were out for the rest of the series with leg injuries. As we go to eat lunch at Edie's Diner in Marina Del Rey on the day of Game 4, Chuck said to me, "I don't know if we win another game and beat them." We won our first championship that night!

2. "Never trust happiness." One of Chuck's favorites, don't become complacent. He liked to use this after a big win, or if we were going to play a bad team. If we won four or five games in a row, he would start practice and say to the team, "Never trust happiness."

1. "You can't fool dogs, kids, or NBA players." This is all about credibility. Players know if you can coach, they are street-smart and have high basketball IQs. You better have a good play in the last two minutes of a game, or else they will think you can't coach. True story: we were playing Portland in Game 5 of the 1990 NBA Finals with 17 seconds to go, the score is tied and it is our ball. Chuck calls play "1C," which is a quick-hitting, last-second play. Isiah and Laimbeer stare at me with a laser look in their eyes. They know we need to take the last shot! I tap Chuck on the knee hard, he looks at me and I say, "Let's run X into 1-4 Flat and take the last shot."

Bob Delaney has been one of the most respected officials in the NBA since his debut in the 1987–88 season. The former law enforcement officer has enforced the rules in over a thousand NBA regular-season games and over one hundred playoff contests, including seven NBA Finals games.

In his own words: "My years as a basketball official began in high school as an intramurals referee. My avocation was put on hold for three years when I became a New Jersey state trooper and went undercover to infiltrate the Mob. I eventually returned to officiating in the Jersey Shore Summer League, which led me to the CBA, and then the NBA.

"This list is a collection of my most memorable NBA coaches. It was not easy naming just 10 because, like officials, coaches are passionate about basketball, and passionate people make for great memories."

11. Doug Moe. My introduction to Coach Moe came in my first game I worked in the Mile High City in 1987 against the Utah Jazz. I was working with Jess Kersey and it was early in the first period when Coach Moe started calling for three-second violations every time Utah was on offense. As a first-year official, I was feeling my way and not inclined to get into a conversation with the Nugget coach and divert my attention from the task at hand. However, he had reached the obnoxious point, so I said "Coach he just got into the lane." Moe responded quickly with a sly smile, "I know, but it is Mark Eaton and it will take him six seconds to get out."

Doug Moe got me. He had the line all teed up and all I had to do was bite.

9 (tie). Jeff and Stan Van Gundy. Jeff and Stan are brothers who happen to have the title NBA coach next to their names. Each has his own story.

Stan's leading line any time he is going to complain about a call is, "I have not complained all night," and then he would. One night in Orlando I heard that line from Coach Stan and it was in the first minute of the game. I looked at Stan in disbelief and asked, "When could you have complained? During the national anthem?"

Jeff provided similar logic during a New York Knicks game he was coaching. I was in the slot position along the sideline in front of the Knick bench. It was midway through the fourth period in a close game. The ball went out of bounds, causing a stoppage in play. Coach Jeff told me that he watches a lot of NBA basketball games and he sees me work often. "I think you are a very good referee," he said. "I just don't think you are very good when you referee my games."

If you ask the Van Gundys, they will tell you they are objective!

8. Jack Ramsay. Dr. Jack, as Coach Ramsay is affectionately called, is an amazing man who has been part of the NBA landscape for generations. His ability to adjust and his energy are two of his many keys to success. One night Jack Ramsay was coaching Portland and a young assistant coach was second-guessing many of my calls. NBA head coaches get more rope than assistant coaches and a technical foul was given. One problem: I did not know the assistant coach's name. So I said, "Technical foul on the assistant coach in the red tie."

Coach Ramsay gave me a look of disbelief, and then sat down next to his assistant coach, Dave Twardzik, who was wearing a red tie and gave a sly smile.

7. John Lucas. One night I was officiating in Seattle and the game was what officials refer to as a "bronco"—we were just trying to hang on. Eventually, Coach Lucas picked up his second technical foul and was ejected from the game. On the way off the floor John walked over to one of the Seattle players and pulled down his shorts like we were in a Globetrotter game.

John's point guard leadership skills carried over to his style of coaching. His enthusiasm for the game was rivaled only by his enthusiasm for the game of life. John Lucas went down a bumpy road during his life. He struggled with addictions. He not only turned his life around but he made it possible for others to turn their lives around. The John Lucas After Care Program in Houston may very well be John's best coaching job ever.

6. K. C. Jones. When I was to work my first Celtic game, I went to the arena early and walked the floor and took time to gaze at the banners and retired numbers. I had to get the spectator out of me because when I walked on the parquet floor it had to be "go to work time."

Later that season I was back in Boston and had a FIRST for my career. The Celtics were losing in the third quarter. As I ran down the court past the Boston bench, their head coach, K. C. Jones, told me to throw him out of the game and that he would give me cause. Next trip down the floor Coach was yelling and waving his hands at me. I gave him a technical foul and ejected him. I recall seeing K. C. as I left the Garden. He smiled and winked. K. C. Jones is a world champion on and off the floor.

5. Pat Riley. Pat Riley is many things. He is a Bruce Springsteen fan, an East Coast guy, and a basketball junkie with slicked-back hair. I too wear my hair slicked back and I am from New Jersey, so I "tawk" funny. Fellow ref Tony Brothers once said I got a "Pat Riley starters kit."

In my first meeting with Coach Riley, a few too many negative comments on my officiating earned him a technical foul. Magic Johnson walked over to me and said, "He doesn't like you being in the league because you got better hair than he does."

The Hall of Fame coach had a great saying, 'Hard work guarantees you nothing, but without it you will not accomplish one thing." Great words from a great leader.

4. Chuck Daly. He may be the best-dressed NBA coach ever. He had a swagger and charisma that said he was in charge, yet he had an uncanny ability to make sure the players were given the ultimate attention. Chuck Daly motivated his players, directed his players, and then got out of the way and let his players play. His teaching was in practice.

He led the Motor City team to back-to-back championships in 1989 and '90. He led the first Dream Team and is the only NBA coach to win a world championship and an Olympic gold medal. Chuck Daly was a class act, a Hall of Famer, and a tremendous representative of the game at every level. He passed away in 2009, but basketball will never forget Coach Chuck Daly, nor will I.

3. Lenny Wilkens. The Coach had a quiet, gentlemanly demeanor. I learned a long time ago that tough guys never have to act tough. Lenny Wilkens is a tough guy who learned the game on the playgrounds of Brooklyn, New York.

He said what he wanted to say in a professional manner—it was short and straightforward. I always listened because he was not the kind of coach who complained on every play, and when he did offer a comment, he was usually right.

He is a three-time Hall of Fame inductee: as a player, a coach, and as an assistant with the 1992 Olympic Dream Team. He was listed as one of the 50 Greatest Players in NBA History and one of the Top 10 NBA Coaches in 1996. OK, go back and read that line again. He was the only person who was on both lists.

2. Phil Jackson. The first time I officiated a Jackson game it was in the CBA and I ejected him. Phil Jackson became an assistant coach to head coach Doug Collins of the Chicago Bulls. A short time later Phil moved over to the No. 1 seat on the Bulls bench and his drive to 11 NBA championships during a run with Chicago and the Los Angeles Lakers began.

He played at the University of North Dakota for Coach Bill Fitch and won two rings playing for Coach Red Holzman during his NBA playing days in New York. Phil parlayed that mentorship into the Zen Master title, which was evident with his players. Yet his style with officials was more geared toward sarcasm and mind games to disrupt versus to encourage. Phil Jackson employed a 21st-century leadership style well before that time period began, and he did it on and off the NBA courts.

1. Bill Russell. The late NBA Director of Officials Darell Garretson was giving a preseason team clinic for the Sacramento Kings and their coach, Bill Russell. The discussion was spirited, with traveling interpretations, and block-charge and goaltending explanations. Listening to Hall of Fame Boston Celtic Bill Russell and one day Hall of Fame officiating guru Darell Garretson discuss the game was like being a student in a doctorate program.

At the 2011 All-Star Game Bill was sitting courtside with his daughter. He smiled and gave me a thumbs-up signal. I responded by saying, "You never gave me that signal when you were coaching, Bill." His daughter never missed a beat and said, "Oh, he was giving you a similar signal, just not with the thumb." I could hear the great sound of Bill Russell's laugh as I ran up the court.

Post Game. *After every NBA game we watch replays of controversial calls to determine if we got the play wrong or right. This chapter will undoubtedly cause the same kind of second-guessing of my calls. I called them there as I saw them, and in writing this list, called them as I experienced them.*

Bill Van Gundy is the father of Jeff and Stan Van Gundy—the only pair of brothers to ever work as head coaches in the NBA. Bill Van Gundy was the head coach at Brockport State College and Genesee Community College.

10. Defense wins. Sell your team on the importance of effective team defense. Teams that are good in transition, dominate the boards, help teammates, and do not commit needless fouls will always have a chance to win. This will prove a real test because players, as a rule, do not like to defend.

9. Do not expect universal love or agreement. If you have a strong need to be universally loved, do not coach! Even when you make decisions that work out well, many will disagree with you. You will always be criticized. You will never satisfy everyone—players, fans, media. Don't try. Do what you think is right. Develop a thick skin.

8. Preparation pays off. Your most important tasks are to plan and conduct practices. Whatever your situation—time, space, help available, etc.—attempt to have your team prepared for anything an opponent might do. This requires work, organization, and solid teaching methods. Preparation is a great motivator. It enables players to play confidently rather than worrying about unknowns.

7. Be demanding. Have high expectations of everyone—players, assistants, and yourself. Demand performance, not talk. Hold people accountable. Never tolerate excuses or alibis. Push each person to be "the best he can be." Everyone can learn and improve. When winning, never accept anything you would not accept when losing.

6. Teach, teach, teach. Anything you want players to know or do, including the rules, must be taught and reviewed. Never assume they "know" something that has not been taught. John Wooden, whom I believe everyone would say was highly successful, believed this. He said that a coach's success would be directly correlated to his ability to devise drills that teach his team to play the way he wants them to play. Encourage players to ask questions. Foster the desire to improve.

5. Winning is all important. Whether or not it should be, winning is the criterion of a coach's success. To keep coaching, you must win!! Everything you do must be pointed toward improving the team's chance to win. Do nothing to appease players, impress other coaches, or simply "for the fun of it." Everyone in the program must focus on winning. Learn from losing but never like it. Move on quickly.

4. Be completely honest. Selfish or sensitive players will have trouble with constructive criticism. They would much rather be flattered. However, flattery will not earn you respect or trust, nor does it guide improvement. Give praise where it is earned, but never where it is not deserved. Be consistent.

3. Work hard. This is a staple of success. Each of us has weaknesses and limitations. However, there is no limit on how hard one can work. Working harder can overcome a lot of deficiencies. Demand that everyone involved—players, coaches, managers—work hard. Set a "hard to equal" example.

2. Trust your gut. Coaches must make many instantaneous and difficult decisions. Thoughtfully formulate a sound coaching philosophy—offense, defense, discipline, motivation—to guide you. When "push comes to shove" always confidently put your trust in your instincts. Do not waste time second-guessing decisions that fail.

1. Be yourself. Take from other coaches—offensive systems, drills, teaching methods, etc.—but do not attempt to be anyone but yourself. Your personality, knowledge, values, and experiences make you who you are. Be that person at practice and in games, when winning or losing. Players need this so that they will always know what is called for.

Top 10 NBA Teaching Coaches
:: by Don Casey

Don Casey has coached in the college and professional ranks for five decades in every capacity possible. He's coached with four NBA teams—the Celtics, Bulls, Clippers, and Nets. Despite all the knowledge and first-hand experience he's gained over the years about his profession, he says he still found it difficult to fill out this list.

"Ranking the best teaching coaches in the NBA is a daunting task," said Casey. "A good teaching coach can take a team with different makeups—whether the roster is full with talent or limited skill, young and raw or experienced but aging—and turn that team into a winner.

"It's over an 82-game season (at its minimum) that a good teacher can connect individuals by convincing them that it will be beneficial to one's personal growth to play within the team concepts. Not an easy task for any coach, but this is what separates the great ones from their peers."

10. Tex Winter. In any field in life there are innovators and adaptors. Tex Winter is an innovator. His greatest innovation was the Triple Post. This scheme was a unique offensive concept that allowed for offensive continuity with players moving with distinct purpose. This is more consistent with the finesse game of the West Coast and contrary to the East Coast style, which was more a street game known for quickness, pass-and-cut, and dribble weave to allow for opportunity.

When Tex introduced the Triangle Offense concept to Phil Jackson's Chicago Bulls, the basketball world took notice and saw the concept flourish. The Bulls spread the offense, applying pressure on the defense through precise, quick movements. The proverb "Read and react" prevailed: read the defense, and then react. An orchestra on the court.

Applying his knowledge and talents as Phil Jackson's assistant with the Bulls and Lakers produced wins and championships.

9. Chuck Daly. Chuck had the unique ability to get players to do what they should be doing and do it well while trying to do better. He won as a coach at each level—from high school, to college, to the NBA, to the Olympics—by teaching sound basketball concepts and instilling his tried-and-true beliefs of teamwork, defensive responsibility (individual and team), and the use of Pick-and-Pop.

Chucks had the innate, uncanny, ability to spot talent not only on the floor, but on the bench as well. He always had outstanding assistant coaches and role players.

Although Charlie was known as the Prince of Pessism, he was also a sharp, classy dresser. He used to say, "No one looks bad in a blue suit." He was right—if they were tailor-made, like Chuck.

8. Alex Hannum. His aggressive personality was assumed by his players. He was the ultimate pro coach. He survived from the early days of the NBA, fine-tuning his craft through the years. In 1967, his greatness was in full showcase when he convinced Wilt Chamberlain to buy into his program by running the offense through the 76ers center, thus forcing the defense to drop and respect the big fella. This allowed guards like Hal Greer to be get open via the cut, and then catch and shoot. Within this adaptive offense, the 76ers thrived all the way to the 1967 championship. Many rank this team in the top five of all time.

7. Pat Riley. Pat is a self-made NBA coach with a great basketball pedigree. He played for the University of Kentucky (in the Rupp's Runts era) in the infamous 1966 NCAA championship game against Texas Western, and later for the championship Lakers in the Jerry West era.

After serving as assistant coach for Paul Westhead of the Lakers, Pat inherited a talented group as new head coach. Many of the players became members of the Hall of Fame. Not bad having all that to work with, but also not that easy for an inexperienced coach.

Pat willed himself to be "that coach"—the one who rises to the level of the Lakers' talent. He adapted to the talent on hand wherever he coached. In LA it was Showtime, with Magic and the fast break; in New York it was Slowtime, with the Knicks grinding it out without a push guard; in Miami it was Zotime, with Riley pushing Alonzo Mourning to become a dominating player, and then returning to combine the talents of a veteran superstar center and an emerging young backcourt superstar to claim another NBA title. But why not? It was about winning—and all of Riley's teams did!

6. Phil Jackson. Phil Jackson learned the basics of his craft by trolling in the CBA as a coach for the Albany Patroons, and later working as an NBA assistant. He built his philosophy around the Triangle Offense (aka the Triple Post), which he learned from Tex Winter, and then combined it with the mantra of team basketball, which was instilled in him by his Knicks coach and mentor, Red Holzman.

Phil's teaching went beyond X's and O's. He introduced his teams to meditation, making each player whole and together as a unit. Phil believed that coaching less is more. This was exemplified by the fact that Phil rarely called time outs. He believed it was up to the players to conquer difficult moments with each other and for each other, and then overcome the challenge.

Many will say, "If I had talented players like Phil Jackson had, I would be a championship coach, too!" Maybe, but more likely no! Coaching the elite is demanding; coaching a superstar is even more so because they want and demand more. Phil coached superstars masterfully by getting them to adopt his teachings and concepts, allowing his teams to soar to heights not seen since the golden days of the Boston Celtics.

5. Dick Motta. A successful coach in college, Motta was feisty by nature and became one of the first coaches to come to the NBA with a new approach. He preached the tried-and-true approach of movement on offense and team defense. But Dick also introduced the "high-post split" that differed from the normal low-post concept; this allowed for tight "scissor cuts" that kept the box area open, allowing for movement and empowering players to improvise and adjust. This was new and different, and teams struggled to defend it.

4. Gregg "Pop" Popovich. The Spurs coach has survived the up and downs of the NBA coaching life to become the longest-serving coach with the same team in major US professional team sports! Pop is a teaching coach who also has a knack for player management that helps his teams win. In his system each player reaches his level while also becoming a "blender" who knows and honors the team concept.

On offense the Spurs are known for their secondary break, which quickly flows into a set offense. On defense the Spurs are known for their team defense that contains, helps, and recovers, completing the full rotation when needed and also taking pride in their individual defense.

Pop knows talent but more importantly knows how to utilize talent, which helps explain why he's one of only five coaches to win at least four NBA championships.

3. Larry Costello. Larry's teams at Niagara University and in the NBA distinguished themselves through their toughness and competiveness. Larry developed into the ultimate offensive-minded coach in his time. Using his innovative spirit he maxed out Kareem Abdul-Jabbar and Oscar Robertson's superstar skills while utilizing the role-playing skills of others. It was more than an art; it was a Monet.

Within his offense he developed a system for feeding the post player, while having players slice and cut to the wing, and then back cut, making defensive coverage very difficult. In the early 1970s Costello's Bucks appeared in two NBA Finals, winning the championship in 1971.

2. Red Holzman. The Knicks mentor was the ultimate coach of team offense and team defense. He had the gift to get a team to do it on both ends of the court. This unique ability allowed both the teacher and coach in Holzman to convince his team to buy into his system while not forcing them to give up their individuality. His continuity offense concepts involved movement with a purpose and enabled his players to be productive for the team and also showcase their individual skills.

1. Red Auerbach. The Celtic coach's greatest skill was teaching his players how to win and what it took to win. Sure, Red implemented an offense to exploit the skills of his players and coupled that with a defense rarely used in the NBA—one that funneled ball handlers toward the middle to the waiting Bill Russell. Auerbach made the game simple and effective. The focus was on how to win and on setting the bar for future generations. Red's way was the original way to basketball coaching excellence.

Red Auerbach's Top 10 Personnel Moves :: by Dan Shaughnessy

Dan Shaughnessy is a longtime *Boston Globe* columnist who has served as the beat writer for the Boston Celtics. Along with fellow *Globe* writers Will McDonough, Peter Gammons, Leigh Montville, Bob Ryan, Ray Fitzgerald, and Kevin Paul Dupont, he was part of what *Sports Illustrated* called the greatest sports staff ever. Here is Dan's list of the greatest moves by the man many consider the greatest sports general manager ever.

10. Sam Jones (1957). Red drafted Jones out of North Carolina Central University with the eighth pick of the 1957 draft.

9. Don Nelson (1965). The former Iowa Hawkeye was released by the Los Angeles Lakers following the 1965 season and subsequently signed by the Boston Celtics, where he was an integral part of five championship teams.

8. Danny Ainge (1981). Drafted the Toronto Blue Jay second baseman Danny Ainge in the second round of the 1981 draft. He then persuaded Ainge to leave baseball and join the Celtics.

7. Gerald Henderson to Seattle (1984). Red traded guard Gerald Henderson, whom he had originally signed from the CBA, to Seattle in exchange for their 1986 first-round pick, which ended up being the second overall pick.

6. Dave Cowens (1970). Drafted future Hall of Famer Dave Cowens with the fourth pick in the 1970 NBA Draft.

5. Dennis Johnson (1984). Auerbach traded reserve center Rick Robey to the Phoenix Suns for future Hall of Famer Dennis Johnson.

4. John Havlicek (1962). Red drafted John Havlicek with the seventh pick of the first round of the 1962 draft. Havlicek is a pivotal player in eight Celtic championships and is voted into the Hall of Fame in 1984.

3. Larry Bird (1979). The forward out of Indiana State with a year still to play in college is drafted by Red Auerbach with the sixth pick under the junior eligible draft loophole.

2. Kevin McHale and Robert Parish (1980). Red traded the first and 13th overall picks in the draft to Golden State for the third overall pick in the draft, Kevin McHale, and Warrior center Robert Parish. The two join Larry Bird to form the Big Three on their way to three championships and the Hall of Fame.

1. Bill Russell (1956). Red traded All-Stars Ed Macauley and Cliff Hagan to the St. Louis Hawks for Bill Russell, who the Hawks had drafted with the second overall selection of the 1956 draft. Russell joined Celtics 1956 draft selections, and fellow Hall of Famers, K. C. Jones and Tom Heinsohn to form the nucleus of the greatest dynasty in sport's history.

In 1999, John Gabriel was awarded the NBA Executive of the Year Award for his work as general manager of the Orlando Magic. He currently serves as director of scouting for the New York Knicks.

10. Jerry Krause. The architect of the Chicago Bulls dynasty, Krause served from 1985 to 2003. During his reign the Bulls won six championships and Krause earned a pair of NBA Executive of the Year Awards. The drafting of players such as Scottie Pippen (Central Arkansas) and Horace Grant (Clemson) along with acquisitions of Toni Kukoc and Dennis Rodman gave Michael Jordan the supporting cast to formulate a powerhouse. In conjunction with such acquisitions, Krause hired minor-league coach Phil Jackson from the Albany Patroons. The one-time baseball scout will go down as one of the winningest executives in NBA history.

9. Mitch Kupchak. The Jerry West disciple was often overshadowed by his mentor, but the student proved to me more than apt. Taking over as a Laker executive in 2000, Kupchak helped steer the team to six championships in the first decade of the century. His acquisitions of Derek Fisher, Pau Gasol, Ron Artest, and Trevor Ariza, along with the drafting of Andrew Bynum, all led to gold in Laker-land.

8. Eddie Donovan. The former head coach of the New York Knicks, whose team once gave up 100 points to Wilt Chamberlain (I was at that game with my dad at six years old) later became the team's GM and put together the 1970 championship team by drafting players such as Bill Bradley, Walt Frazier, and Phil Jackson, and acquiring Dave DeBusschere. Following the championship he took over the Buffalo Braves and built a very impressive expansion team with players such as Bob McAdoo, Ernie DiGregorio, and Randy Smith, while earning an NBA Executive of the Year Award.

7. Don Nelson. Nelly, known for his unorthodox coaching methods, was also a genius in personnel, even though his subordinates held the title GM. The former Celtic built a major power in Milwaukee and had another one up and running in Golden State before constructing the Dallas Maverick team that Avery Johnson took to the finals. Add his accomplishments as a GM to his five championship rings as a player and his being the second-winningest coach in NBA history, with a record of 540-344 (.661).

6. Pat Riley. Riles never really did personnel before Miami, but has excelled at it. He rebuilt a downtrodden Heat team into a power, but never got a chance to show what it can do, due to Alonzo Mourning's health issues. He scooped up Shaq and won a title, and then tore the roster down and won the lottery by getting LeBron and Bosh to go with Wade, forming a power that could run for years. In addition to his NBA title with the Heat as a general manager, the two-time NBA Coach of the Year led the Lakers to four championships.

5. Jerry Colangelo. The no-nonsense GM has always been a fighter driven to unseat the big boys from the moment the expansion Suns came into the league. Since then, the four-time NBA Executive of the Year has led the Suns to two NBA Finals and the playoffs multiple times during his four decades with the Suns.

4. Donnie Walsh. Considered one of the NBA's all-time good guys, he helped build the Denver Nuggets into a powerhouse with Carl Scheer. During his time in Indiana he built a perennial contender that made 17 postseasons, 6 Eastern Conference Finals, and an NBA Finals in 2000. He then went to New York to turn around the Knicks, a task he accomplished in three short seasons before becoming a consultant.

3. Gregg Popovich and R. C. Buford. Pop and R. C. won four titles from 1999 to 2007, and did it with rare humility. They prolonged the run with late picks from overseas like Tony Parker and Manu Ginobili. Even more impressive: they built an organization so admired, that you could work in their front office and be considered for promotion to GM jobs throughout the NBA, as were Sam Presti, Kevin Pritchard, Danny Ferry, Lance Blanks, and Steve Kerr. Popovich served as GM for eight full seasons before turning the job over to R. C. Buford in 2002.

2. Jerry West. West maintained the Showtime team he inherited in the 1980s and was able to rebuild the team from old dynasty to a new one between Magic's retirement in 1991 and the arrival of Shaq and Kobe in 1996. West was named GM of the Lakers prior to the 1982–83 NBA season. During his reign, the Lakers won six championship rings. In 2002, West became general manager of the Memphis Grizzlies and helped the franchise win their first-ever playoff berth. For his contributions, West twice won NBA Executive of the Year, once with the Lakers, and then once with the Grizzlies.

1. Red Auerbach. With his beloved cigar ablazin' Red coached nine championship teams directly and mentored four players—Bill Russell, Bill Sharman, Tommy Heinsohn, and K. C. Jones—who would go on to win an additional seven NBA championships as coaches.

Prior to the 1967 season, Red retired as a coach and named his successor, Bill Russell. As Boston's president and general manger, he then rebuilt the aging Celtics with shrewd draft picks, among them Dave Cowens, Jo Jo White, Paul Westphal, and Don Chaney. In 1979, Red drafted Larry Bird despite knowing that Bird had a year of college eligibility remaining. Two years later he acquired Robert Parish and Kevin McHale to build the greatest front line in NBA history.

My 10 Greatest Influences in the Game of Basketball :: by Jerry Colangelo

Jerry Colangelo is one of the great executives in NBA history. Four times he was named NBA Executive of the Year (1976, 1981, 1989, 1993). In 2004, he was enshrined in the Basketball Hall of Fame. During his career, he has owned the Phoenix Suns, WNBA Phoenix Mercury, and Arizona Diamondbacks.

10. Eddie Gottlieb. Eddie is truly one of the founders of our great game. He developed much of my philosophy towards the game and the rules of the game with his mentoring of me on a personal basis. He instilled in me an understanding of the "the spirit of the rule" whenever rules changes were being discussed.

9. Arnold "Red" Auerbach. His mere presence demanded respect and his track record as a coach and general manager are unparalleled. He raised the bar for the NBA in many ways. An incredible competitor, Red took no prisoners. I learned a great deal from him.

8. Red Holzman. Red helped break me into the NBA back in 1966 with the Chicago Bulls. As we traveled together scouting college basketball prospects, I learned a great deal about the nuances of the game, the game's history, and the characters who played it. Red coached with dignity and always had the respect of his players.

7. Russ Granik. Russ spent three decades in the NBA and many years as deputy commissioner. He made great contributions to the NBA and also, in another capacity, with the Basketball Hall of Fame. In the heated battle of competition, Russ was a soothing influence on relationships inside and outside the game.

6. Wayne Embry. One of the real pioneers representing the African-American community in basketball, as a Hall of Famer, outstanding general manager, and terrific friend. He offered great insights into people and the game. I admire and respect him a great deal. Wayne has always had a passion for the game.

5. Bobby Knight. Another one of the great all-time coaches and students of the game. He is a fierce competitor who shared much of his journey with me because of our personal relationship. He almost coached the Suns on a couple of occasions and I believe would have been a great one in the NBA.

4. Coach Mike Krzyzewski. We have been joined at the hip since 2005 as he helped me restore dignity to the USA Basketball program. A man committed to the game on all levels and without a doubt one of the best leaders of men I have ever met. He represents class beyond being just the winningest coach in college basketball.

3. Pete Newell. A Hall of Fame coach in his own right, Pete served as a mentor to me on a personal basis regarding philosophy of the game and the history of the game. Pete was one of the most intuitive basketball minds of all time and he had great influence on my philosophy, in every regard.

2. David Stern. David is considered one of the great commissioners in the history of major-league sports. He took a great lawyer's mind and made himself a marketing visionary, taking the NBA to incredible heights. My respect for his accomplishments and our relationship is extraordinary. Certainly he will be recognized in the Hall of Fame someday.

1. Cotton Fitzsimmons. Cotton epitomizes what a coach is all about. I don't believe he ever had a bad day because he was one of the most positive people you would ever meet in your life. He made great contributions as a coach and executive to my teams, and he had more of a positive influence on people than one can imagine. One of the great ambassadors of the game we have ever seen or ever will see.

Pat Williams's Top 10 Draft Picks

During my 44-year career in the NBA, I served as general manager for four franchises: the Chicago Bulls, Atlanta Hawks, Philadelphia 76ers, and Orlando Magic. I currently serve as senior vice president of the Magic.

The key to longevity as a general manager is what happens every year in the spring—the college draft. If you can pick it right seven out of 10 years, you'll have a nice career. Anything less, your job is in trouble. Here's a look at my top 10 best selections as an NBA general manger. (I have a bad case of amnesia on the bad picks.)

10. Clifford Ray (third round/40th overall pick in 1971). Bulls
scout Jerry Krause, who would later become the team's general manager, found a real sleeper out of the University of Oklahoma in 1971. Krause first saw Clifford Ray play against Dave Robisch of Kansas. Krause returned from the game shocked that no one in the NBA was talking about this raw center out of Union, South Carolina. The Bulls drafted him in the third round later that year and Ray went on to have a solid, 10-year NBA career.

9. Dennis Scott (first round/fourth overall pick in 1990). Three
D was the franchise's first-round pick in its second year in existence. Scott had a great three-year career at Georgia Tech. He was a long-range bomber who holds the Magic team record for three-pointers, with 981. He wasn't a great athlete and struggled with weight but he could shoot.

8. Nick Anderson (first round/11th overall pick in 1989). Nick
Anderson was the first pick in Orlando franchise history and wore that badge very proudly. He anchored the guard line for years, scoring points and covering the other team's best guard. He rejoined the organization following his playing days and is still a beloved figure in Orlando.

7. Darryl Dawkins (first round/fifth overall pick in 1975). In 1975,
Philadelphia was desperate for a big man. Prior to the draft, we lured an 18-year-old center from Evans High School in Orlando named Darryl Dawkins into the draft and selected him with the fifth pick. At the time this was a radical selection, but we recognized the great upside of the 6-11 center. In the end we didn't get a franchise center but instead a solid center who could break backboards, and established himself as the league's poet laureate and a true character of the game.

6. Lloyd Free (second round/23rd overall pick in 1974). We
selected Lloyd in the second round out of Guilford College in 1975. The Brooklyn

native had amazing leaping ability and never saw a shot that he didn't like. He shot the ball early and often with a great rainbow arc. After three years in Philadelphia, we traded him to the San Diego Clippers for a first-round pick which we later used to draft Charles Barkley.

5. Andrew Toney (first round/eighth overall pick in 1980). Toney was a true Celtic killer who was called the Boston Strangler. Because his career was cut short by foot problems, people sometimes forget how great he was. Danny Ainge once said, "Jordan and Magic keep me up at night, and Toney is right behind them."

4. Mo Cheeks (second round/36th overall pick in 1978). Super scout Jack McMahon spotted Maurice down at West Texas State where he played in a slowdown offense. Jack thought he might be special if we could free him up in an up-tempo system. We drafted him in the second round. He started opening day as a rookie and every game after. For a 10-year period, he was the best pure point guard in the league.

3. Anfernee "Penny" Hardaway (first round/third overall pick in 1993). In 1993, the ping-pong balls fell Orlando's way for the second consecutive year (the league would place restrictions on the lottery after this). With the first pick in the draft, we selected Chris Webber and then traded him to Golden State for the third pick in the draft, Penny Hardaway, and three future first-round picks. Orlando fans were furious that we didn't keep Webber, though over the next three years, Hardaway formed the best young tandem in the league with Shaq O'Neal. Sadly, Penny's knees didn't hold up and his budding Hall of Fame career fell short.

2. Charles Barkley (first round/fifth overall pick in 1984). We used the first-round pick that we received in the Lloyd Free trade to select Charles Barkley, behind Hakeem Olajuwon, Sam Bowie, Michael Jordan, and Sam Perkins. Prior to his arrival, there was no one like Barkley, and there hasn't been anyone like him since. Scout Jack McMahon, who was high on the Auburn forward, described him as 'Wes Unseld who could handle the ball.'

1. Shaquille O'Neal (first round/first overall pick in 1992]. In the early years of the franchise, the Magic experienced significant growing pains. However, it was all worth it for the opportunity to draft Shaq with the first pick in 1992. After three years at LSU, Shaq came to Orlando and made an immediate impact on the team, eventually leading the franchise to the Finals. Sadly, after four years, he left Orlando for Los Angeles, breaking the city's heart. It took the Magic, and its fans, 10 years to recover.

Agents I'll Never Forget Negotiating With :: by Stan Kasten

Stan Kasten was the general manager of both the Atlanta Braves and the Atlanta Hawks. He was twice named NBA Executive of the Year (1986 and 1987). He also led the Braves to 12 consecutive playoff appearances, as well as five pennants and one World Series championship.

11. Steve Kauffman. He's a good guy and still active today. He's always been very involved with his players and treats them like family.

10. Lance Luchnick. He was a real character who had a great run with some top-level players. When Lenny Wilkens was running the Sonics, he told me Lance's real name was Louie. One day I called him that, which didn't go over too well.

9. Norman Blass. He was one of the first agents. He always saw things his way and felt disrespected if you disagreed with him.

8. Ron Grinker. When he was at the University of Cincinnati he wore the Bearcat costume as the school's mascot. He once told me he was the most honest man in the NBA. I thought, "You're not in the NBA. You're a darn agent."

7. Fred Slaughter. His voice-mail message was a riot. It was his son's voice— a real little boy sound. Fred would never answer the phone, so you'd have to keep chasing him.

6. Bob Wolff. He was a real character. He had a smooth style and his office was like a museum with photos and plaques all over the walls.

4 (tie). Donald Dell and David Falk. Those two guys were titans of the industry. You always felt relieved when you got a deal done with them.

3. Herb Rudoy. He was big with the European market. He'd tell you all about the foreign players, but most of us had never seen them play.

2. Arn Tellem. He's been around a long time in basketball and baseball. He's a big-time agent and people treated him that way.

1. Larry Fleisher. He had a regal way about him. He was the union head and you always felt you were in the presence of nobility.

My Top 10 Most Interesting Negotiations
:: by David Falk

David Falk is the most influential player representative in NBA history. During his career he has represented over one hundred NBA players, including Michael Jordan, Charles Barkley, Patrick Ewing, Moses Malone, and Dominique Wilkins. The below list represents some of his more memorable negotiations with team representatives on behalf of his clients.

10. Angelo Drossos/Johnny Dawkins (1986). Long before the big market/small market conundrums that ushered in the 2011 lockout, Spurs owner Drossos became one of the toughest negotiators ever in small market San Antonio and produced entertaining, winning teams. When he "swore on my dead mother's grave" he wouldn't accept our offer, I told him a simple "no" would suffice.

9. Ed Stefanski/Elton Brand (2003). Gentlemanly, somewhat unassuming—and underappreciated GM of the Sixers moved heaven and earth in a matter of hours to create enough room to sign Elton to the "Philly Max."

8. David Checketts/Patrick Ewing (1997). Extremely bright and politically savvy president of the Knicks knew that no team had enough cap room to sign Ewing for more than $10 million but that the Knicks could only replace their franchise center with a minimum player. The deal was closed for $68 million for four years.

7. Geoff Petrie/Mike Bibby (2003). It's not a coincidence Petrie graduated from Princeton. Faced with a free agent who went from 14 points/7 assists per game to red hot in the playoffs, he responded by devising a contract that blended the "outside max" for six years with one year at qualifying offer level to close the deal.

6. Bob Bowman (currently head of MLB Advanced Media)/Patrick Ewing (1985). Had the vision and creativity which he put on display for MLB several decades later, to understand the unique value Ewing had as the first ever No. 1 pick in the draft lottery system. Ewing received the largest contract in NBA history before he took his first dribble at Madison Square Garden.

5. Pat Riley/Juwan Howard/Alonzo Mourning (1996). The very charismatic president of Miami Heat presaged his 2010 coup of LeBron James and Chris Bosh by signing BOTH Howard and Mourning to seven-year contracts for $105 million—the first $100 million deals in team sports history. The commissioner disallowed Howard's contract, returning him to Washington.

4. Red Auerbach/Kermit Washington (1978). Arguably the greatest general manager/president in NBA history (11 championships in 13 years), Red challenged the prevailing concept of no-cut contracts that literally prevented teams from taking a star off the roster by inventing the modern day "guaranteed contract" (money but no roster spot).

3. Jerry Buss/James Worthy (1982). A PhD in chemistry, Buss performed present-value calculations in his head that took me several minutes to do on my HP. That skill enabled him to fund Magic Johnson's 25-year, $25 million contract for $3.2 million shortly after signing Worthy.

2. Dick Watson/Danny Ferry (1989). Perhaps the most cerebral individual I have ever dealt with, Watson envisioned virtually every possible outcome of Danny's career and provided multiple contingencies through "decision trees." Ferry received the highest (and most complex) contract of any player (rookie or vet) in NBA history.

1. Jerry Reinsdorf/Michael Jordan (1996). One of the brightest, toughest, and most savvy negotiators in all of professional sports, Jerry responded to Jordan's insistence that Jerry make the opening offer as a barometer of fairness with the famous question: "Does the first digit start with a 2?" Fifteen years later, no NBA player has ever made $30 million in one year.

Top 10 Clients Who Impacted My Life and Career :: by Keith Glass

Keith Glass is a longtime basketball agent and the author of a wildly popular basketball book, *Taking Shots*.

10. Paul Shirley. I met Paul at the Portsmouth Invitational Tournament in Virginia, after his senior year at Iowa State University. He told me years later that he signed with me because I told him the truth—a novel approach in my business. Well, all these years later the truth is that through all of the various NBA teams and heartaches we endured together, the truth has always been at the core of our relationship. This applied whether we were signing 10-day contracts with the Bulls, Hawks, Suns, etc. or planning his escape from Russia. As a player—and now also an accomplished author and friend—Paul earned a special place with me.

9. Thomas Hamilton. When I met Tommy, he was (and probably still is) 7-4 and weighed close to four hundred pounds. Another distinguishing trait was that he was as skilled a big man as I had seen up close and personal. Tommy, who by the way lived with me briefly and was a person that I really liked, regrettably taught me that it wasn't MY goals that mattered, it was HIS. The impact of Tommy never realizing his potential was that I realized that drive and discipline had to come from within.

8. Chuck Nevitt. The impact of representing Chuck, other than the pleasure of his company, was that through him I was exposed to almost the entire league. He was released and signed so many times that it gave me the opportunity early in my career to network throughout the NBA and make contacts and friendships. Chuck was also one of the funniest guys to be around. When your relationship begins with a guy shooting craps in Vegas on his knees, it does have an impact.

7. Melvin Booker. I know I could be more impressive if I throw in names of players who had better-known careers in the NBA—like Robert Horry or Olden Polynice, for example. But, I was asked who impacted me the most. Even through Mel only played briefly in the NBA, he was one of my favorite people to be with. I loved to watch Melvin play and conduct himself. He played with an intelligence and passion that together were a rare combination. The impact of Mel was that I was always proud of him in every situation where we had signed. It's also nice to represent a friend.

6. Lloyd Daniels. Even though this was another client who obviously never reached his potential, Lloyd had a very large impact on me and members of my family. The impact from him wasn't always a positive one or a particularly productive one, but it was always interesting. I actually can't think of Lloyd without smiling. He was, and still is, fun to be around. Believe me when I tell you that you cannot take a trip to Pesaro, Italy, with Lloyd and not be impacted in a big way. When you talk about a high basketball IQ, Lloyd's must have been off the charts. And, man, could he play!!!

5. Matt Maloney. Matt played in the Ivy League at Penn, not exactly a hotbed for NBA talent. His father, Jim, was a tremendously respected assistant coach at Temple University with John Chaney for some 22 years. Jim asked me to meet him and Matt at a truck stop on the Jersey Turnpike (Exit 8) when they were deciding on who would be Matt's agent. Jim asked me what I thought of Matt as a player, and I said that I didn't think he would get drafted and probably wouldn't make the league right away either. Jim then asked if I had a contract with me and told Matt to sign it. Apparently they had been BS'd enough. Two years later we signed with the Houston Rockets for $18 million after going undrafted and playing in the minor leagues. Jim didn't get to see that contract or see Matt play in the NBA. He tragically passed shortly before those events took place. That had more of an impact on me than probably anything else in my career.

4. Efthimios Rentzias. My 6-11, 19-year-old from Tricala, Greece, affected me in many ways. Even the way I ended up representing him was a story. His career took me through the 1996 NBA Draft (see *Taking Shots* for that chapter), to Denver, to Athens, to Switzerland, to Barcelona, to Siena, Italy, to Istanbul, and back to the Philadelphia 76ers. I can never forget his and his family's trust and loyalty. As a future bonus it was through Efthimios that I ultimately met another one of my favorite-ever clients, Nikos Zissis of Greece. (This is what happens when you're limited to 10—you try and sneak extra guys in!)

3. Mahmoud Abdul-Rauf. Mahmoud's refusal to stand for the national anthem took me through very complex emotions and reactions to those emotions. They ranged from issues regarding religion, patriotism, and freedom of expression, and then ended up as most issues do—to coming down to one thing: money!! As a proud American citizen, I initially was not supportive of this type of behavior. However as Mahmoud's agent, I knew I needed to support him. Finally, as a lawyer, I knew he had the constitutional right not to stand. The twists and turns of this saga taught me many things, and led me down paths I could never have predicted.

2. Scott Skiles. Using the allotted word count to describe the impact of Scott on my career as an agent is cruel and unusual punishment. Having been involved with Scott since he graduated from Michigan State, some 25 years ago, we have obviously been through many times and negotiations together. One thing that will always stand out for me is that I never enjoyed, before or since, actually watching a client play in the NBA like I did with Scott. Particularly his season during his contract year with the Orlando Magic—that was pure fun for both of us. That year was also basically an ongoing negotiation and battle of wits between us and Pat Williams, which to me was priceless. Scott somehow played with such a passion, intelligence, and joy. that it was impossible for me to look away. I miss those games more than I can say.

1. Mark Eaton. Parents will say, "There is something about your first." (Note to second, third, fourth, and fifth children: it's an expression!!) Well, Mark was my "first" client. He was also much more than that. I learned through Mark that sheer determination and persistence is the most powerful tool of all! I had to work at least as hard as Mark did just to be fair. True, Mark was 7-4, but it was his refusal to quit at anything that made him truly special. I have always been grateful to have represented not necessarily the stars of the NBA, but easily the greatest collection of people you could possibly have asked for. For the most part, their loyalty and gratitude for at least what I was trying to do was a constant. I think Mark, being the beginning of things, foreshadowed that for me. It also made me a bit impatient with players who couldn't measure up to his standards as a person as the years went on. That's an impact that has lasted for 29 years!

Top NBA Publicists :: by Jeff Twiss

Jeff Twiss is the vice president of media services for the Boston Celtics, a club he has worked with for over three decades. The University of Vermont alum is known as one of the nicest and most sincere people in the NBA. Here, he pays tribute to his public relations and media relations peers who have helped gain tributes for so many players, coaches, and other people involved with the league, without worrying about gaining any good ink for themselves. Or in his words: "After much thought and deliberation, I came up with this list of the top individuals (or groups of individuals) who have served as NBA publicists—people I will never forget."

17. Every NBA PR person. This final number is held not for any one person or group of PR people but for EVERY PR person who currently works for or who has worked for the National Basketball Association or a particular NBA team. It is not a "me" but a "we" group of skilled and professional people who I have had the distinct privilege of working with—while learning something from each and every one of them.

16. Dennis D'Agostino. Dennis joined the Knicks in the late 1980s and has continues to be a part of the Knicks family as the team's historian and writer. But Dennis does not stop there; he has served as the NBA PR Directors Association treasurer since the organization's inception, or so it seems. When he is not researching, writing, or keeping a close eye on the financial ledger, DD can be found working diligently in the media production center at the NBA All-Star Game or NBA Finals.

15. John White. John was the Portland Trail Blazers' original publicity director. I remember at my first NBA league meetings I was the youngster and I was sitting between John and Harvey Pollack. John would be telling funny stories about incidents that happened over the last season and Harvey would be working on his statistics book. I think I missed a good chunk of what the featured speakers were presenting to us that meeting.

14. Frank Blauschild. Frank was a writer who later worked for the New York Knicks. Frank had some colorful stories as well and had a quick wit, so you had to be on your toes around him.

10. (tie) Tom Ambrose/Jim Foley/Mark Pray/Bill Kreifeldt. Just like the four individuals I mention in the next four list entries, these four are former NBA public relations directors who really helped pave the way for modern PR people. Tom was with the Phoenix Suns, Jim with the Houston Rockets (and later served as Houston's radio color analyst), Mark with the Washington Bullets (later with the Miami Heat), and Bill with the Detroit Pistons and Utah Jazz. All four gentlemen were instrumental in establishing policies and procedures for all NBA public relations directors to work by, and were key in building the NBA PR Directors Association.

9 Cheri Hanson. The daughter of longtime Portland Trail Blazers Publicity Director John White (see below), Cheri has worked for four NBA teams (she's settled back in her native Portland now), as well as for the league office in New York City. She is one of the most respected women in professional sports.

8. Josh Rosenfeld. Josh, the Los Angeles Lakers PR man in the 1980s, and I would see each other twice in the regular season (usually on national television), and again in May and June for the NBA Finals. We would playfully boast that we each had two pretty good players in Larry Bird and Magic Johnson.

7. Kevin Sullivan. Sully was the tireless and creative PR Director of the Dallas Mavericks, and then took his many talents to NBC Universal. But he did not stop there, going on to work for the Department of Education and as White House communications director for President George W. Bush. He is still busy as ever today with his own communications consulting firm.

6. Alex Martins. Like Kevin Sullivan, Alex is a tireless worker and joined the Orlando Magic in the 1980s. He is now the team's Chief Operating Officer.

5. Tim Hallam. Tim has been a mainstay of the Chicago Bulls organization for over 35 years. His calm demeanor and carefree spirit can cut through the most tense and stressful moments with ease. I am amazed that Tim is still standing after "surviving" not one, not two, not three, but six world championship titles (in three-peat fashion, no less, 1991–93 and 1996–98) while working with two Hall of Fame players—Michael Jordan and Scottie Pippen—during that span.

4. Matt Dobek. This is a very emotional entry, as we lost Matt in 2009 after his brilliant 29-year career with the Detroit Pistons organization. Matt and I started in the NBA in the same year, and we were both very fortunate to have been a part of three world championship teams. Simply put, Matt was universally respected and loved by everyone, and is sorely missed every day.

3. NBA Public Relations Department/Communications Group.

The "Big 3" of this group of publicists/public relations/media relations/communications professionals I have worked closely with over my 30 years with the Boston Celtics consists of Brian McIntyre, Terry Lyons, and Tim Frank. Brian came to the NBA from the Chicago Bulls in 1981 and Terry started with the NBA as an intern that same year. Tim began his career with the Houston Rockets in 1994 and came to the NBA in 2001. These gentlemen have been our leaders and voice for all NBA PR Directors for over 30 years.

2. Harvey Pollack.

Harvey, like Howie McHugh, has been with the NBA since the beginning—and I mean that with all due affection and respect. Hall of Famer Harvey is Mr. Stats. Long before computers, spreadsheets, and more data than NASA could use, Harvey had beaten everyone to the punch with his accurate statistics. His yearly, 350-page *Harvey Pollack's NBA Statistical Yearbook* has everything and more for those seeking unusual or forgotten stats or trivia. The veteran Philadelphia 76ers leader also has collected his share of T-shirts and is an astute movie and theater critic.

1. Howie McHugh.

J. Howard "Howie" McHugh was an original Celtic, serving as the team's director of publicity for 38 years, beginning in the club's inaugural 1946–47 season and continuing until his death in 1983. The late Red Auerbach referred to Howie as one of the craziest men he has ever known. Why? Because as a student athlete at Dartmouth College, Howie was the center on the football team, the goalie on the hockey team, and the catcher for their baseball team. He was also a perfect person to learn this business from, a man who was patient, carefree, and gave you just enough direction without overwhelming you. I am proud to call him my mentor.

The All-Time Most Important Promoters of the NBA :: by Andy Dolich

Andy Dolich has been a sports executive in the NBA, Major League Baseball, NHL, NFL, and professional soccer. He is currently the principal of a sports consultant business, Dolich & Associates. Here, he cites a pair of 13s of famous fans, front-office people, players, and others who have been very lucky for the NBA and its efforts to promote itself to the world.

SECOND TEAM

13. Spike Lee. His TV advertising alter ego, Mars Blackmon, and his "Gotta be the shoes" campaign for Nike.

12. Ned Irish. The New York Knicks and Madison Square Garden executive who was the father of NBA Doubleheaders in the 1960s.

11. Jerry Colangelo. One of the NBA's savviest owner/executives during his time with the Phoenix Suns and Mercury. His leadership of USA basketball has grown the game on a global basis.

10. Val Ackerman. First president of the WNBA, serving from 1996–2005. He helped elevate the professional women's game on a national level.

9. Jerry Buss. LA Lakers owner who wrote the check to create Showtime and other exciting chapters of the glitziest team in the NBA.

8. Jerry Reinsdorf. Smart enough to draft a skinny kid from North Carolina and create the Bulls Dynasty.

7. Pat Williams. Been in the league since 1968 and served in many executive positions, including GM of the Bulls, Hawks, 76ers, and Magic. He combined showmanship and basketball business prowess into a winning formula.

6. Rick Welts. NBA league executive credited with turning the All-Star Game into a national showcase of hoops and entertainment.

5. Wilt Chamberlain. "Wilt the Stilt," the greatest all-around athlete in NBA history. The most statistically dominant player and the only one to average 40 and 50 points per season and score 100 points in a game. His epic battles with Bill Russell are the stuff of legend. His larger-than-life personality off the court made him a national celebrity from Hollywood to Harlem.

4. Abe Sapertsein. Owner of the Harlem Globetrotters whose willingness to play doubleheaders with NBA teams in the early days helped popularize the game.

3. Jack Nicholson. The Coolest NBA fan of all (with apologies to Spike Lee).

2. Bill Russell. Eleven championship rings, enough said. He was the ultimate winner in NBA history.

1. Harvey Pollack. "Super Stat" is the only employee hired when the league was formed in 1947 who is still working for the NBA. Harvey is the top stat man in sports.

FIRST TEAM

11 (tie). Bill Davidson, Tom Wilson, and Joe Dumars. One of the NBA's classiest owners and two of its most professional executives created the Detroit Pistons' "Going to Work" years as part of a business plan that energized a city hit hard by economic troubles.

10. The ABA (American Basketball Association). Before its merger with the NBA in 1976, the ABA—with its red, white, and blue ball, three-point arc, ferocious Slam Dunkers, wild uniforms, and some of the most colorful players in all of sports (Terry Pluto's *Loose Balls* is a must-read)—was viewed as the NBA's crazy uncle. The freewheeling ABA style of play was quickly adopted by the NBA after the merger.

9. Mark Cuban. Owner of the 2011 NBA champion Dallas Mavericks, the Broadcast.com founder became a billionaire when he sold to Yahoo. His media-hyped controversies with Commissioner David Stern fit perfectly in today's contentious sports landscape. Cuban is one of the most fan-friendly owners in sports. His proactive use of social media to instantly communicate with his constituencies has become a powerful promotional vehicle.

8. Danny Biasone. The founding owner of the Syracuse Nationals, the club that eventually became the Philadelphia 76ers. Biasone was the driving force behind the NBA's 24-second shot clock. When the league adopted his concept in 1954, professional basketball fans were given a faster, more exciting game that has stood the test of time.

7. Eddie Gottlieb. "The Mogul" was a master promoter. A member of the Basketball Hall of Fame, Gotty helped form the NBA, coached and owned the Philadelphia Warriors franchise, and signed Wilt Chamberlain to his first NBA contract. He was the wizard of doing the complicated NBA schedule for over 25 years. "The Mogul" was basketball's equivalent of baseball's master promoter, Bill Veeck.

6. David Stern. He became the NBA's fourth commissioner in 1984. He guided the league with the touch of a diplomat and the steely focus of a prosecutor. A master of the media, Stern's promotional prowess made the league a global marketing machine. There are few commissioners in sports who have been more identified with the growth of their sport than David Stern.

5. Julius Erving. Dr. J was the maestro of mid-air. His gravity-defying style of play helped legitimize the ABA, which ultimately merged with the NBA. He was the author of the Slam Dunk and a style of play that made him a fan favorite and media favorite. Off the court, Dr. J was a major product endorser and one of the first players to have a shoe named after him. A member of the 50 Greatest Players in NBA History club, fans will always remember his up-and-under balletic baseline move in the 1980 NBA Finals.

4. 1992 Dream Team. The US men's Olympic basketball team was the first American Olympic team to feature active NBA players. This superstar group blitzed the opposition by an average of 44 points a game on their way to gold and global rock-star status. This roster is every coaches dream: Christian Laettner, David Robinson, Patrick Ewing, Larry Bird, Scottie Pippen, Michael Jordan, Clyde Drexler, Karl Malone, John Stockton, Chris Mullin, Charles Barkley, and Magic Johnson.

2. Phil Knight. Owner of the top athletic shoe company in the world, Knight helped glamorize athletic footwear by using Michael Jordan as the face of the company. This move forever charged the world of celebrity sports endorsers. There is no doubt that the money spent by the major shoe companies during "Sneaker Wars" helped draw the world's attention to NBA basketball.

2 (tie). Magic and Bird. The Ivory of Parquet and the Ebony of LALA Land. Magic was the "Swami of Showtime" and Bird was the "Hick from French Lick" with his killer game. From their NCAA title game in 1979 to their last head-to-head on-court duel in 1987, Bird and Magic exemplified the bicoastal rivalry that catapulted the NBA to a higher level of fan interest and media support on a national basis.

1. Michael Jordan. Air Jordan was the ultimate competitor in NBA history. He was the most recognized athlete on the planet, after Muhammad Ali, based on his play and promotional enthusiasm. He elevated the NBA to new heights. Michael combined the best of Elgin Baylor, Connie Hawkins, and Dr. J, and translated it from the schoolyard to the boardroom.

Top NBA Athletic Trainers :: by Tom Smith

Tom Smith has been the head athletic trainer for the Orlando Magic since 2006. Over the past two decades, Smith has also worked for the Atlanta Hawks and Minnesota Timberwolves, as well as a number of minor-league teams and the St. Paul Academy in Minnesota.

Despite all his experience, Smith said, "This list was almost impossible to compile. The only spot that has a rightful owner is No. 1—Joe O'Toole, who worked 28 years for the Atlanta Hawks and never missed a game. Joe is also the only athletic trainer to win the NBA's J. Walter Kennedy Citizenship Award. Mr. O'Toole is respected by every athletic trainer who has had the pleasure of occupying the first seat on an NBA bench. as well as by the coaches who coach this wonderful game and the players who played for his team. Dr. Bob Biel of the Chicago Bulls should be on this list because he lived every athletic trainer's dream in 1974, when he filled in for his suspended head coach and got to coach an NBA game (and his team won).

"There are many NBA athletic trainers who can, and should, be included on the this list. A top 100 list is not enough space for the deserving athletic trainers who should be recognized. The 11 chosen are very special individuals who have left an indelible mark on their players, teams, and the unique medical specialty of being an athletic trainer in the NBA."

Honorable Mention. Jim Gillen (Denver Nuggets); Bill Jones (Sacramento Kings); Fritz Massman (New Jersey Nets); Mark Pfeil (Chicago Bulls, Milwaukee Bucks); Mike Saunders (New York Knicks); Jeff Schedecker (Milwaukee Bucks); Fred Tedeschi (Chicago Bulls); Bob "Chopper" Travaglini (Denver Nuggets); Dick Vandervoort (Houston Rockets).

11. Keith Jones (Los Angeles Clippers, Houston Rockets). Took athletic training to the vice-presidential level of his NBA franchise.

10. Don Sparks (New Orleans/Utah Jazz). Hired the front office staff for his ABA team.

8 (tie). Mike Abdenour (Fort Wayne, Philadelphia, Detroit) and Tom Abdenour (Golden State Warriors). Only brother athletic trainer duo in the history of the NBA.

7. Joe Proski (Phoenix Suns). Thirty-three years with one team and his photo hangs in the Suns arena.

6. David Craig (Indiana Pacers). Thirty-five years in pro basketball.

5. Ed Lacerte (Boston Celtics). Longtime service to the National Basketball Athletic Trainers Association, as well as excellence in athletic training.

4. Frank Furtado (Seattle SuperSonics). The most super of the SuperSonics.

3. Gary Vitti (Los Angeles Lakers). Eight NBA championships . . . need I say more?

2. Ron Culp (Cleveland Cavaliers, Portland Trail Blazers, Miami Heat). Class of the current crop of NBA athletic trainers. Has his own banner in the Heat's arena.

1. Joe O'Toole (Atlanta Hawks). Best single sentence advice ever delivered to a group of athletic training students: "When one of your players gets hurt make sure they know that you are there to help them and tell them that you love them."

Top 10 Essentials for a Basketball Official :: by Don Rutledge

Don Rutledge is the supervisor of officials for the WNBA. He has been an official for three decades and has officiated in two NCAA championship games. In 1991, he was named the Naismith Men's Basketball Official of the Year.

10. Being in Good Physical, Mental, and Emotional Shape. An official must be in the best possible physical condition he can, as "fatigue makes cowards of all of us." Late in the game energy is needed to get to the "open angles" and correctly call plays. An official makes a decision to blow or not blow the whistle every four seconds, and a tired mind makes for slow and bad decisions. An official always must be in an athletic posture that will allow him to move with a purpose, whether walking or running.

9. A Great Knowledge of the Rules of the Game. An official can enhance his understanding of the rules if he understands the spirit and intent behind the rules. All contact is not a foul, all hard contact is not a foul, and some light contact is a foul. Knowing the difference is essential. Use the proper signals and make them crisp, strong and positive.

8. Mastery of the Mechanics of Officiating. Officiating mechanics put officials in the proper position to make quality calls. Dictate your own angle. An official must use his horizontal and vertical field of vision to see all in his primary. Understand each position that you work in during a game: lead, trail, and center. Most plays call themselves. Anticipate the play not the call. Do not guess. Make all calls from an "OPEN ANGLE" as apposed to a "CLOSED ANGLE."

7. Understanding of the Game of Basketball. Develop a "FEEL" for the game beyond the rules, beyond mechanics, beyond officiating technique. It is easy to teach an official where to stand, but it is almost impossible to teach the "FEEL."

Develop pictures of a basketball game. Block/charge, pressing defense, man-to-man defense, fast break, post play, how the rhythm, speed, quickness, and balance of a player can be affected on the floor or in the air. Be the director of the pictures in your mind.

Good officials take the game they are given and make the game better. If it is a good, clean game, leave it alone and let it play. If it is a physical or out of control game, then blow the whistle and clean it up. A good official makes the coaches and players understand what the parameters are and what you will and will not allow in the game.

Understand the coaches; understand the player matchups. Know the time on the shot clock; know the time on the game clock. Is the point guard right-handed or left-handed? Is this player a jump shooter or driver? Don't count the fouls; just call the fouls. Know when and what type of pressure defenses a particular team likes. Is it zone or man-to-man? What type of offense does each team play: pick-and-roll, motion, or triangle offense? Use the pregame warm-up to learn the tendencies of each player and coach.

Video review of your games will give you a great learning experience. It will tell an official what you did and WHY. Know that you cannot out-officiate the video.

Knowledge is power.

6. Officiating Teamwork with Each Crew. Know your partner's strengths and weaknesses. Be able to adjust to any type of partner—passive or aggressive. Lend your credibility to your fellow officials in all situations, especially confrontational situations. Trust your partner to call his primary. Always officiate the fringe of your primary to help a partner when he cannot see from an open angle. If the officiating crew does not get the play right, the game and the crew suffers. Only reach for a call in a secondary area to save the game.

5. Being Observant: See Without Looking, Hear Without Listening, Sense Without Feeling. Use all your senses. Be observant of all around you. Don't be a ball watcher, but use peripheral vision to know where the ball is as well as the competitive matchups in your primary. Have the vision to call a play or not call a play regardless of the consequences. Be able to focus for the entire game, when the ball is alive and when it is dead. Many of our problems are created and started during a dead ball situation.

4. Ability to Handle Adversity and Conflict. Controversy and how you handle it is the crux of officiating. "If you can't take the heat, get out of the kitchen." Confrontation brings stress and negativity. Handle it with anticipation, quick action, and a positive attitude. Do not be afraid to fail. Stay calm, talk softly, and know that you have the "IN CHARGE CARD," but use it judiciously.

3. Willingness to Expose Your Honesty and Character to All. Be a person who tells the truth. You will officiate like you live your life off the court. Have the intestinal fortitude to do the right thing no matter the consequences. Catch the kind of grief you want to catch! Good character, honesty, knowledge and good communication skills will make you, BELIEVABLE!

2. Poise. Have "THE LOOK." Stay calm when all about you is chaos. Stay quiet, keep your emotions under control, don't yell, keep your body language and facial expressions calm and out-think all of the players and coaches when they yell, scream, and stomp their feet and lose their control. As a last resort use a warning, humor, or a technical foul to solve the immediate problem. Do what you get paid to do: Control the Game!

1. Communication Skills (Your Biggest Asset). This is the key element in any human endeavor. Whatever you do, communicate with enthusiasm. Be a good listener. Recognize that the difference in people is more than just their words; it is: what they mean to say; how their thoughts are verbalized; how others interpret what they say. Each official is in charge of his attitude. Exhibit good body language:

As an official you can only answer a coach's question three ways:

I "might" have missed that call (do not say this too often)

I don't know and I don't think you know, so let's look at the video, and then we will both know

I "think" I got that call right

There are no other answers.

Referees I Would Like to See in a Game 7 of the NBA Finals :: by Matt Guokas

Matt Guokas is the son of one NBA player from the 1940s and the nephew of another from the 1950s. He himself has been involved with the NBA as a player, coach, and broadcaster since 1966. Across the last seven decades, Matt Guokas and his family have seen a lot of NBA officials. These are the ones Matt would be happiest to see working the most important game of an NBA season.

11. Richie Powers. Colorful and cocky, Richie worked the famous 1976 triple-overtime thriller between the Boston Celtics and Phoenix Suns that featured lots of confusion and controversies, but Richie was in control all the way. Earlier in his career, his refereeing partner couldn't get in for one game in Syracuse, so Richie asked the players to not overreact, since he was alone. Everyone obliged. A few nights later, he acted as if that cooperation had never happened and was meaner than a junkyard dog.

10. Jack Madden. He had an easygoing demeanor and was tall for a ref (about 6-4). Jack was working an early regular-season game in 1984 between the 76ers and Boston Celtics when he tore up his knee about 10 minutes into the first quarter. Dick Bavetta, his partner, had to go it alone. A few minutes later a nasty fight broke out between Julius Erving and Larry Bird. It brought Red Auerbach onto the floor; Sixers Head Coach Billy Cunningham had his sport coat torn apart; the league was on the phone with Dick, helping him sort things out. But I digress. Jack Madden went on to recover and do a lot of NBA Finals.

9. Ed Rush. Eddie was friendly and always seemed to have a smile on his face—off the court. On it he was all business. In a playoff series between Billy Cunningham's 76ers and Kevin Loughery's New Jersey Nets a lot of complaining and technical fouls went on in the earlier games. Ed brought the two coaches together a couple of minutes before the game and told them in no uncertain terms, "You two coaches, tell the players to play and we'll referee. No talking to us." Case closed.

8. Dan Crawford. Like most young referees, Danny had a tough time earning the respect of players and coaches. He was competent to be sure. Once he showed his personality, things started to get better. He always has a smile on his face and a friendly word for coaches and players before the game. During it he gives everybody a little leeway to air their complaints. But time and experience have made Danny one of the top referees.

7. Darell Garretson. Called every name in the book by players, coaches, and fans, but he was the Supervisor. Anyone that had a complaint for the league office, had to go through him. Darell could be understanding, arrogant, and condescending—all within about two minutes. When he was on the court, no question he was in charge.

6. Steve Javie. When Steve broke in he used the power of the technical foul to keep order and show who was the boss. He infuriated many along the way, but you knew you were going to see him in a big playoff or Finals game. His last 15 years or so, he didn't hear much complaining. Steve became one of the top referees of the 1980s and '90s.

5. Hugh Evans. You always felt good to see Hugh on any game, home or away. He greeted everyone with a warm smile and a friendly hello before a game. He had the knack of not holding any grudges. Hubert would give a little rope to let off a little steam. But when he said, "That's enough" you knew he meant it.

4. Joey Crawford. His father Shag and brother Jerry were outstanding and colorful Major League Baseball umpires, so officiating is in his DNA. In his early years on the job young Joey had an extremely short fuse, and that set the tone for his long and sometimes controversial career. Many times when a coach is standing on the sidelines, continually making comments, Joey's favorite response has been, "Sit the heck down and shut the heck up," (though he may have actually used a different word than "heck").

3. Jake O'Donnell. He was an American League umpire in his early years and then became one of the all-time top referees. There always seemed to be a lot of personal grudges going on, but that didn't change Jake's ability to control a game. As long as you acted and talked with him in a respectful tone, you were OK.

2. Earl Strom. He learned from the top referees of the 1960s. Earl had his battles with coaches, but he outlasted them all. As time went on, he became just about everybody's favorite, because you knew you would get a fair shake from him on the road. Colorful and competent, he would listen to players and coaches without losing control of the situation.

1. Mendy Rudolph. He set the tone for looking professional on and off the court. Never a wrinkle, impeccable at all times. Mendy would wipe some real or imagined sweat off his eyebrow with his pinky finger. Who does that? When Wilt Chamberlain had five personal fouls and Mendy was on the game, Wilt would take himself out of the game. It was unusual because the big fella never wanted to come out. I asked him why and he said that he didn't trust Mendy. "He would want to be known," Wilt believed, "as the only referee to foul Wilt Chamberlain out of a game."

My Most Emotional Moments in NBA History :: by Pat Williams

Over the span of the league's history, there have been moments in time that have transcended the arena and captured the hearts of members of the NBA community, including me. None have done so more dramatically than these 11.

11. Orlando Magic's first game (October 13, 1989). The brand new franchise electrified the sellout home crowd of 15,077 by defeating the defending champion Detroit Pistons in Orlando's first game as an NBA city.

10. Magic Johnson's first game (October 12, 1979). Following a buzzer beater by teammate Kareem Abdul-Jabbar that secured a one-point victory, Magic jumped into his center's arms as if they'd just won the NBA championship. Seven months later they did just that, with Magic taking the place in the paint of the hobbled Kareem and leading the Lakers to the title with 42 points, 15 rebounds, and 7 assists, in a performance for the ages and a sign of things to come.

9. The Lottery Drawing/NBA Draft (1992). Imagine the destiny of a franchise dependent upon the whim of a floating ping-pong ball. I'll never forget kissing the ping-pong ball after the Orlando Magic won the draft's first overall pick, which would end up being Shaquille O'Neal.

8. The 76ers win the 1983 NBA title (May 31, 1983). After a number of bites at the apple, Philadelphia finally brought a basketball title to the City of Brotherly Love, led by center Moses Malone.

7. LeBron James leaves Cleveland (July 8, 2010). In an announcement accompanied by a level of pomp and circumstance usually reserved for royal weddings, LeBron James told a national audience on ESPN, "I am gonna take my talents to South Beach and join the Miami Heat." His proclamation immediately drew the ire of the nation for its perceived vanity and egocentricity. Nowhere was the vitriol more passionate than in Cleveland, where LeBron had played in high school and during his early professional years. Shirts were burned, cynics born, and letters penned by the owner.

6. Derek Fisher: father and basketball hero (May 15, 2007).

Utah Jazz guard Derek Fisher raced to a Western Conference Semifinals game in Utah from New York, where his daughter was undergoing surgery and chemotherapy related to retinoblastoma (eye cancer). By the time Fisher arrived the game was in the third quarter and the Jazz were using a forward at point guard. Fisher would go on to lead the Jazz to a dramatic overtime victory secured by a late three-pointer from the exhausted father, inspiring a raucous Utah crowd to salute its tearful hero.

5. Michael Jordan's first title (June 12, 1991).

After seven seasons of individual excellence and team frustration, Michael Jordan's Chicago Bulls finally won their first of six championships. During the postgame celebration in the locker room Jordan was overcome by emotion and broke into tears as he hugged the championship trophy with his father sitting by his side.

3 (tie). The retirements of Celtic greats Bob Cousy (March 17, 1963) and John Havlicek (April 9, 1978).

Being a fan of a team with so many legendary players also means you have a lot of emotional goodbyes to attend. After a Hall of Fame career Bob Cousy announced his retirement in 1963 and the Celtics held his farewell party in the Boston Garden at the last regular-season game, which happened to fall on St. Patrick's Day. During his farewell speech the Cooz was so overcome with emotion that tears flowed from player and fans until a Celtic fan yelled out, "We love you, Cooz!" The night would later be called, the Boston Tear Party. Cousy would end the postseason on top again, leading Boston to the NBA title—his sixth.

The opening tap for John Havlicek's last game was held up for over 10 minutes by a raucous Boston Garden crowd's standing ovation for Hondo. The 13-time All-Star went out on a high note, thrilling the Boston crowd—as he had so many times before—by scoring 20 points and dishing eight assists.

2. Magic Johnson Announces His Retirement (November 7, 1991).

The man with the radiant smile and gregarious game shocked the world when he announced that he had tested positive for the HIV virus and would retire immediately at a time when the world still perceived AIDS as a death sentence.

Three months after his retirement Magic was voted into the All-Star Game. He not only showed up, he won the All-Star Game MVP Award, after getting 25 points and nine assists. He capped off his performance with a game-ending three-pointer that brought the crowd and players to their feet.

1. Willis Reed leads New York Knicks to title (May 8, 1970).
Ravaged by a devastating leg injury, New York Knicks center Willis Reed refused to be denied in Game 7 of the NBA Finals against Wilt Chamberlain and the Los Angeles Lakers. When Reed walked out of the locker room onto the Madison Square Garden floor, the game was won. Laker announcer, Chick Hearn recalled: "You think the Garden went crazy? Wow! They went absolutely nuts!" Willis Reed hit his first two shots and the Knicks never looked back in beating Los Angeles, 113-99, for their first NBA title. Curt Gowdy would later say, "It was one of the singular most amazing games by an injured player I've ever seen."

Dolph Schayes was a 12-time NBA All-Star and champion with the Syracuse Nationals in 1955. The Hall of Famer scored over 18,000 points in his legendary career and was named one of the 50 Greatest Players in NBA History.

10. War Memorial Coliseum (Fort Wayne Pistons 1952–57). Gym was set up like a bullring. As a result fans were right on top of you.

9. Baltimore Coliseum (Washington Capitols 1946–51). The building was an old armory converted to play basketball. After one guy took a shower there would be nothing but cold water left.

8. Uline Arena (Washington Capitols 1946–51). Nothing but a converted old icehouse. I think I got 48 there one night.

7. Madison Square Garden III (New York Knicks 1946–68). It was a great place to play but after the first half you couldn't see anything. Everybody smoked in those days and the smoke hung over the court. I remember shooting a high, arching set shot that went through the haze and I couldn't see the ball until it came back down and went through the net.

6. Civic Center/Convention Hall in Philadelphia (Philadelphia Warriors 1946–62). I really like the building and had a lot of great scoring nights there.

5. Philadelphia Arena (Philadelphia Warriors 1946–62). Along with the Convention Hall in Philadelphia, we also played games at the Arena. The place was a real Dump with a capital D.

4. Rochester Edgerton Park Sports Arena (Rochester Royals 1945–55). The facility only had seating on two sides of the court, which meant the exits were right under the basket. I remember one night Bob Davies of the Royals ran out the door and came back onto the court with no break in the action.

3. (Old) Boston Garden (Boston Celtics 1946–95). It was old even back in the '50s. The locker rooms downstairs had one hook to put your clothes on. Our locker felt like a boiler room—it was that hot. We were drenched with sweat before the game started. It was usually lights out for us when we were at the Garden anyways. We all felt Red was up to his old tricks. One other thing, the Garden had guide wires that held up the backboard. I was coaching Philadelphia in the famous "Havlicek Stole the Ball" game, which was all set up when Bill Russell hit one of the wires with what would have been a game-ending pass.

2. The Chicago Coliseum (Chicago Zephyrs 1962–63). In order to get to the court, we would have to come up from our locker room and walk through a parking garage. I thought we'd all die from carbon monoxide poisoning.

1. Keil Auditorium (St. Louis Hawks 1955–68). It was a difficult place to play because the building was shaped like a big barn. In those days the Hawks had a great team. Ben Kerner owned the Hawks. He would sit in the front row across from the benches next to his mom, who was a loud and vocal fan. One night we were tied at the end of the game and Bob Pettit was on the line for two shots. He missed the first free throw and the building went silent when all of a sudden you hear Kerner's mother yell, "Bob you're not meant to miss those. My son pays you lots of money not to miss."

My Favorite Old Buildings :: by Jeff Mullins

Jeff Mullins was drafted by the St. Louis Hawks after a stellar career at Duke, where he won ACC Player of the Year in 1964 and had his No. 44 retired. In the NBA he was a three-time All-Star and won a championship in 1975 with the Golden State Warriors.

10. Buffalo Memorial Auditorium. As a child I can remember shoveling snow off a driveway so we could play basketball. But who would have thought that we would have been playing an NBA game outdoors in Buffalo, New York? That's what it felt like when the owners of the Buffalo Braves decided to expand the building by raising the roof and adding a whole new level of seats. The raised roof kept the snow and rain off the court, but it didn't keep the cold night air out of the building. As a visiting team we only had to experience this a few times a year, but I always felt sorry for the Braves players and fans as they toughed it out that year.

9. Seattle's Key Arena. We had some very competitive playoff games with the SuperSonics and I always thought they had some of the best fans in the league. During one hotly contested playoff game, a Seattle fan was unmercifully riding my teammate Rick Barry. At the end of the game we were running out through the stands and the obnoxious fan was leaning over yelling at Rick, unaware that his tie was hanging down. What a surprised look he had when Rick pulled him down and popped him good. We all had a good laugh over that incident!

8. Convention Hall of Baltimore. Downtown Baltimore was my least favorite city to visit during my NBA playing days, and yet I hold very fond memories of their arena. It was there in 1975 that we closed out the NBA Finals against the Bullets. We were underdogs going into that series, and rightfully so, since the Bullets had handily beaten us during the regular season. I'll never forget that Brent Musburger mentioned that he hoped that we would extend the series so that he could get more TV airtime. Little did we all know that we would wrap it up in four games.

7. Cobo Hall. Leaving pleasant San Francisco and arriving in "cold Detroit" was not one of my favorite memories, but I always thought Cobo was one of the cleanest and nicest arenas in the NBA. The Pistons were a talented team, led by Dave Bing and Bob Lanier, and you could always expect a competitive, high-scoring game from them. And despite Bob Lanier's size 21 shoes, you couldn't help but be amazed at his grace, skills, and soft touch.

6. Madison Square Garden. Basketball and Madison Square Garden were synonymous in the 1950s and '60s. But in 1961, college basketball had another gambling scandal that involved four New York metropolitan area schools. Because of that, many colleges, including my Duke University, stayed away from playing in New York. Having heard so much about the Garden, I couldn't wait to play my first game there, and I wasn't disappointed. In those days the Garden hosted many doubleheaders, which for the players meant not only an extra game in New York, but also a reunion of sorts with the players from all four teams. In those days a visit to Madison Square Garden was like a walk through basketball history.

5. LA Sports Arena. To me there was so much to like about the LA Sports Arena. It was a chance to see Hollywood up close and personal, with the likes of Doris Day and James Garner sitting courtside for all the games. When I wasn't stargazing, it was a chance to play against Jerry West, my basketball role model and the reason I wore No. 44 all through high school and college. And who can forget the neon "fan meter" that registered the attendance as crowds filed into the building? What a great marketing tool.

4. Chicago Stadium. Cold and threatening on the outside, with police escorts to your cars after the games, the Chicago Stadium was still one of my favorite buildings to play in. Despite the fact that Chicago's Jerry Sloan and Norm Van Lier were two of the best defenders in the NBA, I had some of my best games in Chicago Stadium. I loved the charm of the old building and always thought that the baskets were very forgiving. Playing in Chicago also gave us the opportunity to visit many of the city's wonderful restaurants, always a special treat.

3. Boston Garden. I never had a chance to see the inside of the Celtics locker room, but I am confident that it was much nicer than the visitors' room. Without question, the Boston Garden visitors' locker room was the worst in the NBA. It was cramped, cold, with old steam heaters that burned if you touched them, wooden benches to sit on, nails to hang up your clothes, and barely enough space for 12 NBA players to maneuver around. That being said, I always loved to play the Celtics because they were the best and you knew you were in for a fast-paced, competitive game.

2. Keil Auditorium. Even though I was drafted by the St. Louis Hawks and played my first NBA game there, my strongest memories of Keil were with my visiting Warrior teams. In 1967 we played the Hawks in the playoffs and during the series my teammate Rick Barry was quoted as saying, "St. Louis has the baseball and football Cardinals and the St. Louis Hawks, which only proves that St. Louis is for the birds." Needless to say that riled up the fans in St. Louis, but we were able to prevail in a tough six game series.

1. Cow Palace. I must reserve my fondest memories for the old Cow Palace in San Francisco. It earned its name over the years because it hosted everything from rodeos, motocross racing, roller derby, and, of course, basketball. It was a long, low rectangular building that gave the impression that the basketball court was extremely long, which suited the Warriors' running style of basketball. In 1975 we won two crucial games in the Cow Palace against the Washington Bullets in the Finals to win the NBA Championship.

My Top 10 Favorite NBA Cities
:: by Adonal Foyle

Adonal Foyle was the eighth overall pick in the 1997 NBA Draft when he was selected by the Golden State Warriors. He had a 12-year NBA career and is a member of the World Sports Humanitarian Hall of Fame for his work off the court. Here are his 10 favorite NBA cities from his playing days to explore off the court and outside the arena.

10. Vancouver. So beautiful and clean that you can eat off the ground, but, alas, they no longer have a team.

9. Washington, DC. Where politics abound and conversations are plenty, so I go to their many museums for silence.

8. Philadelphia. Fabulous cheesesteaks and a city of many firsts for me—from coming to America to experiencing snowstorms and professional sports.

7. Toronto. City of cold, but I can always count on 50 or more family members from the islands to warm me up, for better or worse.

6. Boston. Really good clam chowder. Larry Bird's legacy haunts me every time, making the disappointment of the Celtics fans even sweeter when we win.

5. Los Angeles. City of stars, tall-size fashions that fit me, and the omnipresence of Jack Nicholson's face.

4. Oakland/San Francisco Bay Area. Drafted and played 10 years with the Golden State Warriors—the We Believe team. Place of my summer home and North Beach Restaurant for my Italian food fix. Napa! (Would have been No. 2 if not for my recent property tax bill.)

3. Miami. South Beach (aka Sodom and Gomorrah). Pat Riley's competitive spirit and the team you love to hate, but undeniable talent making for great basketball.

2. New York. Broadway shows, friends, family, and food. Enough said.

1. Orlando. I live and work here. The best arena in all of basketball, land of worlds (Disney, Universal, Lego, Alligator, etc...) and a city on the rise!

Top 10 NBA Cities for Eating Out
:: by Andrew Bogut

The seven-foot center from Australia was the No. 1 overall pick in the 2005 NBA Draft by the Milwaukee Bucks. Since 2007, Bogut has averaged a double-double. At the University of Utah, prior to entering the NBA, Bogut was voted Player of the Year in 2005.

10. Atlanta. Some very good "down south" types of food. Not the healthiest, but you have to indulge once in a while.

9. Chicago. Like all big cities, it's tough to make a decision in Chicago. A heavy Italian community leaves it fairly easy to find a top-notch Italian eatery.

8. San Antonio. With a heavy Hispanic influence it's no surprise you can find some very good Mexican cuisine.

7. New Orleans. This is the place you will see things on a menu that you don't usually see. Alligator, for instance, is very popular in a lot of dishes. Gumbo soup is a must also.

6. Miami. Any city that is "the place to be seen" has good food, maybe a little overpriced and over "Hollywood," but still has great feeds.

5. Boston. The home of the Irish. Some of the best Irish pub-style restaurants you will find in the country. Also some very good seafood, and with good reason.

4. Los Angeles. Cali is very green and health conscious, so as an athlete you can find some great-tasting, low-fat, low-carbs meals. Some great lunch spots mesh well with the sunshine, which is nice if your home team is a cold city.

3. Washington DC. One of my favorite Italian restaurants is in the Georgetown area. Always make a point of going there, sometimes two or three times within two days!

2. Toronto. The Canadian city reminds me a lot of Melbourne, Australia (minus the snow). A melting pot of cultures leads to a great variety of food. Can't go wrong with that, even though decision-making becomes a major problem!

1. New York. Has to top the list merely because of the great variety. Any food, any culture, any nationality—you will find it in NYC.

Teams That Present Best Overall Game Experiences :: by Steve Schanwald

Steve Schanwald is the executive vice president of business operations for the Chicago Bulls. His previous sports promotion experience included head of Sports Marketing for the Air Force Academy and the Pittsburgh Pirates "We Are Family" team.

10. Indiana Pacers. I would go to their games just to walk the concourse and soak up and remember the rich tradition of basketball in the state of Indiana. A brilliantly themed venue and setting for watching an NBA game. When the fans show up, it's terrific!

9. Oklahoma City Thunder. An enthusiastic, supportive, and avid fan base in this one-team pro sports town gets them into the top 10.

8. Dallas Mavericks. They put on a great show and have demonstrated a proclivity for innovation, as exemplified by the ManiAACs (their extra large male dance team).

7. Orlando Magic. Their new arena has raised the bar for indoor stadiums in many ways and should be experienced.

6. Phoenix Suns. The gorilla alone is worth the price of admission, as well as their arena's great sight lines and amenities.

5. Miami Heat. The late-arriving crowd keeps them from rising any higher, but the Miami Heat dancers and the thrill of seeing Wade, LeBron, and Bosh do their thing create a buzz of anticipation and energy that gets them into the top five.

4. Los Angeles Lakers. LA is the birthplace of Showtime, home of the NBA's most iconic dance team (The Laker Girls), and the place in Los Angeles to see and be seen. The celebrity watching alone would be enough to get them into the top 10.

3. Boston Celtics. Latecomers to the party in terms of putting on a show, because of their history and tradition they didn't need much else. Now they put on a terrific show to go with all that history and tradition.

2. New York Knicks. There is an energy and electricity that accompanies any event in New York City. A basketball game played in the "World's Most Famous Arena" is no exception.

1. Chicago Bulls. Widely acclaimed, plus it's my list. Iconic introductions that started a trend throughout the NBA, and Chicago sports fans are the best anywhere and can't be duplicated.

Top 10 NBA Dance Teams
:: by Steve Schanwald

Steve Schanwald is the executive vice president of business operations for the Chicago Bulls. He has won 15 marketing awards during his career and also served as head of sports marketing for the Air Force Academy and the Pittsburgh Pirates.

10. Boston Celtic Dancers. The newest dance team, this group of women has been quick to make its mark among the NBA dance teams and show their Celtic pride.

9. New Orleans Honeybees. The pride of New Orleans, this group of young ladies takes the excitement of Mardi Gras and Bourbon Street inside the New Orleans Arena.

8. Charlotte Bobcats Lady Dancers. Two-time winners of the NBA.com Dance Team Contest, this group of young ladies are athletic and beautiful.

7. Nets Dancers. Very athletic dancers, as the Nets pull from the talent-rich New York area.

6. Chicago Bulls Luvabulls. Highly popular in the Windy City, their high-energy routines echo the team's recent success on the court.

5. Phoenix Sun Dancers. Integrated well into the Suns game presentation, these Desert Divines never disappoint the Suns faithful.

4. Mavs Dancers. Mark Cuban's Mavs Dancers are first-class beauties and have been part of the Mavs family for over 20 years.

3. Miami Heat Dancers. These beauties are an extension of the South Beach lifestyle and their routines are filled with heart-pumping Latin beats.

2. Knicks City Dancers. Drawn from a talent pool second to none, this group represents the Big Apple very well.

1. Laker Girls. Ranked first because they were the first and are the most iconic.

The 10 Most Passionate Celebrity Laker Fans :: by Jeanie Buss

Jeanie Buss is the executive vice president of business operations for the Los Angeles Lakers. She also is the daughter of Lakers owner Dr. Jerry Buss and significant other of coaching great Phil Jackson.

Honorable Mention. Adam Levine; B-Real; David Beckham; Heather Locklear; Ice Cube; Jeffrey Osbourne; Jeremy Piven; John McEnroe; Justin Bieber; Khloe Kardashian; Michelle Kwan; Pete Sampras; Rob Lowe; Snoop Dogg; Tobey Maguire; Walter Matthau (posthumously); Will Ferrell; Zachary Levi.

10. David Arquette. Dresses in outrageous Lakers gear for important games. Most impressive though is when he aided a Staples Center security guard by subduing an unruly fan after a playoff game.

9. Leonardo DiCaprio. Born in Los Angeles, Leo represents all Lakers fans well. The Oscar nominee is known for waiting in line at the concession stand just like everyone else. No wonder he is so cool.

8. Dustin Hoffman. Devoted Lakers fan but always the entertainer, Dustin has made appearing on the "Kiss Me Cam" an art form, even delighting fans by kissing fellow actor Jason Bateman during one time out break.

7. Andy Garcia. His body of work speaks for itself and makes him a celebrity Lakers fan All-Star. He is developing the next generation of fans by often times bringing his daughters to games.

6. Denzel Washington. Seated next to his gorgeous wife, Pauletta, and across from the Lakers bench, this Oscar winner has a calming influence on younger Lakers players who admire him.

5. George Lopez. A lifelong Lakers fan, George in 2010 displayed his loyalty by betting R&B star and Cleveland fan Usher that his Lakers would win a championship. Guess who won that bet?

4. Penny Marshall. A fixture at courtside, Penny even dons a Lakers jersey. Great with Lakers players and fans alike, Penny always supports the charitable work of the Lakers Youth Foundation.

3. Red Hot Chili Peppers. Anthony Kiedis & Flea. These two musicians have shared their Lakers love since the 1980s, often performing the national anthem prior to home games as well as recording a song called "Magic Johnson."

2. Dyan Cannon. She is the matriarch of celebrity Lakers fans and has been devoted for over 25 years. Gotta love her as she brings brownies not only for Dr. Buss and the players but for staff members as well.

1. Jack Nicholson. Jack not only is the greatest celebrity Lakers fan, he is probably the best Lakers fan ever. He has owned his season seats since 1971, and does not jump off the bandwagon when times are tough in Lakersland. Oh, and don't think it is a coincidence he is seated next to the visiting team. Jack is part of the home-court advantage.

Top 10 NBA Mascots I Would Pay to See
:: by Scott Hesington

Scott Hesington knows his stuff when it comes to team mascots. He portrayed Stuff, the Orlando Magic's mascot, until the summer of 2011. Stuff was only the latest in the line of sports mascots that Hesington has embodied since entering the profession in his teens. Of his calling, he says: "When it comes to mascot madness, the NBA is at the top of the pecking order. As a 16-year performer, I should know. I was one of them.

"As a part of this furry fraternity for a huge part of my career, I have witnessed some of the best entertainment, creative minds, and marketing geniuses the world has to offer. I am proud to call them my family, so it is very difficult for me to create a list of only 10, because I would pay to see any of them!

"However, with this task assigned to me, I have done my best to compile my short list and a brief description of my reasoning. Please support my brothers when you witness them next!"

10. Coyote (San Antonio Spurs). One of the most family-friendly mascots in all the NBA, Coyote is extremely creative on the skit side of the show and super at slapstick comedy. He has also flipped the script, because this canine has trained his humans, perhaps commanding more control of his home audience than any other mascot in the league—a phenomenon best seen in his S-P-U-R-S chant. Coyote can silence the San Antonio Spurs crowd with a simple arm gesture at center court, and can start a ruckus just as easily.

9. Gorilla (Phoenix Suns). The inventor of acrodunking (aka dunking from a mini-trampoline), Gorilla earned a lot of attention in the 1990s through winning numerous Mascot Slam Dunk titles at the annual NBA All-Star Game. The support that it has afforded him has been bananas! The Phoenix Suns mascot also holds claim to a tremendous jungle full of props and outfits that few can match.

8. Bango (Milwaukee Bucks). This bouncy buck has risen in fame through recent years due to his physical prowess and daredevil ways. Just as he did on a 16-foot ladder for a dunk during the 2010 NBA Playoffs, Bango stands at the top of the acrodunking food chain, constantly adding a twist to old ideas and creating new ones. When you go to a Milwaukee Bucks game, you want to keep your sights on the deer to see what he serves up next from his menu of moves.

7. Raptor (Toronto Raptors). One of the few mascots who directly represents the team logo and moniker, Raptor is a dynamic dinosaur for the Toronto Raptors, with a broad range of acrobatic skills—from high-flying dunks, head-spinning tumbling, and heart-pounding stunts. Raptor rarely leaves the floor area at his games, thus remaining very visible for the crowd, and is ingenious in his use of simple props—like his cavemen counterparts, making even a simple trash can a crowd-pleasing ploy.

6. Clutch and Turbo (Houston Rockets). Houston's dynamic duo of humor and athleticism was broken up in 2003, as Turbo—the "Godfather of Acrodunk"—pursued a new dream, leaving only the chubby, grey teddy bear. Clutch is tremendous at marketing his oversized persona, as well as promoting his numerous innovative programs provided to the public. He is also a leading innovator of creative skits on video and on the court, injecting them with a certain randomness that adds excitement to his flow. He has been gifted with a lot of time in the spotlight at each game, allowing his antics to be highlighted, but pray none involve you!

5. Bear (Utah Jazz). A true superstar in his Salt Lake City community, Bear could possibly run for mayor and win. It must be noted that he spends an amazing amount of time raising money for charities. Known as the Master of Disaster, Bear is known to cause chaos and leave huge messes in his wake. He has access to practically anything in the area, including helicopters, explosives, and even tanks, making his skits and stunts unparalleled, unpredictable, and often dangerous . . . in a good way.

4. Stuff (Orlando Magic). The most colorful and animated character in the league, this lovable, neon green dragon makes people smile just by being present and showing off his many moving parts. Stuff is probably best known for embodying the clumsy, fat, and mischievous persona. Rising from the ashes in the 2000s, he has also become recognized for his physical humor and unexpected versatility in pratfalls, balance skills, and rigging stunts. Stuff consistently delivers laughs from his lair full of unique toys and fiery outfits that are sure to turn many heads, from center court to the court jester.

3. Benny (Chicago Bulls). This beefy bovine has transformed throughout the years, but has never lost his entertainment savvy. Easily the best mascot dancer in the league, he has moves that are the envy of even his own dance team. Benny is also a fantastic skit writer, with his unique spin on humor, super-quick ad-lib style, and an uncanny ability to personalize his performances to his audience. Once largely invisible, thanks to MJ's shadow at the Chicago Bulls games, he now casts his own long shadow as one of the NBA's elite mascots.

2. Rumble and Squatch (Seattle SuperSonics/Oklahoma City Thunder). When the Seattle SuperSonics uprooted their team, their highly touted Bigfoot mascot, Squatch, was released back into the woods. Thankfully, a very similar bison named Rumble was found to replace him for the Oklahoma City Thunder. He has rapidly become an icon for his excited city, and for good reason. An extremely versatile performer—whether tumbling, swishing half-court shots, or even playing the drums, Rumble gives an action-packed show every time he stampedes onto the stage.

1. Rocky (Denver Nuggets). Quite possibly the most entertaining mascot anywhere, Rocky enthralls fans everywhere with everything from his understated improv, to his heralded accuracy on trick shots from everywhere on the court. Every moment Rocky is on stage he is the star of the show. He brings it every single night and at every event, and like a cat, is always on the move and prowling for his next big thrill. Back when the Denver Nuggets were struggling, the organization advertised this furry feline, Rocky, as the reason to come to a game—and my guess is no one who showed up to see him was disappointed!

Best Game Uniforms in NBA History
:: by Paul Kennedy

Paul Kennedy has been the Voice of Florida Sports dating back to 1988. As an anchor for Fox Sports and Sun Sports, Kennedy had delivered everything from Florida State football to Orlando Magic basketball. He's seen a lot of uniforms—the good, bad, and ugly—during his decades following pro basketball, including the best that he lists below.

12. ABA Uniforms (1967–76). From this incredible universe of high-fashion hues and undaunted by our own audacity, we begin by applauding the promotional chutzpah of the American Basketball Association—a wonderful wisp of wanderlust that transformed hoops into sheer beach-ball entertainment during the Woodstock '60s and Disco '70s, and accented the 2006 World Champion Miami Heat.

11. Atlanta Hawks (1982–92). A very '70s look, in vivid red with yellow-gold piping and angled numbers, accented in white, with the Pac Man Hawks logo on the shorts. "We're in the old Capital Centre playing the Bullets," remembers former Atlanta point guard Doc Rivers, laughing. "Mike Fratello has us all huddled up, game's on the line, and the heckler Robin Finkler is just a couple of rows behind our bench. At the top of his voice he starts singing the Burger King commercial lyrics, 'Hold the pickles hold the lettuce . . . have it your way.'"

10. Seattle SuperSonics (1975–95). From the lush, green forests of the Great Northwest to the sophistication of Seattle's Space Needle skyline, the color scheme and radiating gold design represented one of the very best stops on the NBA tour. "The arched basketball team logo incorporated the scenic skyline of the city and the prominent tower known all around the world," recalls Kevin Calabro, the smooth Voice of the Sonics prior to their 2008 transformation into the Oklahoma City Thunder. "The traditional look of that time and the logo were my favorites."

9. Orlando Magic (1993). "The uniform I wore in Orlando was the favorite of my career," states Shaquille O'Neal, of the work gear of the first club he starred for in his 19-year career. "It was so different from any other. I felt we were pushing the envelope. We had black-and-white pinstripes with stars on the jerseys. No one had a uniform like that."

With the aplomb of a diplomat, Magic founder Pat Williams had merged the traditions of two rival kingdoms in creating the team's game-night attire and playing floor in 1989. With a nod to the tradition of the New York Yankees, he decked the club in those pinstripes and paraded his cast upon a Boston Garden-like parquet court.

8. Cleveland Cavaliers (1972–81). When a young Austin Carr teamed with future Hall of Famer Lenny Wilkens to wear the Cavaliers "wine and gold" ensemble in 1973, they became the first backcourt in league history to each average more than 20 points a game. That they did so with such style and grace on the floor immortalized the fashion statement of a maroon feather floating across the chest of Cleveland's dashing uniform.

"It was the uniform the club wore when it first achieved success," reminds legendary broadcaster Joe Tait—he of 41 NBA campaigns. "Coach Bill Fitch brought the color combination with him from his days at Coe College in Cedar Rapids, Iowa."

7. San Antonio Spurs (1992). San Antonio stands proudly as the Original Team in Black, like Johnny Cash exuding strength from this most-fundamental color scheme. Doc Rivers concluded his playing career with a final roundup at the Alamo. "I've always felt that uniform fit the town as well as any in the game. Tough cowboys—that's what San Antonio is. That is what the Spurs are all about to this day."

They walk the line.

6. Charlotte Hornets (1989). Charlotte's original team president, Carl Scheer, had the foresight to phone Chapel Hill native and global clothing design icon Alexander Julian to increase the buzz in the Hive. What he got was unprecedented teal and lavender with pleated shorts—very long pleated shorts.

5. New York Knicks (1953). Sure, the 1970 Knickerbockers were so Manhattan. Walt "Clyde" Frazier, Willis Reed, Bill Bradley. Dave DeBusschere and Coach Red Holzman with—"Yessss"—Marv Albert on the microphone. The club delivered on a promise to a new generation, blending NBA style with urban chic. Yet, as slick as these Knicks were, history offers us from the league's formative years the 1953 Knights In White Satin Knicks, who were once truly the talk of the town.

Such colors were never more elegantly arrayed than by Coach Joe Lapchick's 1953 cast, as they ruled the interior—with authority—all the while sporting checkered trim and a belted waistband that the team would regally boast until 1967.

4. Washington Bullets (1978). For all the coach-speak about "the name on the front means more than the name on the back," three-time NBA All-Star Phil Chenier remembers his first NBA uniform, one that had his 1971 Bullets resembling those magenta-clad Miami Floridians, only in more patriotic American tones.

"It had a long serpentine stripe from top to bottom, and your first name on the front," recalls Chenier, Washington's longtime popular television analyst who works alongside acclaimed colleague and play-by-play announcer Steve Buchantz.

"It didn't say 'Bullets.' Rather, the jerseys had 'Phil' and 'Wes' and 'Archie' and 'Jack'—that's it. And a rather large stripe on Wes Unseld who would snap rocket outlet passes to flying wingmen, grandly bedecked in the Stars and Stripes.

3. Los Angeles Lakers (1976). Purple is the color of royalty and gold the stuff of kings. Basketball's Midas touch has long been found in Southern California, where NBA stars cheered on by Hollywood moguls have transformed leather basketballs into the glimmering Larry O'Brien Trophy 11 times since arriving from Minnesota in 1960.

"With the uniform's classic lines and slanted lettering, you just look like an athlete," says former Laker center Mychal Thompson, who donned the purple-on-the road, gold-at-home Laker attire for NBA title teams in 1987 and '88.

"When you put on that uniform, with all the tradition, you are a champion, and you are expecting to—and expected to—win.

2. San Francisco Warriors (1967). On a November evening in 1965, while wearing The City attire of the Warriors in San Francisco, Nate Thurmond grabbed 40 rebounds in an NBA game. Only Bill Russell and Wilt Chamberlain could match that stat.

"I would have had 45 if the uniform wasn't so darn heavy," Thurmond laughs now. "That emblem was sewn on, with the Golden Gate Bridge and the cable cars embroidered. When you sweated, it weighed a ton. But it was avant-garde."

1. Boston Celtics (1976). Select any season from the club's inception, and every Celtic team and every Celtic player is wearing the green. Celtic great Tommy Heinsohn said, "The team's first owner, Walter Brown, initiated this, and the kelly green had to do with the Irish. "Red Auerbach was a great follower of Joe McCarthy of the Yankees. Dress like champions. The color green to Red Auerbach—and to all of us—represented class."

"Boston doesn't have a throwback uniform," observes Doc Rivers, who coached the Celtics 2008 NBA title team. "It just has green or white. To me that has symbolized a dynasty. It is the greatest uniform ever."

That's no blarney.

Top 10 Public Address Announcers
:: by Steve Schanwald

Steve Schanwald is the Chicago Bulls' executive vice president of business operations, a position he has held sine 1987. During that time he's overseen ticket sales during the team's 610-game sellout streak and listened to a lot of NBA public address announcers. Here are the 10 he remembers best, excluding the ones he remembers for the wrong reasons.

"Yellers, screamers, and cheerleaders were automatically excluded from consideration—my list; my rules. The show is on the court."

10. Pat Tallman (San Antonio Spurs). His great baritone voice would help whip the Hemisphere Arena crowd into a frenzy.

9. Reb Porter (Indiana Pacers). Reb was the lead P. A. voice of the Pacers from 1976 to 2010. He started in 1968 as the backup P. A. voice and is remembered for his "Two minutes, two-Ahhh," at the end of quarters.

8. Andy Jick (Boston Celtics). The Celtics P. A. announcer from 1980 to 1997 worked three NBA Finals. The successor to Weldon Haire, Andy had a conservative, yet distinctive style.

7. Weldon Haire (Boston Celtics). Weldon was the P. A. voice of the Boston Garden for almost three decades, a tenure that surrounded the original Red Auerbach dynasty era. Anyone who lasts that long merits inclusion on this list, especially considering he was the P. A. announcer for 13 NBA Finals.

6. Mike Walczewski (New York Knicks). The worthy successor to the No. 1 guy on this list knows exactly when to use subtle voice inflection at key moments, and has been exhibiting that art since 1989 for Knicks fans.

5. Ray Clay (Chicago Bulls). His introductions during the Chicago Bulls championship run in the 1990s became legendary.

4. Tommy Edwards (Chicago Bulls). The Bulls P. A. announcer since 2006 has a great sense of timing and how to create dramatic and iconic introductions.

3. Lawrence Tanter (Los Angeles Lakers). He has a great set of pipes, a deep baritone voice, and keeps it simple. For over three decades and counting, he has been the P. A. voice of the Lakers.

2. Dave Zinkoff (Philadelphia 76ers). He's unique, original and memorable—one of a kind. Once heard never forgotten. Who will ever forget the way he introduced "Julius 'The Doctor' Errrrrrving?

1. John Condon (New York Knicks). He's simply the best. John's style was smooth, classy, professional, understated, and elegant. For four decades he was the voice of Madison Square Garden. Truly the Frank Sinatra of P. A. Announcers.

10 NBA Radio Voices I'd Like to Hear Again :: by Al McCoy

Al McCoy has been working longer than any other NBA broadcaster. Winner of the Basketball Hall of Fame's 2007 Curt Gowdy Media Award, McCoy began calling Phoenix Suns games more than 40 years ago, but says he still enjoys listening to other NBA broadcasters. "There have been some great ones through the years, great ones to remember," says McCoy, who has only missed broadcasting one Suns game since he started with the team in 1972. "So when asked to look back at just 10 former play-by-play men, it was a job. But with no present-day or recently retired broadcasters on the list, let's FLASHBACK. Here come the Golden Oldies."

10. Skip Caray. When the name "Caray" is spoken, no question—a top-notch, familiar sportscaster's name comes up: Harry Caray. But Harry's son, Skip, had the Caray name and a style all his own. I loved his call of the Atlanta Hawks. He had a great sense of humor to his approach. If the Hawks were down by 20 in the fourth quarter, Skip's line might have been: 'Well folks, be nice to our sponsors, but it may be time to go walk the dog!!' Unique. Lovable. Skip Caray.

9. Eddie Doucette. When the Milwaukee Bucks came into the NBA in 1968, they didn't have Lew Alcindor yet. But they had Eddie Doucette. And as only Eddie could do, with his excitement and energy, he spread the word to Midwest basketball fans that there was a new team in town. The next season with Alcindor, it was Eddie raising his play-by-play to the rafters. He loved the game and the fans loved him. Eddie's career took him to several other NBA teams, but to Bucks fans, Eddie will always be "their guy."

8. Bill Campbell. If you were ever in Philadelphia listening to games on radio, you heard Bill. He did them all. He was the main basketball man for years for the Warriors and 76ers. Yes, he was in Hershey when Wilt hit 100—it was the game's only broadcast. When I had the chance to listen to Bill, it was a real treat. Bill Campbell was a true pro. He certainly belongs on my list.

7. Johnny Most. To this day, if any NBA fan is talking about the Celtics, Most's name comes up. He WAS the Celts. However, Johnny did work two years on the Knicks broadcasts with Marty Glickman, and it was Marty who recommended Johnny for the Boston job . . . the rest is history. As the story goes, in 1988 the radio broadcast of the NBA All-Star Game featured Most with the Lakers Chick Hearn. Prior to game time, as the two veterans got seated at their

231

broadcast locations, Chick asked Most if he had enough room at the table for his game notes. The reply from Johnny: WHAT NOTES? There are a million stories told about the man with the gravel in his voice.

6. Bob Blackburn. The great Northwest was his haven. Prior to becoming the first play-by-play man for the NBA Seattle Sonics, Blackburn had a career behind him: college sports hockey, minor league baseball, anything in season. His great popularity in Oregon and Washington made him ideal for the Sonics. A twist of fate late in his Sonic days: he was actually replaced. The fans ROARED and Bob came back. A friend of the fans, he made the Sonics come alive. A real "radio guy" and a perfect fit for the new Seattle franchise.

5. Bill King. At one point in time, Bill, who had been in Peoria, Illinois (where so many Midwest broadcasters got their start), was the voice of Nebraska sports. Chick Hearn was still in Peoria doing Bradley games and I was attending Drake University in Des Moines, Iowa working at a local radio station. That was when we three met. Our next stop was the NBA with what was called the "Midwest-style" of play-by-play. Bill did other sports, including the Oakland Raiders and the A's. But to me he was at his best behind the mike for the San Francisco Warriors. I thought basketball was HIS GAME. He referred to the officials as "The paragon of ineptitude." And I believe he was the only NBA announcer to be fined by the league for some of those comments. Remembered as the only announcer I ever knew that could do the game while enjoying a box of popcorn. Best handlebar "stash" in the league.

4. Bill Schonely. Our careers followed the same path: roller derby, hockey, baseball, college sports . . . on and on. Bill had a great following in the Northwest before his NBA days. He was on the air in Seattle when Portland obtained an NBA franchise in 1970. Owner Harry Glickman, knowing Bill from his hockey work and other sports, contacted him about the Trail Blazer job. It was the right time, right place. With Bill's great pipes and tremendous work ethic leading the way, good things followed. And he has a championship ring to prove it. The greatest ambassador the Trail Blazers have ever had. He could be elected Mayor.

3. Hot Rod Hundley. When I started with the Suns some 40 years ago as their play-by-play announcer, the color analyst was already in place. Rod had left his spot alongside Chick Hearn in LA a few years earlier, but he quickly became "MY GUY"!! You know his background: All-American at West Virginia, first-round pick of the Lakers, All-Star and Man About Town. It was Hot Rod who taught me all there is to know about the NBA—ON THE COURT AND OFF THE COURT. Of course, he went on to be the voice of the Utah Jazz. His style was his own. Jazz fans loved him, but then, doesn't everybody?

2. Marty Glickman. When I was honored by the Basketball Hall of Fame in Springfield, Massachusetts, in 2007, in my acceptance speech I cited the two men that devised the unique way to broadcast NBA basketball: Marty in the East and Chick Hearn in the West. The rest of us have followed in their footsteps. No surprise that Marty was the first broadcaster to receive the Curt Gowdy Award from the HOF and Chick was the second. Glickman did a variety of sports, but basketball was "his thing." So many firsts: did the first NBA All-Star Game on Mutual Radio in 1951 and the first NBA game on TV for the Dumont Network. Marty started that list of successful broadcasters coming out of Syracuse University. With his voice and the speed of his play-by-play, he gave the game real identity on radio. And always, smooth and assured. A true legend!

1. Chick Hearn. I was at Drake University, doing some of *their* games when I first met Chick. He was doing Bradley games. When he came into the press box, dressed in his best (as always), and I said my first hello, it was a moment to remember. Chick actually left the Midwest and moved to Los Angeles and was doing college sports, TV shows, etc. before the Lakers came on the scene in 1960. There was no radio in the first year except for the playoffs. Chick was hired to do some games and he just never stopped.

As far as Laker fans are concerned, Chick invented the game. His style can never be duplicated. Just as Glickman had done in New York City, Hearn's approach to broadcasting NBA basketball set the trend. On top of everything: humor when needed, knowing when and how to build excitement, and unfor- gettable phrases. Put all of this talent on the shoulders of one of the nicest men you would ever have the honor of meeting—and that was "Chickie Baby." A classic!!

Top Color Analysts Who Were NBA Players :: by Andrew Herdliska

Andrew Herdliska is a longtime employee in the Orlando Magic's front office who has listened to thousands of NBA broadcasts during his lifetime, and has heard his share of good and great color analysts, many of them former NBA players. Here are Andrew's choices of the best of them, along with his appreciation for the challenges they face.

"It's one thing to drain threes or leap through the air and slam home a dunk; it's another thing altogether to effectively describe those feats and generally articulate the world's most exciting sport in a fashion that is clear, concise and profound—while live on the air. These 10 made the long leap for doing the former to performing the latter with great style and substance."

11. Chris Webber. C-Webb's silky smooth playing style has easily translated to his broadcasting career. He seems to know every player in the Association, and his insights are often echoed by his peers. He easily builds rapport with his fellow broadcasters and seems to have the respect of everyone with whom he works. Webber is the star of NBA TV's studio show and his work for TNT's *Inside the NBA* has earned him some color analyst duties for TNT, as well.

10. Sean Elliott. Broadcasting in the same building where his retired jersey hangs, the Spurs great has either played in or broadcast games during one of the greatest runs by a team in NBA history. His articulate style is appreciated by the audience, but Elliott's best attribute is his knowledge of the Spurs players, coaches, and system. His familiarity offers the audience a level of insight you won't get from color analysts in many markets.

9. Earvin "Magic" Johnson. Magic played the game with infectious joy, but underneath that joy boiled an intense, competitive spirit. Similar to the way he played, Magic's trademark smile and positive attitude dominate his broadcasting career, but that doesn't mean he will not be critical of players or teams, especially anything that has to do with the Lakers.

8. Stacey King. The former Bulls center/forward is now the center of attention on Bulls TV broadcasts. Teaming up with veteran Neil Funk, King may be part of the best duo in local TV broadcasting. King's insightful criticism can be biting, but he balances that out with entertaining stories from the Michael Jordan championship years.

7. Walt Frazier. Broadcasting from the Mecca of basketball, the Knick legend teams up with play-by-play great Mike Breen. Frazier is an entertaining broadcasting poet, often describing the action with rhyming phrases, such as "dishing and swishing," and "posting and toasting," and "shaking and baking."

6. Matt Guokas. When you grow up side-by-side with the NBA as a fan, player and coach, like Matt did, you have a unique familiarity with the game that allows you to correlate the play on the floor with your limitless experiences with the league. From playing with Wilt Chamberlain to coaching Shaquille O'Neal, Matt's breadth of experience allows for insights and stories every generation of NBA fan can enjoy.

5. Mark Jackson. The point guard with the ability to set up teammates and shoot the teardrop runner in the lane joined the ABC/ESPN team of Jeff Van Gundy and Mike Breen to form one of the best trios in announcing. The three perfectly complemented one another, with Jackson adding humor and insight while enjoying a harmonious rapport with the self-deprecating Van Gundy and straight man Mike Breen. Jackson entertained with many of his one-liners, including my favorite describing a defender's poor close-out on a shooter, "Hand down, man down!"

4. Bill Walton. Perhaps the greatest college basketball player of all time, his career was derailed by a myriad of injuries. Walton overcame a stuttering problem to become a top color analyst for NBC. He delighted the audience with "Woodenisms" he learned playing for legendary UCLA coach John Wooden and amused with obnoxious hyperbole. Unfortunately Walton's basketball injuries have also taken a toll on his career as a broadcaster.

3. Tom Heinsohn. The Hall of Fame power forward has excelled at every level of the sport of basketball like no other personality in the sport's history. For over half a century Tommy has excelled as a championship player, two-time championship coach, national analyst, and broadcaster on Celtics television, where he shares his candid thoughts on officials, players, and the game he loves. Even if you haven't seen or heard a broadcast, you probably know what a "Tommy Point" is.

1. Charles Barkley and 1a. Kenny Smith. The TNT tandem entertains and informs like no other combo on TV. The two analysts perfectly complement one another. Barkley is more emotional and unfiltered, telling the viewer exactly what's on his mind. Smith has the ability to break down the game while speaking in a fashion that can be understood by fans of all knowledge levels.

Top 10 Outfits I've Worn While Working for the *NBA on TNT* :: by Craig Sager

Craig Sager has served as a network TV sports broadcaster for over two decades, following his three-year stint at Northwestern University as the school mascot, Willie the Wildcat—still the best outfit he's probably ever worn on a sideline during a sporting event. Working for CBS, CNN, TBS, and TNT, Sager has covered, among other things, college football, the MLB Playoffs, the NFL, the FIFA World Cup, and the Summer Olympics, and also served as the longtime sideline reporter for *The NBA on TNT*. He is known as "America's Sideline Reporter," and as his profession's most audacious dresser.

As "Endorsed" by TNT colleague Charles Barkley: "I don't discriminate against anybody, but when you start hiring pimps to do interviews during the games, I draw the line. We've got a pimp doing interviews with TNT and it's SAGER."

10. Mother's Day 2001. Tickle me Pink coat (Isaia); periwinkle shirt; Dolce Punta polka dot tie; eggshell pants; Liberty Pink and white shoes.

"You're asking me if I'm embarrassed? You should be embarrassed by what you wear." (Isaiah Rider)

9. Christmas Day 2009. Cardinal red coat (Belvest); white red-ribbon shirt; candy cane pants; Santa Claus ornament tie; strawberry lizard shoes.

"Do you want the starting line-up or my wife's Christmas list?" (Mike Brown)

8. A 2007 NBA Playoff Game. Black-and-white checkerboard coat (Valentino); houndstooth pants; black shirt; Swarovski crystal tie; Carrot & Gibbs pocket square; Caiman horn shoes.

"Thanks for the hankie." (Gregg Popovich, as he took the pocket square and wiped his nose).

7. A 2010 NBA Playoff Game. Canary yellow suit (Canali); Amarillo striped shirt; floral tie; Goldenrod pocket square; cobra-skin shoes.

"Will you get away from my huddle, you're blinding my players." (Phil Jackson)

6. A 2010–11 Regular-Season Game. Purple velvet coat (Versace); Wisteria shirt; orchid pants; Pucci tie; deep purple grape alligator shoes.

"Let's go back to the United Center in Chicago. Marv Albert, Steve Kerr, Reggie Miller, and Willie the Wildcat." (Ernie Johnson, Jr.)

5. The 2007 All-Star Game. Violet and plum iridescent coat (Brioni); tangerine shirt; maroon and ebony striped pants; peacock tie; burgundy ostrich shoes.

"That's so bad it needs a new word to describe its horrible awfulness—it's HOR-AWFUL." (Shaquille O'Neal)

4. Thanksgiving Day 2009. Tan, black, brown, gray turkey feather sport coat (handmade); camouflage shirt; mossy oak pants; tree bark tie; python-skin shoes.

"I was looking forward to Thanksgiving dinner, but you've ruined my appetite." (Stan Van Gundy)

3. The 2011 All-Star Game. Black jaguar velvet suit (Georgio Armani); strawberry silk shirt; diamond-studded tie; black and red licorice pocket square; black alligator head shoes.

"You've seen the way Sager dresses. SCARY! Add a pair of alligator shoes—complete with the eye of the alligator staring back at you—and it's understandable why no one would want to go near the guy." (T. J. Simers of the Los Angeles Times)

2. The 2009 All-Star Game. Pink and white carnation sport coat (Isaia); lavender cerulean striped shirt; cornflower spotted tie; magenta pants; Rojo alligator shoes.

"Take this outfit home and BURN it! BURN it ALL! EVERYTHING! BURN IT!" (Kevin Garnett)

1. The 2001 All-Star Game 2001. Black and sliver aluminum suit (Versace); zebra shirt; Timberwolves tie.

"Indescribably hideous gray suit Sager claimed was made by Versace, yeah, Hymie Versace. Last time I saw anyone near something like that was Lloyd Bridges on Sea Hunt." (Tony Kornheiser of the Washington Post)

Top 10 All-Time NBA Personalities to Interview :: by Tim Frank

Tim Frank is the director of communications for the NBA. He has worked in the league for almost two decades. Before coming to the NBA, Tim performed a rare double: graduating from Notre Dame, and then going to work for their rivals at the University of Michigan's sports information department. He's heard and given plenty of interviews in his career, none more fascinating and entertaining than the ones from these 10 NBA figures.

10. Johnny "Red" Kerr. The recently deceased Kerr was known for quick one-liners during his playing, coaching, and broadcast careers, which together spanned over a half century. The Syracuse Nationals first-round pick in 1954, Johnny was the "go-to" guy for reporters in an era when players and media members traveled together. Check any of those sports quote books and you'll see more quotes from Kerr than any other NBA player. For example, when asked why he decided to retire, he answered, "I was driving the lane for a basket and was called for a three-second violation." Asked what his epitaph should be when he died, Kerr responded, "I told you my feet were killing me."

9. Ray Allen. The Professional Basketball Writers Association in the late 1990s decided to establish an award to give high-level players who were the most friendly to the media and public. It, of course, was named for Magic Johnson, and the first recipient was, almost as inevitably, Ray Allen. Ray never gives you a cliché answer—the staple of athletic commentary made famous in the scene from the movie *Bull Durham*. Ray never gives you a quick answer either. He actually listens to the question and thinks about it, and then thinks about an appropriate answer. Ray respects people and the spoken word.

8. Steve Kerr. How many guys can show up to Finals Media Day after playing just 16 total minutes in the entire Conference Finals series and be the center of attention? During his last season in 2003, that's exactly what happened to Kerr. He was always informative, often witty, and established a track record for being available to all. If you spent any time around him during his playing career, you had no doubt that Steve would be on television when he retired. It took him about five minutes to get that job after his last game.

7. Walt Frazier. The Knicks legendary guard has spent the last 40-plus years bringing flash to the media game. As a player Frazier brought his style and his colorful comments to the locker room after a game or practice. As a broadcaster he's become well-known for his use of rhyming catchphrases, like "Styling and

Profiling," "Dishing and Swishing" and "Shaking and Baking," to name a few. Even today when the Knicks come to town, Frazier is the best guy to grab a few minutes with if you're a reporter looking to fill your notebook.

6. Grant Hill. If not for serious foot and ankle injuries that cost him almost six years of his playing career, Hill would have been one of the all-time greats. He certainly was with reporters. Although unable to play for many of his years in Orlando, he was always around to accommodate media members, and told his story of disappointment and frustration to everyone who asked. And he'd always make you feel like you were the only one who ever asked. He looks you in the eye on every question and never runs from the hard ones. Hill would give you insights into the game like few others. He'll certainly have a broadcasting career if he chooses to after he retires, but you figure eventually he'll run the network.

5. Kevin McHale. When a player gets two guest appearances on the all-time great TV show *Cheers*, you know he has to be funny. On a team of great interviews in Boston, McHale stood out for his humor and candor. The power forward always understood that being interviewed could be fun and didn't have to be a chore. Since his playing career has ended he has bounced between the front office, coaching bench, and broadcasting booth, and he still introduces the fun of the game into his sound bites. If you're lucky to get time with him talking about those great Celtics teams, you'd better bring a recorder because you'll be laughing too hard to take notes.

4. Doc Rivers. Rivers was a fantastic interview as a player and may actually be a better one as a coach. Always incorporates humor, emotion, and honesty into his answers. Walk around with him at a game and just watch the number of people he speaks to—from vendors, to fans, to staff members, to referees, to all members of the media. The man loves to talk and the media benefits from his insights. Of course, his best go-to line comes when he's asked an in-depth question about a player's medical condition, and he responds, "You do understand Doc is a nickname, right?"

3. Charles Barkley. For straight entertainment, no one has ever been better than Barkley. The number of moments he's inspired one to think, "No one else could get away with that," are too many to count. How does it get more entertaining than a guy claiming to be misquoted in his own autobiography? The pregame locker room was the Barkley interview room—he just never stopped talking until the media left. He knew almost every NBA media member's name, kids' names, and spouse's name. As former 76ers executive Dave Coskey once said, "There are athletes who are jerks that try to make you believe they are good guys. Well, Charles is a good guy who tries to make you believe he's a jerk."

2. Julius Erving. Bring up Dr. J's name to any reporter and the response is the same: "He would do anything for you." His reputation in professional basketball was obviously built upon his athletic ability, but no one was smoother, more cooperative, or more insightful with the media than Erving. Remember, this was perhaps the greatest star of his era. Yet, if you contacted the 76ers and even if he didn't know you, Doc was on the phone. He'd name a time he'd call and you could set your clock. Reporters of the era tell stories of Doc stuck in traffic and pulling his car over to a pay phone (no player needed the cell-phone era to start earlier than Doc) and calling because he never wanted to keep anyone waiting. That's right, *Julius Erving* didn't want to keep *you* waiting.

1. Magic Johnson. Almost every media member I've been around references Magic Johnson as the standard for players relative to the media game. Magic always offered insight and opinion, but most importantly, he always offered his time. If you missed Magic during the regular media avail, you could catch him at his car before he left for the day. If he knew you needed him, he found a way to reach you. And when you got Magic, you didn't get clichés, you got interesting anecdotes, tidbits, and observations that weren't obvious to you. And it wasn't only about the big guys and big media. Before one NBA Finals game against Boston, there was the usual big crowd around Magic pregame in the locker room, with all the big national newspaper and TV guys, and Magic's telling a million stories, when Magic spotted some kid who covered him back in high school. He shouted out for the kid to come up front, and then introduced the kid to all the big national media reporters and had them all shake the kid's hand. As always, it was a Magic moment.

Best NBA Quotes :: by Brian McIntyre

Brian McIntyre is the senior communications advisor to David Stern for the NBA. He has been an executive with the league for more than three decades, and served a three-year term as director of public relations for the Chicago Bulls. Brian has heard a lot of great quotes from players, coaches, fans, family members, and the media during his years in the NBA. Here are his favorites.

15. "We were so bad that one night someone broke into our box office and returned four season tickets." Johnny Kerr, on coaching the Chicago Bulls in the early 1960s.

14. "In the top story of the day, I've been traded to Portland." NBA forward Kiki Vandeweghe, opening his broadcast while working in the off-season as on-air talent for KABC-TV in Los Angeles.

13. "Sly's not home now and he won't be at practice. There's been a slight death in the family." A male voice, answering the phone at Sly Williams's house, explaining to Mike Saunders, long-time athletic trainer for the New York Knicks, why Sly had missed practice that day. While claiming to be that of Sly's brother, the voice sounded amazingly like the voice of Sly Williams, the talented University of Rhode Island product who played for the New York Knicks in the early 1980s, but had a history of missing practices and being late for team buses.

12. "I am not at all pleased, but I did not do anything for which I should be hung or beaten." Bulgarian Georgi Glouchkov, the first NBA player from the former Eastern Bloc countries, answering a postgame question through an interpreter about the five fouls he committed in just 11 minutes while playing in a game for the Phoenix Suns during the 1985–86 season.

11. "Practice? We talkin' 'bout practice, man. We talkin' 'bout practice. We ain't talkin' 'bout the game, we talkin' 'bout practice, man. . . ." Allen Iverson, after his Philadelphia 76ers coach, Larry Brown, had criticized him for missing practices in 2002.

10. "I can't really remember the names of all the clubs we went to." Shaquille O'Neal, when asked if had been to the Parthenon during a recent visit to Greece.

9. "I'm tired of hearing about money, money, money. I just want to play the game, drink Pepsi, and wear Reebok." Shaquille O'Neal, the loquacious center who has given us so many memorable quotes, it was difficult to choose just one—so I listed two.

8. "If every baby is so pretty, how come there are so many ugly adults?" Charles Barkley, the Hall of Fame forward who may very well be responsible for more memorable quotes than anyone in the history of the league, including one in which he claimed that he had been misquoted in his own autobiography.

7. "Young man, you have the question backwards." Celtic great Bill Russell, when asked by a reporter if he feared playing against Kareem Abdul-Jabbar.

6. "Fo', fo', fo'." Moses Malone, predicting how many postseason games it would take his Philadelphia 76ers to get through the playoffs and win the 1983 NBA title.

5. "Cuz there ain't no fours." Antoine Walker, at the 2003 NBA All-Star Game media availability session, after a reporter asked the quick-triggered forward why he shot so many three-point field goal attempts.

4. "I ain't gettin' in no time machine." Marvin Barnes, after the mercurial forward reviewed the itinerary for a St. Louis Spirits flight and noticed that, because of the time zone differences, the plane was scheduled to land two minutes earlier than the listed departure time.

3. "The ship be sinkin'." Micheal Ray Richardson, the unpredictable New York Knick, commenting on the decline of his team. When asked by a reporter to elaborate and predict how far it could sink, Richardson responded, "The sky's the limit."

2. "Both teams played hard." Rasheed Wallace, with an answer he repeated in response to five different questions during a press conference following a 2003 playoff game between Portland and Dallas.

1. "Don't ever underestimate the heart of a champion." Houston Head Coach Rudy Tomjanovich, after his Rockets won the 1995 NBA Championship.

A Dozen Great Public Speakers from the NBA :: by Pat Williams

Driving into the paint against a waiting Dwight Howard? Holding your ground as Blake Griffin flies at you with the intent to dunk in your face? Stepping to the line with under a minute to play in a tight Game 7 with tens of thousands in the arena screaming at you and millions watching around the world? For many, these daunting challenges barely register on the stress meter compared to getting behind a podium to deliver a speech. But while public speaking ranks as life's greatest fear for many people, these NBA personalities have mastered the difficult, perilous art and enthrall audiences around the world with their spoken words, as well as with their deeds.

12. Clark Kellogg. He does a wonderful job as college basketball's No. 1 color analyst (as he does with the Indiana Pacers). Very smart and presents well whether he is talking about faith, keys to living successfully, or sharing his basketball insights.

10 (tie). Norm Sonju and Walter Bond. Former Mavericks GM Sonju is very enthusiastic when presenting a story, using his hands and voice inflection. When he is finished, every listener is charged up. Former NBA guard Bond is a wonderful career corporate speaker who shares his insights with other athletes so that they may also have careers in the speaking field.

8 (tie). Mark Eaton and James Donaldson. If you are looking for height, these two can dazzle. They have worked hard to take their basketball experiences and share them with the corporate world.

7. Swen Nater. A poet laureate who works his presentation around the lessons he learned from his college coach, UCLA legend John Wooden.

6. Bill Walton. When you ask Bill Walton to speak, make sure you allow for plenty of time. John Wooden used to say that when Walton stuttered they couldn't get him to talk. Now that he doesn't stutter he won't stop talking. He can talk intelligently on many topics from basketball to business to work.

5. Earvin "Magic" Johnson. He lights up a room when he enters with his radiant smile. He sweeps an audience under his spell while speaking on subjects that stretch from his favorite sport to his success as a business leader.

4. Bill Bradley. The formal presentation by the Princeton Rhodes Scholar, New York Knick, United States senator, and former presidential candidate can be a little dry, but it's during the question and answer session that nobody is better. When Bill Bradley's Q&A session is over the audience is left wanting more.

3. Jay Carty. The former Laker who played with Chamberlain, West, and Baylor in the 1968–69 season is a brilliant speaker who can speak smartly on countless topics. He is so good that he teaches other athletes how to present and speak. Unfortunately, Jay now has a throat illness that has curtailed his speaking career.

2. Pat Riley. He enters a room dressed to the nines, strikingly handsome and articulate. His basketball successes are beyond the imagination, so audiences love to listen to him share his experiences.

1. Frank Layden. I envy his use of humor to keep an audience in stitches for 30 to 40 minutes while still being able to deliver a good, strong message. He is my speaking idol. Frank started me on a lifetime of collecting one-liners to use on the spur of the moment.

My 10 Favorite Frank Layden Jokes
:: by Ken Hussar

Ken Hussar is a comedian and a motivational speaker who has coauthored a number of books on life's levity and ways to improve one's plight. Here he offers quotes that do the same, inspired by the witty and wise longtime Jazz executive and coach, Frank Layden, a man who once tried to insert into his second-half starting lineup a fan who had won a halftime shooting contest.

10. "When I coached at Niagara, I had a player who was such a poor foul shooter that when he went to cross himself he missed his forehead."

9. "As a teenager I played in the Catholic Church league. We couldn't afford uniforms, so we had to wear choir robes. It really slowed down our fast break, and the choir smelled funny on Sundays, too."

8. "One veteran reported for training camp so out of shape that his stomach crossed the midcourt line three steps before the rest of his body."

7. "Our team has a great bunch of outside shooters. Unfortunately, we play all our games indoors."

6. "At the beginning of the year we had a booster club. By the end of the season they had turned into a terrorist group."

5. "One sportswriter suggested that we rename our team the Opossums because we play dead at home and get killed on the road."

4. "We're a team in transition. We've gone from bad to worse."

3. "We had a point guard who was so short that he had to stand on a stool while showering. Otherwise the water would be cold by the time it reached him."

2. "I coached a team that was so bad. We couldn't win at home. We couldn't win on the road. I failed as a coach because I couldn't figure out where else we could play."

1. "The worst team I coached lost nine straight and then we went into a slump. On our days off we had a victory celebration."

The below list is a collection of the greatest books ever written on professional basketball. The power of the written word, as presented by these authors, allows the NBA fan to have a more detailed understanding and greater appreciation of the subject matter.

11 (tie). *Maravich* **by Wayne Federman & Marshall Terrill & Jackie Maravich; and** *Pistol: The Life of Pete Maravich* **by Mark Kriegel.** Both books will satisfy the cravings of any Pete Maravich fan. These remembrances capture the spirit and mind of Pistol Pete.

9. *When the Garden Was Eden* **by Harvey Araton.** There were many books written on the great New York Knicks teams of the early 1970s. Araton's book captures the essence of that special era.

8. *West by West* **by Jerry West**. I couldn't believe how transparent this book was by the NBA great. A must read for any psychiatrist and all NBA fans.

7. *Basketball* **by Bill Simmons.** This book is huge, a treasure trove of NBA info and insights. Simmons turned out a book that can literally be sold by the pound, but NBA fans have to read this book.

6. *The Jordan Rules* **by Sam Smith.** This book chronicled Michael Jordan's first championship season. Jordan wasn't happy with the book. But for readers it was a great behind-the-scenes look at one of the league's greatest teams.

5. *Life on the Run* **by Bill Bradley.** The New York Knick great provided a retrospective look at life behind the scenes of an NBA team. He took the reader onto planes, into the locker room, and onto the floor with him and his Knicks teammates.

4. *Tall Tales* **by Terry Pluto.** The great NBA scribe was able to record the world of the NBA in the early days by capturing accounts of former players and assembling them into a mosaic of those pioneer years.

3. *Loose Balls* **by Terry Pluto.** This basketball classic is a written history of the wild and wacky days of the ABA. Pluto's account of the since-gone league is hilarious and thought provoking.

2. *24 Seconds to Shoot* by Leonard Koppett. The erudite *New York Times* writer was able to dig deeply into the first three decades of the NBA and write a sports classic.

1. *The Breaks of the Game* by David Halberstam. When the great David Halberstam wasn't writing tomes on war, politics, or business, he blessed the sports world with his extraordinary writings. This book is living proof of that.

A Dozen Legendary NBA Writers
:: by Pat Williams

The NBA game can be experienced through many mediums, from television to radio to print. The below list is the collection of the greatest writers ever to share their NBA thoughts with the reader in the pages of a newspaper.

11 (tie). Bob Logan and Lacy J. Banks. What a pair these guys were! Bob was an ordinary Philly guy and he carried that mentality to Chicago, where he wrote for the *Chicago Tribune*. Never a clotheshorse, Bob had a good fashion day when he wore matching shoes.

Lacy, a preacher as well as a writer for the *Chicago Sun-Times*, is still one colorful character. Every time he calls I know the conversation will range from the latest NBA gossip, to his sermon from the previous Sunday, to the most recent political scandal in Chicago.

10. Joe Gilmartin. The longtime Phoenix Suns writer has a remarkable sense of humor to go along with his insightful view of the pro basketball world. His legendary quote about the Suns Connie Hawkins still makes me laugh: "The Hawk is a work art. Some nights he's poetry in motion; other nights, still life." Joe once told me: "Here is the deal with the NBA. Two teams play even for 47 minutes and 50 seconds. Then one team goes home ecstatic and the other team heads home despondent. It's a very fine line."

9. Jack Kiser. The former *Philadelphia Daily News* writer covered the 76ers. I arrived with the Sixers in 1968 as a 28-year-old business manager for the team. Jack knew the NBA inside out and could write with a real zing. He was never afraid to tell it as he saw it—every day!

8. George Kiseda. The writer from the old *Philadelphia Evening Bulletin* was a contemporary of Jack Kiser and what a writer he was. Known as the Silver Quill for his snow-white hair, Kiseda had writing talent beyond the typical sportswriter. He later moved to the *Los Angeles Times* to work on the desk, one of the great losses the NBA press corps could suffer.

6 (tie). Leonard Koppett and Terry Pluto. Koppett reminded me of a college professor with his striped suits, upright walk, and tortoise-rimmed glasses. He wrote about the NBA for the *New York Times* in a very professional manner that appealed to a highbrow audience. Years ago he published a book, *24 Seconds to Shoot*, that is still one of my favorites.

Pluto wrote about his Cavaliers for the *Akron Beacon Journal* and *Cleveland Plain Dealer* with passion and gusto, as if they were members of his own family. He still does, with his frank and entertaining columns for the *Plain Dealer*.

5. Mark Heisler. The former writer for the *Los Angeles Times* covered the Lakers for years. I first met Mark when he was covering the 76ers and I was the general manager of the franchise. Mark is a fountain of information. I love to talk with him and pick his brain about all things NBA.

4. Sam Smith. The veteran writer was the Bulls beat man for the *Chicago Tribune* during the Jordan years. Another NBA guru who knew all and wasn't afraid to write about it. He was the perfect writer to be covering MJ's exploits and telling the world what was happening behind the scenes. I loved to read him, and still do.

3. Phil Jasner. The Hall of Fame writer from the *Philadelphia Daily News* died of colon cancer in December 2010. I miss him every day, as does the entire NBA family. You could call Phil day or night to get the latest news, retrieve a long lost phone number, or chat about life in Philly. Phil's son, Andy, carries on in his dad's footsteps and has very big shoes to fill. Nobody covered the NBA like Phil.

2. Pete Vecsey. The legendary columnist writes columns for the *New York Post* that are must-reads for NBA executives, players, and fans. Pete has sources like none other and reveals them in newsy notes that are flush with humor and thought-provoking observations, often funny and insightful at the same time.

1. Bob Ryan. The *Boston Globe* writer is so well established as the *Globe's* all-around sports columnist that we forget he was the *Globe's* Celtics beat writer for years. Mr. Ryan enjoys the NBA scene and still writes about it with a loving, but at times scolding, pen. To really appreciate Bob's basketball writing talents, read his regular column for *Basketball Times*. That's Ryan at his very best.

The 10 Biggest Changes in NBA History
:: by Pat Williams

The more things change in the NBA . . . the more things change. Since its birth in 1949, the league has grown, merged, and changed, changed, and changed some more. Fans who cheered on George Mikan as he led the Minneapolis Lakers to the 1950 NBA championship would have hardly recognized the Jerry West and Wilt Chamberlin–led Los Angeles Lakers of the 1970s, or Magic's Showtime teams in the 1980s, much less the Laker squads that Kobe and Shaq took to titles in the 21st century. But it's hard to believe those early fans would not be amazed and thrilled with how the game of pro basketball has changed over the decades. Here are the 10 most significant changes the NBA has seen along the way.

10. Length of the Season. When I watched the Paul Arizin-led Philadelphia Warriors beat the Fort Wayne Pistons for the NBA championship in 1956 at the Philadelphia Convention Center, the season ended on April 7. Now the season ends in the third week of June, and is soon followed by the NBA Draft, and then free-agent signings. It's truly a year-round league now.

9. New Arenas. Every city has a state of the art facility with all the bells and whistles. Our facility in Orlando, which was built in 2010 for $480 million, is proof of this.

8. League Office Staff. In 1968, when I started in the NBA, the league office employed four people—and that included the commissioner. Now the NBA employs 2,500 staff members around the world.

7. All-Star Weekend. When I first came into the league, the All-Star Game was played on Monday night to get it over with as quickly as possible. The players flew in before the game, had lunch, played, and went home. Now it is one of the premier sporting events in the world. It's so big that only certain cities have enough hotel rooms and convention space to accommodate the crowds that arrive for the four-day festival.

6. Media. When Wilt Chamberlain scored 100 points in March of 1962, there wasn't one writer at the game. Philadelphia Warriors PR man Harvey Pollack had to write the wire reports and every article. Now there is instant information on Twitter and the worldwide web 24 hours a day.

5. Coaching Staffs. In my first year in the league there wasn't one assistant coach. There was a head coach and a trainer who also served as the traveling secretary. Now there are more people working in each team's video room than worked in the league office four decades ago.

4. Salaries. When I was working with the Chicago Bulls in the late 1960s and early '70s, the team's starting center, Tom Boerwinkle, was making $20,000 a year. To secure Chet Walker's services we had to offer him $160,000 over three years and we were scared to death about coming up with that much money. Now our center with the Orlando Magic makes $19.5 million—that's $59,451 for *every quarter of every game* for a whole season.

3. Olympics. When the Dream Team went to the Olympics in 1992, they changed the face of basketball forever. The best players in the world played on the world's biggest stage, and the world watched. Now NBA broadcasts are shown in every almost every country where NBA shirts and hats and other merchandise are bought and worn.

2. International Athletes. The very thought of NBA rosters including players from outside the United States seemed unthinkable back in the 1970s. Now rosters are populated with players from European, African, Asian, Australian, South American, and neighboring North American countries. NBA MVPs Tim Duncan, Hakeem Olajuwon, Steve Nash and Dirk Nowitzki all came from countries other than the US.

1. Value of Franchises. In 1989, the Orlando Magic entered the league at an assessment of $32.5 million. According to *Forbes* magazine, the Los Angeles Lakers are currently valued at $900 million. In cemeteries all over America previous NBA owners are rolling in their graves.

Top 10 Most Colorful NBA Owners of All Time :: by Peter Vecsey

Peter Vecsey is the longtime NBA columnist for the *New York Post*, an analyst on NBA TV, and the 2009 recipient of the Basketball Hall of Fame Curt Gowdy Media Award. Known for his sarcastic wit and ability to deliver the inside scoop, his nickname is "the Viper." A colorful character in his own right, here is his take on the league's most extraordinary owners.

Honorable Mention. Dick Tinkham (Indiana Pacers); Tedd Munchak (Carolina Cougars); Ned Doyle (Miami Floridians); Bill Daniels (Utah Stars); B. J. "Red" McCombs (San Antonio Spurs, Denver Nuggets); John Y. Brown (Kentucky Colonels); Charlie Finley (Memphis Tams); Angelo Drossos (San Antonio Spurs); Roy Boe (New York Nets); Earl Foreman (Virginia Squires); Jackie Moon (Flint Tropics).

10. Donald Sterling (Clippers). An indefatigable self-promoter. Another day, another full-page ad in the *LA Times*—most pertaining to real estate, some listing charities he purportedly bequeaths. Comes off as almost childlike, but is harmless as a harpoon. Diverse discrimination suits and consequent huge settlements appear not to faze him. Bought the franchise in 1981 for half a million dollars less than dismissed coach/GM Mike Dunleavy was awarded June 11, 2011, in an arbitration hearing. Numerous coaches and scouts were similarly forced to sue for non-payment.

In the past few years, Sterling uncharacteristically went deeper into his bottomless pockets to sign or keep free agents. Acquiring Chris Paul to showcase alongside Blake Griffin, matching DeAndre Jordan's $43 million offer sheet and recruiting Caron Butler showed that Sterling, at long last, is ready to compete for real with the Lakers for media attention, fan affection, and marketable adulation.

Heckling his players, humiliating executives and haranguing David Stern at Board of Governor functions, of course, are expected to remain a few of Sterling's favorite things. He can't help being himself, which also means: sincerely asking everyone he comes in contact with for advice about his team and soundly disregarding it; offering phantom jobs to national columnists; and constantly rearranging the courtside seating chart. Depending on the number of demicelebs that show up, you can start the game two chairs removed from The Donald West at tip-off and be escorted by him to the end of the row by the second quarter.

9. Ted Stepien (Cavaliers). He wanted to win in the worst way and didn't hesitate to employ those worst ways. In 1981, he sanctioned the signings of free agents Otis Birdsong, Scott Wedman, James Edwards, and Bobby Wilkerson to unjustifiably lofty contracts, including unprecedented attendance bonuses. That triggered the league's thought process to establish a salary cap at the outset of the 1984–85 season. Another rule activated by Stepien is the prohibition against trading No. 1 picks in successive seasons. He dealt them as if Cleveland had a relentlessly replenishing lifetime supply. However, the masses are loud wrong to indict him for the 1980 trade that sent a first-round choice to the Lakers (who converted it into James Worthy, pick of the 1982 litter) for Don Ford. That was head coach Stan Albeck's doing. He had just arrived from LA, where he'd been infatuated with the faux forward as a three-year assistant under Jerry West.

Stepien's greatest claim to shame? He fired Chuck Daly. The 1981–82 season in Cleveland was Daly's first and last losing experience (9-32) as a professional coach in his 14-year Hall of Fame career.

8. John Y. Brown (Braves/Celtics). In 1964, he obtained Kentucky Fried Chicken from Colonel Sanders for $2 million and built it into one of the world's largest food service companies. Before buying into the NBA for $10,000 cash and a $1.5 million loan, his Hubie Brown-coached ABA Kentucky Colonels won the 1975 championship. His marriage to Phyllis (Miss America) George certainly increased percentage points on name recognition when he entered politics and became Kentucky's 55th governor (1979–83). In retrospect, he turned out to be fairly good and pretty effective at that, so I'm told.

But what John Why is probably best known for is orchestrating the most remarkable trade in professional sports history. After acquiring half ownership of the NBA's Buffalo Braves in 1977, and later buying the rest from Paul Snyder, he explored shifting the franchise to Minnesota. However, upon discovering that Celtics' owner Irv Levin, who lived in California, wanted to move to San Diego, Brown swapped the Braves (deferrals and all) for the Celts straight up. A year later, he acquired Bob McAdoo from the Knicks without Red Auerbach's knowledge, much less approval. Red on Roundball was so hot he "seriously" entertained accepting an offer from Madison Square Garden President Sonny Werblin to run the Knicks. With the city of Boston in riot gear, John sold the Celtics to minority partner Harry Mangurian.

7. Ted Turner (Hawks). A rapacious risk taker. Knows when to hold 'em. Not known to fold 'em. America's Cup challengers and contenders in promotional contests attest to his competitive soul. Ted loved to enter celebrity contests. The Braves staged one in which an active player lined up at first base with Ted at third. They'd race to home pushing a baseball with only face and nose; no hands or feet allowed. A picture of his wild-eyed, winning smile, bloody from head to chin, was on the cover of his first bio.

Ted toyed with the idea of making Hubie Brown coach of the Hawks and manager of the Braves, an inspiration probably not taken that seriously by Brown. Clearly, it was not an idle thought, as evidenced by Stan Kasten being named president of both Atlanta teams. CNN was just getting off the ground and in need of funding (a lot of bankers hung around the Mouth of the South in the '80s) when Kasten proposed an acquisition of great magnitude at a board meeting in late summer of 1982. A studly rising rookie was available for $1 million cash. Utah Jazz owner Sam Battistone urgently needed the money to keep his franchise afloat. Turner turned to the CFO and asked, "Can we get a million from the bank?" The CFO responded definitively, "No!" Turner turned to Kasten and said, "Get him!" Dominique Wilkins led the Hawks to eight playoff appearances in 11 seasons, became a nine-time All-Star, and was branded the Human Highlight Film.

6. Harold Katz (76ers). Employees called his fiscal approach Katzonomics. He was the first owner to cut out food in the press room. "Why should I feed the media when they're on expense accounts?" he reasoned. Head coaches, assistants and scouts might've been more upset with that policy than members of the media.

To his credit, Harold went deep into his pocket for players. Moses Malone's $13.2 million, six-year free-agent contract was the NBA's richest in 1982. To his discredit, he commanded at least one coach to reduce a player's daylight during a down season when he got close to earning a sizeable perk for averaging x-amount of minutes.

Harold was infamous for his equal opportunity rages following painfully unacceptable defeats and no-sweat efforts. Within minutes, he'd rip the GM outside the locker room, the coach inside it, and get in the faces of players. Harold's specialty, though, was meddling morning, noon, and night. He really wanted Charles Barkley in the 1984 NBA Draft. However, once he got him, his coach, Billy Cunningham, stuck with Marc Iavaroni at power forward; Cunningham wanted Sir Cumference to win the starting spot on merit, not get it as a gift. After three weeks, Harold called GM Pat Williams and told him to relocate Iavaroni. A dozen games into the season, Marc was sent to San Antonio.

5. Jack Kent Cooke (Lakers). Nobody's sure why a Canadian would buy a basketball team. Legend has it he was convinced it'd be a good investment after driving around LA and seeing many homes with hoops in driveways. A Fabulous Forum usher once found a $20 bill after a game. He brought it to Jack the next day and said he worked Section 6 and maybe fans in that area could be asked if anyone lost it. Jack praised him and said he was proud to have such an honest employee. He told the guy to look for something extra in his next paycheck. But the pay was the same. Then the guy saw something else in the envelope. It was an autographed picture of Cooke.

Some people delicately label Jack "quite frugal." The less subtle in the species brand him "cheap in seven languages." When Bill Sharman became the Lakers' coach he asked Jack if he could hire an assistant, and was told, "I have at least fifty employees and I don't have an assistant, so I don't see why you need one." He finally gave in. Bill hired K. C. Jones.

Bill Sharman was one of the first coaches to use film to pinpoint errors and perfectly executed plays. Bill Bertka was hired to handle that chore. He'd stay up all night to splice footage together so it could be shown at the team meeting the next day. The old projector had hiccups. Bertka often had to hold a pencil in the reel to make it work. Sharman asked Cocke for a new projector and was told, "Now, Bill, no one else in the league does this so I don't know why we have to spend money on a new one." When Bill reported back to the staff he'd been turned down, Chick Hearn said, "Let me talk to him. I'm sure I can convince him." After his meeting, Hearn came back to Sharman and said, "Wow, is he tough! No projector!" So, during the Lakers' 33-game winning streak in 1971, Sharman and Bertka were forced to show film to the players while holding the projector together with a pencil.

4. Larry Miller (Jazz). No owner has ever been more emotionally and wholesomely committed to his state, city, and fans than this swashbuckling entrepreneur who regarded the team as a community asset. Hence, his rejection of numerous offers to sell it at a colossal profit (he purchased half the franchise in 1985 from Sam Battistone for $9 million and bought the remainder a year later) from groups poised to relocate it.

Larry went from being a stock boy in an auto parts store to becoming the tenth largest U.S. automotive dealer. Sensitive to seismic proportions, appropriately, he would cry at the blink of a brake light. Mistaking that as a weakness was a reckless underestimation. He was equally likely to get it on in a flash with those who displeased, crossed, or challenged him. Stories about his father-son battles with Karl Malone remain a mesmeric topic of conversation, as is the Mailman's tender hospital care of Larry when he was dying.

Larry's impulsive bursts from his nearby courtside seat into a Jerry Sloan huddle to criticize players' lack of effort/execution prompted Stern to order Miller to the opposite side of the arena. He quickly rescinded his decree; it seems Larry was listening in on opponents' huddles.

When traveling with the team, he would wear a Jazz uniform on the charter. When the team was home, Larry would shoot around and sometimes join his players on the layup line. Frank Layden never tires telling how Miller would sing in the shower, and then come out butt-naked and talk to one or two players as he was giving his pregame speech.

3. Mark Cuban (Mavericks). His biggest challenge is himself. The forward-thinking, self-synchronized billionaire relishes his regular-guy reflection: weight room workout fanatic; decent pregame jump shooter who frequently attended Michael Jordan's Las Vegas fantasy camp; steady scruffy look—T-shirt, jeans, tennis shoes, unruly hairstyle—regardless of pomp or circumstance; and a seemingly strategized unwillingness to undertake the practices that being good in a boardroom setting require . . . which means a slower, more intimate, last-century, consensus-building process that conflicts with his 4G, hi-def, 3-D world view.

As a result, Mark's impulsive proposals lobbed into NBA Board of Governors meetings, without the benefit of a presale, freak out the older and more conservative businessmen, directing his most poisonous barbs at Commissioner David Stern and others (particularly Stu Jackson) in the league office. Contrary to his image, Mark often is right about the issues he takes issue with—referee training and evaluation, team websites, the use of third-party writers to get a message out about his team, etc. Over the long haul, those seeds often take root and grow into real change, albeit without any credit to his efforts. If he ever became smooth in the way of boardroom politics, he'd be a killer. Regarding their adversarial relationship, Stern quipped, "I don't take it personally or seriously. It's all shtick with Mark. If I didn't exist, he would've invented me."

2. Jerry Buss (Lakers). The Hall of Fame owner knows his limitations, and then tries to exceed them. Has anyone ever spotted him without a barely legal feline by his side? And another beauty two years younger on his other side? Or surrounded by a Staples Center suite of 'em?

The majority of owners park behind their team's bench or at courtside. In 1979, when Buss bought the franchise, the Fabulous Forum and NHL Kings from Jack Kent Cooke for $67.5 million, he couldn't afford to give away the most valued locations to friends and family. So he blocked off 60 seats to the very rear of the press at the visitor's end. That's where he entertained. Whenever fans complained about paying $100 for on-the-floor sight lines, he'd tell them the Lakers had $7 tickets available. "Who'd want to sit there?" was the common response. "I do." One night his guest list included Muhammad Ali. Early on, he moved down to courtside and commandeered a front-row spot. Afterward, the Champ thanked Buss for his hospitality, "but you sit in the worst seats."

Buss was first to recognize the reward of a high-octane presentation (Showtime) orchestrated by a maestro (Magic Johnson) and marketed it accordingly. People in the business of being seen at exclusive events shelled out once-unimaginable sums ($2,500 per game) to be on top of the winning (the operative word) action that began with a title (ten altogether) in Buss' baptism season. In 1990, Mike Dunleavy replaced Pat Riley and radically changed the team's offensive style from run 'n' stun to pick-and-roll. It wasn't a smooth transition, with one victory in five games. Following the fourth defeat, by one point, at home to the Suns, the rookie coach told the players, "We're getting better and better each game. I believe in you and I believe in our half-court line of attack." Before he could finish, a ball boy notified him, "Dr. Buss wants to see you in his office." Dunleavy braced for a cold wind. "A month ago," Buss began, "We thought we were some of the smartest mother-bleepers for hiring you. Well, we still think we are. Relax and coach the way you see fit." The Lakers won eight of their next ten and lost to the Bulls in the Finals.

1. Franklin Mieuli (Warriors). The precursor of Mark Cuban. An offbeat character who once showed up at a game in bare feet and always boasted a boisterous black beard and Sherlock Holmes cap. Franklin often walked the beach at Half Moon Bay—an hour from San Francisco, past the Santa Cruz mountain range—picking up assorted shells, colored pebbles . . . who knows, maybe seaweed.

In his office on Golden Gate Avenue he housed two dozen figurine statues of hands. Yes, hands! Small ones, large ones, medium-sized, wooden, glass, plaster of paris, etc. Nobody had the nerve to ask him why. His collection seemed almost sacred. Old writer friends called him, "Mule-y" because of his stubborn pursuit of Rick Barry after Have Jump Shot, Will Travel absconded to the ABA.

Before the three-point shot was introduced into the NBA, debates on its merits and downside took place. Prior to the final vote at a Board of Governors meeting, Franklin made an impassioned plea in opposition. Former Utah Jazz owner Sam Battistone vividly recalls his closing remarks: "We cannot tamper with the family jewels of NBA basketball." David Stern remembers him saying, "We don't need another earring on the pig. If the three-point shot is voted into the game, this will be the last meeting I will attend," he proclaimed. Stern and Battistone confirm Franklin never returned.

The Top Milwaukee Bucks
:: by Eddie Doucette

Eddie Doucette has broadcast NBA basketball games for over three decades, including almost two decades of broadcasting for the Milwaukee Bucks. He compiled the following list after evaluating the overall contributions of Bucks players, coaches, and owners—through either their achievements on the floor, their front office decision making, or their presence in the community. Coming up with the top 10 was no easy task. "Some of the players I've chosen made the list over others who may have had better career statistics," said Doucette. "But when measuring all the things done while representing the organization, they got the nod. After doing this list, I know now how difficult it is for coaches and management to cut down "on-the-bubble" players.

"Apologies to Brian Winters (whose number is retired), Marques Johnson, Ray Allen, Glenn Robinson, and a few others who merited serious consideration. Thank you for the thrills you provided Bucks fans."

12. Bob Dandridge. The Greyhound was a fourth-round draft pick in 1969. Bobby played eight-plus seasons for the Bucks and is one of the most unheralded players in league history. He was on the Kareem-Oscar NBA title team in 1970-71, when he averaged 18.4 per game (19.0 for his entire Milwaukee career). As good as he was offensively, he was that good or better at the defensive end, drawing the toughest opponent to guard each game. One former member of the championship team said, "We don't win it without Bobby Dandridge."

11. Bob Lanier. For his 14 seasons in the NBA, this eight-time All-Star scored 19,248 points and was inducted into the Basketball Hall of Fame. Big Bob was a major contributor to five consecutive division titles in the 1980s by the Bucks. He was the "hub" of Don Nelson's most successful Bucks teams.

10. Junior Bridgeman. Came to the Bucks as part of the trade that sent KAJ to the Lakers. In the sixth man's nine and a half years in Milwaukee he played in more games than any player in the team's history. He totaled almost 10,000 points and was a key contributor to five consecutive Central Division titles. A quality individual, his number is retired. His post-playing career has been exemplary in the business and community world.

9. Sidney Moncrief. Played for the Bucks during some prolific years in the '80s. His Bucks teams won 50 or more games and appeared in the playoffs in seven straight seasons. Sid played both ends of the floor adroitly, but defense was his specialty. He was voted to the NBA's All-Defensive first team four times.

He was the league's first-ever Defensive Player of the Year Award winner. He also was a five-time NBA All-Star and remains third on the Bucks' all-time scoring list. Moncriefs's No. 4 jersey has been hanging from the Bradley Center rafters since January 1990.

7 (tie). Jim Fitzgerald and Herb Kohl. Fitz purchased the team in 1976 from the Pavalon ownership group. Jim would dub his early ownership era and the young team the "Green and Growing." Eventually, the Don Nelson-coached Bucks won five consecutive Central Division titles. The Fitzgerald group eventually took less money to make sure the team stayed in Wisconsin. He sold to local businessman and future US Senator Herb Kohl in 1985. Kohl has been extremely patient and not afraid to spend money for talent. Both native Wisconsinites are to be applauded for their efforts to bring a winner to their home state.

6. Jon McGlocklin. The "original Buck" came to the team as an expansion draft player in 1968, and went on to become the club's first All-Star and a significant link on the 1971 championship team. No Buck has had more impact on the community or is more respected for his off-court works than Jonny Mac, the cofounder and president of the MACC FUND (Midwest Athletes Against Childhood Cancer). He is Mr. Buck.

4 (tie). Larry Costello and Don Nelson. The first and second coaches in Bucks history amassed 1,029 regular-season and playoff wins between 1968 and 1987. Coach Costello devised an offense that made Oscar Robertson and Lew Alcindor a devastating duo, and then built the supporting cast that complemented their skills, resulting in the 1971 championship and a near second title in 1974, when the Bucks lost in seven games to Boston in the Finals. In a little over eight years as coach, Costy won 447 games and a ring. He gave his rookie assistant Don Nelson a brief education in '76 before turning over the coaching responsibilities to him. Nelson and the "Green and Growing Bucks" grew together, wining five consecutive division titles. Nellie is the Bucks' winningest coach, with 582 victories.

3. Wes Pavalon and Partners. The original ownership group headed by Wes Pavalon had the vision to bring an expansion NBA franchise to Milwaukee in 1968. They combined their arrival with winning the coin flip for the rights to Lew Alcindor (aka Kareem Abdul-Jabbar), and then convinced Oscar Robertson to join the team, selling him on it being his best chance to win a much coveted ring. Wes and his partners made all the right moves while leading the franchise through its most successful era.

:: **Dirk Nowitzki.** This is a *fantasy selection*. Dirk was selected as the Bucks first-round pick in the 1998 draft. The Bucks then traded his rights, the 19th selection, and Pat Garrity, to Dallas for Robert "Tractor" Traylor, who had been the sixth overall selection. Milwaukee fans have run the "what-if" drill through their minds ever since. Combine his talents with a city that prides itself as the home of a huge German population and it would have resulted in instant magic. Oh well!

2. Oscar Robertson. The Big O was arguably the best big guard to ever to play in the league. Oscar joined the Bucks in Lew Alcindor/Kareem Abdul-Jabbar's second season, and they immediately formed a devastating KO combination, leading the Bucks to the 1971 NBA championship and NBA Finals in 1974. In his four years in Milwaukee, the Bucks averaged 62 wins a season. Oscar gave the Bucks the leadership they needed. He never took defeat kindly and was a coach on the floor at all times. He is the biggest reason the Bucks won the ring he wanted so badly before his playing days ended.

1. Kareem Abdul-Jabbar. He joined the Bucks as Lew Alcindor for the franchise's second season in 1969 and led the Bucks to 56 wins—a 29-win improvement from the season prior to his arrival. At the time it was the biggest one-year turnaround in NBA history. Boy, it was fun! The next year the Bucks won 66 games and dominated the playoffs to win the NBA championship, with KAJ receiving the first of three NBA MVP Awards that he earned in his six years with the Bucks. He averaged 31.7 points and 16 rebounds a game in only his second season. He remains the team's all-time leading scorer and rebounder, with averages of 30 points and 15 rebounds a game. There's no question that the attention he drew created sports-world awareness for the Bucks, the city of Milwaukee, and the state of Wisconsin.

Top 10 Chicago Bulls of All Time
:: by K. C. Johnson

K. C. Johnson has covered the Chicago Bulls since 1990—including the magical three-peat years of 1996 to 1998—for the *Chicago Tribune*. As for the contents of this list, he offers "apologies to early franchise stalwarts like Jerry Sloan, Bob Love, and Johnny 'Red' Kerr, but six championships earn the most cache. Thus, Michael Jordan, Scottie Pippen, and Phil Jackson, occupy the top-three spots."

10. Chet Walker. The Michigan graduate played for the Bulls from 1969 to 1975. During that time, he averaged over 20 points a game while being selected an All-Star four times.

9. Artis Gilmore. The A Train, Gilmore, entered the Hall of Fame in 2011, a long overdue acknowledgement of the gentle giant's achievements and supreme scoring ability.

8. Norm Van Lier. Originally drafted by the Bulls in the third round of the 1969 draft, Van Lier was traded to the Cincinnati Royals only to be traded back one year later to Chicago. As a Bull, he was chosen to play in three All-Star Games and was first-team or second-team All-Defensive seven times.

7. Jerry Krause. Though a polarizing figure, and one who inherited Jordan, Krause did manage six title teams with shrewd acquisitions like Toni Kukoc and Scottie Pippen.

6. Bob Love. Love isn't in the Hall of Fame, but his Bulls jersey is retired for his silky smooth scoring ability through much of the 1970s.

5. Johnny "Red" Kerr. Kerr was the face of the franchise before his passing. He topped his own stellar playing career for other teams by guiding the expansion 1966–67 Bulls to the playoffs as a coach, and later serving as business manager and longtime passionate broadcaster for the team.

4. Jerry Sloan. Speaking of passion, the fiery Sloan, whose jersey is retired, served as the defensive backbone of the Bulls near-miss teams in the mid-1970s. Sloan also later coached the franchise.

3. Phil Jackson. Undeniably the most decorated coach, Jackson won six titles with the Bulls and would go on to win five more with the Lakers.

2. Scottie Pippen. The seven-time All-Star is arguably the most versatile defender ever to play the game. The Hall of Famer was selected to eight NBA All-Defensive teams.

1. Michael Jordan. The five-time MVP is arguably the greatest player in NBA history. Over his career, he led his Bulls to six championships. The 14-time All-Star was not only one of the greatest offensive players, but one of the league's greatest defenders, earning eight selections to the NBA All-Defensive team.

Top 10 Individuals to Impact the Cleveland Cavaliers :: by Terry Pluto

Terry Pluto is a columnist with the *Cleveland Plain Dealer*. He has written over twenty books, including *Loose Balls*, which is ranked 13th on the *Sports Illustrated* list of greatest sports books. He has twice been honored by the Associated Press as the top national columnist amongst his peers.

10. World B. Free. No one knows the Cavs better than Joe Tait, and he says Free belongs on this list because he brought a ray of hope coming out of the darkness of the Ted Stepien era.

9. Lenny Wilkens. Hired by Wayne Embry, Wilkens won more games than any other Cavs coach. He also played 149 games for the team in the early years, averaging 18.5 points and 7.4 assists a game.

8. Wayne Embry. The classy general manager brought about one of the best eras of Cavs basketball in the late 1980s and early 1990s by bringing in the likes of Brad Daugherty, Mark Price, and Larry Nance.

7. Brad Daugherty. The team's second-best player after James, but had his career cut short, retiring at age 28 because of a back injury.

6. Nick Mileti. The owner who brought the Cavs to Cleveland. He'd be higher, but he sold the franchise to Ted Stepien, which nearly led to the end of pro basketball in Cleveland.

5. LeBron James. The best player in team history would be No. 1 on the list had he not left the team in such an insulting fashion.

4. Mark Price. The most beloved Cavs player, regaining that title after LeBron James bolted.

3. Bill Fitch. The team's first coach and general manager put together the Cavs first playoff team—the 1975–76 squad known as the "Miracle of Richfield."

2. Gordon Gund. He purchased the team from Ted Stepien, who nearly ruined the franchise.

1. Joe Tait. A broadcaster who was there from the beginning and the person most associated with the Cavs in the minds of the fans.

Steve Bulpett has served as a beat writer covering the Boston Celtics dating back to the days of the original Big Three in the 1980s. He observed that "trying to fit the contributors from 17 NBA championship teams onto such a list is roughly the equivalent of asking Shaq to squeeze into his rookie uniform." But he did it.

Honorable Mention. Owner Walter Brown; Dennis Johnson; K. C. Jones; Bill Sharman; Robert Parish; Kevin Garnett. And what about Johnny Most, whose raspy-throated homerism marketed the team to generations, through dark days into glory?

10. Kevin McHale. While there are those who insist the last great low-post skill set retired with him, McHale was most valuable to the Celtics in another way. It was his ability to guard small forwards that allowed Larry Bird to roam and occasionally relax on defense. Things were never the same for the Celts after McHale played on a broken foot in the 1987 postseason.

9. Paul Pierce. He'll look even better with time and perspective, but no one can deny he's been perhaps the most well-rounded scorer in franchise history. He gets extra credit for embracing the team's history (after growing up a Lakers fan) and sticking things out through the bad times.

8. John Havlicek. Measured against Woody Allen's quote that 80 percent of success is showing up, Havlicek would be an all-time great, having played the most games in Celtic history. But he was so much more than that. This talented and tireless player bridged the championship eras of the 1960s and '70s.

7. Sam Jones. Sadly, he is often overlooked in the Celtic pantheon, but Sam Jones was the key offensive counterpoint to Bill Russell's work at the other end of the floor. And when the game was on the line, everyone on the team knew where the ball was going.

6. Tommy Heinsohn. Older folks know him as a Rookie of the Year, six-time All-Star, and Hall of Famer. Younger people know him as the team's TV color commentator, dispensing Tommy Points through green-colored glasses. In between, he found time to coach the Celtics to two championships, winning more than 61 percent of his games along the way.

5. Dave Cowens. He pulled the Celtics out of their post-Russell funk with a rugged work ethic that made him a league leader in floor burns. Listed at 6-9 (yeah, right), he never backed down against larger opponents—even when he was backing them down into the post for his killer drop-step move.

4. Bob Cousy. Red Auerbach refused to draft this "local yokel" out of Holy Cross, but fate smiled on the Celtics when owner Walter Brown picked Cousy's name out of a hat after the Chicago Stags folded. The Cooz made the Celts relevant in the area until Russell came along. Then he helped make them champions.

3. Larry Bird. His game appealed to the purists. His down-home nature and fierce attention to preparation endeared him to all. It is not hyperbole to say Bird and Magic Johnson rescued the NBA at a critical time, and Larry's litany of clutch shots elevated him to magical heights of his own. The Hick from French Lick became the toast of The Athens of America.

2. Bill Russell. His pride and strength as a human being cannot be separated from the man in sneakers. Bill Russell became the greatest winner in team sports history (11 championships in 13 seasons) because he had to live up to his own high standards. And while others put up better numbers, Russell's intellect allowed him to see through the stats to the heart of the game. It was there that he made himself great by making his teammates better.

1. Red Auerbach. A cantankerous brat of a man, he succeeded through the ages by finding players who shared his pathological disdain for losing. As coach and general manager, he guided the franchise to glory by laying down the law, and then empowering his players to enforce it. Along the way, he got the best from Russell and made him the coach, and then drafted Bird as a junior-eligible. Auerbach will forever be known as the patriarch of the franchise.

The 10 Most Memorable Clipper Personalities :: by Ralph Lawler

Ralph Lawler has been the radio and television voice of the Clippers dating back to 1978, when the team played in San Diego. Over his tenure he has called over 2.500 Clippers games. Here are the 10 figures he's seen make the greatest impact on the Clippers franchise.

10. Cedric Maxwell. Only with the Clippers for a colorful season and a half after winning two championships in Boston, but it was a memorable season and a half. One night, with the game on the line, he was bringing the ball in bounds in front of my broadcast. I suggested on the air that the ball was likely going to Marques Johnson. Max turned to me, shook his head 'No,' and said: "Nixon."

9. Derek Smith. A sad tale of what might have been. His career was transformed by Coach Jimmy Lynam, who turned the former Golden State power forward into a shooting guard. He was a bigger, stronger version of a young player named Michael Jordan. Derek was averaging 28 points a game when a serious knee injury in 1985 stripped him of his explosiveness. He was never again close to being the same player.

8. Danny Manning. The Kansas Jayhawk star was a reluctant Clipper when he was drafted first overall by the team in the 1988 NBA Draft. A series of knee injuries kept him from a possible Hall of Fame career. Still, he was a two-time All-Star with the Clippers, and later an NBA Sixth Man of the Year Award winner in Phoenix. A class act all the way.

7. Ron Harper. Harp was a stutterer, but he never let that keep him quiet. He was fun to be around and teammates loved playing with him. Younger fans, who remember him only for his time in Chicago and with the Lakers, are surprised to learn he averaged over 20 points a game in four separate seasons in his early years.

6. World B. Free. As colorful as the name he adopted after being born Lloyd Free. He was a forerunner of bigger-than-life stars such as Shaq O'Neal and Ron Artest. Oh, and he could score. He averaged over 20 points a game for eight straight seasons. In his two years with the Clippers in San Diego, he poured in 28.8 and 30.2 points per game!

5. Blake Griffin. Make that "No. 5 and rising." This young man's future knows no bounds. He is blazing new trails with the fervor of Lewis and Clark. We had to wait a year for his rookie season because of an injury in the preseason in 2009. He started impressively the following year but exploded into the public consciousness when he stunned the Knicks and the New York media with a 44-point, 15-rebound, 7-assist rookie masterpiece in only his 14th game as a pro. His dry sense of humor makes him a media "Natural."

4. Elgin Baylor. Truly one of the game's all-time great players, Baylor served as general manager for the Clippers for over 20 seasons. He was named NBA Executive of the Year in 2006. But I'll remember him as a master storyteller and as a man who never turned down a free game of golf; Elg once told me that he didn't like the game enough to pay for it. He was truly one of a kind.

3. Larry Brown. I'm not sure there's ever been a better coach of the game of basketball. The Clippers were a disappointing 22-25 when Larry replaced Mike Schuler as head coach in February of 1992. They were a better team the minute Brown assembled them on the practice floor. They won their first five games under Coach Brown and finished the season winning 23 of their final 35. The man can coach.

2. Donald T. Sterling. The longtime team owner is a master moneymaker. His defiant smuggling of the Clippers from San Diego to Los Angeles in 1984 was a bold and brilliant move. The fabulously successful real estate investor admits that owning a pro sports team is the most difficult challenge of his professional career.

1. Bill Walton. He is a Hall of Fame player who became a leading television sports commentator after overcoming a debilitating stuttering affliction. The Clippers made him the game's first million-dollar-a-year player as a free agent in 1979. He won two NBA championships and was a league MVP. Still, I'll remember him as a great friend and a truly great man who gives more to every relationship than he gets.

The 10 Most Important Figures in Grizzlies Franchise History :: by Geoffrey Calkins

Geoff Calkins, from the newspaper the *Commercial Appeal* in Memphis, was a lawyer from Harvard before entering the world of journalism. Within his "new" career, he has twice been named Best Sports Columnist in the country by the Associated Press and three times been named the Green Eyeshade Award for Best Columnist in the South.

10. Don Poier. Could go a lot of directions with No. 10. Tony Allen became the symbol of the grit-grind Grizzlies. Andy Dolich was the team president who oversaw the construction and development of FedExForum. But we'll go with Poier, the eloquent voice of the Grizzlies both in Vancouver and Memphis, who died of a heart attack during a road trip in 2005. Poier was a Canadian, but he grew to love his new Southern home. His warm, passionate style would have fit anywhere. And it was Poier who gave the team its first tag line, when Jason Williams hit a 3-pointer to win an early exhibition game. "Only in the movies and in Memphis," he said. When Battier hit a considerably more important 3-pointer to win that first playoff game in San Antonio, everyone remembered Poier's words.

9. Jerry West. Don't forget, the guy won the Executive of the Year Award for steering the Grizzlies into the playoffs for the first time. His smartest, most coura-geous decision was to hire Hubie Brown as coach. West himself will tell you that he was ultimately disappointed in his tenure in Memphis, but his willingness to sign on with the franchise and move to the city meant a lot to Memphians.

8. Pau Gasol. The team's first all-star, Gasol led the Grizzlies to three straight playoff appearances. But his deferential, team-first personality made him a better fit as a second option in Los Angeles.

7. The Pursuit Team. This group could rank higher, honestly. It's the collec-tion of Memphians who got it in their heads that the city could attract an NBA team. Pitt Hyde and Staley Cates were the two central figures, but there were plenty of others involved. Their original idea was to buy a franchise themselves, but they settled for coaxing Heisley to move to town. If Heisley ever decides to sell or move the team, you can be certain they'll reemerge.

6. Hubie Brown. Memphis loved the guy. He became a civic grandfather—except this grandfather could coach. Ask any Grizzlies fan to rank the top five moments in franchise history, and they'll include the night that Brown accepted the Coach of the Year Award before the team's first home playoff game.

5. Chris Wallace. You won't find Wallace ranked above Jerry West on many lists, but he unquestionably outperformed the Logo as general manager of the Grizzlies. It was Wallace who engineered the much-maligned trade that sent Pau Gasol to the Lakers in exchange for (among other things) Pau's little brother, Marc. The trade also gave Wallace the cap space to deal for Randolph's contract. Pau won two titles with the Lakers, but Marc and Z-Bo became the guts of the new Grizzlies.

4. Shane Battier. Maybe the most beloved Memphis player ever. He was picked behind Gasol in the team's first draft in Memphis, but it was Battier—the National College Player of the Year out of Duke—who gave the team instant credibility in a new market. When Battier was later traded to Houston for the pick that became Rudy Gay, he said his only regret was that he didn't win a playoff game in Memphis—something he took care of during a brief second tour with the team, when he hit the winning 3-pointer to lift the Grizzlies over the Spurs in the 2011 playoffs.

3. Zach Randolph. After three other NBA stops, Z-Bo found a home in Memphis. He may or may not be a better power forward than Pau Gasol, but he's a better fit with this hardscrabble city. And unlike Gasol, he led the Grizzlies to their first playoff victory.

2. Lionel Hollins. For the longest time, Hubie Brown ranked as the most significant Grizzlies coach, but Hollins has surpassed him. The Grizzlies were floundering in Memphis before Hollins came in and fashioned a blue-collar, winning culture.

1. Mike Heisley. He's blunt and bombastic, but he's changed nearly everything about the franchise, including its location. Among his greatest hits: hiring Lionel Hollins as head coach when nobody else would; dealing for Zach Randolph; handing fat contracts to Randolph, Rudy Gay and Marc Gasol; persuading Jerry West to move to Memphis as team president. All that, plus Heisley sang the national anthem at the team's first home playoff game.

The 10 Atlanta/Milwaukee/St. Louis/Tri-Cities (Black)Hawks Who Left the Biggest Imprint on the Franchise :: by Bob Rathbun

Bob Rathbun has been the voice of the Atlanta Hawks since 1996. He has been awarded Sportscaster of the Year in both Virginia and Georgia. He gives kudos to the top figures in the long history of one of the NBA's original franchises.

10. Joe Johnson. Many have scoffed at the Hawks for giving Joe a max contract, but he has been one of the most productive players in Atlanta history. Joe is one of only 10 active players, through the 2011–12 season, to be selected to play in the NBA All-Star Game in six consecutive seasons.

9. Wayne "Tree" Rollins. The Hawks have a tradition of great centers, and Tree stood among the tallest. Tree still holds the franchise record for most blocks in a career (2,283), in a season (343), and in a game (12).

8. Steve Smith. Although his Hawks tenure was relatively brief, Smitty made quite an impact on the franchise. During his five years with the Hawks he was named an Eastern Conference All-Star in 1998. After his playing career, he rejoined the Hawks as a TV analyst and has made Atlanta his home since his playing days here.

7. Glenn "Doc" Rivers. Long before his coaching days in Orlando and Boston, Doc Rivers was the Hawks coach on the floor. One of the greatest point guards in Hawks history, Doc still holds the team's all-time assist record. Originally a 1983 second-round pick of the Hawks, Doc was an All-Star in Atlanta and won the Walter Kennedy Sportsmanship Award.

6. Lou Hudson. He earned his nickname "Sweet Lou" from his silky jumper. Hudson joined the Hawks in St. Louis in 1966 and became one of Atlanta's biggest stars when the franchise moved to Georgia in 1968. Hudson is the third-leading scorer in franchise history, and was a six-time All-Star for the Hawks. His No. 23 has been retired.

5. Dikembe Mutombo. The man with the NBA's longest name had a far-reaching impact when he arrived in Atlanta as a free agent in the summer of 1996. He won two of his four NBA Defensive Player of the Year Awards with the Hawks, and had fans wagging their index fingers after every block. Deke still holds Philips Arena records for most rebounds (29) and blocks (11) in a game.

4. Pistol Pete Maravich. After his amazing college career at LSU, Pete took Atlanta by storm in 1970. He averaged 23 ppg as a rookie, and by his fourth season was at 27 ppg. Despite the fact that chemistry issues derailed his time as a Hawk, his four-year run here was spellbinding. The Hall of Famer passed way before his time, at age 40, less than two decades after the Hawks made him the third overall pick in the NBA Draft.

3. Bob Pettit. The man who invented the position of power forward in the NBA, Pettit played all of his time as a Hawk in Milwaukee and St. Louis. He was the centerpiece to the franchise's only NBA championship, won over the Celtics in 1958. One of the 50 Greatest Players in NBA History, Petit still holds the Finals record for points in a deciding game—the 50 he scored in the clinching Game Six of the 1958 NBA Finals against the Celtics.

2. Lenny Wilkens. Lenny edges out Pettit for second because of his overall impact. Wilkens was a Hall of Fame player for the Hawks in St. Louis in the 1960s and returned to coach the team in Atlanta in the 1990s. While with the Hawks, he became the NBA's all-time winningest coach, breaking Red Auerbach's record in 1995. He added the Hall of Fame's highest honor as a coach, and was the only man named as both one of the Top 10 Coaches and 50 Greatest Players in NBA History.

1. Dominique Wilkins. No denying the top spot to the Human Highlight Film. Even today, almost two decades after he last played a game for Atlanta, Nique remains the franchise's top personality. Wilkins was a nine-time All-Star, two-time Slam Dunk Contest winner, and a former league scoring champion. He remains the Hawks all-time leading scorer. Wilkins is still employed by the Hawks as a team vice president and serves as the color analyst on its television broadcasts.

The 10 People Who Left the Deepest Impact on the Miami Heat :: by Ira Winderman

Ira Winderman has covered the Miami Heat for over two decades for the *South Florida Sun Sentinel*. Below, Ira offers his take on the top 10 figures in the short but significant history of the Miami Heat—a franchise that's grown in a quarter century from being an expansion team, to an NBA champion, to a destination of choice for top players.

10. Rony Seikaly. The center out of Syracuse not only was the franchise's first draft choice, but also stood as the face of the franchise over the team's formative years. In many ways, his growth as a player coincided with the franchise's growth from its infancy. In 1990, he was named the NBA's Most Improved Player, one of only two Heat players ever to receive the honor (Ike Austin was named in 2006). As cosmopolitan as Miami itself, the European-raised center was the perfect fit at the franchise's inception.

9. Ira Rothstein. The franchise's first coach not only oversaw the team's first three seasons, but later returned to Miami to guide the Heat-owned Miami Sol of the WNBA, with his third go-round with the Heat coming as an assistant coach at Pat Riley's side during the team's 2005–06 championship run. Rothstein, in fact, has served as an assistant under three Heat coaches: Riley, Stan Van Gundy, and Erik Spoelstra.

8. Billy Cunningham. While theatrical impresario Zev Bufman and longtime NBA executive Lewis Schaffel stood at the heart of the franchise's expansion bid in 1988, it was the likeable former Philadelphia 76ers forward who stood as the focus of that effort, later moving into a lead personnel position in the front office. While many Heat fans had never heard or Schaffel or Bufman, Cunningham was coming off a successful run as 76ers coach, lending instant credibility to the Heat.

7. LeBron James. By the time his Heat tenure is over, James certainly could rise to the top of this list—if his and his team's expectations are met. When James agreed to leave the contending Cleveland Cavaliers to join the Heat as a free agent in the 2010 offseason, it showed just how impactful the allure of South Beach and a Pat Riley-led front office had become. James' signing clearly stands as the most significant free-agent signing over the team's first 23 seasons.

6. Tim Hardaway. Hardaway arguably stands as the most impactful player in franchise history, considering the amount of big shots and big plays he made as point guard in the late 1990s. While Alonzo Mourning was viewed as the face of the franchise over that period, it was Hardaway who orchestrated the team's most memorable offensive possessions. From the killer crossover to the look-down three-pointer, Hardaway left an enduring impression.

5. Shaquille O'Neal. After so many years of contending, it was only after O'Neal was acquired from the Lakers in the 2004 offseason that the Heat made the final step to becoming NBA champions, with O'Neal anchoring the 2006 title team. He was still near his peak when added at the considerable cost of Lamar Odom, Caron Butler, and Brian Grant. O'Neal offered the needed inside component to complement the perimeter game of Dwyane Wade.

4. Alonzo Mourning. Beyond the blocked shots, the dunks, the defensive tenacity, the passion that made Heat-Knicks of the late '90s the NBA's ultimate theater, Mourning emerged as the franchise's first community icon, with his charitable efforts that established a youth center not far from the Heat's home court, as well as the attention he drew to organ transplant with his emergence from his kidney transplant.

3. Micky Arison. While prudence and patience were the bywords of the franchise's early years, once Micky Arison took over controlling operation of the team in 1995, he seemingly threw all of his Carnival Cruise force into the franchise, acquiring big contracts and even bigger talents, with no signing bigger than the addition of Pat Riley as coach and team president mere months after Arison assumed control. Unlike his father, Ted Arison, an initial franchise investor, Micky Arison entered with a passion for the game.

2. Dwyane Wade. From the moment he was selected with the fifth pick of the 2003 NBA Draft, the guard out of Marquette changed the face of the franchise. A year later, Shaquille O'Neal was added in a blockbuster trade with the Lakers, with Pat Riley returning to the bench just over a year after that to guide the Heat to the 2006 NBA title. For all Glen Rice, Steve Smith, and Tim Hardaway had done for the franchise, the Heat had never possessed a perimeter presence of such dynamic capabilities until Wade's arrival.

1. Pat Riley. Prior to Riley's September 1, 1995, arrival as coach and team president, the Heat, over the franchise's first seven seasons, had recorded just one winning season, advanced to the playoffs twice, and had recorded a grand total of two playoff victories. Since then there have been three berths in the conference finals, two trips to the NBA Finals, as well as the 2006 NBA championship. Over Riley's 16 years as the face of the franchise, there have been 13 winning seasons.

The 10 Most Impactful Hornets Personalities :: by Gil McGregor

Gil McGregor is the longtime Hornets broadcaster with 21 years of experience with the team. Here, he highlights the people who have been most important to the Hornets' relatively brief but unique and wide-ranging history.

11. Gene Littles. He was the first Charlotte Hornets coach in 1988. He came and did a good job, and as a result passed the torch onto the coaches who succeeded him.

10. Dell Demps. He represents the future of the NBA and the Hornets franchise. Dell is part of the NBA management tree and proving the league to be an equal opportunity employer. Dell's biggest challenge is to prove that a small-market franchise like New Orleans can be successful.

9. Glen Rice. He was an NBA superstar without the fanfare. When he was named the MVP of the 1997 All-Star Game, he really put Hornets basketball on the national map. The team has never replaced him at the 2-guard slot. Rice was that good. In fact, he was as talented at his position as any other Hornets player has been at his.

7 (tie). Anthony Mason and Bobby Phills. Mason brought toughness to the team and Phills brought the class you wanted in an NBA player. It took two guys to bring both elements to our franchise, but it worked. The Hornets are still trying to get over the shocking January 2000 death of Bobby Phills.

6. Chris Paul. When the Hornets drafted Paul out of Wake Forest, they got a great floor general and one who could do it all from the point guard position. However, they also got one of the best leaders in NBA history. He led the team from Charlotte to New Orleans, and then from New Orleans to Oklahoma City and back to New Orleans. All of these moves rested squarely on the shoulders of Chris Paul.

5. Bob Bass. When Bob came to Charlotte as the general manager, he took his marching orders from the owner and made it work. Bob was faced with financial restrictions, but he was smart enough to know how to get things done and produce a successful team.

4. Dave Cowens. When Dave was named Hornets coach, his name and the Celtics history he brought with him made you believe he knew what it took to win. We all believed he had brought some of Red Auerbach's mystique with him, and we became the Celtics of the South.

3. Larry Johnson. When he became the first overall pick in the 1991 NBA Draft, it gave us legitimate hope for our future. ('The best player in the draft is coming to Charlotte! Wow! We're going to be on after this!') Larry was a tough guy but when he took on "Grandmama" as his alter ego, it made it easy for fans around the country to start following the team.

2. Muggsy Bogues. We'll see some 7-3 NBA player, but never again will we see another 5-3 guy. Muggsy had more heart than size. He inspired all the little guys out there and embarrassed all the big guys. When Muggsy was at Wake Forest, Dean Smith, coach of the University of North Carolina, said, "If you don't see him, pick the ball up."

1. George Shinn. If not for him, the Hornets would not exist today. Pro basketball would never have returned to North Carolina. George was a visionary leader and had a tenacious side to him. And a footnote: because of George's vision the NFL came to Charlotte and the NBA found a permanent home in Oklahoma City.

Steven Luhm is a longtime writer from the *Salt Lake Tribune*. Here, he writes about the figures who have had the most impact on the Jazz, a franchise that made the unlikely move from New Orleans to Salt Lake City, and thrived.

10. Hot Rod Hundley. Hundley was the voice of the Jazz for three decades. After working for the Phoenix Suns, LA Lakers and CBS, he joined the expansion New Orleans Jazz. In 1979, he followed the team to Salt Lake City, where he became as popular with the public as almost any Jazz player. Hundley's words and opinions became gospel to a generation of Jazz fans, many of whom gained much of their NBA knowledge from him. Hundley retired in 2009, but his legacy remains. The EnergySolutions Arena pressroom is known as the Hot Rod Hundley Media Center.

9. Mark Eaton. A fourth-round draft pick after rarely playing at UCLA, mountainous Mark Eaton found a home in Utah. He stood 7-4 and weighed 290 pounds. He anchored the Jazz's defense during the decade when the franchise evolved from laughingstock to contender. He gave Utah a chance when matched against All-Star low-post centers like Kareem Abdul-Jabbar, Artis Gilmore, Moses Malone, and Hakeem Olajuwon, who once called Eaton his most difficult opponent. Eaton still holds the NBA record for average blocks per game in a season (5.6) and in a career (3.5).

8. Phil Johnson. Few assistant coaches can be considered franchise cornerstones, but Phil Johnson isn't a typical assistant. He was a Dick Motta protégé and the NBA's Coach of the Year in 1975 with the Kings. When Jerry Sloan took over as head coach of the Jazz in 1988, the first call he made went to Johnson, who took the job as Sloan's lead assistant. Despite a handful of chances to leave over the years, Johnson stayed with Sloan and the Jazz for nearly 23 seasons. NBA general managers named him the league's top assistant five times between 2002 and 2010.

7. Sam Battistone. In 1974, Sam Battistone joined a nine-man partnership that paid $6.15 million for the expansion New Orleans Jazz. By 1979, the team was looking for a new home. Battistone and co-owner Larry Hatfield considered Albuquerque but decided on Salt Lake City. Despite adding limited partners, moving a handful of home games to Las Vegas, and improving the team on the court, the Jazz continued to struggle financially. But Battistone stayed committed to Utah. After buying out Hatfield, he resisted offers from out-of-town buyers and kept the Jazz in Salt Lake until local car dealer Larry Miller was able to purchase the team.

6. Adrian Dantley. Acquired from the Lakers one month before the Jazz's first game in Utah, Adrian Dantley gave the franchise star power (injury-plagued Pete Maravich came to Utah with the team, but played in just 17 games and was waived). Dantley spent his most productive seasons with the Jazz. He was a two-time scoring champion, a six-time All-Star, and an important piece of the puzzle when the Jazz won their first division title in 1984. Dantley didn't always get along with GM/Head Coach Frank Layden, but he took major steps toward his eventual Hall of Fame induction in 2008 while playing in Utah.

5. Jeff Hornacek. The Jazz acquired Hornacek from Philadelphia in a pre-deadline deal on February 24, 1994. Before the trade the Jazz had reached one Western Conference final in their history. After Hornacek's arrival, Utah reached two Western Conference finals and two NBA Finals over the next five seasons. In his five full seasons with the Jazz, the team averaged 59.2 regular-season wins. Clearly, Hornacek's long-range shooting, passing ability, tenacity, and team-first approach to the game made him the perfect complement to All-Stars John Stockton and Karl Malone.

4. Frank Layden. When the Jazz moved from New Orleans to Utah, acceptance came slowly. When fans called and asked General Manager Frank Layden what time that night's game would start, he'd reply, "When can you be here?" Asked why he drafted John Stockton in 1984, Layden said, "He's Irish, he's Catholic, he laughs at my jokes, and his father owns a bar. What's not to like?" Layden's sense of humor was the Jazz's trademark in those early years. His ability to build and eventually coach a contending team captured the fans' fancy and cemented his legacy in Utah.

3. Jerry Sloan. When Frank Layden resigned as coach of the Jazz on December 8, 1988, his assistant Jerry Sloan replaced him. He kept the job for nearly 23 seasons. Along the way the Jazz became a model of consistency, known for offensive execution and the same toughness that made Sloan a feared defender during his playing career. When he resigned midway through the 2010–11 season, Sloan was third on the all-time list for coaching wins. He is the only coach to win 1,000 games with the same franchise. Under Sloan, the Jazz reached the playoffs 19 times in 22 years, including 16 postseason appearances in a row from 1988 to 2003.

2. Larry Miller. The Jazz would have survived—perhaps even prospered—without Larry Miller. But it would not have happened in Utah. When outsiders sought to buy the financially struggling Jazz and move the franchise, Miller stepped forward. The Salt Lake City car dealer bought 50 percent of the team on April 11, 1985. Fourteen months later he bought the remaining 50 percent. Miller saved the Jazz for Utah, built a new arena in 1991, and presided as the once-struggling franchise became a model small-market operation. He died in 2009.

1. John Stockton and 1a. Karl Malone. No way to separate these two first-ballot Hall of Famers. John Stockton is the NBA's all-time assists and steals leader. Karl Malone is the league's No. 2 all-time scorer. Both attended small colleges—Gonzaga and Louisiana Tech, respectively. Both were drafted in the middle of the first round—16th and 13th overall. Both became one of the greatest to ever play their positions—point guard and power forward. With Stockton and Malone, the Jazz went to the playoffs 18 straight times, reached the conference finals five times in a seven-year span, and played in consecutive NBA Finals in 1997 and 1998.

Top Individuals to Impact the Sacramento Kings :: by Ailene Voisin

Ailene Voisin is a columnist for the *Sacramento Bee*. The Brooklyn native came to Sacramento by way of Las Vegas, where she attended UNLV before taking a detour to law school and San Diego. She has covered everything from the NBA to volleyball during her journalism career, and worked around the US for numerous papers, including the *Atlanta Journal-Constitution* and the *Los Angles Herald-Examiner*. Below, she lists the people who have most affected the Kings leading up to and during the franchise's time in Sacramento.

Honorable Mention. Before it became the Sacramento Kings, this franchise put some fine teams onto the court in its home cities of Rochester (where the team was known as the Royals and won the 1951 NBA title), and then in Cincinnati, and then in Omaha/Kansas City (where the Kings nickname began). It also boasted some very fine players, including Sam Lacey (the franchise's all-time leader in rebounds, blocks, steals and games played), as well as Hall of Famers Bobby Wanzer, Arnie Risen, Jack Twyman, Bob Davies, Nate "Tiny" Archibald, Jerry Lucas, Oscar Robertson, and Maurice Stokes.

11. Peja Stojakovic. Fans actually booed when David Stern announced the Kings' first-round draft pick in 1996. Then they saw him shoot. He was so well thought of that one woman I know named her cat, Peja.

10. Ron Artest. Before he devoted himself toward the pursuit of world peace, Ron-Ron was better known for his participation in the famous brawl at the Palace of Auburn Hills. He also was acquired from the Pacers shortly thereafter (for Peja) and bullied a moribund squad into the playoffs. He played with the Houston Rockets before signing with the Lakers and (gasp) allowing inner Ron to emerge. His improbable three-point shooting was critical to the Lakers title run against the Boston Celtics.

9. Jason Williams. He grew up a few blocks away from Randy Moss and over the river from the basketball rim once graced by West Virginia's iconic Jerry West. Unfortunately, if not exactly a flash in the pan, JW II was too flashy for his own good. He was sort of like Ricky Rubio, but without the judgment. He was fun, though, and a magician in the truest sense of the word. Once, he performed his magic tricks at a fan fest.

8. Mitch Richmond. He deserves to take a bow, and then another bow. The first legitimate star of the Sacramento era also made possible the arrival of the first legitimate superstar: Chris Webber. In a painfully one-sided move, Kings President Geoff Petrie traded his aging, aching, disgruntled guard for a younger, healthy, disgruntled power forward who was just as eager to change locations. Webber didn't count on Sacramento. Richmond didn't last in DC. But, hey, both players had their jerseys retired in the building formerly known as Arco Arena. Assuming a new arena is built in Sacramento, both jerseys will make the trip.

7. Jerry Reynolds. The longest-tenured Kings official, Jerry is the ultimate utility player. He has been a head coach, assistant coach, player personnel director, television commentator, and general manager (of the now defunct WNBA Sacramento Monarchs). He tinkered with the Monarchs roster that won the WNBA Championship in 2005 and reached the finals the following season. More significantly, the immensely popular Reynolds is probably the second-best sports figure from French Lick, Indiana. (If you might have forgotten, the No.1 ranking belongs to Larry Bird).

5 (tie). Joe and Gavin Maloof. When the Maloof family purchased majority shares in the Kings in 1999, the two oldest siblings thought this was how it worked. Teams were talented. Teams reached the playoffs. Teams contended for championships. Then the refs whiffed Game 6 of the 2002 Western Conference finals, depriving the Kings of a first-ever trip to the Finals. Webber blew out his knee a year later. Coaches came and went. The Maloofs fortune came and went. The team almost went to Anaheim in April 2011. This NBA life. It's tough out there.

4. Geoff Petrie. He was the architect of the Sacramento Kings' first playoff appearance and the brains/muscles behind the hugely talented and wildly entertaining teams that featured some combination of Webber, Stojakovic, Divac, JWill, Mike Bibby, Doug Christie, Hedo Turkoglu, Gerald Wallace, Bobby Jackson, and Brad Miller, among others, and should have reached at least one NBA Finals. But Petrie never seemed to recover from Webber's career-threatening knee injury. He went through coaches, acquired bad contracts, and, most recently, assembled a toxic roster. The owners are big fans, but the problem is, the fans are no longer such big fans of Geoff Petrie.

3. Gregg Lukenbill. Back in the 1980s, no one except a young, eccentric Northern Californian thought Sacramento had a chance of landing an NBA franchise. Well, Lukenbill put together an ownership group to buy the slumping Kansas City Kings; relocated them two years later to Sacramento; and financed a temporary facility (Arco Arena I), and then the current barn (Arco II) that is hopelessly outdated, but is still standing. Then there was the night he crawled onto the rafters and, with a horrified crowd watching, plugged a leaky roof that threatened cancellation of a game. He was crazy, true. But sometimes crazy is necessary.

2. Vlade Divac. This is the most beloved of all Kings. Whether he was talking about his underwear (he responded to Utah Jazz fans who accused him of wearing women's underwear by saying he wore no underwear, "men's or women's"), or maneuvering for one of his instinctive post moves, or throwing one of his ridiculous passes, this was the player who stole Sacramento's heart. Unfortunately, he also tapped the ball back to Robert Horry for the three-pointer of 2002 infamy.

1. Chris Webber. The best player in the Sacramento Kings history also has the most tortured history. He is a former Rookie of the Year (with Golden State) who endured league suspensions, legal troubles relating back to his days in Ann Arbor, bad relationships with two teams (Warriors, Wizards) that led him to Sacramento, where he rehabilitated his reputation, revived a franchise, and then shredded a knee while in the prime of his career. When Webber crumbled to the court during the Kings-Mavericks playoff series in 2003, his career crumbled right along with him. He underwent microfracture surgery but was never the same player, and limped through his final seasons with the 76ers and Warriors.

Shaun Powell is a longtime New York sportswriter. He was formerly a columnist for *New York Newsday* and now writes for ESPN New York. Here he picks the top 10 figures in the history of one of the NBA's most prominent and storied franchises.

10. Dick McGuire. The less loquacious of the McGuire brothers (Al was the talker in the family) Dick was the first great Knicks player as a top-flight playmaking point guard. At his peak, he was second only to the great Bob Cousy, and both had similar styles. Tricky Dick was tough to figure out; he was usually one step ahead of his defender when it came to decision making and running an offense. Born and raised in New York, McGuire was one of the league's early influences. McGuire was a seven-time All-Star and led the league in assists as a rookie. He had been a member of the organization in various capacities for almost 50 years when he died in 2010.

9. Joe Lapchick. He was regarded as the grandfather of New York basketball because of his coaching stints with St. John's, and then the Knicks, a team he guided to three straight appearances in the NBA Finals during the infancy of the league. The Knicks also had eight straight winning seasons under Lapchick, and because of that, basketball took off in the city and gave New Yorkers a team to root for other than the Yankees and Dodgers. Lapchick was an emotional coach at a time when coaches stayed under control and remained in their seats; because of that, he was a man well before his time. His techniques and philosophies were borrowed by many future coaches who cited Lapchick as a mentor and inspiration.

8. Red Holzman. No coach has ever been more influential in New York basketball circles than Red, a two-time championship winner whose success, unfortunately for Knick fans, hasn't been matched since. Holzman was the right man for the right time because he allowed his players to be themselves and stay true to their separate personalities, as long as they unified on the court. The Knicks had free spirits (Phil Jackson) and scholars (Bill Bradley) and country-raised players (Willis Reed), but managed to enjoy amazing chemistry. Even when Earl Monroe joined Walt Frazier after the first championship, there was no friction or clash of egos.

7. Sweetwater Clifton. Along with Chuck Cooper and Earl Lloyd, Clifton was a pioneer who helped break the color barrier in basketball. That alone is why

Sweetwater makes the list. His contributions to basketball went beyond mere numbers; he ushered in a new era for the game and helped popularize it among African-Americans, who dominate the sport today. As a player, Clifton certainly was among the better talents of his time, making the All-Star team in the 1956–57 season (at 34, he was then the oldest player in history to do so) and helping the Knicks reach the championship round for the first time in franchise history. He averaged almost 10 rebounds a game for an NBA career that didn't begin until he was 27, as he had previously resorted to playing for the Globetrotters until given the green light to integrate the NBA.

6. Dave DeBusschere. A ferocious power forward who adored the dirty work, DeBusschere began with the Pistons but only realized basketball greatness during his six seasons (1968–74) in New York, where he won two championships with the Knicks and paved the way for his Hall of Fame induction. DeBusschere was a solid and amazingly consistent rebounder who averaged 11 boards a game for his career and in double-figures every season except his first two. And in his final season, he scored 18.1 points per game, second-highest of his career. More than anything, DeBusschere was a tremendous teammate who stuck to fundamentals and left the flash to others. He was the player you hated to play against but would love to play next to.

5. Bernard King. He played for six teams but most famously with the Knicks for four epic seasons beginning in 1982. Born and raised in Brooklyn, King became a symbol of an asphalt prince, someone who learned the game on the hard courts of the gritty city and beat the odds to enjoy a long and distinguished professional career. A major scorer, his 32.9 point-average in the 1984–85 season was one of the best by a small forward and it turned King into a star. However, his explosive first step was stolen by a torn ACL, back when a torn ACL was a career killer. Nonetheless, King made a triumphant return in Washington and made the All-Star team. He'll forever be immortalized in New York for his 50-point games on consecutive nights, and for then scoring 60 on Christmas Day.

4. Bill Bradley. The Senator was a consummate gentleman, scholar, and athlete—a combination you don't often see in sports. And yet Bradley took enormous pride in fulfilling all three sides to his makeup to achieve a dreamy adult life as a basketball star, a politician, and presidential candidate. From a basketball standpoint, Bradley was fluid, dependable, and obviously clever. In other words, he was a perfect fit for a Red Holzman-coached team that brought glory to New York basketball. He was only an All-Star once and his lifetime numbers (12.4 points, 3.2 rebounds, and 3.4 assists per game) certainly weren't glamorous, but Bradley was one of the top role players of his era and was big on two championship teams. Plus, he's in the Hall of Fame.

3. Patrick Ewing. He did everything for the Knicks except win a championship. There will always be that vacancy in Ewing's soul, but not because he didn't do everything he possibly could to fill it. Pat Riley was fond of calling Ewing "a warrior" and from a basketball standpoint, the description fit. Ewing was an example of a star who stayed in shape and came to play every night. Few centers in NBA history had his offensive game, and despite never having a Hall of Fame teammate, Ewing had the Knicks in the title hunt almost every season during his prime. He was denied by Michael Jordan and Hakeem Olajuwon, no shame there. A championship probably would've catapulted Ewing to the top of this list.

2. Walt Frazier. With the exception of Joe Namath, no athlete personified the New York experience quite like "Clyde." Really, now: Frazier dressed the part, talked the part, played the part. He was all style and all substance, the perfect fit for a cosmopolitan city that thrived on both. Frazier knew how to win games—two titles with the Knicks—and he knew where to go after games. He could spend the day in Harlem and the evening at a five-star restaurant, and be welcome in both places. Of course, as a player, his only peer was Jerry West. And Clyde outplayed the great West in the 1970 Finals with 36 points, 19 assists, and 7 rebounds in one of the greatest Game 7 performances of all time.

1. Willis Reed. It would be wrong to whittle what he meant to the Knicks down to his famous walk from the tunnel at Madison Square Garden in the 1970 Finals. Obviously, Reed was much more than an iconic symbol of playing through pain. He won an MVP Award and was a seven-time All-Star. He was one of the best big men of his era, willing to challenge Wilt Chamberlain and Nate Thurmond and others despite being on the short end, height-wise, in those battles. In his prime, Reed averaged over 20 points and 10 rebounds per game, and, above all, was respected for his leadership. That said, there's nothing wrong with being famous for being gutsy and taking one for the team. It's called "pulling a Willis Reed."

For almost a half century, writer Mark Heisler has captured the essence of sports in print. The majority of his career was spent with the *Los Angeles Times* covering the Lakers and the NBA. In 2006, he was the recipient of the Naismith Basketball Hall of Fame's Curt Gowdy Award. Below is his list of the 11 people who most impacted the Lakers franchise.

10 (tie). Owners Jack Kent Cooke and Jerry Buss. I'm cheating by including them both, but this list would be a farce without either. Cooke sprinkled stardust on the franchise, writing the manual for owners in all sports, building his own arena when politicos running the Sports Arena dared him to find a better deal. Buss invented Showtime, not to mention the Laker Girls, to appeal to local movie stars, succeeding beyond anyone's dreams but his own. His Lakers replaced the Dodgers as the hot local ticket in the 1980s when the O'Malleys were still in charge and the team still won world championships. Since, with no world championships for the Dodgers and no NFL team, it's LA as in Lakers.

9. Wilt Chamberlain. His demand to the 76ers to trade him to Los Angeles started the Lakers on their way to becoming the superstars' destination of choice. Only five seasons in LA, but what seasons! In Game 7 of the 1969 Finals, his Lakers were stunned by the aged Celtics under Cooke's balloons. In Game 7 of the 1970 Finals, the Willis Reed-inspired Knicks routed them. During the 1971–72 season, LA won a record 33 in a row and romped to the Lakes' first title in LaLa Land.

8. Shaquille O'Neal. May actually have been Most Dominant Ever, as he billed himself, among other things (Big Aristotle, Big Pythagorean Formula, et al.). Although Laker coaches said the key to his career was the fact he won only two MVPs. Indisputably Most Fun Ever, leading the Lakes to three titles in eight seasons, even if they left a few more of those on the table, too.

7. Phil Jackson. Won five titles in 11 seasons in LA, even if he was more of a law unto himself than a Laker. Said whatever he wanted about whomever he wanted to (like Jim Buss) while living with the owner's daughter (Jeannie Buss). Unlike any other coach, he acknowledged ongoing issues, forcing players to work things out and giving the press a field day in the interim.

6. Elgin Baylor. Greatest player fans never saw, lighting up the pre-national TV era. Put up huge numbers, but wasn't the same after tearing up a knee in

1965. Julius Erving before Julius Erving with unheard-of hesitation, "hang in the air" moves.

5. Chick Hearn. Holy trinity of announcers: Vin, Marv, and Chickie. The Lakers didn't have a big two in the 1960s, when they went from the bumpkins that Minnesota trucker Bob Short left on the Sports Arena doorstep, to glamour franchise, but three: Elgin, Jerry, and Chickie. An indefatigable hot dog, Chick knew the game inside and out, and would rip the Lakers. Lived to work, doing 3,338 Laker games without missing one over 20 years until his death at 85 while also performing side gigs, like calling UNLV games.

4. Kareem Abdul-Jabbar. Hated fame as much as Wilt and Shaq loved it. Thorny with press—although he was highly intelligent, a great quote, and a journalist in his own right. Went well beyond prime to get his record 38,387 points at 42, but his Skyhook was as much the game's ultimate weapon at the end as at the beginning.

3. Kobe Bryant. Lightning rod for controversy, more admired than beloved, even by Laker fans, but ask Jerry West who's the best of them all! High-wire sensibility makes him the most spectacular player since Julius Erving in the ABA. Ultra-gamer, never-before-seen 365/24/7 dedication. Five titles tie him with Kareem and Magic for most as a Laker.

2. Magic Johnson. This is some franchise if he's not No. 1. Undisputed as game's best playmaker, had charisma coming out of his ears. Beloved by teammates, coaches, press people, and anyone else who knew him. His five titles were no accident. As West said: "Somewhere out there, there's a kid out there who will be a better player than Magic Johnson, but no one will ever be a better leader."

1. Jerry West. Tortured genius, nonetheless born for icon-hood as NBA logo and as Mr. Laker. His heart-on-his-sleeve style endeared him as much to opposing players and fans. As GM nonpareil, he kept the Showtime team he inherited on top through the 1980s, then pulled off a miracle, going from Magic's retirement in 1991 to the arrival of Shaq and Kobe in 1996. Said Magic, capturing West perfectly at the unveiling of his statue at the Staples Center before an overflow, star-studded crowd, "I know Jerry was saying, 'No one will be there.'"

The Most Impactful People in Magic History :: by David Steele

David Steele has been a play-by-play announcer for the Orlando Magic since the team first took the court in 1989. In 2010, he was named the Florida Sportscaster of the Year by the National Sportscasters and Sportswriters Association. Below, he lists the top dozen figures in the history of the Orlando Magic, a franchise that has made a significant impact on the NBA despite its relatively brief history.

11 (tie). Bo Outlaw and Darrell Armstrong. Bo and Darrell. Darrell and Bo. For Magic fans during the late 1990s, the two are inseparable. For years they represented the team's identity both on and off the court. Heart and hustle was their calling card on the court, community service was their mission off it. Today Outlaw continues to impact central Florida working as a community ambassador for the team; and as for Armstrong, if a poll was taken today for the most popular player in team history, he just might win.

10. Matty Guokas. Guokas's hiring as the first head coach of the Magic in 1989 brought immediate credibility to the franchise. He had played for Philadelphia's NBA title team in 1967, and later was head coach of the Sixers. As coach of the expansion Magic, Guokas provided a steady hand for four seasons before stepping away from the coaching profession. In 2004, Guokas returned to the franchise as a commentator on Magic TV broadcasts.

9. Tracy McGrady. TMac was the face of the Magic franchise from 2000 to 2004. He led the NBA in scoring in 2003 and 2004, and still holds the franchise record for points in a game (62 against Washington in 2004). McGrady earned Eastern Conference All-Star status during all four of his seasons in Orlando. TMac was also named first team All-NBA twice, joining Penny Hardaway and Dwight Howard as the only players in Magic history to have been selected first-team All-NBA.

8. Nick Anderson. The first player taken in the college draft by the Magic, with the 11th pick in 1989, Anderson still holds the franchise record for games played (692) and points scored (10,650). Nick will always be remembered for one of the greatest plays in Magic history, stealing the ball from Michael Jordan during the 1995 playoffs. Like Bo Outlaw, Anderson now works for the team as a community ambassador.

7. Otis Smith. A fan favorite as a player for the Magic from 1989 to 1992, Otis Smith has made his most significant impact on the franchise in the team's front office. After retiring as a player, Smith spent two years as the Magic's community relations manager, and in 2003 became the team's director of player development. Smith played a key role in drafting Dwight Howard with the No. 1 pick in 2004 (not a clear-cut decision at the time), and was the team's general manager from 2006 to 2012. In this role he presided over the franchise's second trip to the NBA Finals in 2009.

6. Shaquille O'Neal. Shaquille O'Neal's arrival in 1992 as the first overall pick in the draft put the Magic on the map as a serious NBA contender in just its fourth year as an NBA franchise. Shaq made the Eastern Conference All-Star team all four seasons he played in Orlando, and, along with fellow All-Star Penny Hardaway, led the team to the NBA Finals in 1995.

5. Penny Hardaway. Played six seasons for the Magic (1993–99) and for a time in the mid-'90s was a top five talent in the NBA. Hardaway made four All-Star teams and was twice named first-team All-NBA with the Magic. A youthful Penny and Shaq led the Magic to their first NBA Finals in 1995. Hardaway's popularity reached its zenith in 1996 with the nationwide introduction of Lil Penny into the world of sports marketing.

4. Alex Martins. Martins began his career with the Magic in 1989 as the team's public relations director, left Orlando in 1998, and then returned in 2005 to oversee the day-to-day direction of the club. Now president of the Magic—and one of central Florida's most influential people—Martins is largely responsible for the building of the spectacular Amway Center in downtown Orlando, and has been instrumental in creating a championship culture throughout the organization.

3. Pat Williams. Simply put, if not for Pat Williams, there would be no Orlando Magic. In 1985, Williams and local businessman, Jim Hewitt, set out to bring an NBA franchise to central Florida. More than four years later, the Orlando Magic took the floor at the Orlando Arena, changing the area's sports scene forever. Williams presided over the drafting of Shaquille O'Neal and the acquisition of Penny Hardaway, and was the team's general manager until 1996.

2. Dwight Howard. The overall top pick in the 2004 draft is a perennial All-Star, Defensive Player of the Year, and first-team All-NBA center. In addition to his amazing abilities on the court, Howard is a worldwide marketing wonder, and is one of the franchise's hardest workers in the community, having won five Rich and Helen DeVos Community Enrichment awards for his efforts in the central Florida community.

1. The DeVos family. The DeVos family purchased the Magic in 1991, and since that time, operation of the franchise has truly been a family affair. Club Chairman Rich DeVos sets the tone for the organization, running a first-class business operation while also setting high standards for the franchise in the community. Rich and his wife, Helen, also chair the Orlando Magic Youth Foundation, which has raised and distributed more than $15 million to nonprofit organizations through the years.

Eddie Sefko is the Dallas Mavericks beat writer for the *Dallas Morning News*, and has been an NBA reporter for over a quarter century. His list is a collection of individuals who have most impacted the Dallas Mavericks since the team's 1981 founding. Sefko emphasizes that the people on the list appear in no particular order.

10. Don Nelson. The coach who first molded Dirk Nowitzki into the player who would become MVP of the league and of the NBA Finals, Nelson was there for every step from the dregs that were the 1990s, to that ultimate reward, even though Nelson was long gone before the team's NBA championship was realized. He changed the culture of a losing team and will forever be remembered for his innovative strategies.

9. Donnie Nelson. He merely dug up the most important asset in franchise history. It was the younger Nelson who first set eyes on a thin, seven-footer from Germany named Dirk Nowitzki. He went so far as to try to hide Nowitzki so other teams wouldn't get onto him. So certain was he that Nowitzki was the real deal that he laid his job on the line to convince ownership to draft him. Nelson continued to make smart personnel decisions that ultimately led the Mavs to an NBA title.

8. Mark Cuban. There are NBA owners. There are controversial NBA owners. And then there is one NBA owner on the executive equivalent of steroids. Cuban made billions in the dot-com boom, and then bought the Mavericks and unleashed never-before-seen brashness against the league establishment. If there was an issue that he felt was not being addressed, Cuban let Commissioner David Stern hear about it. And he spent money to fix problems. Fans love owners like that.

7. Dirk Nowitzki. The kid with the really bad haircut showed up in Dallas after the 1998 NBA Draft and years later reached the ultimate level of consciousness: Dirk became as popular as some of the greatest Dallas Cowboys of all time. In a football town, there is no greater compliment. Nowitzki simply was the key to the franchise finally winning the NBA championship. He'll go down as one of the greatest players in NBA history.

6. Donald Carter. The original owner wore a big hat and epitomized all things Texas. Along with Norm Sonju, he brought the NBA to Dallas, and under his stewardship the franchise became a model for other expansion teams. There's a reason why Mark Cuban allowed Carter to receive the 2011 championship trophy. He's still revered for his style of running the team.

5. Jason Kidd. Arguably the best draft pick in franchise history (remember, Nowitzki was a draft-night acquisition via a trade with Milwaukee). Kidd had a Swiss Army Knife of assets on the court, and the one thing he didn't possess when he got to the league, a jump shot, he worked on and eventually became one of the top three-point shooters of all time, in terms of triples made. His two terms with the team were capped with the 2011 title.

4. Brad Davis. Never an All-Star caliber player, he nonetheless was the face of the franchise in its formative years. The 180-pound guard never played at anything less than 100 percent and endeared himself to fans with his style of play, not to mention his wavy blond hair. Davis and Rolando Blackman were the first two Mavericks to have their uniform numbers retired and, to date, remain the only ones.

3. Norm Sonju. As right-hand man to the Mavs original owner, Donald Carter, Sonju was instrumental in laying the groundwork for the franchise coming to Dallas. He also made a ton of shrewd personnel decisions in the early years, adding players like Mark Aguirre, Jay Vincent, and Rolando Blackman to the roster as the Mavericks developed an effective blueprint for other teams starting from scratch.

2. Rick Carlisle. The veteran head coach's calm, cerebral approach turned out to be exactly what the Mavericks needed after the volatile, heavy-handed management style of Avery Johnson. Carlisle built a strong relationship with key players—Jason Kidd in particular—and the give-and-take between coach and point guard ended up being a tipping point in the championship run of 2011. Carlisle always found ways to turn trouble spots into advantages—or at least opportunities.

1. Dick Motta. They don't come any more old-school than Motta, whose no-nonsense approach and dry wit were the perfect combination for an expansion team that was looking to make a splash. Hiring Motta as the first coach of the franchise supplied instant credibility. Not surprisingly, the product on the floor quickly followed suit. Within three years the Mavericks were competitive and began a long run of playoff appearances.

The 10 Greatest Moments in Nets Franchise History :: by Herb Turetzky

Herb Turetzky has served as the official scorer of the Nets since the franchise's early years in the mid-1960s, when the team was known as the New Jersey Americans. Along the way, he's achieved his profession's ironman streak of serving as official scorer for 1,000 straight games. He's also been inducted into the New York City Basketball Hall of Fame, published a book of poetry called *BASKETBALL and Life*, and witnessed countless great moments in Nets history, the top 10 of which he recounts here.

10. The 1990 drafting of Derrick Coleman with the first overall pick. While his career did not match his potential, Coleman's drafting joined him with veteran center Sam Bowie, outstanding small forward Chris Morris, and rapidly blossoming shooting guard Drazen Petrovic, and prepared the Nets for a possible run at NBA championships. With Petrovic's leadership, both Coleman and the next season's first-round pick, Kenny Anderson, became All-Stars and might have continued in that mold for their careers had Petrovic not perished in a 1993 car crash. Without Drazen's incredible work ethic and will to win, which forced both stars to practice and play harder than they did at any other point in their careers, Coleman and Anderson resumed their previous relaxed approach to the game and they, and the Nets, once more became mediocre competitors.

9. First-ever ABA game (October 23, 1967). The New Jersey Americans, with Brooklyn legend and former St. John's All-American Tony Jackson, faced the Pittsburgh Pipers, with fellow Brooklyn legend and former Globetrotter Connie Hawkins, at the Teaneck Armory. Both stars were overshadowed by the incredible, career-high, 41-point performance by Americans' center and former Augsburg College and AAU player Dan Anderson, a feat he never again approached in his brief ABA career.

8. The 1976 merger of NBA and ABA teams. The inclusion—along with Denver, Indiana and San Antonio—of the Nets as one of the four ABA teams to be integrated into the NBA offered the team the chance to showcase the talents of their ABA championship squad, including quite possibly the game's most entertaining and talented young forward, Julius "Dr. J" Erving, to millions of fans across the country.

7. The 1992 Eastern Conference Playoffs triple-overtime victory. The victory over former ABA nemesis, the Indiana Pacers, propelled the Nets to their first-ever NBA Finals appearance.

6. Trades for Rick Barry (1970), Julius Erving (1973), and Jason Kidd (2001). Players who, respectively, led the Nets to their greatest heights of the 1972 ABA Finals, the 1974 and 1976 ABA championships, and the 2002 and 2003 NBA Finals.

5. The 2003 NBA Finals. Jason Kidd's leadership carried the Nets to challenge the Spurs in a hard-fought six-game series, won by San Antonio.

4. The 1974 ABA Championship. Led by league MVP, Julius "Dr. J" Erving, the Nets defeated the Utah Stars for their first-ever championship.

3. The 2002 NBA Finals. In 2002, the Jason Kidd-led Nets made their first-ever NBA Finals, where they took on the Shaquille O'Neal and Kobe Bryant-led Los Angeles Lakers, who swept the Nets in a four-game series on the way to their third straight NBA championship.

2. The 1976 ABA Championship. Again led by MVP Julius Erving, the Nets defeated the Denver Nuggets in the final ABA game, coming from behind to win, thanks to 16 fourth-quarter points from Erving's teammate Super John Williamson. The title paved the way for the Nets inclusion as one of the four ABA teams in the NBA-ABA merger later that year, and their first-ever season in the NBA.

1. The 2011–12 Building of the Barclays Center in Brooklyn. The state-of-the-art arena is set to open for the 2012–13 NBA season, when the Nets will finally become one of the NBA's major-market franchises. Led by the trio of point guard Deron Williams, center Brook Lopez, and power forward Kris Humphries, the Nets could challenge the New York Knicks for supremacy in the New York City region. Under the ownership of Russian billionaire Mikael Prokhorov, the team will spread the Brooklyn Nets and NBA brands around the world, while giving Brooklyn, the nation's fourth-largest "city," its first major professional sports franchise since the baseball Dodgers left for Los Angeles in the 1950s.

Carl Scheer was the first president and general manager of the Denver Nuggets. He also served as NBA's deputy commissioner and is now an executive with the Charlotte Bobcats.

11. Rocky. Through thick and thin, name changes, logo changes, and uniform changes, one thing remained the same for two decades with the Nuggets—Rocky, the team mascot. Rocky was the consummate entertainer, especially when it was necessary to pay less attention to what was happening between whistles.

10. Bill Ringsby. Bill owned the Denver-based Ringsby Rocket Trucking System. He added ownership of the city's first pro basketball team to his portfolio in 1967. The ABA franchise didn't look far for a nickname (the Rockets) or a logo (borrowed from the side of one of Ringsby's trucks).

9. Spencer Haywood. Haywood was the first player in pro basketball history to play professionally before his college eligibility had expired. To the chagrin of the NCAA, NBA, and several ABA teams, the Rockets signed Haywood after his first season at the University of Detroit, where he had averaged 32.2 points per game in 1969. The Rockets explained that it was a "hardship" exception. Haywood was spectacular in Denver, scoring 30 points per game and easily winning the ABA Rookie of the Year Award. But Haywood inflicted "hardship" on the Rockets when he bolted the ABA the very next season for the NBA's Seattle SuperSonics due to a contract dispute.

8. Larry Brown. The scrappy and intuitive point guard from the University of North Carolina had handed the Rockets defeats in their first two playoff appearances as a member of the New Orleans Buccaneers and Oakland Oaks. The Rockets remedied that problem in 1971 when they acquired Brown in a trade with the Virginia Squires. Three years later Brown was named head coach of the repurposed Denver ABA franchise, now called the Nuggets. He is the only coach to ever guide a team to an NBA championship as well as an NCAA championship. His Nuggets coaching record stood at 251-134. Brown was named to the Basketball Hall of Fame in 2002.

7. Alex English. English was the first post-merger star for the Denver Nuggets. The eight-time NBA All-Star was the league's leading scorer in the 1980s. English set 31 Nuggets records in his 10 years with the franchise. Alex became a Hall of Famer in 1997.

6. Dan Issel. Marvin Webster's misfortune became Dan Issel's good fortune. The Morgan State rookie contracted hepatitis prior to the 1975 Nuggets season, prompting the Nuggets to enter and win a bidding war for Issel, the Kentucky All-American who was being offered around by the disorganized Baltimore Claws. Issel was a six-time ABA All-Star and represented the Nuggets in the 1977 NBA All-Star Game. Another Denver entrant into the Hall of Fame in 1993, Issel coached the Nuggets to an NBA first when in 1994 his Nuggets became the first No. 8 seed to knock off a No. 1 seed in the playoffs when Denver chased Seattle in five games.

5. Red McCombs. The pride of Spur, Texas, McCombs became the third owner of the Denver Nuggets in 1978. After Larry Brown left as coach in 1979, the Nuggets faltered. Under McCombs' watch, Doug Moe was hired as coach in 1980 and the Nuggets flourished on and off the court, making the Western Conference Finals in 1985. McCombs sold his stake in the Nuggets later that season. The Nuggets were one of three sports franchises McCombs has owned, the others being the Minnesota Vikings and the San Antonio Spurs (twice). He also was a giant in the automotive and broadcasting industries.

4. Chopper Travaglini. Chop was the legendary Nuggets trainer who bridged the franchise from the ABA to the NBA. The roll call of ankles he's taped in his 14 years in Denver is legendary. He championed the safety innovation of the breakaway rim and was a champion of the people who raised over $11 million as president of the Denver Nuggets Community Fund. Travaglini died in 1999 at the age of 66.

3. George Karl. At midseason in 2005, Karl took over a floundering Nuggets team with a 17-25 record and sitting a full six games out of the last NBA Playoff spot. He cajoled them to a 32-8 finish, which was good enough for seventh place in the West. Now in his seventh season, he is the second-longest tenured coach in Nuggets history and became just the seventh coach in NBA history to win 1,000 games. He's not only battled NBA teams, but took on cancer and won in 2010, coaching every game of the 2010–11 season.

2. David Thompson. The Skywalker preceded Michael Jordan as the icon of above-the-rim play during his seven seasons with the Nuggets from 1975 to 1982. He's third on the Nuggets all-time scoring list, soaring his way to 11,992 points. Thompson was the only player to be named All-Star Game MVP in both the ABA and NBA. DT was named to the Hall of Fame in 1996 and presented Jordan into the Hall in 2009.

1. Doug Moe. The longest-tenured coach in Nuggets history, Doug Moe brought the Nuggets more success than anyone prior or since. His 10-year term brought 432 wins to the club. Moe coached three Hall of Famers (Issel, English, and Thompson). His teams had a penchant for scoring, as they averaged 114.6 points per game. Affectionately known as Big Stiff, Moe coached Denver, San Antonio, and Philadelphia to 628 career wins.

The Most Influential People in Indiana Pacers History :: by Bob Kravitz

Bob Kravitz is a columnist for the *Indianapolis Star*. Over his three-decade career, he has worked across the country, writing for local papers and *Sports Illustrated*. Here, he lists the most important figures in the history of the Indiana Pacers, a history that has taken the team from an early 1970s mini-dynasty run in the ABA to the brink of greatness in the NBA.

11. Rick Smits. The final person on this list was a tough one to choose. Scores of Pacers fans were asked to ch me in with their choices, and they offered several suggestions: Byron Scott, Larry Bird, Mark Jackson, Detlef Schrempf, Jermaine O'Neal. For the sake of argument, let's go with Smits.

The 7-4 Dunking Dutchman never became the dominant force he was expected to become, limited by constant injuries to his feet. He was the second overall pick in the 1988 NBA Draft, ard slowly improved before becoming the Pacers No. 2 option to Reggie Miller through the Pacers playoff years. In his final season (1999-2000), he helped take Indiana to the NBA Finals, where they lost to the Los Angeles Lakers in six games.

10. George McGinnis. McGinnis is widely viewed as one of the greatest high school basketball players, if not THE greatest high school basketball player, in Indiana history. He was also a dominant force at Indiana University. He first played for the Pacers from 1971 to 1975, winning two ABA titles, earning playoff MVP and regular-season MVP honors, and making the All-Star team three times. He went to Philadelphia for a few seasons, was traded to the Denver Nuggets in 1978, and two years later was reacquired by the Pacers for Alex English. McGinnis was a shadow of his former self in his second incarnation as a Pacer, and English went on to become one of the NBA's greatest scorers.

9. Roger Brown. Talk to Bob Leonard and some of the old ABA hands who remember the early Pacers, and they will recall Brown as a precursor to Michael Jordan and other legends of the modern-day game. He was a great player who played above the rim, but we'll always wonder how great he could have been if not for his off-the-court issues. In 1960, he was banned from the NCAA and NBA when it was learned he'd been introduced to a gambler who was involved in point shaving. Brown was never accused of engaging in point shaving, but Brown was still forced to wait until 1967 before he signed with the ABA's Pacers. In eight years in the ABA, with three teams, Browns won three titles, made four All-Star teams, and scored 10,498 points. Brown was one of seven players unanimously selected to the ABA All-Time team.

8. Mel Daniels. Before Reggie Miller, there was Mel Daniels. He was among the best centers, if not THE best center, in the ABA and the NBA. Like Slick Leonard, he belongs in the Basketball Hall of Fame. Like Leonard, he is not. Daniels was a 6-9 center who'd played at the University of New Mexico and chose to play in the then-fledgling ABA. He was the league's Rookie of the Year with the Minnesota Muskies, and then was traded to the Pacers. He was the league's MVP in 1969 and 1971, and led Indiana to three ABA titles. Some other résumé notes: Mel Daniels played in seven ABA All-Star Games, led the ABA in rebounding three separate seasons, and is the league's all-time leader in total rebounds and rebounding average. Daniels is one of four players—along with Reggie Miller, George McGinnis, and Roger Brown—whose jersey has been retired by the Pacers.

7. Larry Brown. After years of struggling around the .500 mark, the Pacers were led out of the desert of mediocrity by the itinerant but brilliant head coach. Brown was brought to Indiana for the 1993–94 season, and the Pacers won their first-ever NBA playoff series, sweeping the Orlando Magic. They then upset the Atlanta Hawks in the next round. They eventually lost to the Knicks in seven games in what was the first of several memorable "Hicks vs. Knicks" postseason showdowns. The next year, the Brown-led Pacers got past the Knicks in the play-offs, but lost in the Eastern Conference Finals to the Magic in seven games. Eventually, he left for another job—because he's Larry.

6. Ron Artest. He was, no arguing, one of the most influential Pacers, although not in a particularly good way. The moment Ron-Ron went into the stands at the Palace of Auburn Hills in 2004, it not only altered the fate of that particular season—the Pacers looked like a Finals-contending team—but ruined the franchise for years to come. The Brawl destroyed the Pacers, ruining Reggie Miller's last chance to win a ring, and forcing management to run off several of its best, but most problematic, players. Artest has since found help for his emotional issues and turned his life around, but during his time with the Pacers, he was a full-time headache who ultimately left the franchise in tatters.

4 (tie). Herb and Mel Simon. The Simon Brothers, who are Indy-based mall magnates, saved the franchise in 1983 at a time when there were rumblings the team was at risk of moving to another city. The brothers presided over the slow rise of the franchise into an NBA Finals runner-up in 2000. The Simons didn't particularly need the Pacers to get or stay rich, but they stepped forward out of a sense of civic responsibility. Herb remains the primary owner; his brother, Mel, died in 2009.

3. Donnie Walsh. Walsh was The Architect, the brains of the operation. He took over as the franchise's general manager in 1987 and made several spectacular decisions, including the then-unpopular choice of UCLA sharpshooter Reggie Miller over IU fan favorite Steve Alford in the 1987 Draft. He also did something quite rare in the modern-day, cap-constrained NBA. Walsh completely rebuilt a veteran team that reached the 2000 Finals without losing much ground and returning to the draft lottery. He traded for Ron Artest, Reggie Miller, and Jermaine O'Neal, among others. If not for The Brawl, that team might have returned to the Finals, and even won it all. Walsh took a franchise mired in post-ABA mediocrity—and worse—and slowly built it into an NBA Finals team.

2. Bob "Slick" Leonard. It's a minor crime against humanity that Slick isn't in the Basketball Hall of Fame. He should be a no-brainer, especially when his record is compared with some of the coaches who've been inducted. Is there an anti-ABA bias? Sure looks like it. Slick was a legendary player at Indiana University, and then as a coach led the Pacers to three ABA championships (1970, '72, and '73). He continues to be one of the faces of the modern-day franchise, working as the team's radio analyst.

1. Reggie Miller. It's acceptable that Reggie didn't make the Hall of Fame on the first ballot in 2011, but how did he fail to advance to the second round of voting when compared with Dennis Rodman, Ralph Sampson, and Jamaal Wilkes? Really? How does this make sense? Miller will always be remembered as one of the most bloodless, clutch players in NBA history, a rare performer whose postseason statistics were better than his regular-season numbers. Just ask Spike Lee and the New York Knicks. Miller's eight-points-in-8.9-seconds blitz at Madison Square Garden in the 1994–95 playoffs remains one of the sport's most remarkable feats.

Top 10 Most Influential People in Pistons History :: by Tom Wilson

Tom Wilson, a native of Detroit, worked for the Detroit Pistons franchise for over three decades, during which time he rose to the rank of team president and CEO.

Honorable Mention. Dennis Rodman, Vinnie Johnson, Larry Brown, Fred Zollner, George Blaha, Doug Collins, Dave DeBusschere, Richard Hamilton, Bob Lanier, George Yardley.

10. Grant Hill. You often hear the cliché: he's a better person than a player. But for Grant it was true. Supremely talented, he was a triple-double threat every single night for the Pistons, with his great quickness, ease at getting to the basket, and the ability to create. As a point forward, he made everyone better. Upon arrival he became the spokesman for the team. He exuded class. It was a loss for the NBA, and its fans, when he broke his foot and missed portions of four years recuperating. It was unfortunate that we were never able to surround Grant with enough talent to win while he was with the Pistons.

9. Dave Bing. When the Pistons lost a 1966 coin flip for University of Michigan star Cazzie Russell, Dave Bing became a Detroiter. Bing was a pure player who led the league in scoring his second season, invoking shouts of "BING-O" that would echo around a vacant Cobo Arena as he hit shot after shot. Until the arrival of Bob Lanier, Dave was pretty much out there by himself.

Articulate, passionate, committed to the team and the community, Bing applied those qualities on the court and to starting his own company, Bing Steel, and later to becoming mayor of the City of Detroit, an incredibly difficult and challenging position that he embraced, simply because he wanted to make a difference.

8. Chauncey Billups. Mr. Big Shot was a well-deserved nickname for the player who probably hit more big shots than anyone who ever played for the Pistons. Came to Detroit after bouncing around with four other NBA teams, and found a home here. He was the glue who never panicked, always under control, and played and lived with a class that was respected throughout the league. He made it all work—positioning the team on the floor, riding the hot hand, and doing all the little things that you could ask from a point guard. When he won the 2004 NBA Finals MVP Award, the whole city shared it with him. He could lie dormant for an entire game, waiting for the opportunity to win it, and, invariably, he would.

7. Bill Laimbeer. Tough. Competitive. Mean. Laimbeer was the conscience of the Bad Boys. He set the tone, and was an enormous piece of Jack McCloskey's puzzle. Truly, the player you hated, unless he was on your team. Laims cared not at all for opponents. He and fellow Bad Boy Rick Mahorn were best friends until Rick was sent to Minnesota in the expansion draft of 1989. After that, Bill would not talk with him. He was the sponge that absorbed the hatred from other teams and fans. He took it so that his teammates could play their games. He was ridiculed because he couldn't jump, heckled for his lack of athletic ability—but all he cared about was beating you. His mental focus was crucial for him, and when he retired, it wasn't because his physical ability was gone; it was more because he was just burned out of his passion. He was there every night, playing almost 900 games in a row before being suspended by the league (he would tell you it was the other guy's fault).

6. Ben Wallace. Ben came to Detroit from Orlando for Grant Hill. Oh, were we criticized for that deal. But in 12 months Ben became the icon of the reborn Pistons. With his mop of unruly hair, his ability to block almost any shot, and his 48-minute attitude, he endeared himself to everyone in Detroit. Defensively, he was the eraser in the golf bag. Everyone played a little harder because he did. Teammates played tougher D because Ben had their backs. He was symbolic of a city that didn't have all the advantages of others, but made up for it by just strapping it on every day and "Goin' to Work."

5. Jack McCloskey. Trader Jack came to town as a coach who had never sat in the GM's chair. He tore the team down and started over, making a hundred trades—some good, some bad. But the good ones, oh, my!!! Bill Laimbeer, Vinnie Johnson, Rick Mahorn, Adrian Dantley, Mark Aguirre, James Edwards. Add to that his drafting of Isiah, Dumars, Rodman, and Salley. At one point Jack had drafted 14 first-round players and ALL of them were still in the league!! But competitive—he was Isiah in a sports coat. He absolutely hated to lose. Tearing up the equipment room. Throwing everything not nailed down around the training room. Keep your distance!! But that's what you loved about him. Piece by piece, he assembled the Bad Boys—the best team to never be appreciated by anyone not from Detroit.

4. Chuck Daly. Seldom has the perfect coach met the perfect team for him. The Pistons mix of toughness, arrogance, and talent needed someone who could orchestrate that mixture and keep it pointed in the same direction. Daly said that it was like coaching a dozen corporations, with ego and money to burn. Daddy Rich always said the key to his success was the ability to go deaf. "Never listen to the players complain when you pulled them. Always remember that it's a long season, and you need the players for 82 games." It was a volatile balance of somehow being their equal yet their boss. Equally cool. Equally calm. Equally giving. And he made it seem soooooo easy.

3. Joe Dumars. While his backcourt partner Isiah Thomas was so visibly passionate, Joe Dumars played in his shadow—every bit as talented and every bit as competitive, but every bit of it hidden behind a facade of calm and cool. He was the best defensive player of his era. His MVP performance in the 1990 NBA Finals against Portland—while dealing with his father's passing in the middle of the series—is what he will always be remembered for. A remarkable shooter not prone to ups and downs, he would wipe the sweat of his brow, tug up his shorts, and laser focus on the man he was supposed to be guarding that night.

After his playing days Joe ascended to the Pistons GM position and put together the 2004 "Goin' to Work" NBA champions. He even had the NBA citizenship award named after him. A well-deserved honor.

2. Isiah Thomas. The point guard from the University of Indiana was the key player in reversing the fortunes of a long-suffering organization. He was perhaps the most intense competitor in Pistons history, which drove him to be bold, audacious, daring, and to do whatever it took to win games. I saw him saw a cast off a broken hand so he could play. I saw him sit in a vat of freezing water for a severely sprained ankle for days, and then wrap that ankle until it was like concrete, so that he could play in Game 6 of the NBA Finals against the Lakers in 1988. Time and again, he'd take the big shot when every player, every coach, and every fan knew what was coming—and deliver more often than not. HE WAS the Bad Boys. No one was allowed to get hurt or be selfish with Isiah; it was always about team. The Palace was truly the house Isiah built. Inch for inch, arguably as good as anyone who has played.

1. Bill Davidson. Perhaps the consummate owner. His passion for the game, and for those who worked for him in pursuit of excellence, and championships, was second to none. He was brilliant but didn't wear it on his sleeve. He was a self-made man who took great pride in overcoming the odds. It was his vision to take a moribund franchise from a tiny, empty arena in downtown Detroit to the Pontiac Silverdome and its 80,000 (mostly empty, for a number of years) seats. Then, because he wanted HIS team to play in an arena befitting its talents, he funded what was, at the time, the most expensive privately financed arena in history—The Palace of Auburn Hills. He also was the first to buy a private plane to give his team every chance to succeed. Players and staff worked hard to return his demonstrated passion for them.

The 10 Most Important Individuals in Toronto Raptors History :: by Matt Guokas

Matt Guokas has been part of the NBA as a broadcaster, head coach, and player for four decades longer than have the Toronto Raptors—the 1995 expansion franchise whose most impactful players and front office folks he lists below.

10. Isiah Thomas. The team's first general manager brought with him all the star power a new franchise needs, along with all the commotion that only Isiah can create.

9. Jose Calderon. The point guard from Spain has played all seven of his NBA seasons in Toronto. He is in the top five in points and first in assists in franchise history, and has finished in the league's top 10 in assists four times.

8. Tracy McGrady. Toronto drafted the high school senior with their first pick in the 1997 NBA Draft. He played three years in Toronto, where he refined his craft, before launching into superstardom in Orlando and Houston.

7. Morris Peterson. The left-hander from Michigan State has played in more games (542) as a Raptor than anyone. He had his best season in 2005–06, when he averaged 16.8 points a game.

6. John Bitove, Jr. His family, which controlled JB Big Boys and Roy Rogers, headed the ownership group that secured Toronto an NBA expansion franchise in 1995.

5. Sam Mitchell. Sam is the winningest coach in Raptors history. In his five seasons of coaching the team (2004–09), he led Toronto to two playoff appearances and was named NBA Coach of the Year for his efforts in the 2006–07 season.

4. Bryan Colangelo. The son of the great Jerry Colangelo, Bryan came to Toronto from Chicago to serve as the Raptors president and general manager. Twice he has been named NBA Executive of the Year.

3. Damon Stoudamire. The University of Arizona product was the seventh overall pick in the 1995 NBA Draft. During his time in Toronto he was named NBA Rookie of the Year for the 1995–96 season and finished in the league's top 10 in assists three times.

2. Vince Carter. The Tar Heel product could jump out of the gym and throw down a windmill dunk on his way back down, or pull up and take a three-pointer. He has the highest points per game average (23.4) in franchise history. His seven years playing north of the border included five NBA All-Star Game appearances.

1. Chris Bosh. The only player to score over 10,000 points as a Raptor, the Georgia Tech center with the smooth left-handed stroke also leads the franchise in rebounds. He averaged 20.2 points and 9.4 rebounds a game, and played in five All-Star Games during his seven seasons (2003–10) as a Raptor.

Top 10 Most Impactful People on the Houston Rockets Franchise :: by Jim Foley

Jim Foley spent 39 years in the NBA. After three years (1969–72) as public relations director of the Milwaukee Bucks he worked 36 years with the Houston Rockets (1972–2008)—15 years as the team's public relations director and 21 years as its radio color commentator. He retired in 2008.

10. Carroll Dawson. CD joined the Rockets in 1980 and remains connected with the team. Dawson was an assistant coach in Houston for 16 years, during which time the Rockets reached four NBA Finals. In 1996, he became general manager, a position he held for 11 years and used to acquire players Charles Barkley, Scottie Pippen, Steve Francis, Yao Ming, and Tracy McGrady. Since retirement in 2007, he has served as a senior consultant. He was inducted in the Texas Sports Hall of Fame in 2003.

9. Clyde Drexler. Though he played just a quarter of his 16 NBA seasons with his hometown Rockets, Clyde "The Glide" Drexler is one of the most popular players in Houston sports history. He played at Sterling High School and with the University of Houston's Phi Slamma Jamma teams. During the 1995 playoffs he averaged 21 points per game, as the Rockets became the first No. 6 seed to win an NBA title. For the past seven years he has been part of the Rockets television crew. He was inducted into the Basketball Hall of Fame in 2004.

8. Leslie Alexander. Only a few NBA owners have been around as long as Rockets owner Leslie Alexander. His teams won back-to-back titles in 1994 and 1995, and only three Rocket teams during his 18-year tenure have had losing seasons. Perhaps his biggest achievement was to convince Harris County voters to approve a new arena—the state of the art Toyota Center, which opened in 2003. Mr. Alexander also founded the Clutch City Foundation, which has raised over $12 million for local charities since 1995.

7. Elvin Hayes. In January 1968, a crowd of 52,693 watched Elvin Hayes and the Houston Cougars beat UCLA in the "Game of the Century" at the Astrodome. Three years later a Houston group purchased the San Diego Rockets—with their top player, Elvin Hayes—and moved the team to Houston. Hayes was an instant star in the NBA, but after a year back in Houston and the team playing and drawing poorly, he was traded. The Big E not only spent his first four pro years as a Rocket and brought the "big leagues" to Houston, he would put the finishing touches on a 16-year Hall of Fame career by returning to Houston for his final three seasons.

6. Ray Patterson. Ray Patterson became the chief operating officer of the Rockets in 1971 and remained in the job for 18 years. In the early years he often dipped into his own pocket to help with team expenses. The opening of the Summit helped the team over the hump. During Patterson's first decade with the Rockets, the franchise changed ownership six times. Most agree that without Ray Patterson there would not be an NBA team in Houston. All but four of Patterson's last 17 teams made the postseason, and two (in 1981 and 1986) reached the NBA Finals.

5. Calvin Murphy. The 5-9 "Pocket Rocket" spent his entire 13-year NBA career as a Houston Rocket, with only Hakeem Olajuwon playing more years in Houston. One of the most exciting players of his era, Murphy averaged over 20 points per game in five seasons and had a career scoring mark of nearly 18 points per game. One of the top free throw shooters ever, he had a career accuracy of .892 and shot .958 (206 of 215) from the line for the 1980–81 season. Despite his prominence as a scorer, Murphy remains the Rockets all-time assist leader. He went into the Hall of Fame in 1993.

4. Moses Malone. Moses Malone played the first half dozen of his 17 NBA seasons with the Rockets and remains the franchise's all-time leader in scoring average (24.0 ppg) and rebounding average (15.0 rpg). His 31.1 points per game in 1981–82 is the only time a Rocket averaged 30 or better for a season. Twice with the Rockets he was voted the NBA's MVP, in 1979 and 1982. He led the Rockets to the NBA Finals in 1981, only the second time a team got there after posting a losing record in the regular season. Straight out of Virginia's Petersburg High School to the pros, Malone was inducted into the Basketball Hall of Fame in 2001.

3. Yao Ming. As the top choice of the 2002 NBA Draft, Yao Ming immediately brought aboard a billion new Rockets fans—his fellow Chinese. The best Chinese player of all-time, as well as the best player ever over 7-2, the 7-6 Yao Ming averaged 19 points and nine rebounds and was a six-time All-Star during his eight NBA playing years. His career was cut short at age 29 by foot injuries. The consummate teammate will be remembered not only for his talent but also for his many humanitarian efforts, both in this country and in his homeland.

2. Rudy Tomjanovich. Rudy Tomjanovich spent 33 consecutive seasons with the Rockets, starting as a player in 1970. In 11 playing seasons, he averaged 17 points and eight rebounds per game, while ranking third in career games and points. Five times he was named to the All-Star Game. In 1981, he joined the Houston coaching staff and worked under Del Harris, Bill Fitch, and Don Chaney before being named the Rockets head coach a decade later. In 12 seasons, he became the winningest head coach in team history, with 527 wins and a winning percentage of .559. His 1993–94 team set the club mark for best season, with a 58-24 (.707) mark. That team, along with the 1994–95 team, won back-to-back NBA titles, beating New York in seven games in the 1994 NBA Finals and sweeping Orlando in the 1995 Finals.

1. Hakeem Olajuwon. Hakeem "The Dream" Olajuwon is the greatest Rocket of them all. His accomplishments over 17 seasons with the team are unequaled. In 1994, he was named the NBA's MVP. In 1994 and in 1995, he was named the MVP of the Finals in honor of his leading the Rockets to back-to-back NBA championships. Six times he was first team All-NBA and five times first team All- Defensive, including two seasons when he was named Defender of the Year. He is the Rockets all-time leader in nearly two dozen statistical categories and is at or near the top in several all-time NBA categories (first in blocked shots; eighth in points and steals; 11th in rebounds). Named one of the 50 Greatest Players in NBA History in 1996, Olajuwon was inducted into the Basketball Hall of Fame in 2008.

Top 10 Individuals to Impact Philadelphia Professional Basketball
:: by Jim Lynam

Jim Lynam first coached in college before going to the NBA, where he was a head coach for ten seasons in the 1980s and '90s with the Philadelphia 76ers, Washington Bullets, and Los Angeles Clippers. He also served as the general manager of the 76ers. Here, he lists the most important individuals in the history of pro basketball in Philadelphia, a city that has hosted two NBA franchises, four NBA championships, and lots of great players, coaches and front-office people.

Honorable Mention. Pat Croce; Larry Brown; Alex Hannum; Harvey Pollack; Andrew Toney.

10. Paul Arizin. Pitchin' Paul spent all 10 seasons of his storybook NBA career in his native town with the Philadelphia Warriors. Cut from his La Salle High School team, he was a walk-on at Villanova University. In his senior year he led the nation in scoring and was selected by the Warriors with their first pick in the 1950 NBA Draft.

In 1950–51, he was Rookie of the Year. The guard/forward would twice lead the NBA in scoring, first in the 1951–52 season, and then again in the 1956–57 season after returning from two years service for the US Marines during the Korean War. Arizin played in 10 NBA All-Star Games, was first team All-NBA on three occasions, and was inducted into the Basketball Hall of Fame in 1978.

9. Hal Greer. He was one of the linchpins of the Philadelphia 76ers first championship team in 1967, averaging 22.1 points per game during the regular season and 27.7 during the postseason. Greer is the all-time leading team scorer. He played in 10 straight NBA All-Star Games and was second team All-NBA seven times. He is ranked by many as the third-best guard to play in the 1960s, behind Oscar Robertson and Jerry West. He still holds the record for the most points scored in a quarter in an NBA All-Star Game (19), setting the mark in 1968 when he was the game's Most Valuable Player.

8. Harold Katz. A former high school basketball player who loved the game, he became the ultimate fantasy league player when he bought the 76ers in 1982 for $12 million. He immediately made an impact on the franchise when he signed Moses Malone to the richest contract in the league, turning an NBA Finals team into an NBA championship team the following season.

Katz had reenergized the fan base and made his Sixers the No. 1 sports topic in the city of Philadelphia. One year later he would draft an undersized/overweight power forward from Auburn by the name of Charles Barkley against the recommendations of many. Katz saw a future Hall of Fame talent in Barkley, and again he was right on the money.

7. Eddie "The Mogul" Gottlieb. Gotty not only put pro basketball on the map in Philadelphia as general manager and owner when he bought the Warriors in 1952 for $25,000, he was also one of the driving forces that established the NBA as a major professional sports league. Up to his passing in 1979 he had been solely responsible for drawing up the NBA schedule for the previous 30 years (and if rumor is correct, he did it all in longhand on a yellow legal tablet). He was also the head of the NBA rules committee for 25 years and the author of the famous "territorial draft" rule that allowed the Philadelphia Warriors to secure the rights to Wilt Chamberlain because he played high school in Philadelphia (the only time that a "territorial" pick was based on high school location). Longtime Temple Head Coach and Hall of Famer Harry Litwack once said of Gottlieb, "He's about as important to the game as the basketball itself."

6. Billy Cunningham. The Kangaroo Kid has the unique distinction of being the only person to have both played and coached on a Philadelphia 76ers NBA championship team. The No. 7 overall pick in the 1965 NBA Draft, Cunningham was fiery and exciting on the court, with his slashing, high-flying style. He was named first team All-NBA in 1969, 1970, and 1971. In his eight seasons (1977–85) as the Sixers coach, he would lead his team to the Finals three times and win the championship in 1983. Billy C's 454 wins as a head coach ranks him 12th on the NBA's all-time wins list while his coaching record and winning percentage put him at the top of the list in Philadelphia 76er annals.

5. Charles Barkley. Sir Charles burst onto the Philadelphia 76er scene in the 1984–85 season. He joined the likes of Moses Malone, Julius Erving, and Mo Cheeks, making one of the league's top teams even better. He immediately became a fan favorite based not only on his amazing combination of athleticism, quickness, and strength, but also for his off-the-court personality.

He was a terrific ball handler, underrated passer, and relentless rebounder (he led the NBA with 14.6 rebounds per game in 1986–87). During his final six All-Star seasons in Philadelphia he averaged 25 points and 11 rebounds a game. He finished his career as an 11-time NBA All-Star, was selected first team All-NBA on four occasions, and won the league's Most Valuable Player Award in 1993.

4. Allen Iverson. AI came to the 76ers as the top pick in the 1996 NBA Draft. Night in, night out, he entertained the Philadelphia faithful with his non-stop, frenetic style. Despite his diminutive stature he was among the most dynamic and fearless men to ever wear an NBA uniform. Always on the attack, he shot an astounding 8,168 free throws over his 14-year NBA career (averaging over nine per game). He was a 10-time NBA All-Star, led the league in scoring in four seasons, and was the NBA's Most Valuable Player in 2000–01, when he led the Sixers to the NBA Finals. In the history of the NBA his playoff scoring average (29.6 ppg) is second only to Michael Jordan's.

3. Moses Malone. Moses Malone arrived in town in 1982, his blue-collar work ethic a perfect fit in Philadelphia. He served as the missing link, leading the Sixers back to the NBA Finals in 1983 for their fourth Finals appearance in seven years. But this time Malone was the difference as Philadelphia won its first NBA championship in 16 years as he dominated the Lakers and Kareem Abdul-Jabbar by averaging 26 points and 16 rebounds in the four-game sweep. Before the playoffs Mo had predicted sweeps in all three playoff series with his famous "Fo', fo', fo'" line. He missed by one game, as the 76ers went 12-1 in the postseason.

2. Julius Erving. When The Doctor came to Philadelphia in 1976, he took the NBA game to another level—literally. He was in a class by himself when it came to electrifying the crowd with thunderous dunks and on-the-court/off-the-court grace and elegance, making him as one of the great ambassadors of the game.

Erving was the league MVP in 1981 and a five-time NBA All-Star after an amazing ABA stint in which he led the league in scoring on three occasions and was a two-time MVP. He was inducted into the Hall of Fame in 1993 and was selected as one of the 50 Greatest Players in NBA History.

1. Wilt Chamberlain. Wilt began his amazing career as a Philadelphia Warrior in 1959. To say that he is the greatest force in the history of the game would be an understatement. He averaged 37 points and 27 rebounds per game *in his rookie year*.

Some more of Chamberlain's statistical accomplishments that will endure for the ages:

On March 2, 1962, he scored 100 points in a game against the New York Knicks

He averaged over 50 ppg for the *entire* 1961–62 season

On November 24, 1960, he grabbed 55 rebounds in a single game vs. the Boston Celtics and longtime nemesis Bill Russell

He led the league in field-goal percentage nine times

In 1967 he set a record by scoring on 35 *consecutive* field-goal attempts

During the 1966–67 season, Chamberlain, at the urging of Coach Alex Hannum, played a more team-oriented game and submitted arguably one off the most productive NBA seasons ever, averaging 24.1 points (a career low at that time), a league-leading 24.2 rebounds, and 7.8 assists per game (third best in the NBA) while shooting 68 percent from the field. The stunning numbers earned him the league's Most Valuable Player Award, and he led the team to his first NBA title.

Longtime Temple Head Coach and Hall of Famer John Chaney may have summed up Wilt the best when he said, "Forget about all the records that he set, the Big Fella's real legacy is the number of rules that they changed or put in the books just to try to contain him."

Most Impactful Individuals in Spurs History :: by Mike Monroe

Mike Monroe is the NBA beat writer for the *San Antonio Express-News*, where he also covers the San Antonio Spurs. Here he lists the most important players, coaches, and executives to serve the franchise, from its 1971 inception in the ABA as the struggling Dallas Chaparrals, to its current life as a 21st–century powerhouse that regularly competes for, and often wins, the NBA title.

10 (tie). Bob Bass and R. C. Buford. Bass served the Spurs for almost two decades as an assistant coach, head coach, and general manager. He drafted David Robinson and Sean Elliott, among others, and was named NBA Executive of the Year for the 1989–90 season.

Buford, a Spurs assistant coach from 1988–92, returned to the club in 1994 and has remained with the team since, becoming the Spurs general manager in 2002 and president of sports franchises for Spurs Sports and Entertainment in 2008. As GM he has had oversight of a roster that has been one of the NBA's best for more than a decade.

9. Sean Elliott. One of seven Spurs players whose numbers have been retired, Elliott's "Memorial Day Miracle" shot, a game-winning three-pointer against Portland in the 1999 Western Conference Finals, ranks as one of the most memorable plays in club history. After the 1999 NBA Finals he received a kidney transplant and in 2000 became the first player to play in the NBA after a major organ transplant.

8. Tony Parker. The 28th overall pick of the 2001 NBA Draft, Parker came to the Spurs as a 19-year-old and almost immediately became the team's starting point guard. A four-time All-Star, he was MVP of the 2007 NBA Finals after making 56.7 percent of his shots from the floor and averaging 24.5 points per game. During the 2011–12 season he became the team's all-time leader in assists.

7. Manu Ginobili. A second-round draft pick and 57th overall pick in 1999, Ginobili became a key member of the Spurs Big Three, along with Tim Duncan and Tony Parker, after joining the team in 2002–03. A two-time All-Star, Ginobili's fiery style of play has made him a community favorite and one of the most popular players in club history.

6. Peter Holt. Since Holt became chairman and CEO in 1996 of what ultimately became Spurs Sports and Entertainment, the team has won four championships. Of equal importance, Holt engineered a successful campaign for a new arena, which opened in 2002 and may well have kept the team in San Antonio. Twice the Spurs have been named the best organization in all of pro sports (2003 and 2005) and six times as the best franchise in the NBA by *ESPN the Magazine's* Ultimate Standings.

5. Angelo Drossos. The Spurs would not be in San Antonio had not Drossos and several other San Antonio businessmen leased the ABA's Dallas Chaparrals in 1972 and brought them to South Texas. Drossos also secured George Gervin from the Virginia Squires as that team was being dismantled. He was also instrumental in the merger of the ABA and NBA while making sure that San Antonio would be one of the only four ABA teams that survived.

4. George Gervin. The franchise's first legitimate superstar, George "Iceman" Gervin won four NBA scoring titles and appeared in 12 NBA All-Star Games, but his importance is magnified given the role he played when four ABA teams were merged into the NBA in 1976. He is third on the team's all-time scoring list with 19,383 points, fourth in games played (709), and the all-time leader in combined ABA-NBA points, with 23,602 in 15 seasons. Gervin was the first Spur elected to the Naismith Memorial Basketball Hall of Fame.

3. Gregg Popovich. In his 16 seasons as head coach, Popovich has guided the Spurs to four championships and a winning percentage of .675, the third highest in NBA history. He is one of only 14 NBA coaches with more than 800 wins. He also served as the Spurs GM until 2002 and remains president of basketball operations. Popovich is credited with creating the atmosphere for success that still permeates the Spurs organization.

2. David Robinson. Before Duncan arrived the Spurs became one of the NBA's elite teams because Robinson was a Hall of Fame center whose physicality and athleticism allowed him to dominate games. A member of two Spurs championship teams, he is the club's all-time leader in blocked shots, and second in points, rebounds, and games played.

1. Tim Duncan. Until the two-time MVP power forward arrived, the Spurs had never won a championship. By the end of his eighth season, they had won four titles. An All-Star each of his first 14 seasons (except 1999, when there was no NBA All-Star Game) he was/is the linchpin of the Spurs teams that won 69.9 percent of their games, second-best in NBA history.

Most Important Individuals in Suns History :: by Matt Guokas

Veteran NBA broadcaster and former Magic and 76ers head coach Matt Guokas entered the NBA as a player in 1966, three years before the Phoenix Suns joined the league. In the succeeding decades he's watched the Suns make the playoffs 29 times and post the fourth-highest winning percentage of all NBA franchises. That success is due to the club's fine management team and the players they scouted and developed into some of the NBA's best. Here are the members of the Suns organization Matt rates as the most vital to the franchise's proud history.

11. Al McCoy. The voice of the Suns has been a constant with the team since 1972. You can't have one without the other.

10. Connie Hawkins. The Hawk swooped into Phoenix in 1969 and became the Suns first superstar. He led the team in scoring and rebounding through some of the franchise's early years, and played in four straight NBA All-Star Games before knee injuries derailed his game.

9. Cotton Fitzsimmons. Fitzsimmons won NBA Coach of the Year in 1989, when he led the Suns to the Western Conference Finals versus the Lakers. He is second on the team's all-time wins list, with 341.

8. John MacLeod. MacLeod is first on the team's all-time wins list, with 579. He was the Suns head coach from 1973 to 1989, and led the Suns to the NBA Finals in 1976.

7. Alvan Adams. The center in a forward's body played all 988 games of his NBA career as a Sun and is second on the team's all-time scoring list, with 13,910 points. In the 1975–76 season he was named Rookie of the Year, played in the All-Star Game, and led the Suns to the NBA Finals—a series that included the historic triple-overtime Game 5 in the Boston Garden.

6. Charles Barkley. He was only in Phoenix for four years of his 16-year Hall of Fame career, but they may have been his best. An All-Star in each of his seasons in Phoenix, he averaged over 23 points and 11 rebounds a game for the Suns. He won the league's MVP Award for the 1992–93 season, which ended with the Suns losing in the NBA Finals.

5. Kevin Johnson. The great point guard could distribute, score, and help charities. Four times in his career he averaged a double-double (points-assists) for the season and played in three All-Star Games. He was vital to a dramatic Suns turnaround that saw the team nearly double its winning percentage to .671 for his first full season in Phoenix, and average an even higher winning percentage over the course of the next six seasons.

4. Walter Davis. The smooth shooting guard/small forward came to Phoenix from the University of North Carolina. The six-time All-Star was named Rookie of the Year in 1978 and is the franchise's all-time leading scorer, with 15,666 points.

3. Dick Van Arsdale. Known as the Original Sun, Van Arsdale was chosen by the Phoenix Suns in 1968 in their expansion draft. He scored the franchise's first basket and played in three All- Star Games. He was the heart of the team. To this day, he remains involved with the Suns in the front office.

2. Steve Nash. The two-time MVP from South Africa by way of Canada is in the middle of a Hall of Fame career that began in Phoenix in 1996, and then traveled to Dallas for six seasons. As a Sun he has been voted to five All-Star Games and led the league in assists six times. His return to Phoenix from Dallas for the 2004–05 season sparked a remarkable Suns revival, as the team more than doubled its winning percentage from the previous season while going from sixth place to first place in the Pacific Division.

1. Jerry Colangelo. At age 28, Jerry Colangelo was named general manger of the Suns in the franchise's maiden year. He continued in that capacity for over three decades and led the group that bought the team in 1987. He has established himself as one of the league's shrewdest talent evaluators, drafting stars like Walter Davis, Alvan Adams, Steve Nash, and Amare Stoudemire, and trading for others like Kevin Johnson and Charles Barkley. Over his tenure the Suns played in two NBA Finals and posted the league's fourth best all-time winning percentage.

Top 10 SuperSonics of All Time
:: by James Donaldson

James Donaldson is a former NBA All-Star center who scored over 12,000 points and grabbed almost 2,500 rebounds during his career. The 7-2 author of *Standing Above the Crowd* is also a veteran entrepreneur who works as a motivational speaker. He played the first three of his 14 NBA seasons for the Seattle SuperSonics, a team that was in the NBA from 1968 to 2008 before renaming itself the Thunder and moving to Oklahoma City. During its time in Seattle, the franchise put some great players on the court, especially these 10.

10. Marvin Webster. The Human Eraser gave the Sonics a much-needed presence in the middle in the late 1970s as they were building towards a championship team. Marvin was one of the few players in the league who could match up one-on-one against the other great centers of the NBA. A shot blocker extraordinaire!

9. Paul Silas. Not known for his athletic ability, Paul Silas provided leadership on and off the court for many of the younger players around him. A true gentleman and mentor (but also a fierce competitor), Silas provided the lead that the other guys on the Sonics always followed.

8. Fred "Downtown" Brown. If the three-point line had been around during the early part of this terrific marksman's career, he would have been one of the leading scorers in the league, year after year. Brown gave the Sonics explosive firepower, especially coming off the bench. A big contributor to the 1978–79 championship team.

7. Gus Williams. Gus was probably the fastest player in the league in his prime. He could go baseline to baseline like no other. Because he had defenders constantly "backpedaling," he would pull up and hit the midrange jumper when needed. A fun-loving guy who many of the championship players gravitated towards, Gus kept things loose while at the same time giving the 1978–79 championship team terrific athletic ability and scoring from the guard position.

6. Spencer Haywood. Woody was the forerunner of the prototype power forward. He also set the stage for underclassmen to enter into the NBA. A great player who could score, rebound, run the floor, and play defense. People tend to forget how great he was. He alone was probably more responsible than anyone for establishing Seattle as a great NBA city.

5. John "JJ" Johnson. Johnson gave the title-winning championship Sonics the versatility the team needed to free up the other players to be more effective. He was among the first of the small forwards with the ability to play either guard position and run the offense effectively. He created the "point forward" position. His selflessness and leadership on the court was one of the reasons that the Sonics were able to win the NBA championship in 1979.

4. Jack Sikma. Sikma confounded and caused difficult matchups for most big men in the league. Known as the Banger, he wasn't afraid to mix it up inside, but his true strength came from his ability to execute an "inside pivot jump shot" that was almost impossible to block. A smart, team-oriented, and consistent player, Sikma was an integral part of the great championship team.

3. Shawn Kemp. Kemp brought true excitement throughout the 1990s to some very good and dominant Sonic teams. There's never been a player who played "above the rim" and was able to run the court the way that the Reign Man did. In his prime he was truly one of the best power forwards in the league.

2. Gary Payton. Gary "The Glove" Payton was the best "true point guard" the Sonics ever had. He led the team flawlessly, night after night, and year after year. With breakneck speed, he was able to score at will and play "lockdown" defense on any guard in the league. He was also known for his nonstop chatter on the court, as he was either barking out orders to his teammates or trash-talking an opponent. He was part of the great Seattle teams throughout the 1990s.

1. Dennis Johnson. DJ was "the rock"—a steady presence from the guard position, as he played along with the great players on the Sonics NBA title team. At 6-4, with very long arms and the ability to quickly move his feet, he played terrific defense on whomever he was matched up against—and never shied away from taking on the other team's most explosive scorer. Whenever you talk to one of the championship players from the Sonic team, without a doubt, the conversation circles back around to Dennis Johnson and how valuable he was to their championship team.

Top 10 People Who Helped Make the Thunder Such a Quick Success Story
:: by Berry Tramel

Berry Tramel has been a sportswriter and editor for the *Oklahoman* since 1991. He was born and raised in Norman. Here, he lists the people most responsible for bringing an NBA team to his home state, and for making the Oklahoma City Thunder such an instant success story.

10. Rick Horrow. The sports business consultant helped Oklahoma City (OKC) leaders push through the sales-tax vote in 1992 that brought many new structures to the city, including the arena that became the Ford Center. When the Hornets went looking for a temporary home, OKC was ready.

9. Chris Paul. When the Hornets came to OKC in September 2005, they brought a just-drafted point guard who became an immediate impact player. Paul made the Hornets competitive and helped create a hunger in Oklahoma City for a permanent NBA team.

8. Brad Keller. The Seattle attorney was the star of the showdown lawsuit in which Seattle tried to keep the franchise's chairman, Clay Bennett, from moving the team. Keller's theatrics eventually prompted a settlement, which allowed Bennett to move the Sonics to OKC.

7. Scotty Brooks. In their maiden season in OKC, the Thunder, under Head Coach P. J. Carlesimo, was 1-12 after 13 games. Carlesimo was fired, Brooks was promoted to head coach, and the team has been ascending ever since.

6. Russell Westbrook. Durant, everyone saw coming. But who knew Westbrook would develop into an NBA All-Star in just his third season? Westbrook's development gave Durant a sidekick and OKC the talent to become a title contender.

5. George Shinn. OKC's first taste of the NBA was an excellent experience, in part because the Hornets owner always had made a commitment to entertainment. The Hornets' game presentation was superb, and the team wasn't half bad, either. Oklahoma City quickly fell for the NBA.

4. Sam Presti. The young general manager, hired by Clay Bennett in Seattle, quickly remade the roster with financial prudence, setting up the Thunder for long-term success.

3. Mick Cornett. The Oklahoma City mayor was long a conduit for NBA Commissioner David Stern, letting him know the city still was in the market for a franchise. Cornett is a symbol of OKC's strong government/business leadership, and was a big reason OKC voters passed a sales-tax referendum to renovate the Ford Center.

2. Kevin Durant. A lovable superstar is never a bad starting point for a franchise, and Durant provided the Thunder a face for the franchise and an elite scorer.

1. Clay Bennett. The Thunder chairman helped put together the business leaders who made the Hornets an immediate economic success upon their relocation after Hurricane Katrina, and then formed the group that bought the Seattle SuperSonics and eventually moved them to OKC.

Timberwolves Personalities Who Have Most Impacted the Franchise
:: by Tom Hanneman

Tom Hanneman is the television play-by-play announcer for the Minnesota Timberwolves. He has been with the team since the Timberwolves first broke into the league in 1989.

11. Kevin Harlon. The original voice of the Wolves, Kevin called games on radio and TV for the Timberwolves' first nine seasons. At first listeners didn't know what to make of this young announcer, but by the time he departed the team for the national stage, Harlan had become a legend. His machine-gun, high-energy calls were unlike any that fans in the Upper Midwest had ever heard. Tony Campbell hit shots "right between the eyes," while Kevin Garnett demonstrated "no regard for human life." Harlan made a struggling young franchise must-hear radio and must-see TV.

10. Ricky Rubio. It's too early to determine what impact Rubio might ultimately have, but based upon his start, Ricky could rocket to the top of the list. Timberwolves fans waited two seasons for the young Spaniard to arrive, and when he did, Rubio reignited their pure passion for the franchise. Not only in Minnesota, but around the globe. Fans quickly learned not to take their eyes off the baby-faced 21-year-old guard with the most amazing court vision in Wolves history.

9. Bill Musselman. A team often takes on the personality of its head coach. That was the case with the inaugural edition of the Timberwolves. Bill Musselman was intense. A do-whatever-it-takes-to-win personality. His first roster was filled with tough but inexperienced competitors. Musselman got the most out of every one of them. His drive to succeed impacted many of those players and a young assistant to pursue coaching careers of their own. Five of them became NBA head coaches. Three of them went on to earn the NBA Coach of the Year Award: Sam Mitchell in 2007 with Toronto; Scott Brooks in 2010 with Oklahoma City; and Tom Thibodeau, the Chicago Bulls head coach in 2011.

8. Flip Saunders. The most successful coach in Timberwolves history. In his nine seasons at the helm, Flip produced the team's first eight playoff appearances, capped by a trip to the Western Conference Finals in 2004. Saunders is the only head coach to direct the Wolves to the playoffs. Flip is the Timberwolves all-time leader in coaching victories, with 411 wins (358 more than the runner-up).

7. Kevin McHale. After he closed out his Hall of Fame career with the Celtics, McHale returned home to Minnesota, first as a television analyst for the Wolves, later as the team's GM, and then as president of basketball operations and head coach. McHale struck out on some draft picks, but he also hit some home runs—most notably with Kevin Love and Kevin Garnett, the two greatest players in Timberwolves history. Not only did he bring them to Minnesota, but he also helped launch their careers by sharing his considerable NBA experience on and off the court.

6. Sam Mitchell. Sam Mitchell was a Timberwolves original. He scored the first points in franchise history and helped shape a kid out of high school into a future Hall of Famer. Tough, intense, and talented, Mitchell was the Wolves vocal leader during his 10 years in Minnesota. He commanded respect and demanded total commitment from his teammates. Sam and fellow veteran Terry Porter were instrumental in teaching a teenager named Kevin Garnett how to do things the right way from the start. It was the most important double-team in Timberwolves history.

5. Glen Taylor. Seeing the franchise faced with the prospect of new ownership and a move to New Orleans in 1994, NBA Commissioner David Stern was determined to keep the Timberwolves in the Land of 10,000 Lakes. His search for a local owner ended when Glen Taylor stepped forward and purchased the team in 1995. The former Minnesota state senator from Mankato ensured that Minnesota wouldn't lose another NBA franchise. It was the greatest save in Timberwolves history.

3 (tie). Marv Wolfenson and Harvey Ratner. Without Marv and Harv, the Timberwolves never would have existed. The founders of the franchise brought the NBA back to Minnesota for the first time in 29 years following the Lakers departure for Los Angeles. After drawing over a million fans to the Metrodome in the team's inaugural 1989–90 season, Wolfenson and Ratner built the Target Center, which has served as the Wolves home ever since. Marv and Harv struck a deal to sell the franchise and relocate it to New Orleans in 1994. The NBA blocked the sale a month later.

2. Kevin Love. When Kevin Garnett was traded to Boston in 2007, the Wolves lost their identity. It took a quantum leap by Kevin Love three years later to put the team back on track. Love put together some impressive numbers en route to earning the NBA's Most Improved Player Award in 2011. He produced the league's first 30-30 game in 28 years. He delivered a double-double in 53 consecutive games, won his first NBA rebounding title, and became the first player in 28 years to average at least 20 points and 15 rebounds a game. Love offered hope to a franchise that had been in a tailspin.

A year later Love continued his climb and was hailed as the best power forward in the game. In 2012, he became just the second player in team history to earn multiple All-Star invitations. Timberwolves fans have been hit hard by the power of Love.

1. Kevin Garnett. The greatest player in Timberwolves history, KG was more than just the face of the franchise for 12 seasons. Minnesotans watched him evolve from an ebullient 18-year-old tenderfoot to the best player on the planet, as the NBA's MVP in 2004. Garnett owns virtually every individual franchise record. He led the NBA in rebounding four consecutive seasons.

KG's intensity on the court and pure passion for the game made him the most popular athlete in the Upper Midwest since Kirby Puckett (his childhood idol).

Garnett delivered some legendary performances, none greater than his 32-point, 21-rebound Game 7 masterpiece on his 28th birthday, May 19, 2004, in a victory that sent the Wolves to the Western Conference Finals and is still considered by most as the greatest win in franchise history.

No one has ever impacted the Timberwolves more than Kevin Garnett.

Top 10 Portland Trail Blazers Personalities :: Kerry Eggers

Kerry Eggers is a longtime Portland sportswriter and lifelong Oregonian. He has written four sports books and is an award-winning writer who currently works for the *Portland Tribune*. Here, Kerry lists the stars of Portland's long-time romance with its Trail Blazers.

Honorable Mention. Buck Williams, the swashbuckling power forward who proved the final piece to the puzzle to get the Blazers to the NBA Finals in 1990 and 1992 (and is currently an assistant coach); the late Stu Inman, the architect of Portland's 1977 NBA championship as director of player personnel; Geoff Petrie, the 1970–71 Rookie of the Year and two-time All-Star guard who later served as general manager for the 1992 team that reached the finals.

10. Maurice Lucas. Luke's defining moment was his altercation with Philadelphia's Darryl Dawkins in Game 2 of the 1977 NBA Finals, but that was only part of his legacy as a Blazer. His partnership with Bill Walton in the trenches was the key to Portland's drive to the franchise's only world title that season. A three-time All-Star during his run with the Blazers, he was the ultimate enforcer on a team that had everything else. He was an assistant coach until his death from cancer in 2010.

9. Brandon Roy. Roy arrived on the scene in 2006 as the Blazers were trying to repair their reputation in the community and around the league after the "Jail Blazer" era. A breath of fresh air, he quickly became one of the most popular players in franchise history, earning Rookie of the Year honors in 2006–07. Roy made the All-Star Game three times (2008–10) as one of the game's most promising young shooting guards before a degenerative knee condition forced him to retire in 2011.

8. Larry Weinberg. A real estate developer in Southern California, Weinberg was one of three men who in 1970 paid $3.7 million to secure an NBA expansion franchise for Portland. Weinberg quickly jumped to the forefront of the ownership group and became team president in 1975, presiding over the team's only NBA title in 1977. He remained in the position until he sold the club to Paul Allen in 1988. The Blazers honored Weinberg by retiring a No. 1 jersey in his name in 1992.

7. Rick Adelman. A starting guard on the original 1970–71 Trail Blazers (he spent three seasons in a Portland uniform), Adelman apprenticed as an assistant coach under Jack Ramsay and Mike Schuler before taking over as Portland's head coach midway through the 1988–89 season. In his first full season, Adelman took the Blazers to the 1990 NBA Finals and made it there again in 1992. The Blazers reached the playoffs all six years Adelman was at their helm.

6. Paul Allen. The Microsoft cofounder and billionaire took over ownership from Larry Weinberg in 1988 and quickly saw results as the Blazers reached the NBA Finals in both 1990 and 1992. He provided the resources for Portland to run its playoff streak to 22 years and put up the bulk of the funds to ensure construction of the Rose Garden in 1995. Allen remains owner of the franchise that is regarded as one of the most stable in the NBA.

5. Bill Schonely. The original radio play-by-play broadcaster of the franchise remains an icon in Oregon and southwest Washington, and arguably the most popular figure ever associated with the team other than Clyde Drexler. The Schonz, who coined the phrase "Rip City" that is now synonymous with the team and the city, called games until 1998. He has since served as broadcaster emeritus and goodwill ambassador for the club, emceeing functions, delivering speeches, and maintaining legendary status in the community.

4. Jack Ramsay. The Hall of Fame coach had the greatest season of his long career in 1976–77, when he took a Trail Blazer franchise that had never made the playoffs to the pinnacle with an NBA championship. Ramsay served the longest term as coach in franchise history—10 years (1976–86)—and is by far the winningest coach the team has had, with a 453-367 record.

3. Harry Glickman. The man most responsible for bringing the city of Portland to the major leagues was Glickman, a local sports promoter who put together the ownership group and spearheaded the drive to gain an NBA expansion franchise in 1970. Glickman served as general manager and president of the club for 25 years.

2. Bill Walton. Walton's star shined for only a short time in Portland, but what a burst of light that spread over the region. The injury-plagued center put it all together in the 1976–77 season, becoming the spiritual and physical force behind the franchise's only NBA championship. Walton was even better the next season, earning the league's Most Valuable Player Award, as Portland started the season 50-10 and appeared on its way to a second successive title. Alas, Walton suffered a leg injury, the Blazers were eliminated in the first round of the playoffs, and, two years later, he was gone.

1. Clyde Drexler. Drexler arrived in Portland as an alumnus of the University of Houston's Phi Slamma Jamma fraternity and left 11 years later as the greatest player in franchise history. Clyde the Glide owned the city for many years. He was an eight-time All-Star who guided the Blazers to NBA Finals appearances in 1990 and 1992. Drexler was a member of the Dream Team that won Olympic gold in 1992 and still holds franchise career records in many categories, including games played, scoring, and steals.

Top 10 San Francisco/Golden State Warriors (1962–Present) :: by Jim Barnett

Jim Barnett was drafted in the first round by the Boston Celtics in 1966. He played in the NBA for over a decade, and then became an analyst for the Golden State Warriors for the last quarter of the century.

The Warriors are one of three charter members of the NBA, along with the Boston Celtics and the New York Knicks. They won the inaugural NBA championship in 1947 while in Philadelphia and a second title in 1975 after moving to the West Coast. In the following list, Barnett celebrates those who have had the most influence on the franchise since its move to San Francisco before the start of the 1962–63 season.

10. Tom Meschery. Tom Meschery was a homegrown San Francisco Warrior who attended Lowell High in San Francisco, and then St. Mary's College. He was drafted by the Philadelphia Warriors before traveling home with the team to San Francisco in 1962. Tom, who played along with Wilt Chamberlain, averaged 16 points and 10 rebounds in the team's first California season.

The wildly popular Warrior was nicknamed the "Mad Russian" because he was such an intense competitor. Meschery was a fan favorite and personal favorite of new owner Franklin Mieuli. Upon his departure, his No. 14 was retired by the franchise and also placed on every Warriors game jersey.

9. Alex Hannum. Coach Hannum, an enforcer as a player, took over the Warriors coaching job following the team's last-place finish in its inaugural season. The no-nonsense coach proceeded to transform the Warriors into a defensive-minded team, and then led them to the championship series against the Boston Celtics in 1964. San Francisco lost the series, but Hannum was named Coach of the Year. After three years in San Francisco, Hannum followed his star center Wilt Chamberlain to Philadelphia, where they won the NBA championship together in 1967.

8. Tim Hardaway. Chosen in the 1989 draft with the 14th overall pick, the point guard with the electrifying crossover dribble brought excitement back to the Warriors. For two of his years with the Warriors he teamed up with Chris Mullin and Mitch Richmond to form Run TMC. Hardaway was a three-time All-Star and finished in the top 10 in assists in five straight seasons.

7. Wilt Chamberlain. Wilt brought immediate credibility to a brand new team in the Bay Area. He had just come off the highest-scoring season in NBA history when he averaged 50.4 points per game during the 1961–62 season. During his two and a half seasons in a Warrior uniform, he continued to dominate, averaging 44.8, 36.9, and 38.9 ppg. His mere presence on a new roster, in a new city, was more than enough to place him on this list. A member of the Naismith Hall of Fame and one of the 50 Greatest Players in NBA History, Wilt had his No. 13 retired by the Warriors.

6. Don Nelson. Don Nelson became head coach of the Warriors in 1988 and proceeded to coach the team to five playoff appearances during two separate tenures. He was named Coach of the Year following the 1991–92 season. His unconventional "smallball" approach produced high-scoring, running basketball teams that twice led the league in scoring and finished second on another occasion. Don finished with the second-highest number of games coached in Warriors history, and in the process became the NBA's winningest coach of all time, with 1,335 victories.

5. Nate Thurmond. Nate Thurmond was the third overall pick in the 1963 NBA Draft. In his rookie season he and Wilt Chamberlain led the Warriors to the NBA Finals. Thurmond's play during that year (he averaged 10 rebounds per game) allowed the Warriors to trade Chamberlain the following season.

During Thurmond's 757-game career with the Warriors, the team made the playoffs six times while he averaged 17 points and 17 rebounds per game. The durable, defensive-minded center made six All-Star Game appearances and was named to the All-NBA Defensive Team five times. Named as one of the 50 Greatest Players in NBA History, Nate was inducted into the Naismith Hall of Fame in 1985. His No. 42 was retired by the Warriors.

4. Franklin Mieuli. The eccentric but shrewd businessman who dressed in casual clothes (including his ever-present deerstalker) brought the Warriors to the West Coast in 1962. In the early years, the team struggled with attendance, finances, and minority investors until he took over as sole owner. During his 24 years as owner, the team made three NBA Finals appearances and won its only West Coast title in 1975.

Fiercely loyal, he treated everyone like family, including "favorite son" Tom Meschery, and prodigal son Rick Barry, whom he brought back from the rival ABA, leading to the Warriors 1975 NBA championship. Franklin was without prejudice in racial terms, making African-American Alvin Attles a player-coach midway through the 1969–70 season. Ten of the dozen players on the championship roster were black men. Without the perseverance of Franklin Mieuli the franchise could have easily ended up in another city.

3. Alvin Attles, Jr. Alvin Attles is "Mr. Warrior." He has been a Warrior for over six decades as a player (711 games in 11 years), coach (1,075 games in 13 years), general manager, and consultant. He originally was a fifth-round pick from North Carolina AT&T in 1960. As a player Al was known as the Destroyer because of his aggressive, defensive-minded style of basketball. Al's No. 16 is retired by the Warriors.

Attles served as player-coach and spent his entire coaching career with the Warriors. During the 1974–75 season, Coach Attles used an unconventional platoon system, often going 10 players deep to win games, and leading his underdog Warriors over the heavily favored Washington Bullets to sweep the NBA Finals and win the championship.

2. Chris Mullin. Perhaps the most popular player in Warriors history. Mullin was a player that people could identify with—someone not blessed with great speed or athleticism. He arrived in 1985 and played 13 seasons and 807 games—more than any other Warrior. He also ranks first on the all-time Warriors list in steals, second in minutes played, second in free throw percentage (.862), and second in points scored (16,235). He averaged over 20 points per game during his Warriors career and had five straight seasons when he averaged over 25 ppg.

Chris shot a remarkable .513 from the field throughout his Warrior years. His shining moment came in the 1991 playoffs when he led the Warriors to their first postseason victory in Los Angeles since 1969 while scoring 41 points. Chris later served as the Warriors executive vice-president of basketball operations and was inducted into the Hall of Fame in 2011. Chris's No. 17 is retired by the Warriors.

1. Rick Barry. Rick Barry is simply the greatest player in Warriors history. Drafted with the fourth overall pick in 1965, he burst onto the NBA scene by averaging 25.7 ppg and winning Rookie of the Year honors. The following season he led the league in scoring (35.6 ppg) and took the Warriors to the NBA Finals, where they lost in six games to the great Philadelphia team. After a five-year sabbatical in the ABA, Rick returned to the Warriors and played another six years. In 1975, he led the Warriors to their only West Coast NBA title as they defeated the Washington Bullets in four straight games in the NBA Finals. He was named Finals MVP.

Barry is the Warriors all-time leading scorer with 16,447 points, for an average of 25.6 ppg. He had 13 games of 50 or more points while wearing a Warriors uniform. Considered the greatest free throw shooter in NBA history, he shot .896 from the line with his underhand style as a Warrior. Rick was an eight-time All-Star during his Warrior years and was named as one of the 50 Greatest Players in NBA History. He was inducted into the Naismith NBA Hall of Fame in 1987. His No. 24 is retired by the Warriors.

10 Most Impactful Bullets/Wizards of All Time :: by Steve Buckhantz

Steve Buckhantz is in his second decade as the Washington Wizards play-by-play TV announcer. He is known for his clever catch phrases such as "dagger" and "backbreaker."

The Washington Wizards franchise has been known by several different names, and played in a number of locations, since its inaugural 1961 season as the Chicago Packers, the NBA's first expansion team. The team changed its name to the Zephyrs the following season, and then a year later moved to the East Coast and became the Baltimore Bullets. The club moved to Landover, Maryland, in 1973 and changed its name to the Capital Bullets, and then the Washington Bullets the following season. The club later moved into DC and, in 1997, became the Washington Wizards.

The franchise has also been known for having some of the greatest players, coaches and front-office people in NBA history. Here are the top 10:

10. Dave Bing. While he was with the team for only two seasons, Bing, one of the 50 Greatest Players in NBA History, just has to be on this list. He was a Bullet AND was born in Washington, DC. Bing is or a long list of elite stars from the District, graduating from Spingarn High School in 1962.

9. Bobby Dandridge. Bobby D played four seasons for the Bullets, but clearly the most impactful was his first. In fact, he may have been as responsible as anyone for the franchise's lone NBA championship. Dandridge came to the squad in 1977, averaged nearly 20 points and six rebounds a game, and was likely the difference maker in the 1978 NBA Finals that garnered the Bullets their only NBA title.

8. Gus Johnson. Anyone who calls themselves a true Bullets fan knows of the Honeycomb. Gus Johnson was shattering backboards long before it became fashionable. A five-time All-Star and ferocious rebounder, he averaged 17 points and nearly 13 rebounds a game for his career. Gus passed away in 1987 and was elected to the NBA Hall of Fame in 2010.

7. Phil Chenier. Please excuse any hint of bias, because Phil has been my TV broadcast partner for the past 15 years. But he is still regarded as one of the greatest Bullets of all time. I watched him (on TV) drop 53 points against the Trail Blazers in 1972. He had one of the sweetest, smoothest jump shots in league history. Even more importantly, he is among the classiest and most friendly human beings you will ever meet.

6. Gilbert Arenas. His legacy will forever be shrouded in controversy, but in his prime Gilbert Arenas was one of the most electrifying players in the NBA. His impact on the team was immense, on and off the court. He led the Wizards to four consecutive playoff appearances, after they had advanced just once to the postseason in the previous 16 years. His 60 points against the Lakers in a 2006 overtime win in Los Angeles was a Washington franchise best. A normally good-hearted person, Arenas saw his reputation permanently tarnished after bringing guns into the Wizard locker room on Christmas Eve 2009.

5. Michael Jordan. Statistics notwithstanding, Michael Jordan makes an impact whether he's playing basketball, driving a golf ball, or getting off an elevator. To many folks his playing time in Washington will be marked with an asterisk, but there is no arguing how his presence changed the perception of the Wizards around the league. He regularly sold out all 30 arenas and helped earn the franchise close to $60 million. He also averaged 20 points and 6 rebounds a game, at AGE 40!

4. Earl Monroe. You may get an argument from Knicks fans, but for a kid growing up in the DC/Baltimore area in the late 1960s, Earl the Pearl was the coolest thing for a Bullets fan to put on a uniform, and Monroe donned his own Bullets jersey upon induction into the Hall of Fame. Bad knees and all, Earl Monroe did unimaginable things with a basketball. He was magic before Magic ever handled the rock and once said, "You could put me in a phone booth with five guys and they couldn't guard me." As a player he is my all-time favorite Bullet.

3. Elvin Hayes. It is not a stretch to call him the greatest NBA power forward of all time, but suffice it to say, the Big E knew how to get it done in the clutch. With a 16-year career average of 21 points and 12.5 rebounds a game, he helped the Bullets to three NBA Finals, and to win it all in 1978.

2. Wes Unseld. It is quite possible that no other 6-7 center wreaked the kind of havoc during his NBA career that Wes Unseld did. He wrestled down rebounds, fired laser-like passes, and set picks that shook foundations. He is one of only two players in league history to be named Rookie of the Year and NBA MVP in the same season. Inducted into the Hall of Fame in 1987, he is the greatest Bullet player of all time.

1. Abe Pollin. He was proof you need not wear a uniform to have the greatest impact on a sports franchise, let alone a city. Pollin not only built two different arenas with his own money, he also revitalized a dormant downtown DC area. And while his 46-year tenure was the longest of any owner in the NBA, Pollin was known as much for his philanthropic efforts as he was for his ownership. As much as any Washington-area businessman, Abe Pollin changed lives and the landscape of our city. Pollin passed away in November 2009.

Top NBA Teams of All Time
:: by Dr. Jack Ramsay

Note: Dr. Jack Ramsay led the Philadelphia 76ers to the 1967 NBA title as general manager and the Portland Trail Blazers to a championship as head coach 10 years later. During his Hall of Fame NBA coaching career the Philadelphia native won 864 games. A great student of the game who has been around since the earliest days of the NBA, Ramsay is likely as qualified to write this list as anyone alive, but still found it difficult, saying:

"To select the top NBA teams of all time is a daunting task—especially when one considers that every championship team is a great one. I've been in the enviable position to watch every great team since the league began. My selections are made with care and with confidence.

"I offer apologies to teams like back-to-back winners at Detroit (1989 and 1990) under Chuck Daly and Coach Rudy Tomjanovich's Houston Rockets (1994 and 1995); to Milwaukee's 1971 champions, led by Oscar Robertson and Kareem Abdul-Jabbar; to Miami's 2006 title winner, led by Dwyane Wade; and to the great, never-give-in Mavs of 2011. I also want to humbly acknowledge the Portland Trail Blazers, an incredibly wonderful group of team players, led by Bill Walton and Maurice Lucas, that won the title over Philadelphia in 1977; this team was even better the next season (1977–78), when it led the league with a 50-10 record until a rash of injuries short-circuited its hopes for an extended championship run."

11. San Antonio (2002–03). This was the best of the Spurs teams that won four titles between 1999 and 2007. San Antonio was led by: two stellar big men, Tim Duncan and David Robinson; two excellent penetrators, Tony Parker and Manu Ginobili; a defensive stopper, Bruce Bower; and an astute coach, Gregg Popovich. Coach Pop got good help from bench players Steve Kerr, Steve Smith, Danny Ferry, Malik Rose, and Kevin Willis. The Spurs were 60-22 in the regular season and beat each playoff series opponent, 4-2, including New Jersey in the NBA Finals.

10. New York (1972–73). The Knicks (57-25) finished second to Boston (68-14) in the regular season, but edged the Celtics, 4-3, in the Eastern Conference Finals. Coach Red Holzman had a starting lineup of future Hall of Famers: Walt Frazier and Earl Monroe in the backcourt; Bill Bradley and Dave DeBusschere at forwards; and Willis Reed at center. Another Hall of Famer, Jerry Lucas, came off the bench. The Knicks played Holzman's team offense with sharp precision and also stuck to its opponents with glue-like, aggressive defense. The Knicks beat Baltimore, the Celtics, and Los Angeles (4-1) to win the NBA championship.

9. Minneapolis (1952–53). The Minneapolis Lakers won five NBA championships between 1949 and 1954. George Mikan, the game's first dominant big man, owned the six-foot wide lane on offense and defense, and was also the league's leading intimidator. Mikan received great help from Jim Pollard, a marvelous, fluid 6-7 small forward; a lightning quick point guard, Slater Martin; and a powerful big forward, Vern Mikkelsen. John Kundla was the coach during the team's lengthy run of championships.

8. Los Angeles (1971–72). The Lakers moved from Minneapolis to Los Angeles for the 1960–61 season. The franchise won its next championship in Los Angeles in 1972 with a unique team featuring point guard Jerry West, who led the league in assists (8.7 apg), and a center, Wilt Chamberlain, who led the league in rebounding (19.2 rpg) but didn't finish in the top 20 in scoring. This team was brilliantly coached by Bill Sharman, who got great performances from remaining starters Gail Goodrich, Happy Hairston, and Jim McMillian, as well as outstanding contributions off the bench from LeRoy Ellis, Pat Riley, and Jim Cleamons. The Lakers beat Chicago and Milwaukee in the playoffs, and then New York (4-1) in the NBA Finals.

7. Los Angeles (2001–02). This Lakers team was good in the regular season (56-26), but came on strong in the playoffs. Shaquille O'Neal and Kobe Bryant were magnificent leaders under Coach Phil Jackson's careful direction, and the team got abundant help from Ron Harper, Robert Horry, Rick Fox, Brian Shaw, and Horace Grant. The Lakers dominated playoff opponents, sweeping the first three rounds, and then losing only once to Philadelphia in the NBA Finals.

6. Philadelphia (1982–83). This was a great 76ers team, coached by a Hall of Fame player, Bill Cunningham, and stocked with a powerhouse roster. Moses Malone (24 points and 15 rebounds per game) was their intimidating big man; Mo Cheeks ran the offense and harassed on defense; Julius Erving ran the break; Andrew Toney scored inside and out; and Bobby Jones was their defensive stopper. The Sixers were 65-17 in the regular season and lost only one playoff game (to Milwaukee). In the Finals, Philly swept Los Angeles.

5. Boston (1956–57). I once asked Red Auerbach which was the best of the eight championship Celtics teams that he coached. He answered without hesitation that it was this team. He explained that it was Bill Russell's first NBA season and that Bill had joined the team later in the season because of his involvement with the US Olympic team. Bob Cousy, Bill Sharman, Frank Ramsey, and Tom Heinsohn had played on good Celtics teams, but hadn't won anything. Russell changed all of that by providing the team with a game-changing defensive style of shot blocking and rebounding never before seen in the NBA. The Celtics became a relentless fast-breaking, high-scoring team that ran opponents off the court. With his adroit use of Ramsey off the bench, Auerbach also introduced the sixth-man concept that became a part of every NBA team's game tactic, and remains so to this day.

The Celtics swept Syracuse to open the playoffs, and then outlasted a strong St. Louis team to win the NBA Finals in seven games. Russell went on to play on 11 championship Celtic teams in his 13-year NBA career.

4. Los Angeles (1984–85). This was LA's best Showtime team—a spectacular, fast-breaking, high-scoring group coached by Pat Riley and featuring the scintillating floor generalship of Magic Johnson. Kareem Abdul-Jabbar was yet a dominant center, and James Worthy, Michael Cooper, Byron Scott, Kurt Rambis, Mitch Kupchak, and Bob McAdoo chimed in significantly, whether as starters or off the bench. The Lakers were 62-20 in the regular season and finished 15-4 in the playoffs. LA beat Boston, 4-2, in the NBA Finals.

3. Boston (1985–86). Boston started a front line of Larry Bird, Robert Parish, and Kevin McHale, with Dennis Johnson and Danny Ainge in the backcourt, and Bill Walton and Scott Wedman coming off the bench. Coached by K. C. Jones, the Celtics were 67-15 in the regular season. In the playoffs Boston swept Chicago, lost once to Atlanta, swept Milwaukee in the Conference Finals, and then beat Houston, 4-2, in the NBA Finals. Bird was the focus of the Celtics' game—shooting threes, posting up, making deft passes to open teammates, and then getting steals and rebounds on defense. McHale had the best back-to-the-basket moves in the league, Parish looped in face-the-basket jumpers or outran his matchups for layups, and Walton showed his great passing skills from the post.

2. Philadelphia (1966–67). This 76ers team, which finished the regular season with a 68-13 record, was named the best team of the first 50 years of NBA basketball by a panel of media experts. Coached by Alex Hannum, the Sixers had no weaknesses. Wilt Chamberlain, who had averaged over 50 points a game five seasons before, refined his game to become an excellent passer from the post and continued to be a dominant rebounder. Luke Jackson, a 6-9 powerhouse, helped Wilt with rebounding and had a deadly touch from the perimeter. Chet Walker and Hal Greer were effective scorers from anywhere on the court, and Wali Jones did a masterful job of running the offense after Larry Costello tore his Achilles tendon early in the season. Billy Cunningham was a dynamite sixth man, and Dave Gambee, Matt Guokas, and Billy Melchionni filled in adequately off the bench.

The Sixers beat the Celtics decisively (4-1) in the playoffs—a first-time experience for them, as Chamberlain outplayed Russell, another first. The NBA Finals were somewhat anticlimactic after the win over Boston, but Philadelphia won it (4-2) over a stubborn San Francisco team led by Nate Thurmond and Rick Barry.

1. Chicago (1995–96). The best of Chicago's six championship teams, these Bulls won an amazing 72 games and lost but 10. Led by the overall dominance of Michael Jordan and the deft control of game tempo by Coach Phil Jackson, Chicago was solid in every department. Scottie Pippen and Dennis Rodman joined Jordan in establishing a lockdown defense; Ron Harper ran the triangle offense with purpose and poise; Toni Kukoc, Steve Kerr, and Jud Buechler made open shots consistently; and Luc Longley, James Edwards, and Bill Wennington shut down the middle against opposing big men and cutters through the lane. But Jordan was the team's rock. He seemed to make every big shot or assist with the game on the line and to come up with the defensive stop to preserve a victory. This team was the best of the best.

Top 100 NBA Players of All Time
:: by Pat Williams and Michael Connelly

The players listed here were not selected on the basis of which players in NBA and ABA history would fare best in a one-on-one tournament. They were chosen as the players who had the greatest positive impacts on their eras, teams, leagues, and the game of basketball itself.

Honorable Mention. Paul Westphal; Marques Johnson; Chris Paul; Jack Twyman; Joe Fulks; Mark Jackson; Connie Hawkins; Vlade Divac; Sam Lacey; Jack Sikma; Chauncey Billups; Walter Davis; Chet Walker; Spencer Haywood; George McGinnis; Tom Chambers; Charles Oakley; and Kevin Willis.

100. Tracy McGrady. The amazing talent was on the cusp of top 25 of all time greatness after scoring over 15,000 points by age 27, but was hampered by injuries the second half of his career. He twice won the scoring title (2003 and 2004) and was a seven-time All-Star.

99. Dave DeBusschere. The foundation of the New York Knicks two championship teams, No. 22 was an eight-time All-Star, six-time All-Defensive Team selection, and a player with an elite tangible and intangible skill set.

98. Mitch Richmond. The sharpshooter from Kansas State scored over 20,000 NBA points. He was named Rookie of the Year in 1989, played in six All-Star Games, and won an NBA championship in a supporting role with the Lakers 2002 title team.

97. Kevin Johnson. The point guard of the Phoenix Suns could shoot, get to the hoop, distribute to teammates, and give to charities. One of the true good guys in the league, Johnson scored over 13,000 points while dishing almost 7,000 assists.

96. Sidney Moncrief. The leader of the 1980s-era Milwaukee Bucks, Moncrief guided his team to 10 straight postseasons and played in five All-Star Games.

95. Gail Goodrich. The guard from UCLA stayed home in Los Angeles to play on those great Laker teams of the late 1960s and early '70s. He was a key part of LA's 1971–72 championship season that included a record 33-game winning streak. For his career he scored over 19,000 points and played in five All-Star Games.

94. Vince Carter. One of the greatest athletes to ever play in the NBA, Carter came from the University of North Carolina and was a magnificent offensive force. He has scored over 20,000 points, many through spectacular dunks and reverse layups. He was the Rookie of the Year in 1999 and has played in eight All-Star Games.

93. Paul Silas. One of the great offensive rebounders the game has seen, Silas collected over 12,000 total rebounds during his career and was part of three championships. The Celtics were never the same after their owner wouldn't pay him his due and traded him to Denver.

92. Gus Johnson. The five-time All-Star center of the Baltimore Bullets averaged 12.1 rebounds and over 16 points a game. In the 1970–71 season he averaged 17.1 boards a game. He was one of the first highfliers in the NBA. During his playing career, he broke three backboards.

91. David Thompson. Skywalker only played to age 29, but his amazing skills allowed fans to see the game played at its pinnacle when this five-time All-Star (one in the ABA; four in the NBA) had the ball in his hands.

90. Bill Sharman. The 10-time All-Star (and MVP of the 1955 All-Star Game) and four-time NBA champion was the perfect piece of the early Celtics dynasty puzzle. The 6-1 guard was a strong defender, proficient free throw shooter, and a seven-time top 10 scorer in the league.

89. Ed Macauley. The ultimate compliment for Easy Ed was that he was traded to St. Louis for Bill Russell (along with Cliff Hagan). The seven-time All-Star won a title in St. Louis and is a Hall of Famer.

88. Maurice Cheeks. As the point guard of the 76ers 1983 championship team, Mo was the ringleader who put the great players around him in best position to succeed. The four-time All-Star had over 7,000 assists.

87. Tony Parker. The San Antonio guard has three championship rings and was voted MVP of the 2007 Finals. He has played in three All-Star Games and seems to have his best moments in the biggest games. The point guard scored over 13,000 points before the age of 30.

86. Bob Lanier. The big lefty with the sweet touch was the foundation of the emergent Detroit Pistons of the late 1970s and Milwaukee Bucks of the early 1980s.

85. Guy Rodgers. The point guard out of Temple University was a four-time All-Star for the Warriors and Chicago Bulls. He was either first or second in the league in assists in eight different seasons and averaged 7.8 assists a game for his career.

84. Alonzo Mourning. The former Hoya was a defensive force who twice won NBA Defensive Player of the Year honors (1999 and 2000). He battled health issues during his career, but played on seven All-Star teams and earned a championship with the Miami Heat in 2006.

83. Earl Monroe. The four-time All-Star was a star in Baltimore, where he won the 1963 Rookie of the Year Award. But his game was destined for New York, where he won a championship with the Knicks and cemented his legacy of greatness while wowing the Garden crowd with his style and spin moves.

82. Buck Williams. The power forward that starred primarily for the Nets grabbed over 13,000 rebounds and scored almost 17,000 points in his career.

81. Grant Hill. The amazing talent from Duke was slowed most of his career by injuries, but when he has played, he has been special. During his years of good health, Hill displayed many moments of brilliance. He played in seven All-Star Games and has scored over 17,000 points.

80. Derrick Rose. Jumping ahead a little bit, but the Chicago Bull guard seems destined for greatness, with an MVP Award already on his mantle (he's the youngest ever to win it). He is an unstoppable force when he wants to get to the hoop.

80a. Kevin Durant. Three straight scoring titles and led team to 2012 Finals. 2008 Rookie of the Year in Seattle. Three-time NBA scoring champion.

79. Bill Walton. One of the greatest to ever play the game, Walton was unfortunately saddled with foot and ankle injuries that stole so much of his career. He won a championship in Portland in 1977 and the MVP Award the following year. Years later, he came to Boston with a second lease on basketball life and won a second championship in 1986 while earning the Sixth Man of the Year Award. His revival finally put a smile on his face as he found a true appreciation of the game. If not for injuries, Walton would likely be in the top 10 of this list.

78. Carmelo Anthony. The four-time All-Star scored over 16,000 points by age 28 and, if he stays healthy, Melo could threaten the 25,000 mark. At times a malcontent, he left Denver for New York, where the pressure of performing and delivering under the big lights will weigh on his shooting hand.

77. Chris Webber. The mercurial talent with unlimited potential was moved from team to team in an effort to find the right fit. His best days were in Sacramento, where he helped his team advance to within reach of the championship.

76. Pistol Pete Maravich. The LSU sensation came to the NBA and wowed crowds with his entertaining passes, offensive arsenal, and flamboyant, Bohemian appearance during a time of nonconformity in America. During his career he scored over 15,000 points and was probably the greatest H-O-R-S-E player the sport will ever know.

75. Tim Hardaway. The point guard with the "killer crossover" spent a career breaking the ankles of defenders while scoring over 15,000 points and setting up teammates over 7,000 times.

74. Robert Parish. Part of Boston's original Big Three, the even-keeled (except when he was playing against Bill Laimbeer) center rebounded, blocked shots, and consistently hit the 12-footer all the way to three championships.

73. Dan Issel. An ABA superstar in Kentucky, Issel brought his game to Denver and was annually amongst the league's top scorers. In the ABA and NBA he scored over 27,000 points and averaged over 20 points a game with Denver.

72. Adrian Dantley. The guard/forward from Notre Dame scored over 23,000 career points, and twice won the NBA scoring title (1981 and 1984).

71. Chris Mullin. The lefty with the sweet stroke ran the floor in Golden State, shooting 18-footers and dominating opponents with his superior basketball IQ. He scored almost 18,000 points and played on the original US Dream Team.

70. Artis Gilmore. The lefty center dominated in both the ABA and the NBA, scoring almost 25,000 points and grabbing over 16,000 rebounds. He won a title in the ABA and played in 11 All-Star Games.

69. Ray Allen. The greatest long-distance shooter in NBA history, Allen has scored over 23,000 points. The sharpshooter from the University of Connecticut started with Seattle and came to Boston to win his championship ring while sustaining his excellence. One of the best offensive players off the ball working through picks.

68. Neil Johnston. A star from the 1950s, the three-time scoring champ and one-time rebound leader won a championship with Philadelphia in 1956.

67. Bernard King. One Christmas he gave NBA fans the gift of witnessing his greatness as he scored 60 brilliant points and brought down the house in Madison Square Garden. The forward was impossible to cover. He could face up to the hoop and hit the 15-footer or put the ball on the floor and go by his defender with ease.

66. Hal Greer. The guard played alongside Wilt Chamberlain in Philadelphia, where he won a championship in 1967. He played in over a thousand games while scoring 21,586 points and dishing out 4,540 assists.

65. Dikembe Mutombo. With his wagging finger, this multilinguist could reject an opponent's shot in any language. He led the league in rebounds four times, in blocks five times, and four times was named NBA Defensive Player of the Year.

64. Paul Arizin. The guard won the scoring title twice with the Philadelphia Warriors and led his team to the 1956 championship. He sacrificed two years of his prime to join the Marines during the Korean War.

63. Joe Dumars. The quiet, steady force of the Detroit Pistons Bad Boys was no complementary piece. He could shoot (16,401 career points) and shut down the opposing team's best scoring guard (four-time NBA All-Defensive Team). After his playing career he became a top team executive.

62. James Worthy. The athletic forward from the school of Dean Smith ran the break alongside Magic and could either finish at the rim or shoot the midrange jumper with great proficiency.

61. Lenny Wilkens. The quiet point guard scored almost 17,000 points and dished out over 7,000 assists—twice leading the league—in his NBA career. Following his playing days he moved down the bench to the head coaching seat, where he won over 1,300 games.

60. Dennis Johnson. DJ went from prolific scorer in Seattle, where he was the 1979 NBA Finals MVP, to Phoenix, to Boston, where he became a shutdown defender and the point guard of the 1980s Celtic dynasty.

59. Dennis Rodman. He was a rebounding machine wrapped in unique packaging. He was dogged in his pursuit of every loose ball. He won in Detroit and Chicago and San Antonio. Complex? Yes. A great rebounder? Also, yes.

58. Paul Pierce. The Truth spoke the truth in the 2008 Playoffs, when he put the Celtics on his back and carried them to their 17th championship during a post-season run that included his memorable duel with LeBron James in Game 7 of the Eastern Conference Finals. For his career the 10-time All-Star has scored over 22,000 points.

57. Wes Unseld. The 6-7 center/forward was a rebounder extraordinaire who used his wide frame. He could start the fast break and defend in the paint. He averaged over 14 rebounds a game and was a key piece of the Washington Bullets 1978 championship team.

56. Dominique Wilkins. The Human Highlight was a prolific offensive force with unparalleled athletic skills. He went toe-to-toe with Larry Bird in the NBA Playoffs one Sunday in 1988 and scored 47. For his career, he scored 26,668 points.

55. Alex English. The silky smooth Nugget was the engine of the high-powered, high-altitude Denver offense. He scored 25,613 points during his eight-time NBA All-Star career.

54. Gary Payton. The Glove had some of the quickest hands known to the league, stealing over 1,000 wayward passes or dribbles while dishing out almost 9,000 assists. Payton won a title with the Miami Heat in 2006 and was a tenacious defender.

53. Willis Reed. The ringleader of the Big Apple circus was the undeniable leader of the New York Knicks glory years. The center with the huge heart rebounded, limped, and willed his team to championships in 1970 and 1973.

52. Reggie Miller. With unlimited range, the UCLA product put the Indiana Pacers on the NBA map with his three-point shooting and steely resolve in the biggest moments. Reggie scored over 25,000 points, and who could forget his dagger-in-the-heart performances in Madison Square Garden, right in Spike Lee's face?

51. George Gervin. The San Antonio swingman laying the ball toward the basket from one of his patented finger rolls was a thing of a beauty. The Iceman scored over 26,000 points in his pro career and won four scoring titles.

50. Walt Bellamy. The well-traveled center recorded over 14,000 rebounds and almost 21,000 points in the NBA. In his first three years in the league the 1961–62 NBA Rookie of the Year averaged over 17 rebounds and 28 points a game.

49. Billy Cunningham. The five-time All-Star (four times in the NBA; once in the ABA) won an NBA championship with Wilt in 1967, scored over 16,000 points, and then won a championship as head coach of the Sixers in 1983. The forward was a great defender and cutter to the basket before injury derailed his career.

48. Bob McAdoo. He bounced around the league to any team in need of an offensive assassin. He was the best player on some underrated Braves teams in Buffalo, where he was Rookie of the Year (1973) and MVP (1975). He later won two championships in Los Angeles as a coming-off-the-bench scorer.

47. Tom Heinsohn. One of the great forwards in NBA history, the Hall of Famer possessed a deadly hook shot that he could take from the corner or on a drive to the hoop. The Celtic forward deserves a "Tommy Point" for earning a championship ring for each finger (eight as a player and two as a coach).

46. Sam Jones. The clutch guard from the Boston Celtics dynasty years earned a ring for each finger just as a player. The bigger the moment, the better he was, with Jones once scoring 51 points in a playoff game. His signature play was the around-the-picket-fence game-winner against the Lakers in the 1969 NBA Finals.

45. Walt Frazier. Clyde the Glide was a New York superstar in every sense of the word. He led the Knickerbockers to two championships. Whether wearing a fur coat downtown or the blue and orange on the Garden floor, Frazier had style and grace. A great two-way player whose star always shines.

44. Dave Bing. The gentleman who could score or distribute. The seven-time All-Star and 1967 NBA Rookie of the Year carried the Pistons franchise on his back during its lean years. The successful entrepreneur and current mayor of Detroit might be having an even more amazing career after leaving the NBA.

43. Jason Kidd. The triple-double threat (Kidd has registered over one hundred triple-doubles in his career) is a creative leader capable of putting all of his teammates in the perfect position to succeed. He finally won an elusive NBA title with the Dallas Mavericks in 2011.

42. Nate Archibald. Tiny was the consummate point guard. He played in six All-Star Games, won a championship with the Boston Celtics in 1981, and led the NBA in scoring AND assists in the 1972–73 season with the Kansas City-Omaha Kings.

41. Patrick Ewing. The New York Knick center did everything he could do to bring a championship to the Big Apple. He played with voracity while scoring over 24,000 points. He was one of the greatest college players of all time and lived up to his potential in the NBA.

40. Dolph Schayes. The epitome of a power forward, Schayes led the Syracuse Nationals to the 1955 championship, scored over 18,000 points, and grabbed 11,256 in rebounds during his time in the NBA.

39. Clyde Drexler. The Phi Jamma Slamma alum electrified Portland and the NBA with his graceful approaches to the basket. He scored over 22,000 points, played on the Dream Team, won a championship back in Houston, and participated in 10 All-Star Games.

38. Nate Thurmond. Nate the Great is the most underrated of the great centers in NBA history. He collected exactly 15 rebounds (14,464) and 15 points a game (14,437) over his 14-year NBA career that included seven All-Star Game appearances, and he did it all competing during the league's era of great centers.

37. Julius Erving. The good Doctor was an ABA sensation whose game translated nicely to the NBA. He was the league MVP in 1981 and won a championship with the Moses Malone-led 76ers in 1983. His game had a lot of flash and a great deal of substance.

36. Steve Nash. The Canadian wowed the NBA with his special ability to score, get to the hoop, and deliver to teammates. The two-time MVP and eight-time All-Star has led the league in assists five times.

35. Dwyane Wade. The scoring guard out of Marquette was the driving force of the Miami Heat's 2006 championship team. He is one of the extraordinary triumvirate in Miami that has the potential to establish a dynasty . . . but that story is still being written.

34. Dirk Nowitzki. The seven-foot German with the small forward game cemented his legacy with a 2011 championship in Dallas. But he became a star long before that. He is a 10-time All-Star who won the league MVP Award in 2007.

33. Dwight Howard. Known as Superman, the Orlando superhero is a specimen the likes this league has never seen. The 6-11 center moves like a guard and has shoulders broad enough to carry a franchise on while averaging 13 rebounds and over 18 points a game during his first eight seasons.

32. Jerry Lucas. The power forward who realized his ring with the New York Knicks in 1973 was a relentless rebounder who tallied over 15 boards a game for his career while scoring over 14,000 points and becoming a seven-time All-Star.

31. Kevin Garnett. Straight out of high school, this intense power forward was a star in Minnesota before coming to Boston and winning a championship. He is a 14-time NBA All-Star with over 24,000 points and over 13,000 rebounds in his career—and an immeasurable number of scowls and glares.

30. Allen Iverson. The fearless guard of the 76ers could shoot, fake, crossover, and defy an opponent into capitulation. At just 165 pounds the former Hoya was an NBA MVP (2001) and four-time scoring champion who twice led the league in steals.

29. David Robinson. The Admiral was what you expect out of the Naval Academy—classy, proficient, and results personified. During his career he won MVP, Rookie of the Year, and Defensive Player of the Year Awards, and was an integral member of two San Antonio Spurs championship teams. The lefty center was one of the greatest athletes to play the position.

28. John Stockton. The guard out of Gonzaga might be the greatest pure point guard to ever play the game, and—along with Utah Jazz teammate Karl Malone—part of maybe the greatest duo in NBA history. Stockton, who led the NBA in assists nine times, has more steals (3,265) and assists (15,806) than anyone in NBA history.

27. LeBron James. He came out of high school in Ohio destined for greatness. LeBron is maybe the greatest athlete to play the game in league history. He brought Cleveland to the edge of a title, only to "bring his talents to South Beach." If he stays healthy, he could challenge for Kareem's all-time NBA points record.

26. Kevin McHale. The greatest low-post player in NBA history, No. 32 was part of the famous original Big Three in Boston that won three championships. He could come off the bench or start, and either way dominate at the big forward position, where his long arms and soft hands made him deadly on both ends of the court.

25. Rick Barry. The shooting forward led the Golden State Warriors to their lone championship in 1975. Eight years before he won the NBA scoring title in just his second season. He was also the most prolific scorer in ABA history (30.5 a game). Barry was one of the great free throw shooters in league history, using the underhand method to achieve virtual perfection from the line.

24. Elvin Hayes. The star from the University of Houston team that upset the UCLA Bruins in January 1968 in front of 52,693 in the Astrodome came to the NBA later that year. He went on to lead the league in rebounding twice, score over 27,000 points, and lead the Washington Bullets to the 1978 NBA championship.

23. Karl Malone. He is second in career scoring, with almost 37,000 points—many coming on his patented pick-and-roll play with teammate John Stockton. The Mailmen didn't deliver Utah a championship, but was still a legacy player.

22. Scottie Pippen. He was taken fifth overall in the 1987 NBA Draft out of the little-known University of Central Arkansas. And though he would exist in the shadow of Michael Jordan, this two-way triple-threat star was a seven-time All-Star and six-time NBA champion who established his own place in NBA history.

21. Dave Cowens. The fiery, 6-9 redhead center outplayed, outworked, and outhustled bigger opponents, night in and night out, while pulling down 13.6 rebounds a game. He won the MVP in 1972–73, played in seven All-Star Games, and earned two championship rings.

20. Charles Barkley. The Round Mound of Rebound could do things on the basketball court that no man his size had ever done. He was a tireless rebounder who could dribble the length of the court and distribute the ball or pull up and make a three-pointer. He scored over 23,000 points and grabbed over 12,000 rebounds. He was an 11-time All-Star and won the league MVP Award for the 1992–93 season.

19. Bob Cousy. The Houdini of the Hardcourt revolutionized the game under the watch of mentor Red Auerbach, whom he lovingly called Arnold. He led the fast-breaking Celtics to six championships as their leader and point guard.

18. George Mikan. The first great big man, the bespectacled one carried the Minneapolis Lakers to five NBA championships in the late 1940s and 1950s while leading the league in scoring three times and rebounding twice. He was the best player of his era.

17. Isiah Thomas. The sweet-faced point guard with an assassin's spirit led the Bad Boys to two championships in the 1980s. He scored over 18,000 points, played hurt, and hated to lose to his core.

16. Shaquille O'Neal. An immense human whose carefree personality endeared him to fans. In the first half of his career, he could dominate the game simply with his superior size. As his career developed his game evolved. He won an MVP in 2000 and four championships over his equally immense career.

15. Tim Duncan. The quiet superstar from Wake Forest was the driving force behind four San Antonio Spurs championships. With an old-school game that included first-class decorum, the center/power forward used his soft-touch elbow jumper and great length to carve out his place in NBA lore.

14. Moses Malone. A relentless machine on the boards, Moses came straight from high school to professional basketbal, where he won three MVP awards and led the Philadelphia 76ers to a championship in 1983.

13. John Havlicek. Hondo played for the great 1960 Ohio State team before coming to Boston, but only after being cut by the Cleveland Browns. In his early years he popularized the sixth-man role before evolving into a star of his own. He was part of nine Celtic championships, scored over 26,000 points, and played on 13 All-Star teams.

12. Elgin Baylor. The Laker great started in Minneapolis and traveled to Los Angeles with the team in 1960. He scored over 23,000 points and grabbed over 11,000 rebounds in the NBA. He never won a championship, but that fact hasn't diminished his contributions to the game. His jump shot and ability to suspend himself in the air to improve his vantage point were legendary. He scored at least 40 points in 87 different games.

11. Bob Pettit. The power forward of the St. Louis Hawks took his team to the NBA championship in 1958. He was a two-time MVP and led the league in scoring twice. During his career he scored 20,880 points and averaged over 16 rebounds a game.

10. Jerry West. The symbol of the perfect NBA player, Jerry West lent his image to the center of the NBA logo. He played in Los Angeles with grace and skill. There was no shot too big for the 14-time All-Star and one-time champion (1972) known as Mr. Clutch. He was the only man in NBA history to win Finals MVP on a losing team. He led the league in scoring (1969–70) and assists (1971–72).

9. Hakeem Olajuwon. The Dream went from Nigeria, to Phi Jamma Slamma at the University of Houston, to the Houston Rockets—the team that the big man led to two championships. He could do it all: block shots, hit turnaround jump shots, face the basket, and rebound.

8. Kobe Bryant. The son of NBA alum Joe "Jellybean" Bryant, the Laker great has been the force behind five LA championships. He has scored 50 points or more in a game 24 times, including an 81-point performance. His complete game has gained him nine All-Defensive Team selections.

7. Oscar Robertson. The Big O had a triple-double for the ENTIRE 1961–62 SEASON, when he averaged 30.8 points, 11.4 rebounds, and 12.5 assists a game. The man also known as Horse starred for the Cincinnati Royals before teaming up in Milwaukee with the next guy on this list to win the 1971 NBA championship.

6. Kareem Abdul-Jabbar (aka Lew Alcindor). He changed names and changed teams but was always great. With goggles in place and his skyhook loaded and ready, the center from Power Memorial won six championships and was named league MVP six times. Along the way he scored over 38,000 points and secured over 17,000 rebounds.

5. Larry Bird. The Hick from French Lick played the game of basketball the way it was supposed to be played—with sincerity, a relentless desire to win, and the ability to shoot, pass, rebound, and play defense. He led the Boston Celtics to three championships, revitalized a city, and saved the drowning league with the help of his friend and rival, Magic Johnson.

4. Bill Russell. The five-time MVP is the greatest team player in sports history. He has 11 NBA championship rings (two earned as player-coach). Sure, his numbers might not have been as good as a certain other center of his era, but No. 6 was less concerned with stats than with winning—and win he did!

3. Earvin "Magic" Johnson. The director of Showtime could win as the point guard running the offense or as the stand-in center stealing the show (see Game 6 of the 1980 NBA Finals). He was one of those rare players who made everyone around him better with his magical passing, ever-improving offensive game, and winning spirit and attitude. The three-time MVP was the driving force behind five Laker title runs.

2. Wilt Chamberlain. The Big Dipper has more NBA records than any other player. He dominated as a scorer, rebounder, and shot-blocker. He even led the league in assists one year. No player has ever been able to exert his will upon a team sport the way Wilt Chamberlain did.

1. Michael Jordan. His Airness was not only the greatest offensive player in basketball history but also one of the great defenders, being named to the All-Defensive team nine times in his career. The five-time MVP was more than vertical (and sometimes horizontal). It was the amalgamation of talent, hard work, and an unquenchable will to win that allowed him to hug the NBA championship trophy six times.

Pat's Acknowledgments

With deep appreciation I acknowledge the support and guidance of the following people who helped make this book possible:

Special thanks to Alex Martins, Dan DeVos, and Rich DeVos of the Orlando Magic.

Thanks also to my writing partner, Michael Connelly, for his superb contributions in shaping this manuscript.

Hats off to three dependable associates—my trusted and valuable colleague Andrew Herdliska, my creative consultant Ken Hussar, and my ace typist Fran Thomas.

Hearty thanks also go to my friends at the Perseus Books Group. Thank you all for believing that we had something important to share and for providing the support and the forum to say it. Special thanks to Greg Jones for your continued support and encouragement.

And finally, special thanks and appreciation go to my wife, Ruth, and my supportive children and grandchildren. They are truly the backbone of my life.

Michael's Acknowledgments

I would like to extend my sincere thanks to all the players, executives, coaches, and celebrities who submitted lists to the book. To Greg Jones of Running Press Book Publishers, thank you for bringing this project to fruition. To Hank Guenthner for organizing the town basketball leagues. To Mr. Tobin for bringing me to those thrilling Catholic Memorial–Don Bosco games. To Rick Kuhn, who named me captain of the St. Theresa Juniors. To Jay Parker and Mike Radley, with whom I have played basketball for over 30 years. To Steve Alperin, the lefty who won games of H-O-R-S-E and forgave debts. To my junior varsity coach at Catholic Memorial, Paul Capodilupo, who chose me for the team. And lastly, to my coauthor, Pat Williams—I can't thank you enough for sharing your amazing network of friends with me and with the readers. It is an honor to participate in this project with you.